I0753988

HISTORIC PHOTOS OF THE MANHATTAN PROJECT

TEXT AND CAPTIONS BY TIMOTHY JOSEPH, PH.D.

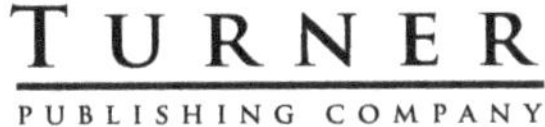

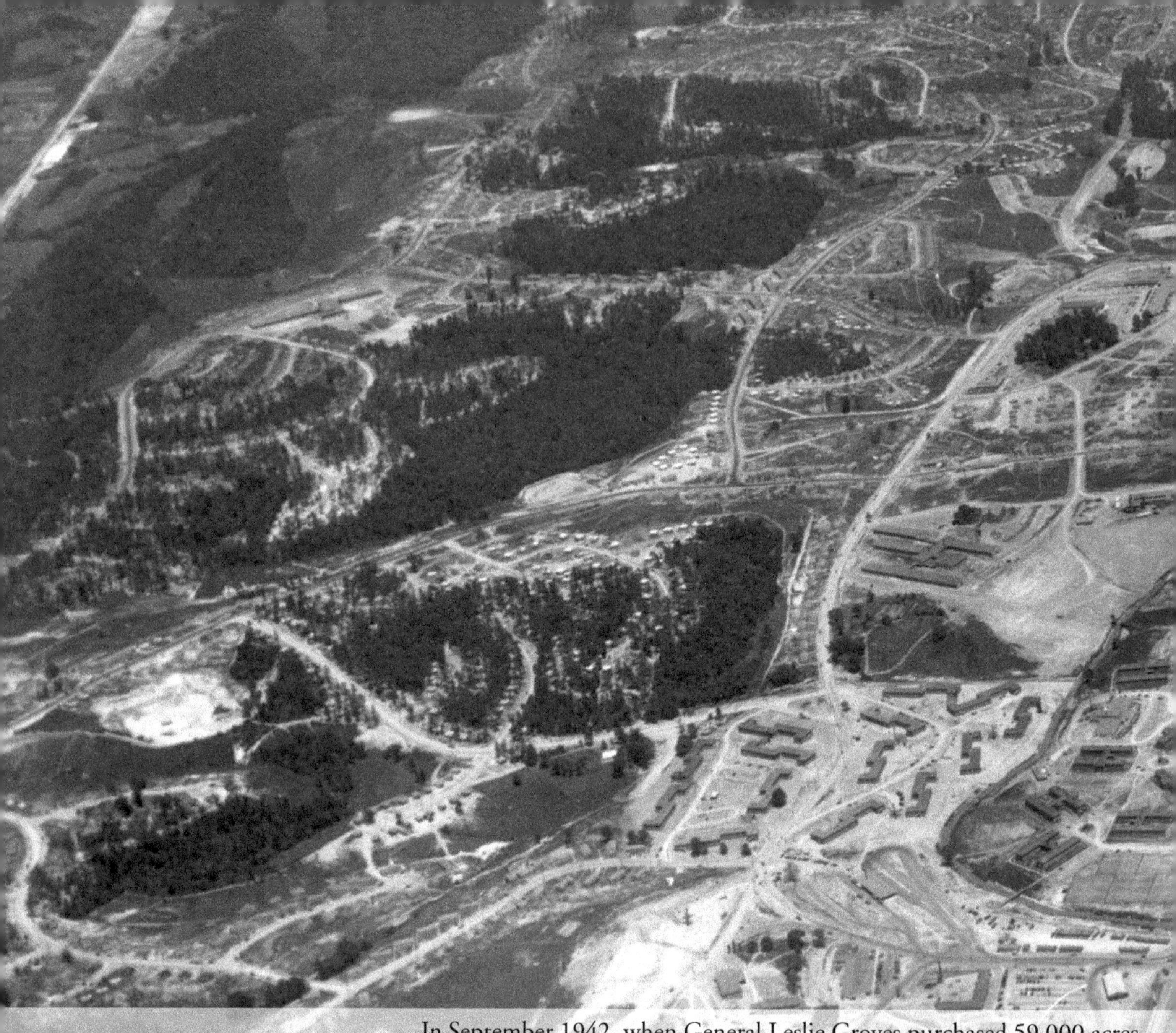

In September 1942, when General Leslie Groves purchased 59,000 acres between Black Oak Ridge and the Clinch River as the first federal reserve for manufacturing nuclear material for the atomic bomb, there were only about 3,000 residents on rural farms in those valleys. By 1945 there were 75,000 people living in 10,000 family dwellings, 13,000 dormitory spaces, 5,000 trailers, and 16,000 barracks, forever changing the countryside.

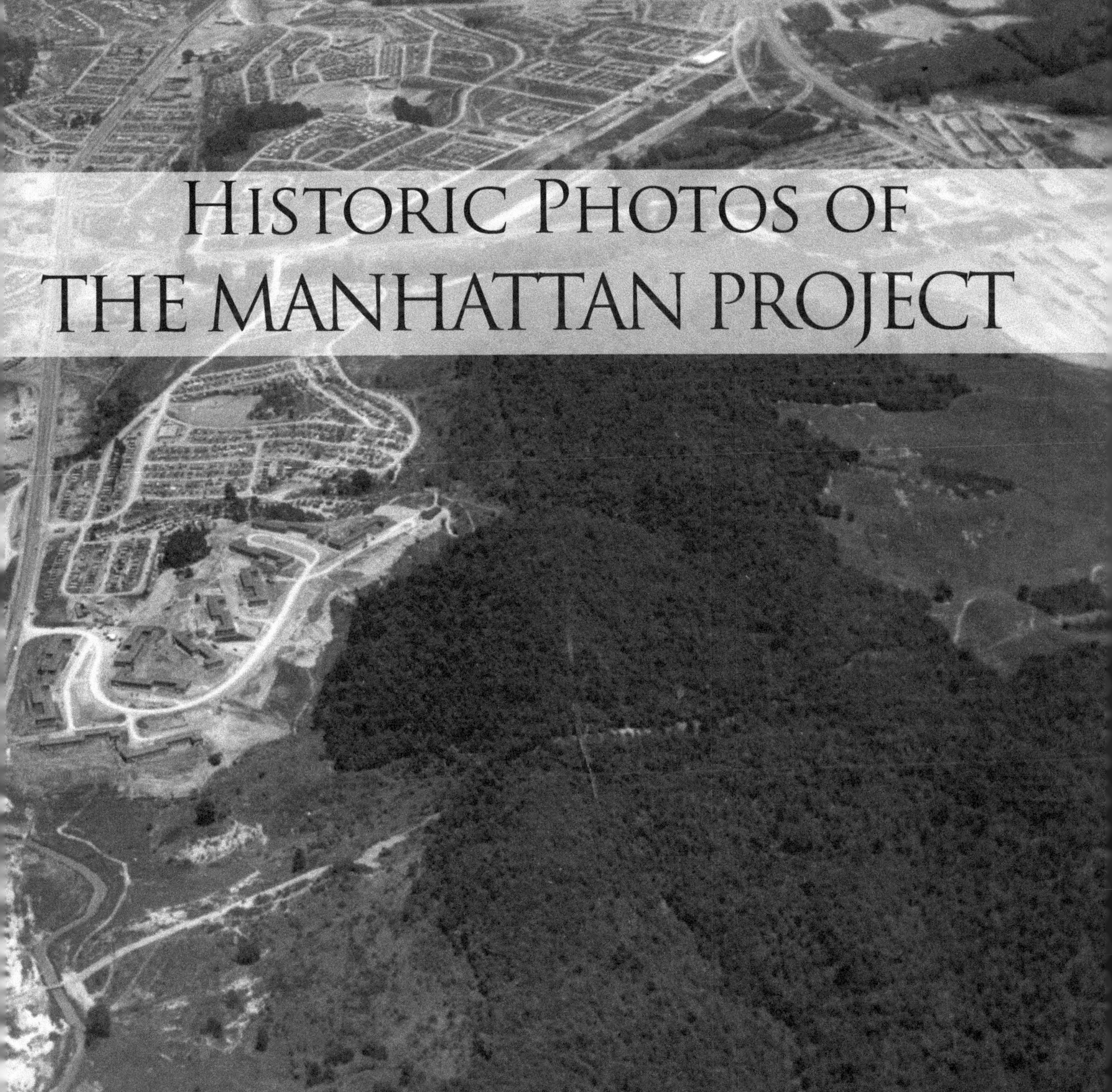
HISTORIC PHOTOS OF
THE MANHATTAN PROJECT

Turner Publishing Company
www.turnerpublishing.com

Historic Photos of the Manhattan Project

Library of Congress Control Number: 2008910973

ISBN-13: 978-1-59652-521-4

ISBN 978-1-68442-074-2 (hc)

Contents

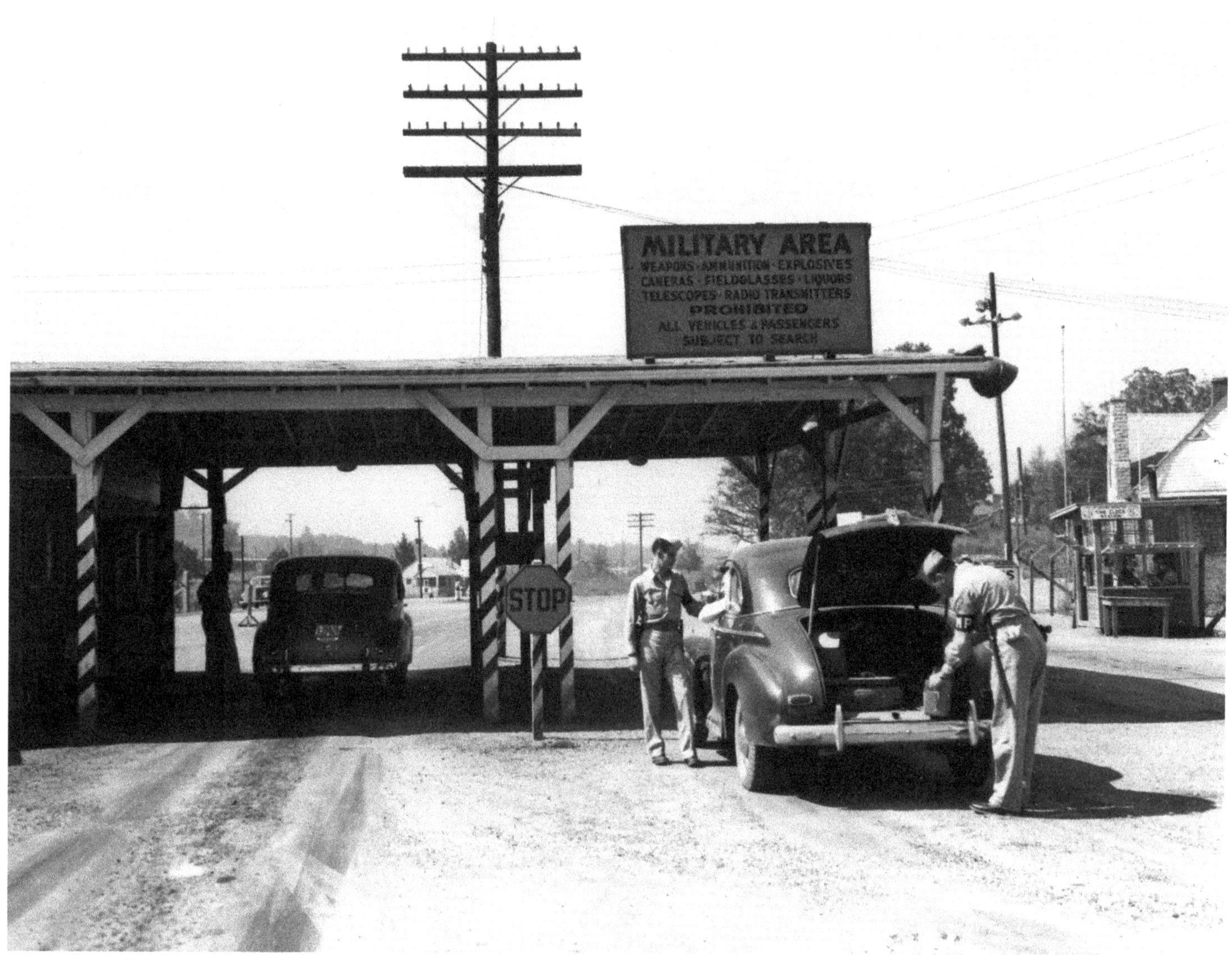

Automobiles are being checked before passing through the Elsa Gate portal into the Secret City of Oak Ridge. The home seen through the portal still stands today. The building to the right housed a business which had to be sold because it was inside the controlled area.

Acknowledgments

This work, *Historic Photos of the Manhattan Project,* was made possible with photos from the National Archives; the Library of Congress; the United States Department of Energy, Washington, D.C.; the Oak Ridge Public Library; the United States Department of Energy, Oak Ridge Office; Argonne National Laboratory near Chicago, Illinois; and the personal files of George D. Kerr, Knoxville; I appreciate their stewardship of this important and irreplaceable historical national resource.

This book is a visual journey pursued through the eyes and work of those individuals who gave so much to the Manhattan Project effort. It documents in historical photos what can only be described as the most significant and far-reaching challenge the United States ever embarked on. This historical essay is dedicated to two peoples: the Americans who made it a success, and the ill-fated Japanese who suffered the consequence.

The honor of achievement belongs to every scientist, military and political leader, and every individual worker involved in the Manhattan Project. Although the project ended the war, it did so at a great cost to innocence. This journey is presented with utmost respect and sadness for every individual who unwillingly paid the price of war. Every American celebrated peace, while at the same time shed tears for those innocent people who died and suffered to bring about that peace. If only wisdom could wipe war from the face of the earth as quickly as were so many innocent souls.

Preface

Philosophers and laymen alike, past, present, and to come, have, and will continue to debate the decision that was made to use nuclear bombs on two Japanese cities. What cannot be debated is whether or not nuclear weapons would have been created—the answer is clear—for even before such a weapon entered the minds of scientists in the United States, Germany was working hard to understand nuclear chain reaction in order to develop the worst of all weapons. What is debatable is what would have happened had our nation ignored the possibility that such a weapon could be created, and thus failed to undertake the enormous challenge to create this horrific technology. Had our enemy constructed the bomb first would it have been dropped on New York or San Francisco? Where would our nation be today had history unfolded differently? That is for all of us to ponder.

One cannot help associating the use of these dreadful weapons with the killing of thousands of innocent people, forgetting that far more innocent civilians were tragically killed using standard weaponry: guns, cannons, conventional bombs. The only difference between loss of life by thousands of small bombs during hundreds of bombing raids, or two enormous bomb blasts, is the magnitude of the explosion, the length of time required, and the simple fact that no conventional bomb could deliver enough of a threat to end the war.

Those two bomb blasts cost the lives of thousands, yet saved untold thousands. Many estimates have been made of the number of American and Japanese soldiers and civilians who would have lost their lives had not the war ended with the dropping of the second nuclear weapon, but the numbers far exceed the casualties inflicted by those two terrifying events. Too, there is no debate that bringing into play such a devastating device resulted in the unconditional surrender of the Japanese on August 14, 1945, a day of celebration around the world to announce that peace was finally real.

This book is a visual recounting of a single project like no other the world had ever seen. Never had so much been accomplished so quickly by so many. The statistics of time, manpower, organization, conditions, and construction were in and of themselves staggering, but equally so was the inconceivable pace in the advancement of the sciences required to make success possible. Perhaps the most bewildering aspect of this project was the construction of enormous industrial facilities to produce what no one knew how to produce when construction began. It is unheard of today to erect even a small building without detailed engineering drawings. But to build super-factories on the fly while the processes to go on in those facilities were still under development remains a prodigious achievement. Yet this is exactly what was done. So little was known about nuclear physics, nuclear chemistry, fission-fusion chain reactions, and reactor science that facilities utilizing different "possible" processes needed to be constructed simply because researchers could not wait for the proof that a process would achieve the intended result.

While working on this book I was asked by a woman, "When did the Manhattan Project actually begin?" I told her of various dates of official actions such as the August 13, 1942, establishment of the Manhattan Engineering District in New York City, and the June 17, 1943, decision by President Franklin D. Roosevelt to build the pilot plant. Then I said to her, "Actually, now that you've made me think about it, here's when I believe this incredible project actually began." I picked up a copy of a letter and handed it to her.

On August 2, 1939, Albert Einstein wrote to FDR, explaining that Nazi Germany was working to create a gruesome weapon of mass destruction, and telling the President that in his view, our nation should pull together the best scientific and industrial minds in the country and push theoretical physics into reality—we needed to build a nuclear bomb and we needed to build it first. Roosevelt recognized the wisdom of Einstein and entered this nation into the most important race in world history.

—Timothy Joseph, Ph.D.

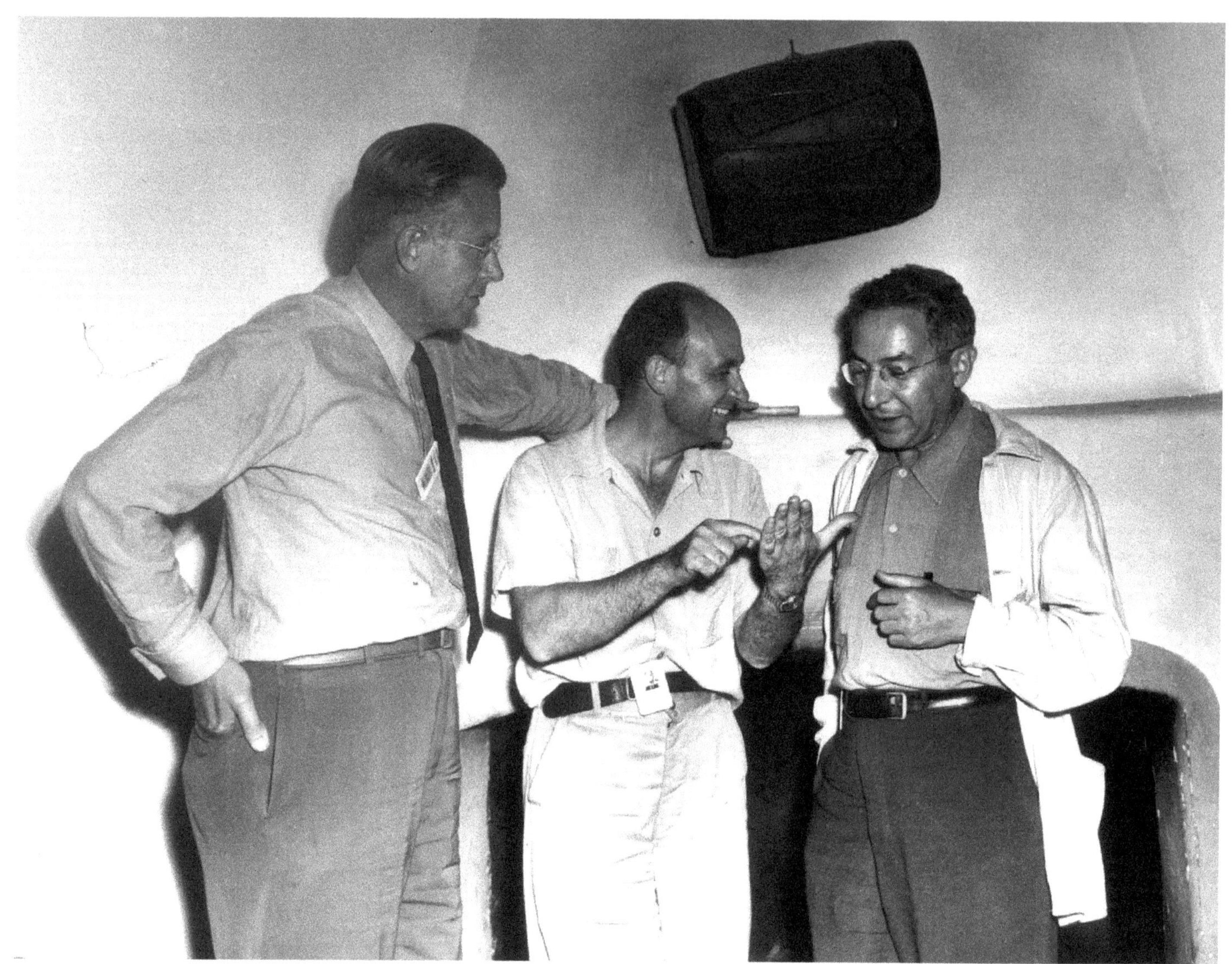

Shown here at Los Alamos, these scientists played key roles in discovering how to construct a nuclear bomb. Dr. Earnest Lawrence (left) received his Ph.D. in physics from Yale in 1925, and in 1936 became Director of the Radiation Laboratory at the University of California, Berkeley. Dr. Enrico Fermi (center) was the project's lead scientist. Dr. Isidor Rabi received his Ph.D. in 1927 from Columbia University and was Associate Director of the Radiation Laboratory at the Massachusetts Institute of Technology. All three were awarded a Nobel Prize. (National Archives)

Leaders, Scientists, Decisions, and War

How and Why the Manhattan Project Was Born

Nazi Germany invaded Poland in September 1939, France and Britain immediately declared war on Germany, and World War II was under way, yet the United States remained neutral. That changed with the Japanese invasion of Pearl Harbor on Sunday morning, December 7, 1941. Suddenly the United States found itself in a world that was in war, with chaos and killing nearly everywhere. Immediately upon entering World War II the goal of the United States was to end it.

Wars are won in two ways—killing and fear of being killed. In the seven months before the two nuclear bombs were released on Japan, American bombing raids destroyed most of 67 Japanese cities killing hundreds of thousands, yet no end to the war was in sight, only more aggression. Changing conventional bombing raids to two single-nuclear-bomb drops instilled enough fear in the Japanese to bring about surrender and the end of the reign of terror on both sides. Estimates vary, but it is thought that as many as 500,000 Japanese died and some 5 million more were made homeless by war's end. Worldwide, it is estimated that more than 70 million people, most of them civilians, were killed in World War II, the deadliest conflict in all of human history.

The two bombs that brought about the Japanese surrender were conceived, designed, and built in one undertaking—the Manhattan Project. It formally began on August 13, 1942, when the Manhattan Engineering District was established and given the mission to do whatever it took to construct industrial-size plants to synthesize the plutonium and uranium needed for nuclear bombs, to design a nuclear bomb, and to build a nuclear bomb—and do it fast. Secretary of War Henry L. Stimson appointed Brigadier General Leslie R. Groves (who had overseen construction of the recently completed Pentagon) to head the project.

Genesis of the project occurred long before it was given a name. In secrecy, speculation, intense fear, and a clear necessity to win a race no one knew how to run, the seeds of this incredible undertaking were planted. Little was known about chain reactions or critical mass, but by 1939 theoretical physicists understood that the ability to split the nucleus of an atom could yield a massive explosion. Shortly after Adolf Hitler took power on January 30, 1933, more than a thousand university professors emigrated from Germany in fear (most to Britain and the United States), including 10 physicists and 4 chemists who had won or would win the Nobel Prize. Many had formed a strong association, and they brought with them knowledge that German nuclear research was advancing rapidly.

Building on the work of Leo Szilard and Enrico Fermi, Otto Hahn and Friedrich Strassmann in Germany bombarded uranium atoms with neutrons in December 1938, concluding that the nuclei had burst—they had discovered nuclear fission. A manuscript describing these events led Szilard and Fermi to conduct an experiment at Columbia University in Manhattan, discovering neutron multiplication in uranium, proving that a chain reaction was possible. Szilard later said that he knew the world was headed for sorrow.

It was Szilard who approached his good friend Einstein, and together they drafted the letter sent to Franklin D. Roosevelt in 1939. That letter led to the establishment of government research into nuclear fission. Fermi and Szilard, along with a number of renowned scientists, took their discoveries to the next level in an abandoned racquet court of the University of Chicago where they built the first crude reactor about 25 feet wide and 20 feet tall called Chicago Pile-1, or CP-1. When work was completed, it held 771,000 pounds of graphite, 80,590 pounds of uranium oxide, and 12,400 pounds of uranium metal. Fermi calculated it would go critical, and it did. The first controlled chain reaction took place at 3:25 P.M. on December 2, 1942.

The race was on.

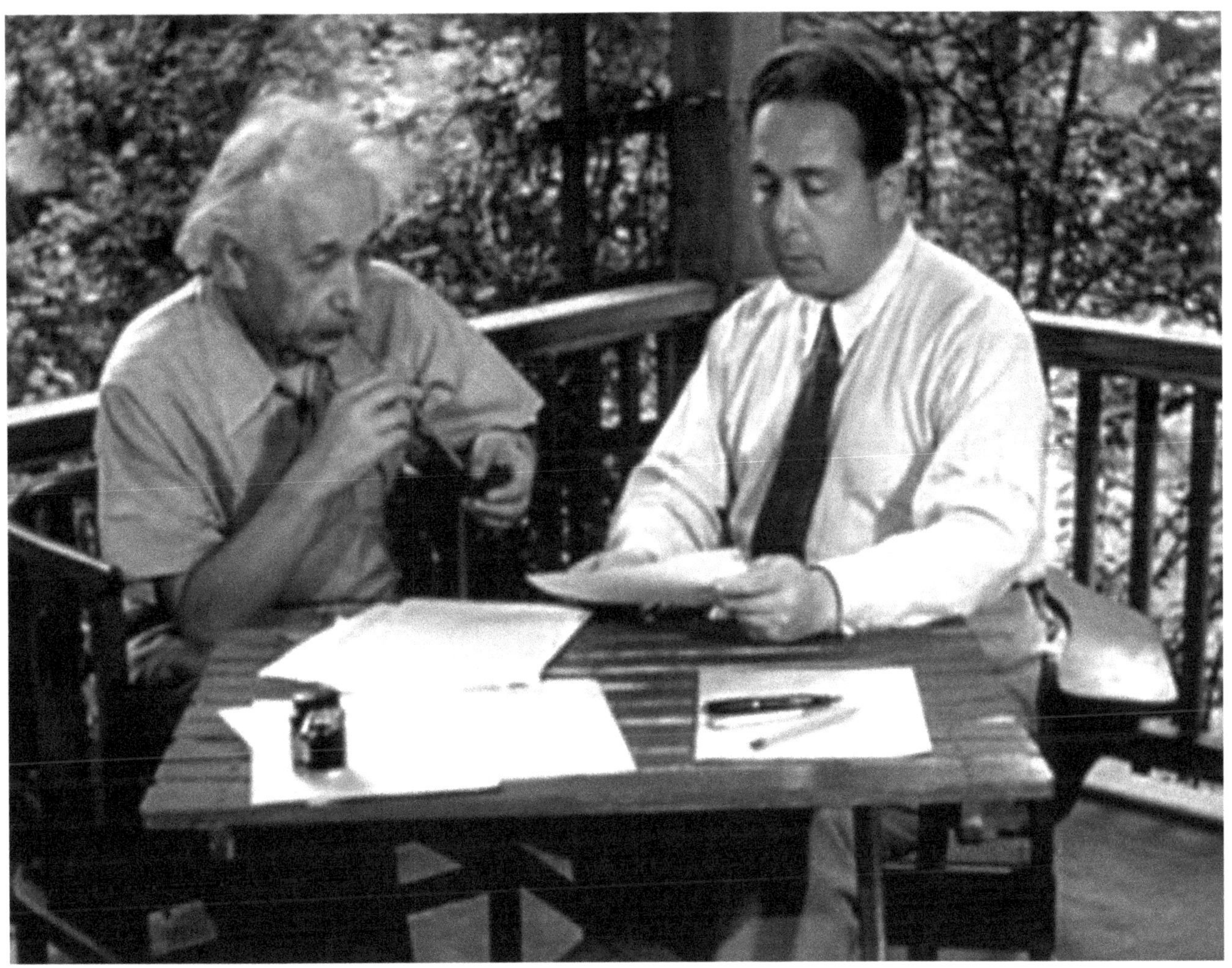

With the discovery of uranium fission and his knowledge that Nazi Germany was working on concentrating uranium most likely for producing a fission weapon, Leo Szilard (at right) was troubled that America seemed not to care. He turned to his friend Albert Einstein. On Einstein's back porch on Long Island, the two men wrote a letter to be hand-carried to President Roosevelt. Reaching the president on October 11, 1939, the letter yielded but two immediate results: a recognition of the remote possibility of a bomb being developed by the Nazi's, and creation of a "Uranium Committee" with $6,000 to buy graphite and uranium for Szilard's experiments.

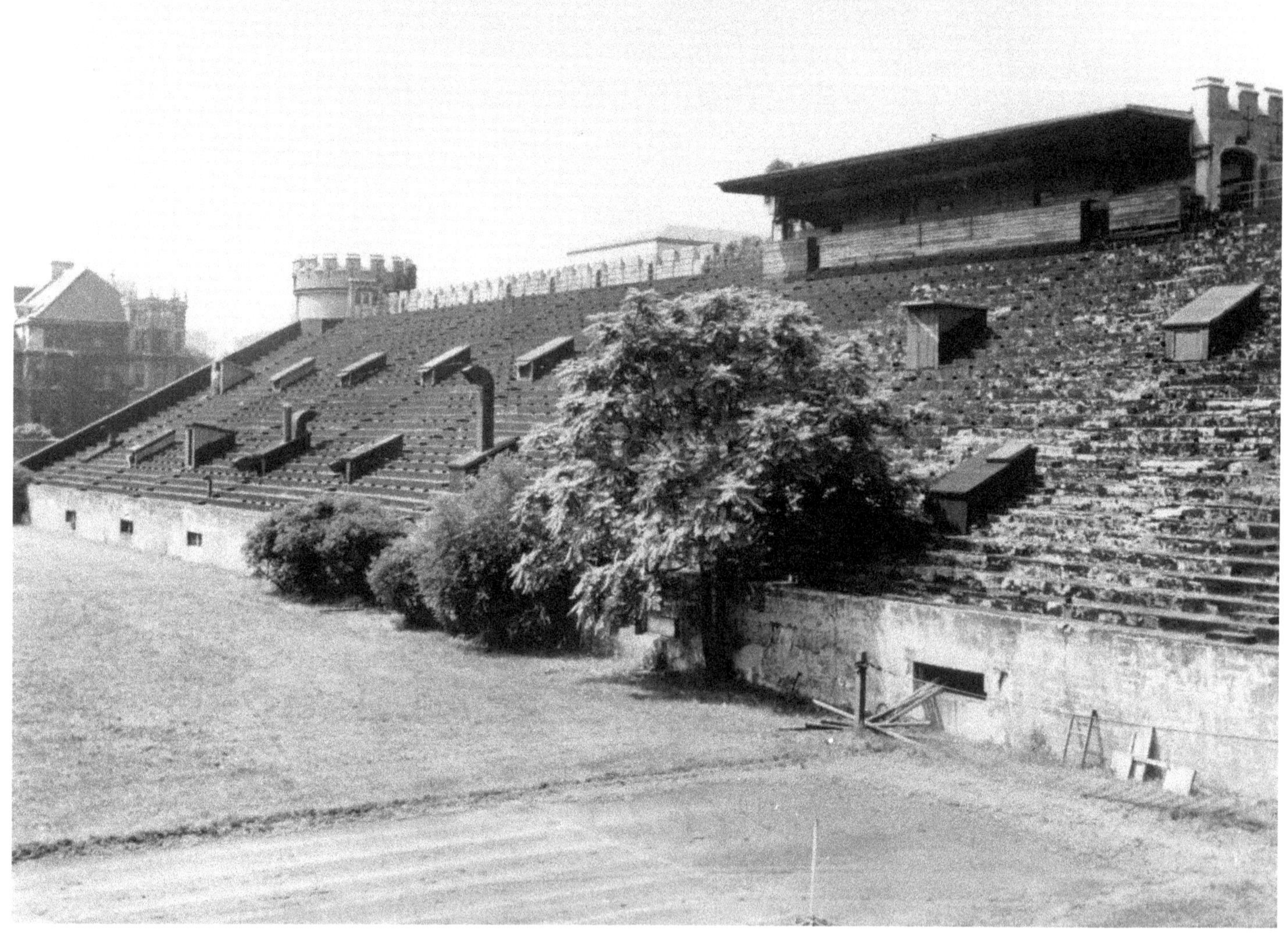

The first self-sustaining controlled nuclear chain reaction occurred at 3:25 P.M. on December 2, 1942, in a most unlikely place—an abandoned racquet court under these stadium seats at the University of Chicago's Stagg Field. It produced merely half a watt of energy, yet ample proof for the feasibility of building what then could not even be imagined—a nuclear bomb.

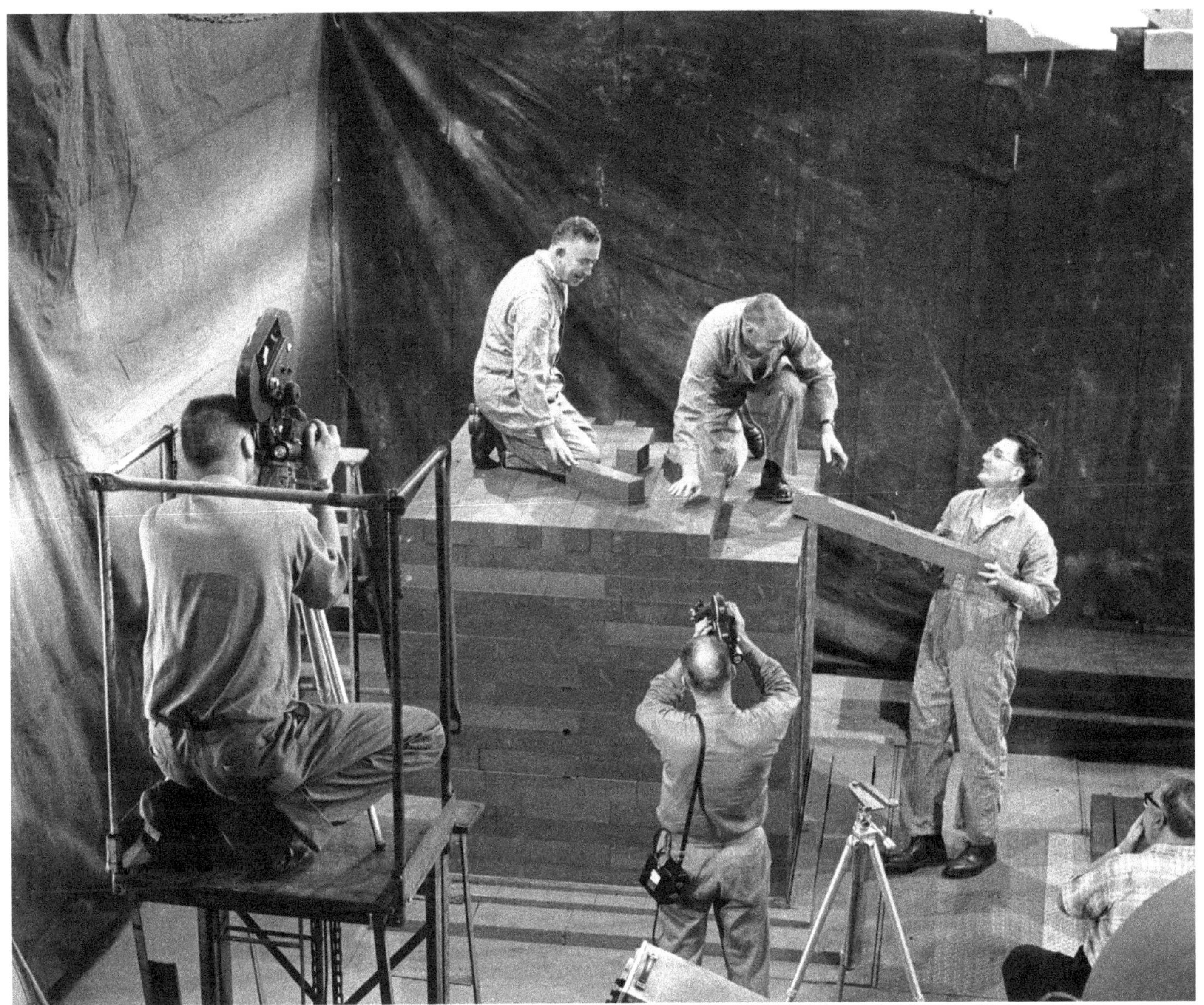

In 1942, these workers have no idea of the historical significance of what they are building. The graphite blocks shown here were stacked according to specifications to become the world's first nuclear reactor, the model for many more to follow. This crude device proved a self-sustaining nuclear chain reaction was possible, and that it could be controlled.

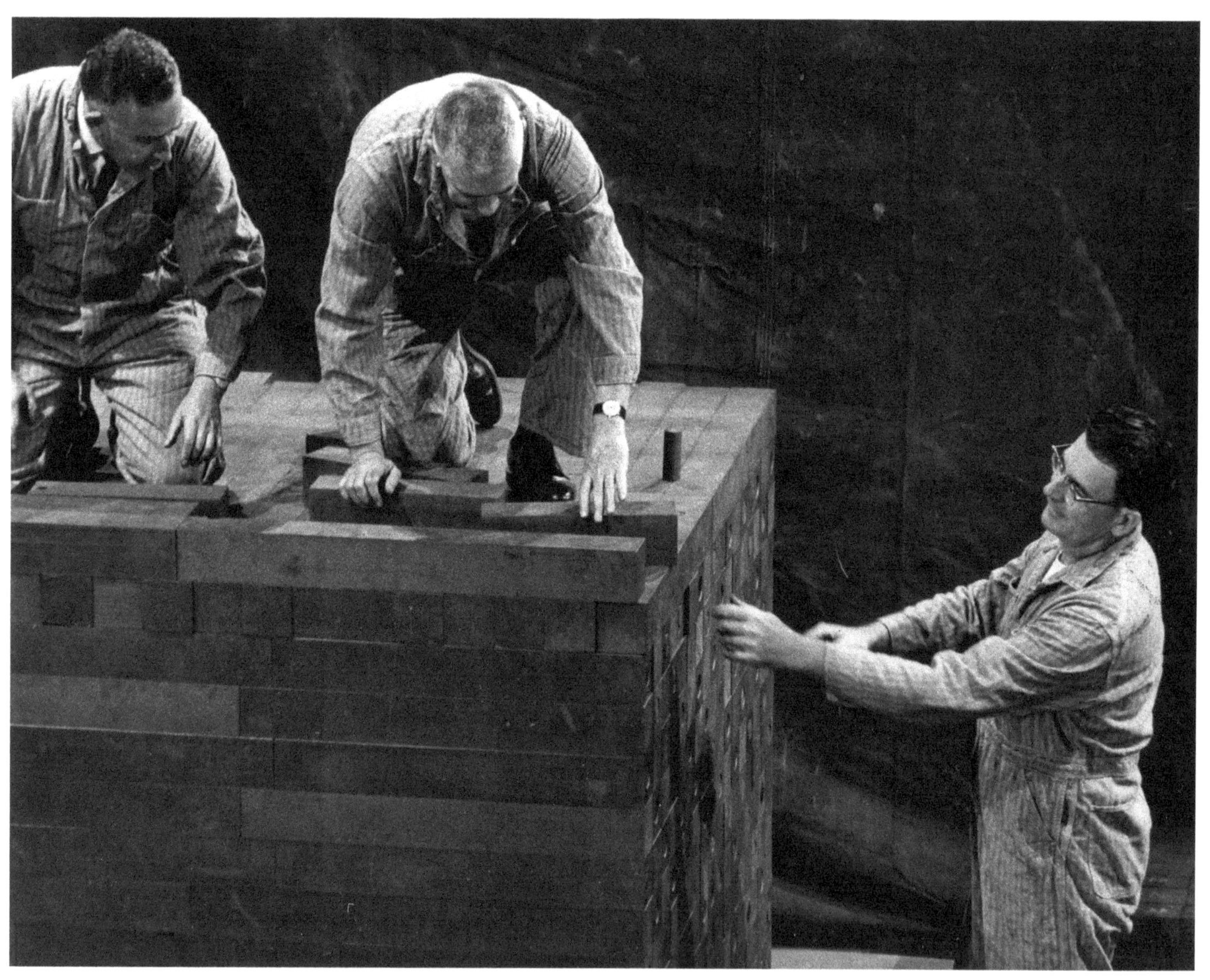

A close-up of the blocks of solid graphite being stacked into a precise configuration. When completed the reactor was about 25 feet wide and 20 feet tall. The holes in the front face are for the uranium metal plugs. The final pile of graphite weighed 771,000 pounds. When it went critical it contained 80,590 pounds of uranium oxide and 12,400 pounds of uranium metal. The cost was roughly one million dollars.

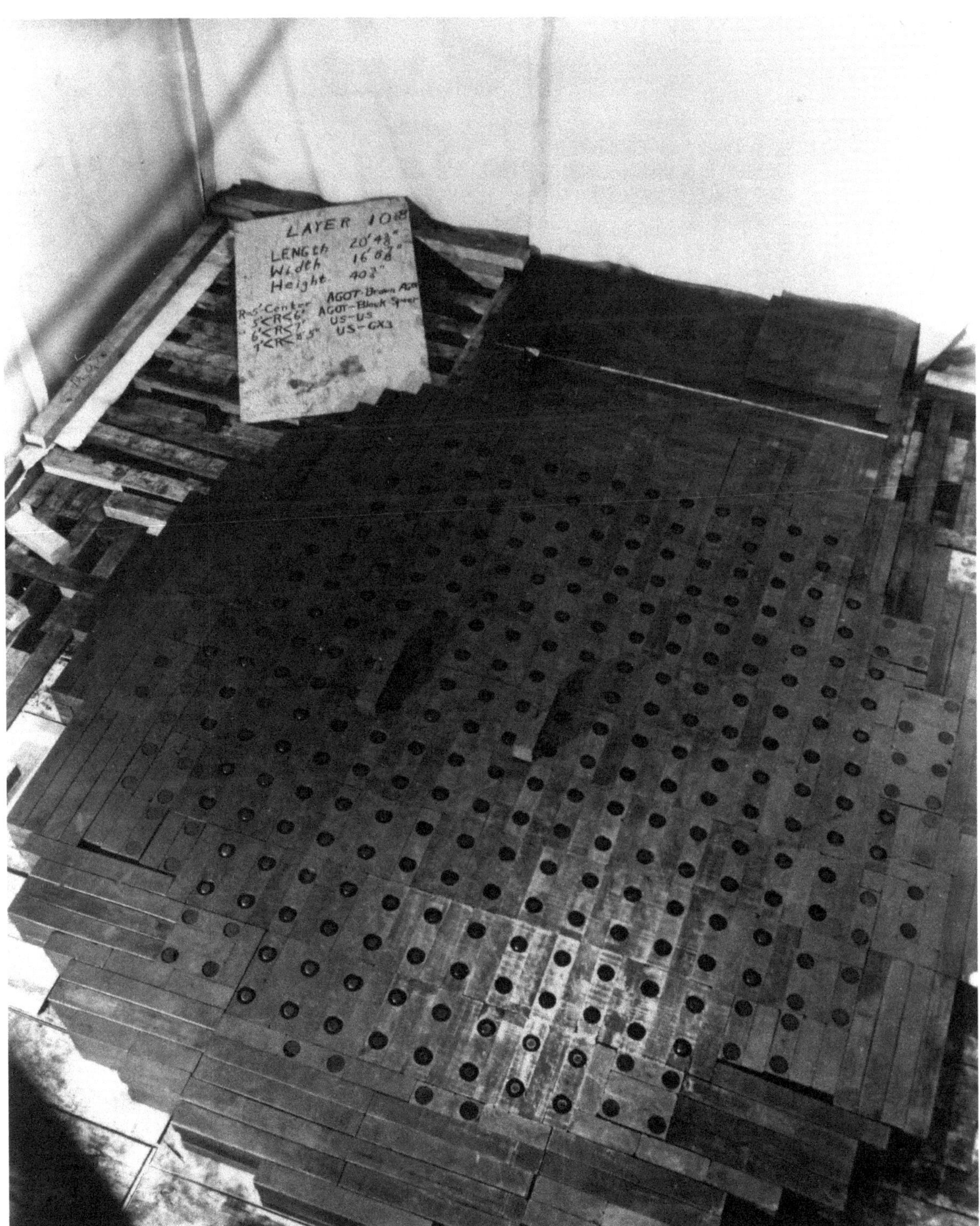

Another view of the graphite blocks, carefully numbered and stacked. It was called Chicago Pile-1 (CP-1) and was the world's first nuclear reactor. Lead scientist Enrico Fermi and his team kept the chain reaction going in this "crude pile of black bricks and wooden timbers" for 28 minutes. In doing so they began the nuclear age. CP-2 was built a short distance away at what is now Argonne National Laboratory, outside Chicago, Illinois.

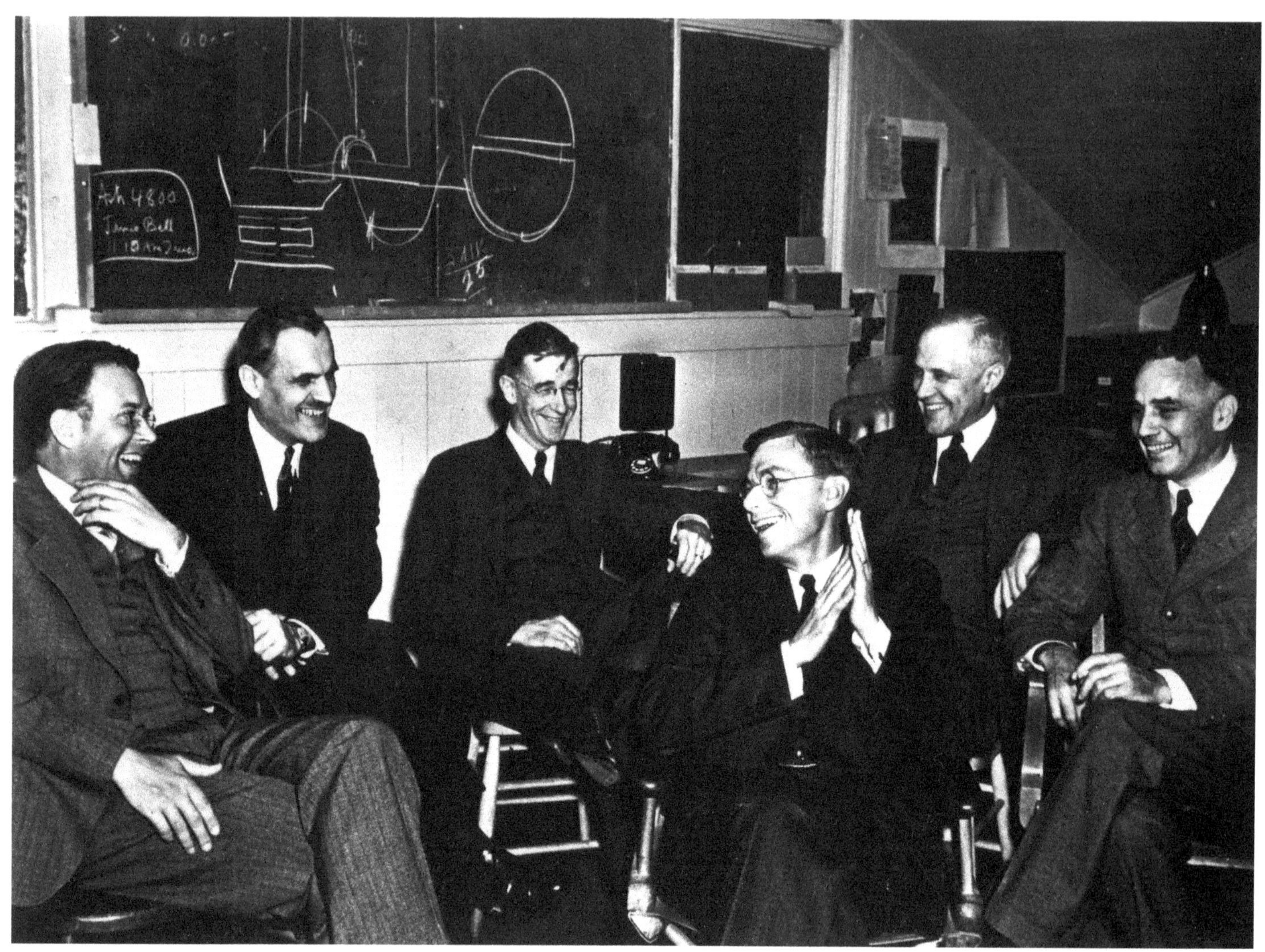

Many scientists contributed to the birth of the nuclear age. Ernest O. Lawrence, director of the Radiation Laboratory, University of California, believed that the U.S. would certainly be drawn into World War II. He pushed to speed up research, for he and other scientists knew that Germany was making progress toward a bomb. In this photo, left to right, are Lawrence, Arthur Compton, Vannevar Bush, James Conant, Karl Compton, and Alfred Loomis.

Julius Robert Oppenheimer was born in New York, on April 22, 1904. He entered Harvard at age 17, and as a freshman received permission to take graduate courses. In 1927 at age 23, he earned his Ph.D. In June 1942 General Leslie Groves appointed him Scientific Director of the Manhattan Project, a role that would earn for him what he considered the dubious distinction "Father of the Atomic Bomb." In 1947 he was made Director of the Institute for Advanced Study at Princeton University and later held the position of Senior Professor of Theoretical Physics. He considered this position an honor, for it was the former position of his old friend Albert Einstein.

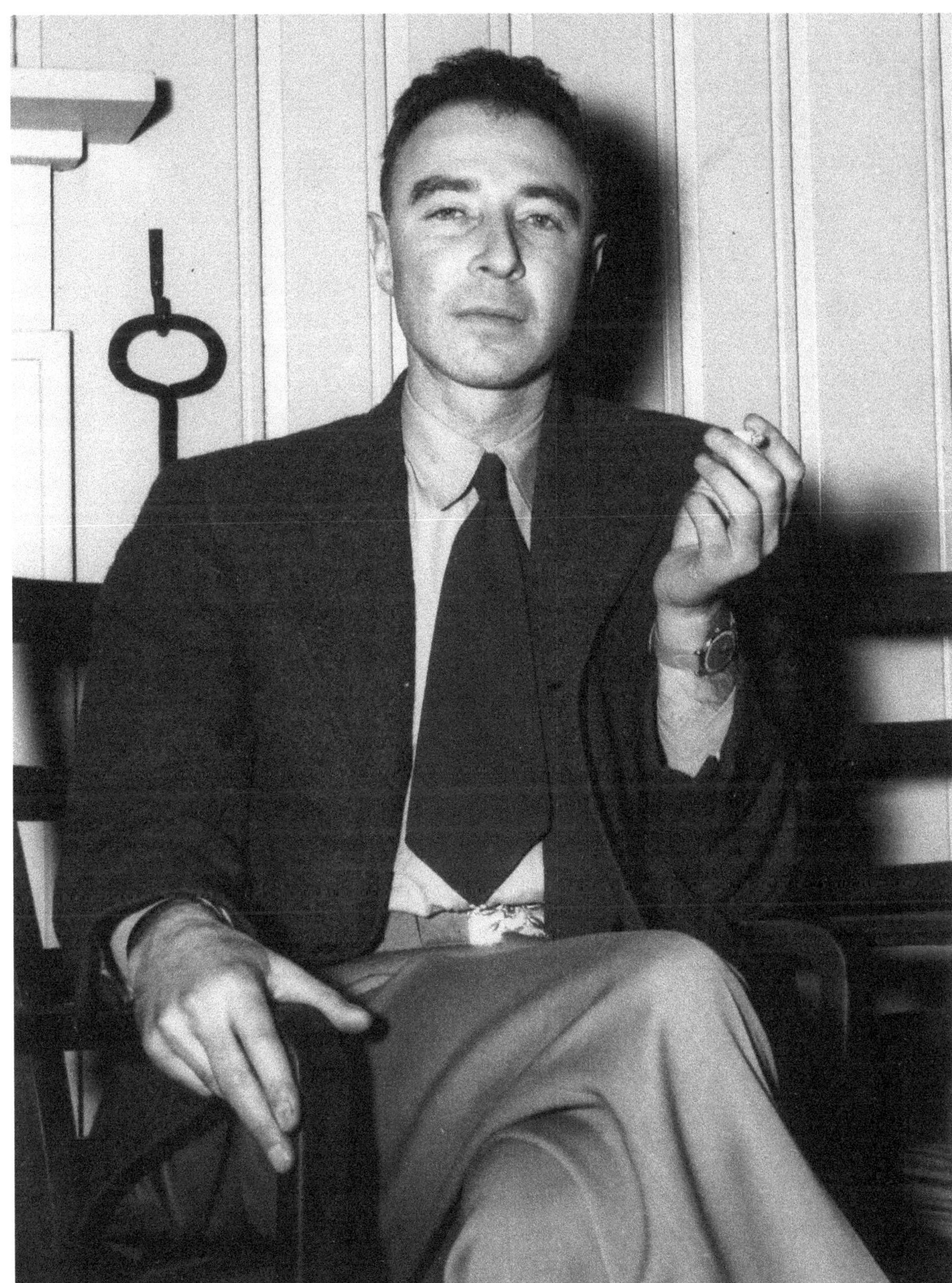

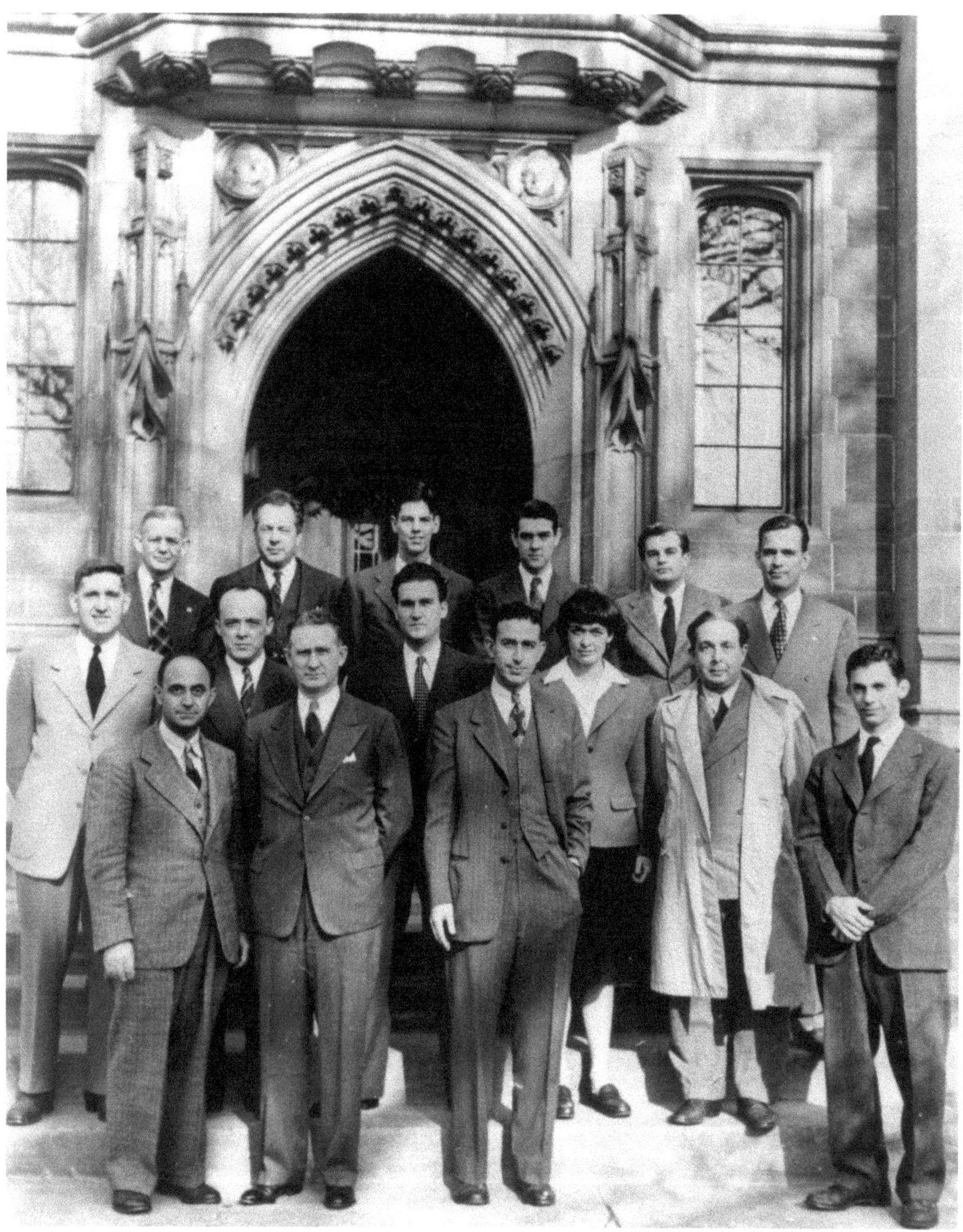

These scientists were involved in the first nuclear chain reaction at CP-1. This photo was taken on the steps of Eckhart Hall, University of Chicago, on December 2, 1946. Back row (left to right): N. Hilberry, Samuel Allison, Thomas Brill, Robert Nobles, Warren Nyer, and Marvin Wilkenig; middle row: Harold Agnew, William Sturm, Harold Lichtenberger, Leona W. Marshall, and Leo Szilard; front row: Enrico Fermi, Walter Zinn, Albert Wattenberg, and Herbert Anderson.

The key administrative figure in the Manhattan Project was Leslie R. Groves. Born in 1896 in Albany, New York, son of an Army chaplain, he graduated from West Point in 1918, fourth in his class, and went to work for the Corps of Engineers. A man of integrity, excellence, and duty to country, under his supervision the Pentagon was built in less than a year and a half. It was this accomplishment in particular that led to his appointment as chief of the super-secret Manhattan Project, in pursuit of which he was given an enormous budget. Groves immediately set out to build huge manufacturing facilities across the United States.

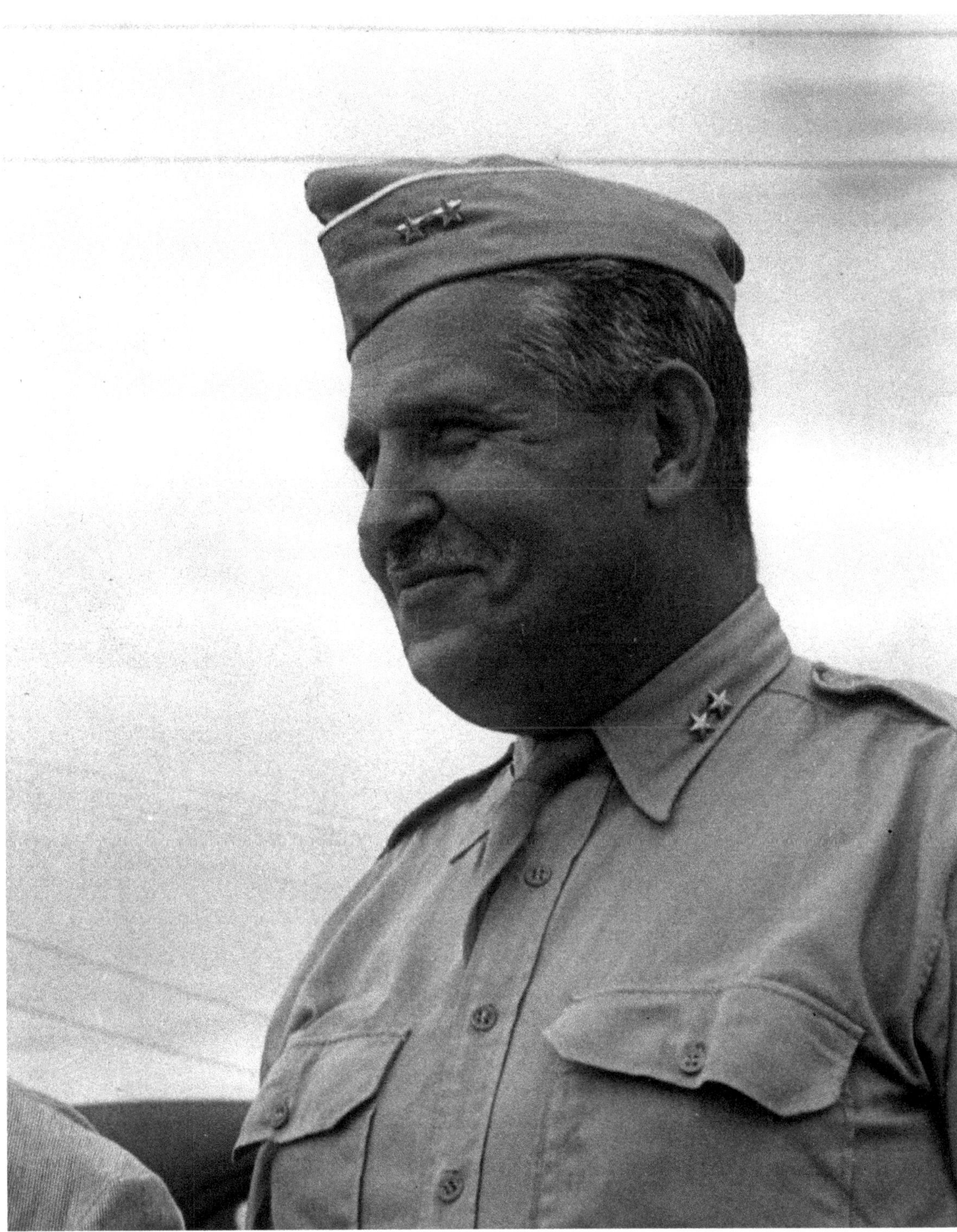

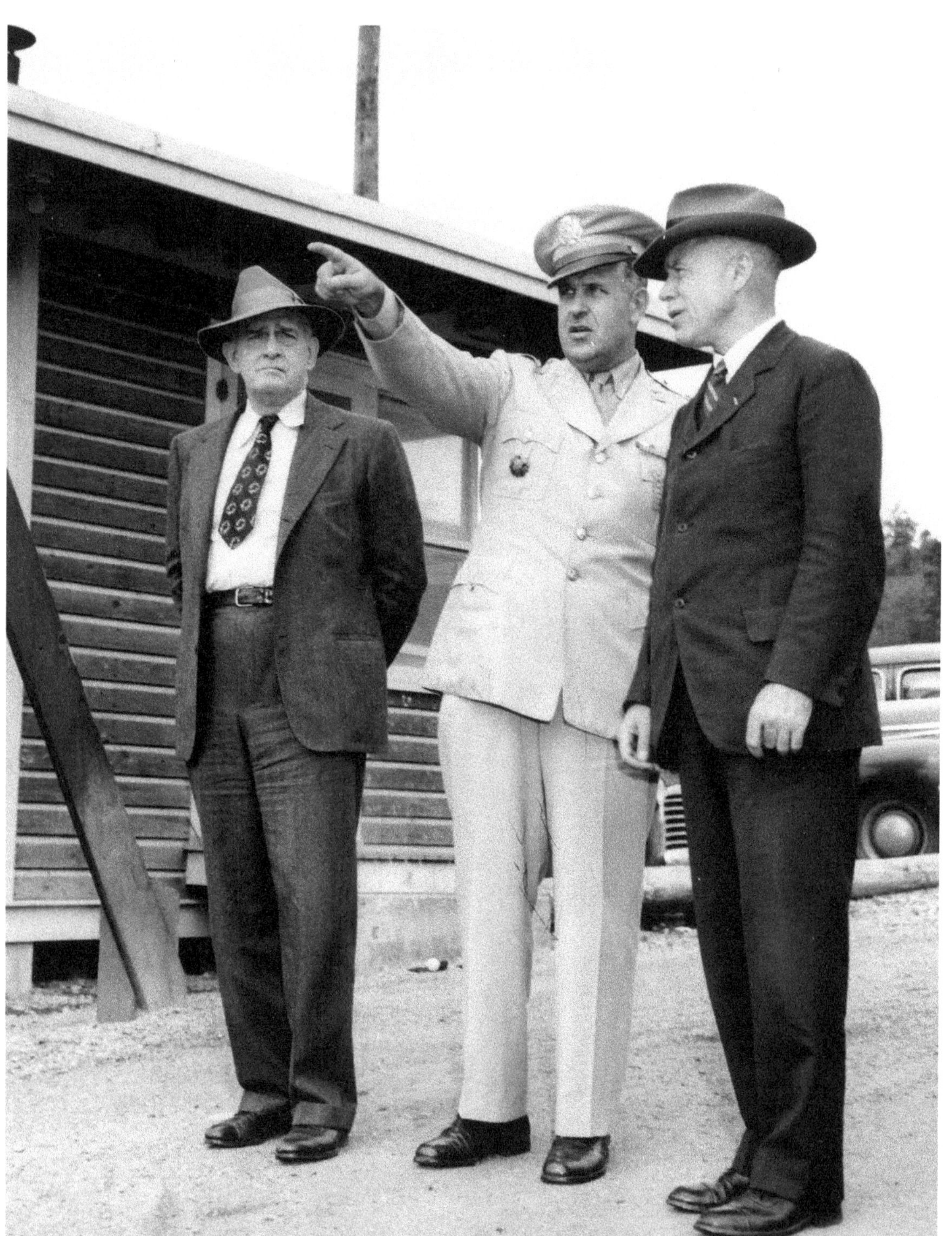

Leslie Groves at the Y-12 site in Oak Ridge, Tennessee, with Secretary of War Robert Patterson and Senator Tom Stewart, September 29, 1945.

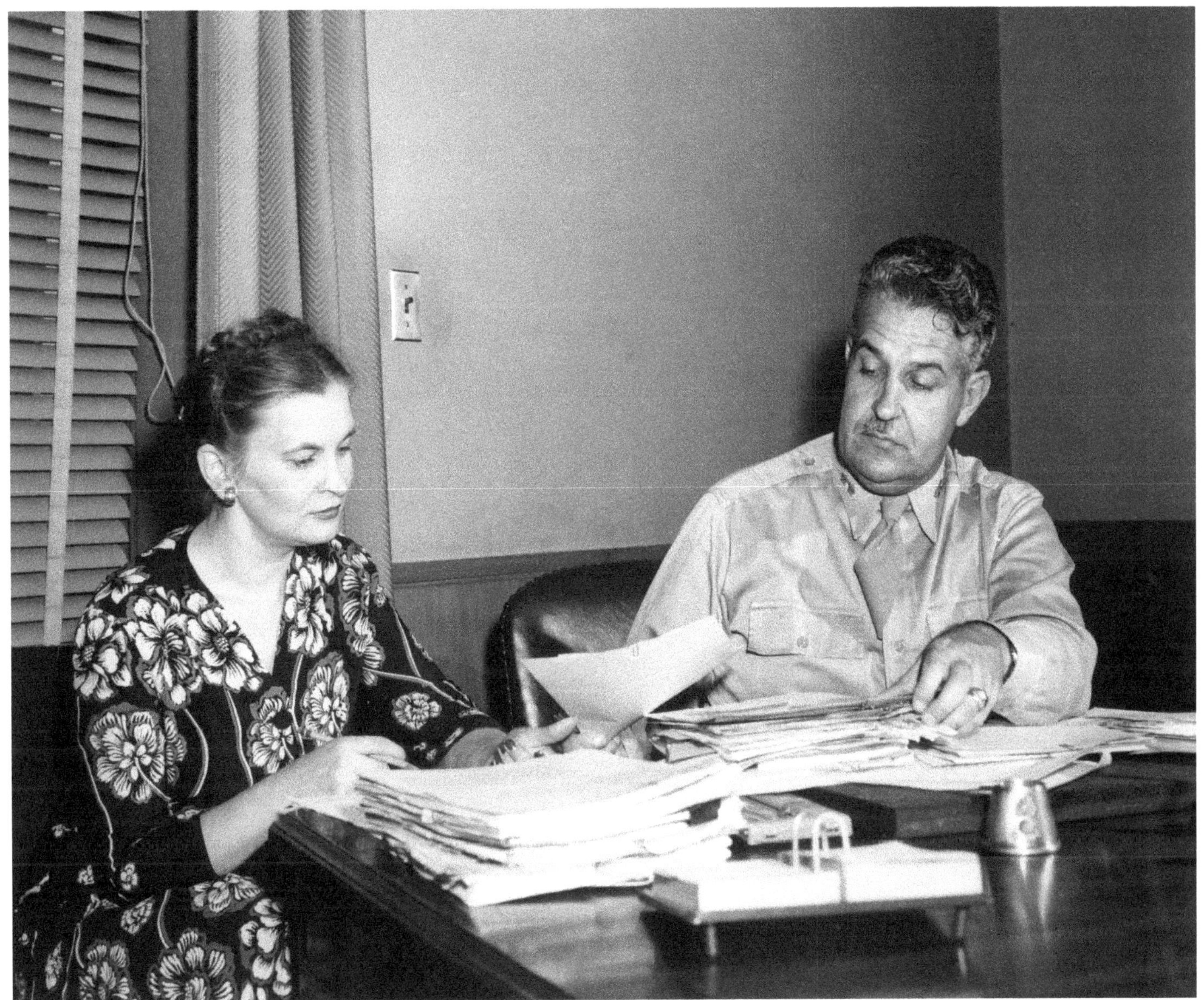

Only two or three people knew the full scope of the Manhattan Project, where all the secret facilities were located around the U.S., and what the mission actually was. Groves knew it all of course, and the second-most-knowledgeable person on the project was his secretary, Mrs. J. M. O'Leary, called "Jeanne."

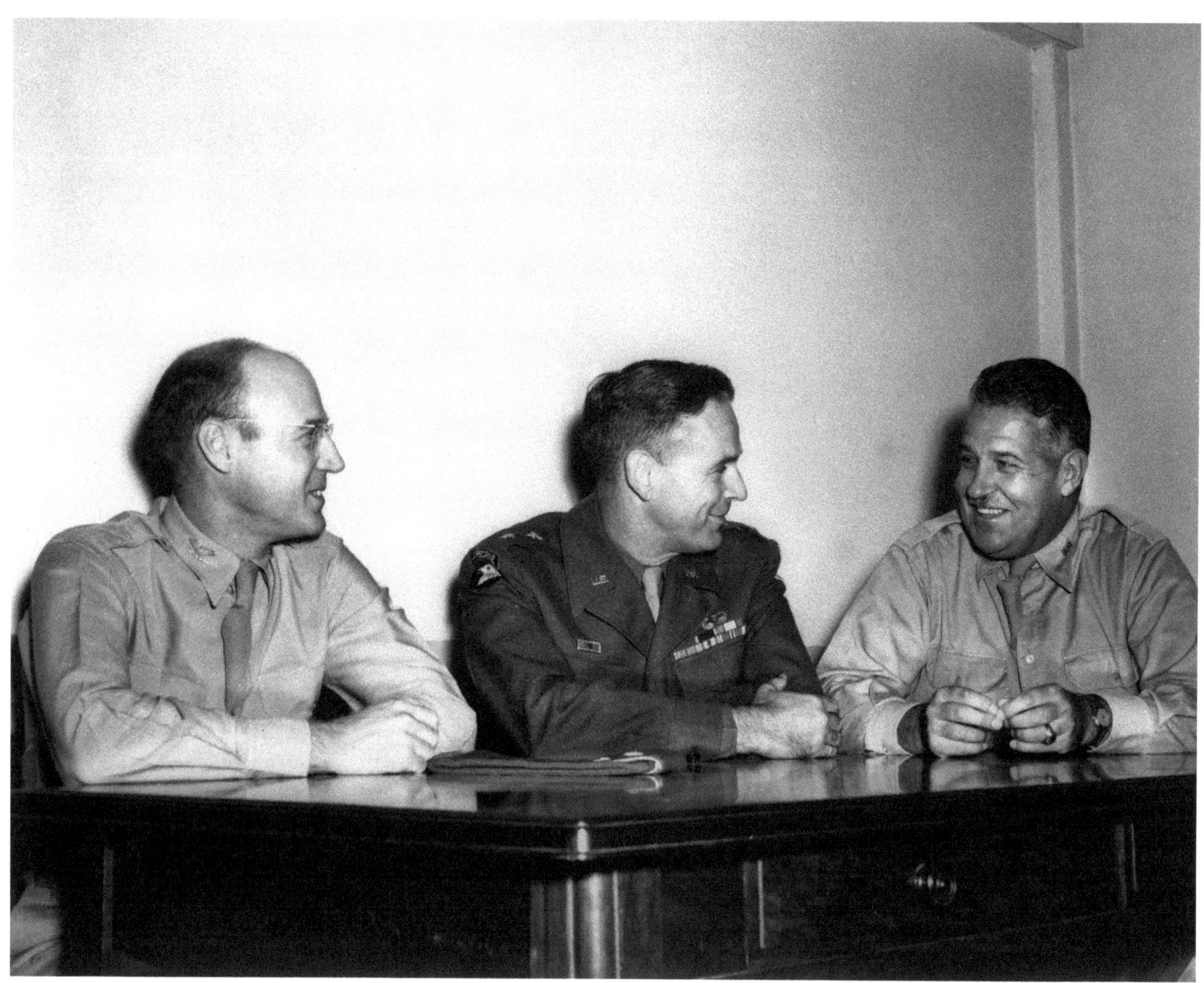

On the left is Colonel Kenneth Nichols, the deputy to General Groves. He was based in Oak Ridge during the project, but was also responsible for the facilities in Hanford, Washington, playing a key role in the construction of those facilities. At center is General Maxwell Taylor, U.S. Army 82nd Airborne Division. The three men are shown at a press conference held January 10, 1946.

How and Where to Build the Unknown

An Unimaginable Construction Challenge

General Leslie Groves was charged with a mission: to do the impossible. No chemical or physical method for producing large amounts of uranium or plutonium was known, much less how much of the stuff would be required for a bomb. An equally profound mystery was how to build the bomb itself. Yet the aim of the Manhattan Project was clear—to do just that.

Groves immediately pulled together the best physicists, chemists, and industrial leaders the world had to offer, including the scientists who had done the original research. He made Dr. Enrico Fermi the lead scientist. Two things were immediately clear: first, there was the very real possibility of an uncontrolled nuclear chain reaction or massive explosion and the release of radioactivity; and second, each potential method would require its own full-scale industrial plant so that mistakes, which were inevitable, would not halt progress. Groves and the scientists knew that these huge plants would have to be constructed while research was being done into the very processes they were to utilize. Groves focused his team in several directions at the same time and immediately set out to determine what facilities were needed and where they should be located.

The need for extreme secrecy and the real possibility of a radiation accident meant that the team should seek remote locations only. The sites chosen were:

- Oak Ridge, Tennessee—selected on September 23, 1942, for the enrichment of uranium. Construction began on February 18, 1943.
- Los Alamos, New Mexico—selected on November 25, 1942, as the bomb-design research facility. Construction began in April 1943.
- Hanford, Washington—selected on January 16, 1943, as the site for the production of plutonium by using full-scale nuclear reactors. Construction began on August 27, 1943.

Because so little was known, four, large, distinct facilities were constructed at Oak Ridge and located apart from one another in three distinct valleys. The Y-12 Plant was constructed to house an electromagnetic process for separating and enriching uranium using devices called "calutrons." Construction began in February 1943, cost $427 million, required 13,200 construction workers, and had an operating force of 22,842 employees in 1945. Y-12 began shipping bomb-grade highly enriched uranium to Los Alamos in early 1945.

The X-10 Plant, a Graphite Reactor, was built for the large-scale production of plutonium-239 from the fission of uranium so that scientists could research and develop chemical and physical methods to separate the isotopes of plutonium needed to produce weapons-grade plutonium. Work began in February 1943, less than two months after Enrico Fermi and his colleagues at the University of Chicago successfully operated the world's first, crude nuclear reactor CP-1. After nine months of construction the Graphite Reactor was loaded with uranium and achieved criticality. The plant cost $13 million and had a peak construction workforce of 3,247 employees.

The K-25 Plant was constructed to separate uranium isotopes by diffusing uranium hexafluoride gas through porous barriers. The first units began operating on February 20, 1945. The K-25 building was a huge U-shaped structure that if straightened out would have run to nearly a mile in length. The interior was 400 feet wide with walls 60 feet tall, and each arm was 2,450 feet long. It was said to be the world's largest building at nearly 44 square acres. The construction workforce reached 25,000 employees in May 1945.

The S-50 Plant was built to separate uranium by liquid thermal diffusion. Construction began on June 21, 1944, and took just 75 days to complete. Located on the Clinch River in the same valley as the K-25 Plant, the S-50 Plant began operation in October 1944. Problems led to halting the operation shortly after the plant went full-scale. It was shut down September 9, 1945, and demolished the following year.

It should be remembered that the Oak Ridge, Los Alamos, and Hanford facilities were each full-scale industrial complexes all under construction at essentially the same time and in three different parts of the United States. Little was proven, research was ongoing during construction, and scientific theories and applications were opening uncharted territory. And all of this was being orchestrated by one man, Leslie Groves.

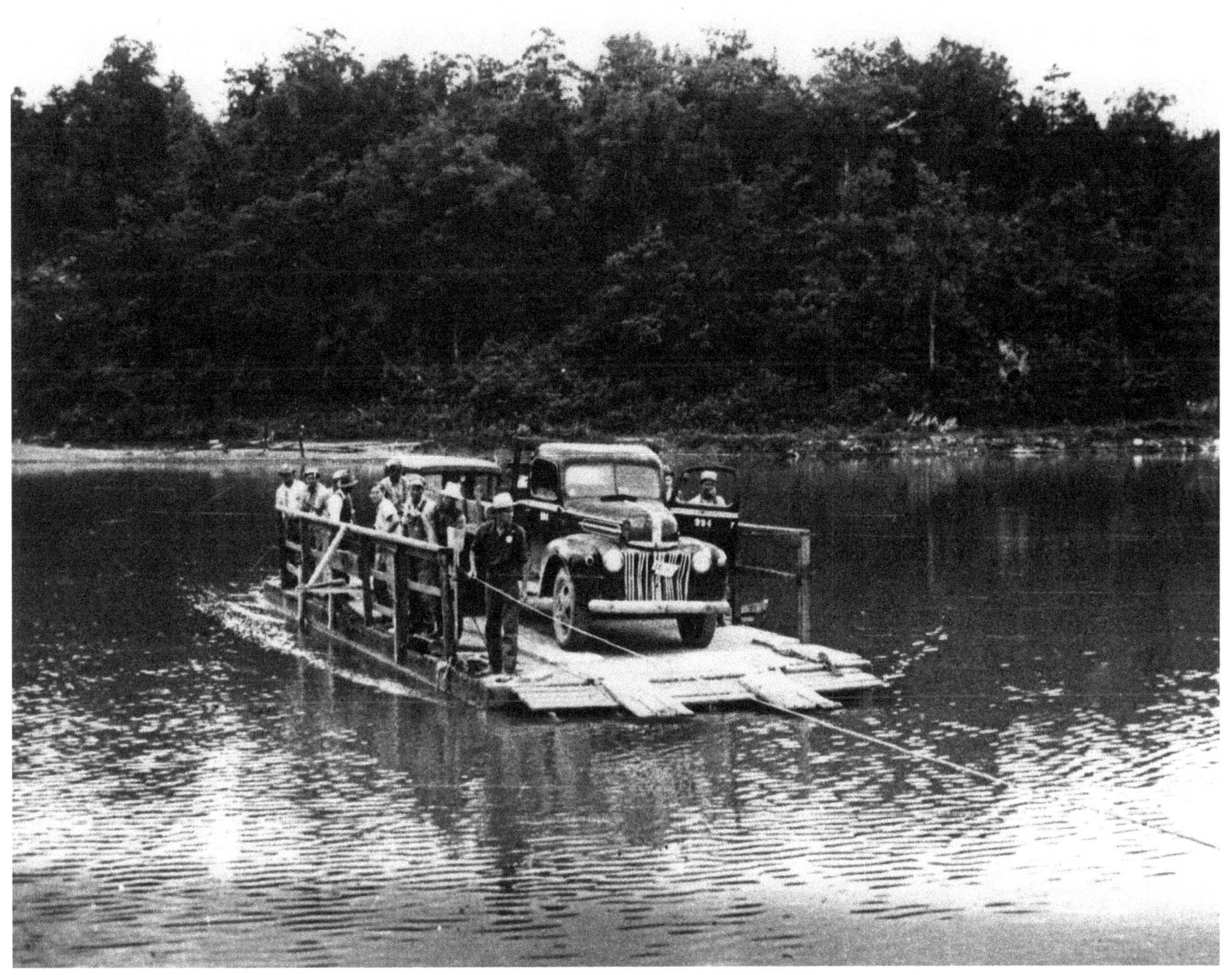

There weren't many bridges in the rural areas around Oak Ridge in the 1940s. This pull-ferry across the Clinch River carried people and vehicles to K-25. When the Gallaher Bridge was built, the ferry ended its runs across the river.

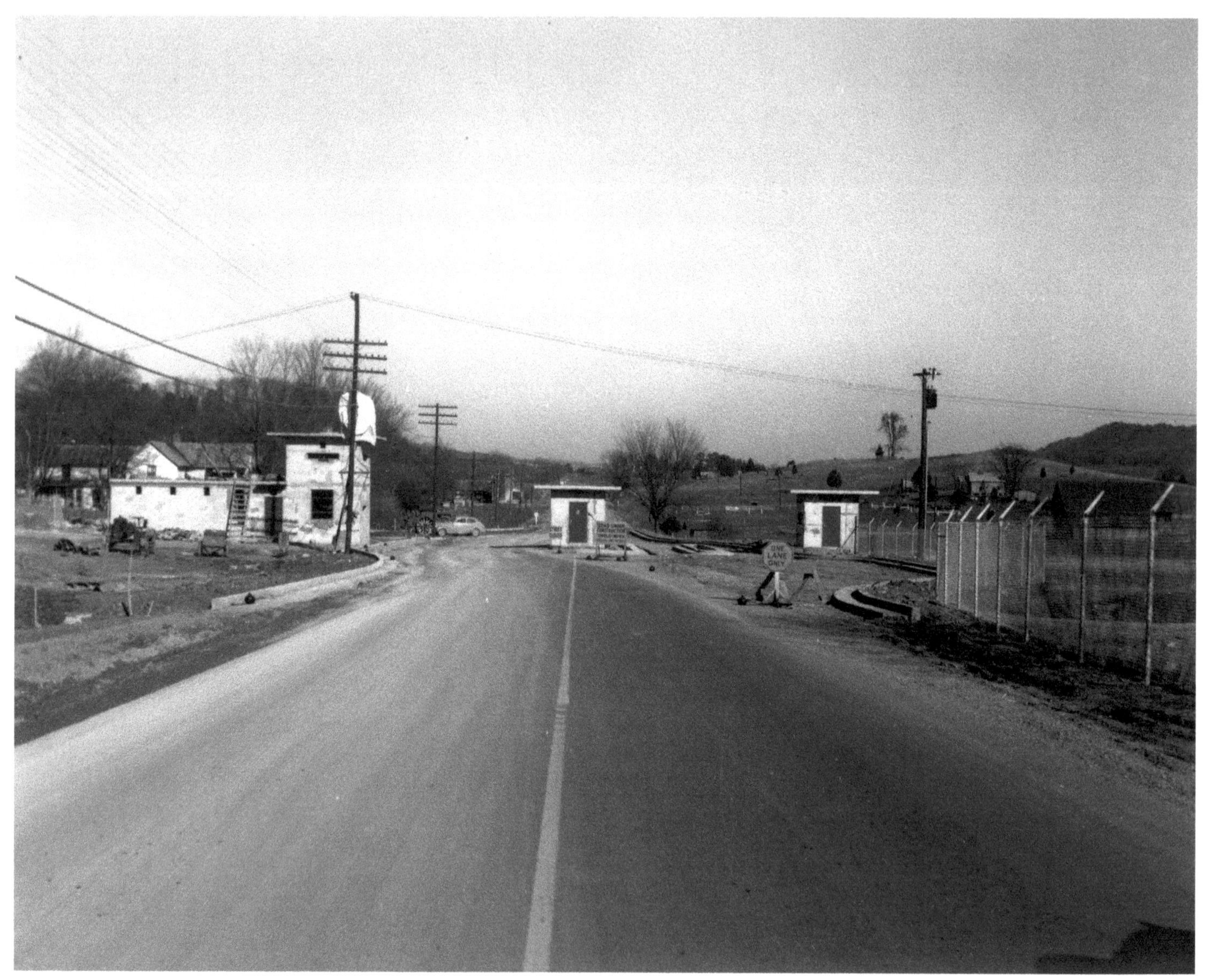

When completed, the Oak Ridge Reservation would have four separate facility areas (K-25, S-50, Y-12, and X-10) in three distinct valleys and would be completely cut off to public access. The only way in was through a number of security stations or gates, one of which is shown here. Armed guards were posted on the second floor of the taller building to the left. The long, narrow windows were gun slots from which the guards monitored activity. Three of these gates still stand in Oak Ridge today and are used by residents for meeting facilities.

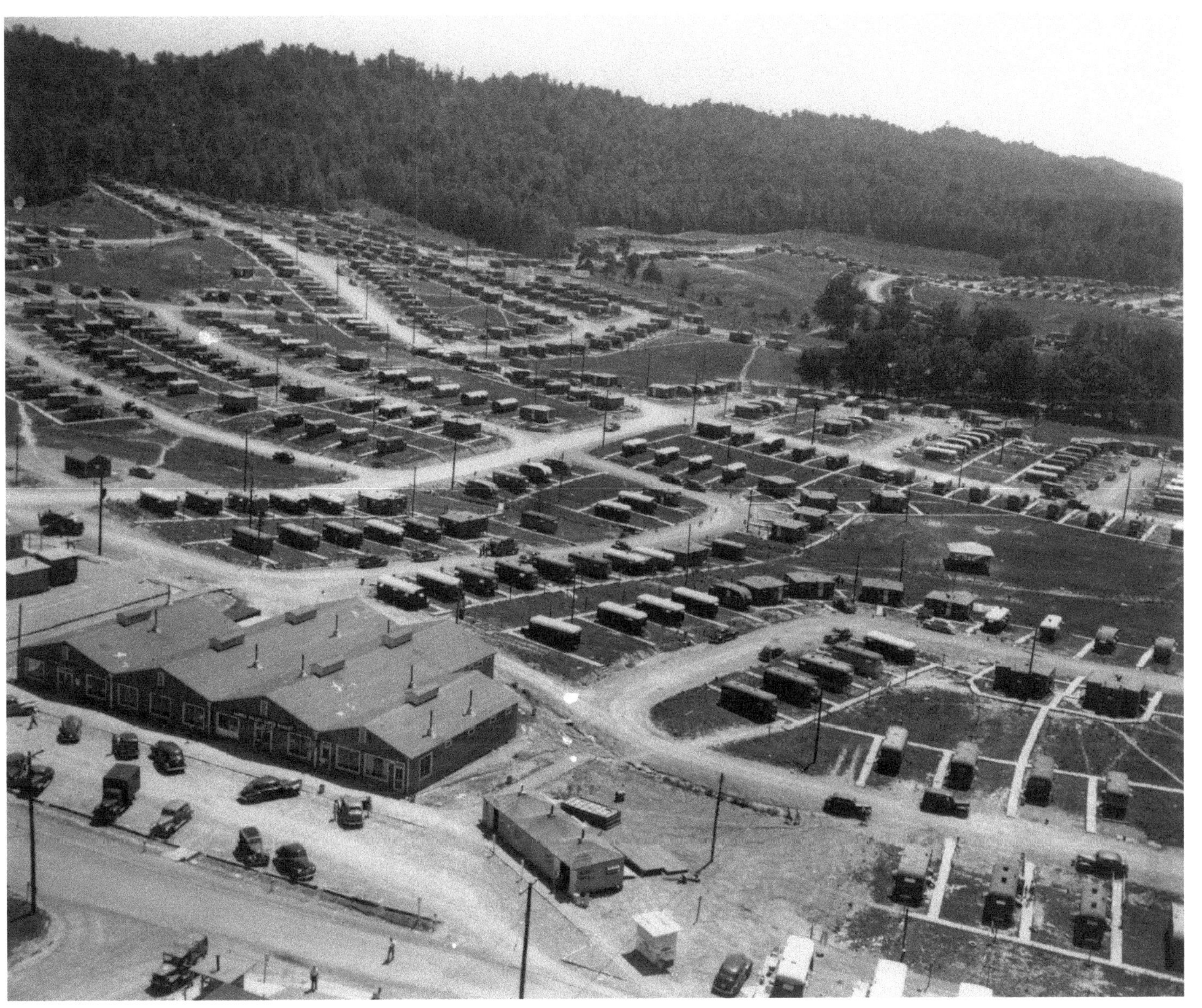

Land was being cleared everywhere for construction of the production facilities. At the same time schools, theaters, medical units, and living quarters of all kinds were being built to accommodate the families and workers. This is a 1945 aerial view of trailers in Gamble Valley, just one of the many living areas.

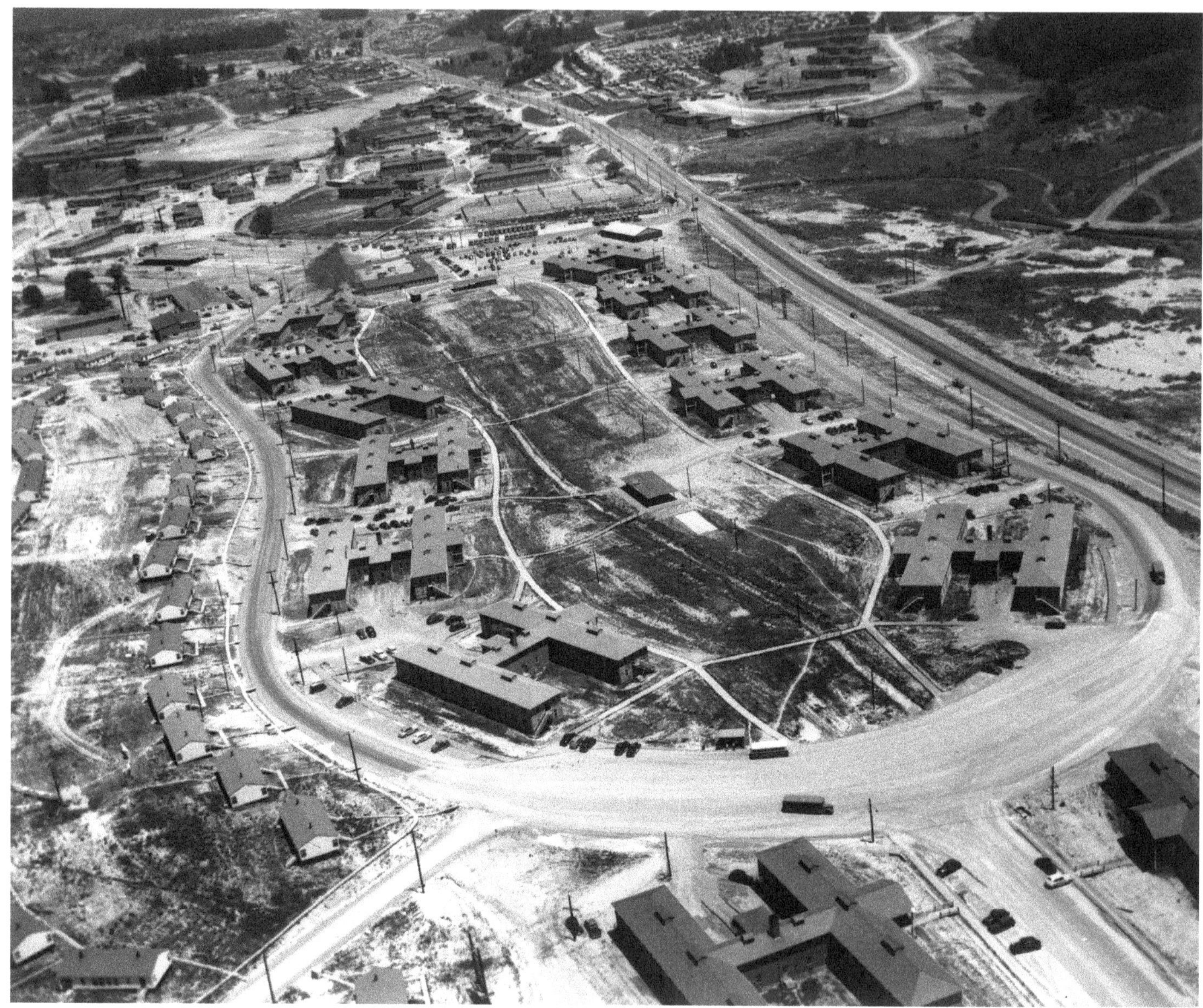

This 1944 aerial photo shows more than a dozen dormitories built to house men and women workers. A single room ran $15 a month, a double ran $20. A two-room apartment sharing a bath with another apartment cost $25. These dorms and apartments included maid service, linens, towels, and soap. An A-house with two bedrooms, living room, kitchen, and bath went for $38. All rentals included coal for heating, water, electricity, and other services.

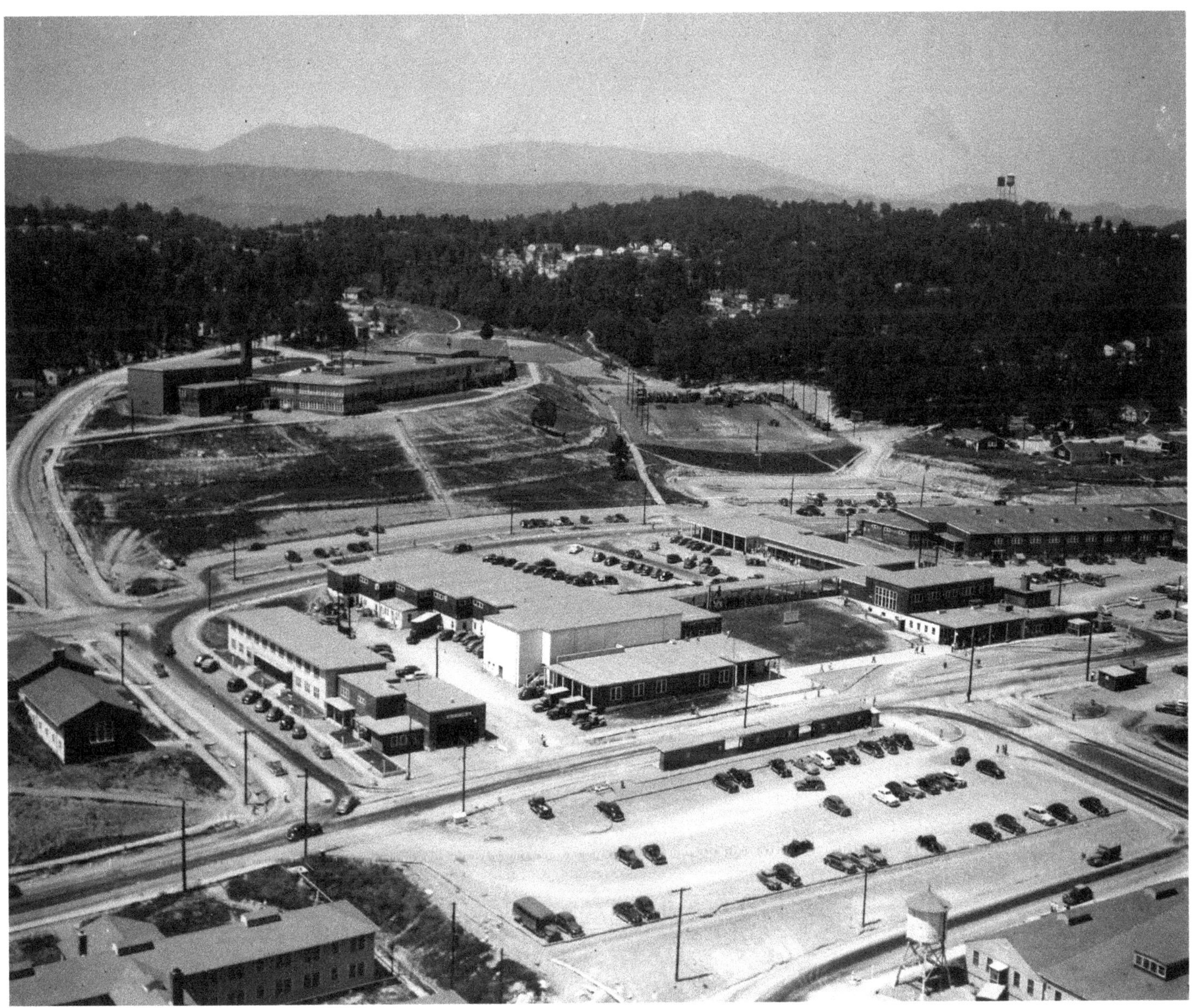

Jackson Square was the center of business activity in Oak Ridge. Its stores, bank, theater, and other city offices made it a popular gathering place. The Oak Ridge High School is visible in the background with the athletic field to the right. By 1944 there were 50,000 people living and working in Oak Ridge.

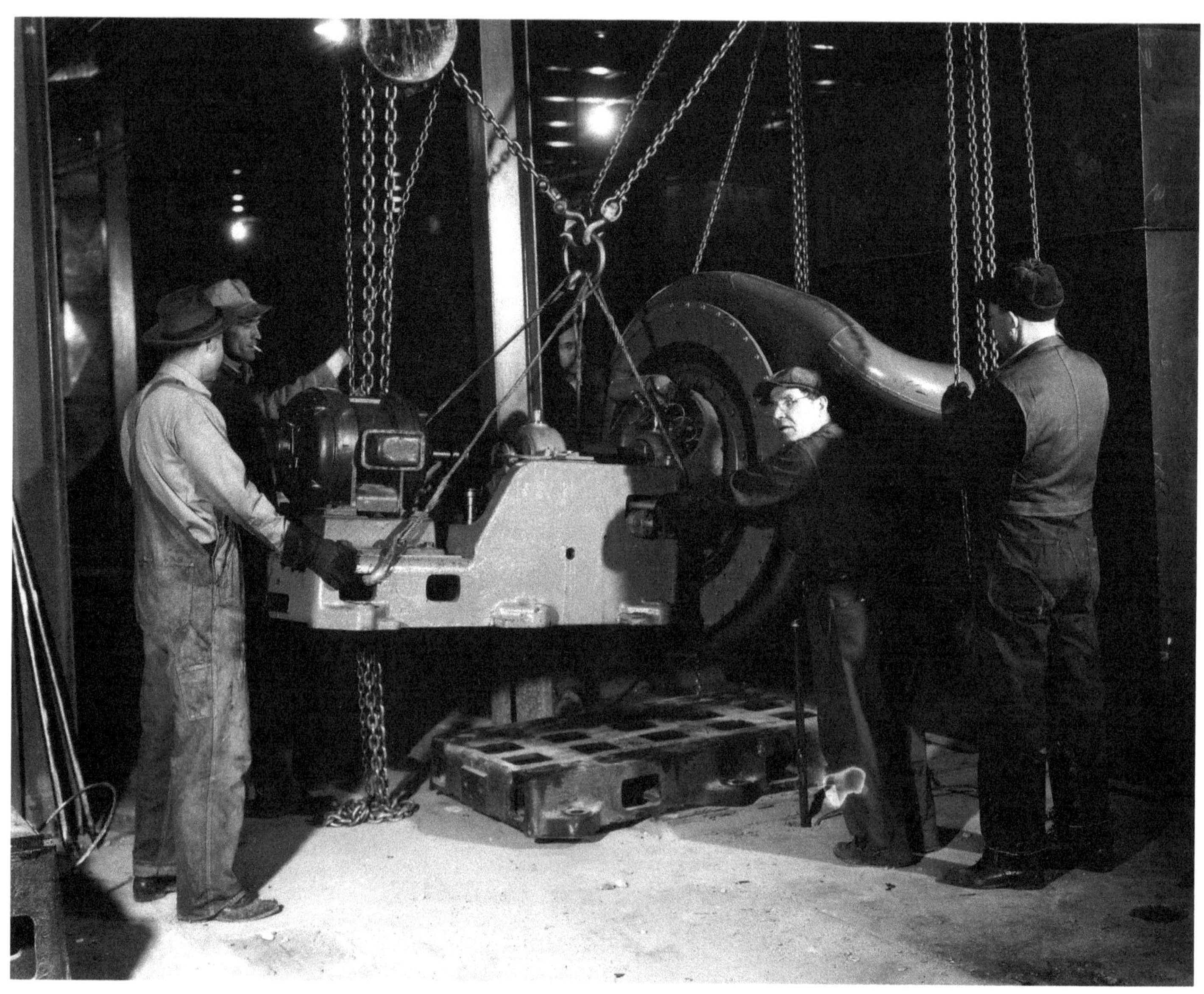

A maintenance crew sets one of the hundreds of vacuum pumps in the gaseous diffusion building at the K-25 Site in Oak Ridge.

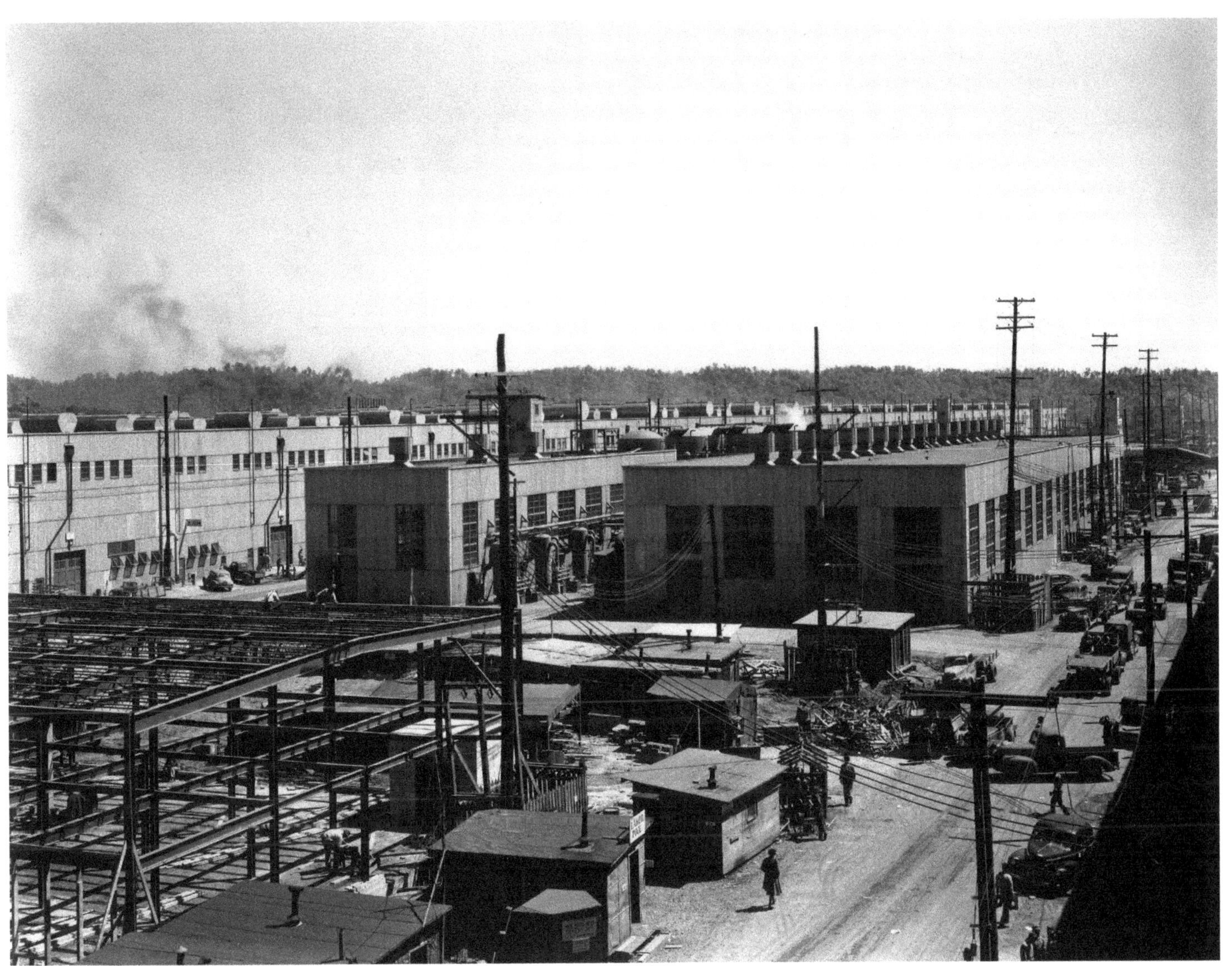

A complex gaseous diffusion process separated uranium using a porous barrier, but it took many repetitions and a huge number of units called cascades. Though the K-25 facility was massive, it could yield weapons-grade uranium only in quantities measured in grams because it was trying to physically separate isotopes of the same atom. An isotope of any element has a different number of neutrons in its nucleus, which means the difference in the atomic weight of the atom is extremely small, merely the weight of the neutrons, rendering isotopes enormously difficult to separate from one another. The building was larger than the Pentagon, and at the time was the largest single building in the United States. It consumed enormous amounts of electricity. This and the other facilities in Oak Ridge at the time consumed one-seventh of the power produced in the U.S.

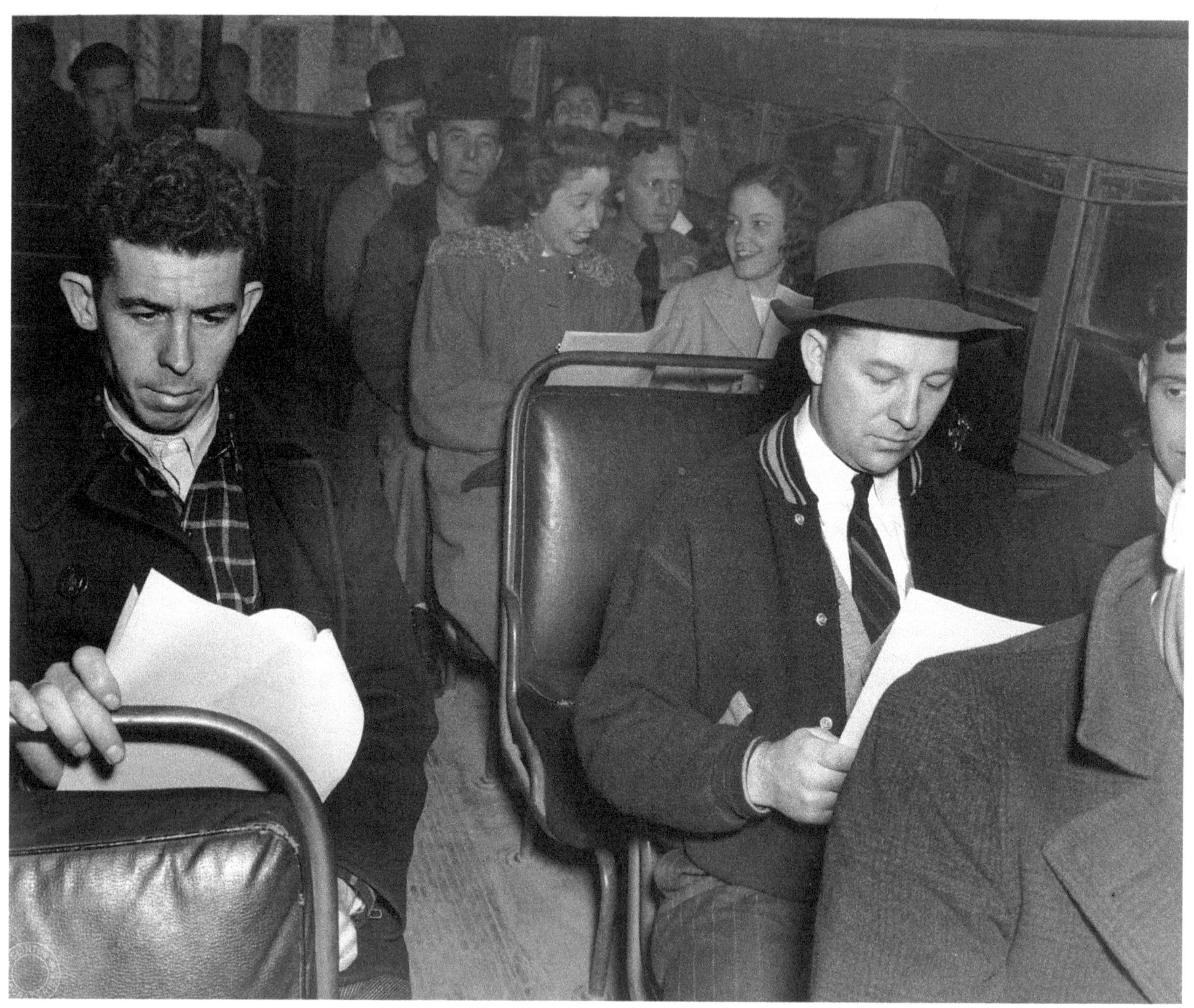

At each of the "secret facilities" around the country, every project employee knew that the specific work he or she performed, whatever it was, could not be discussed with anyone, not even a spouse. In this photo, workers on their commute to and from the plants at Oak Ridge remain silent, read, or share idle chatter.

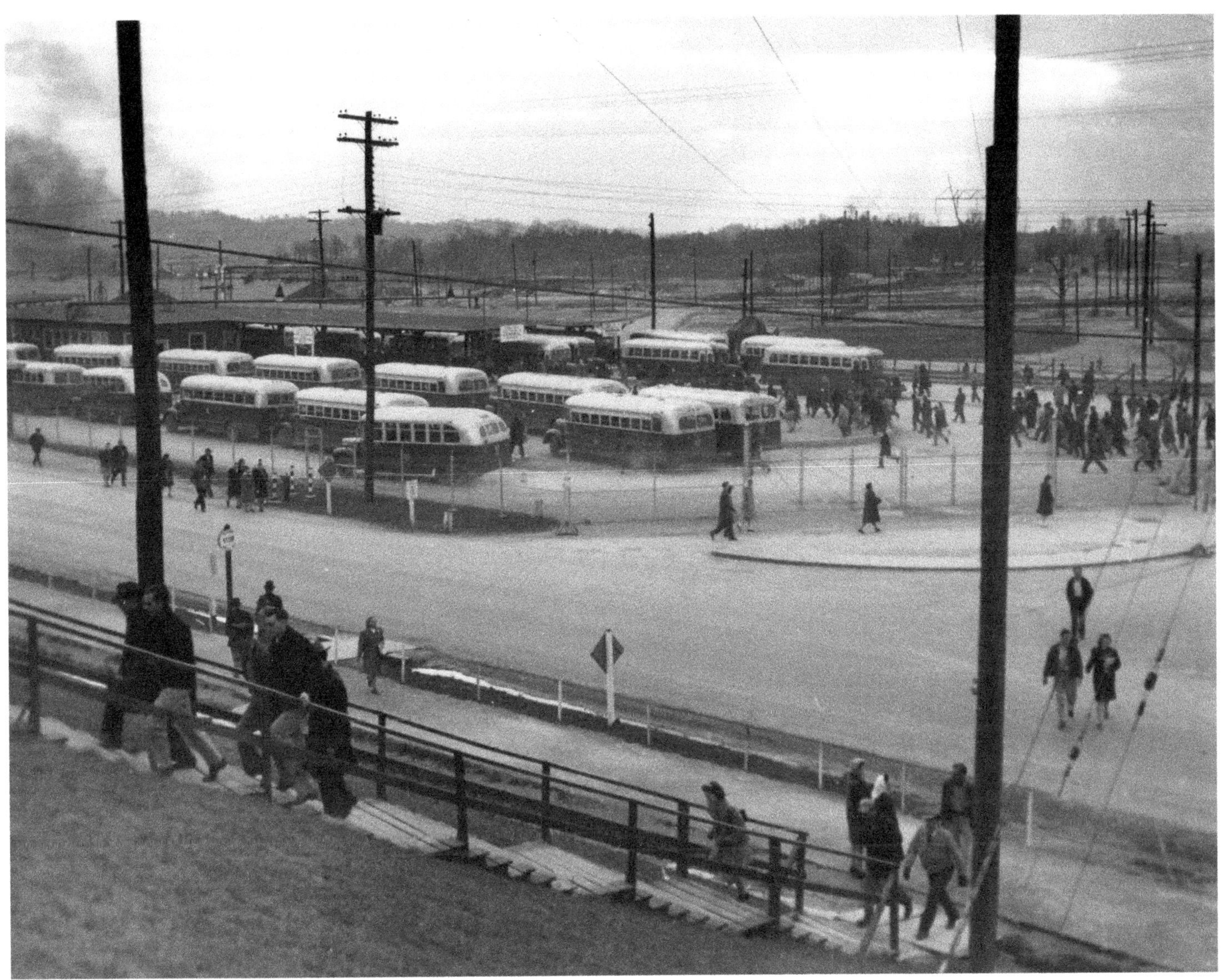

The Oak Ridge sites, including K-25, had one of the single-largest bus fleets in the U.S. to bring workers from the residential areas, apartments, and dorms to the facilities. This bus terminal at K-25 is just one of the many terminals throughout the secret city.

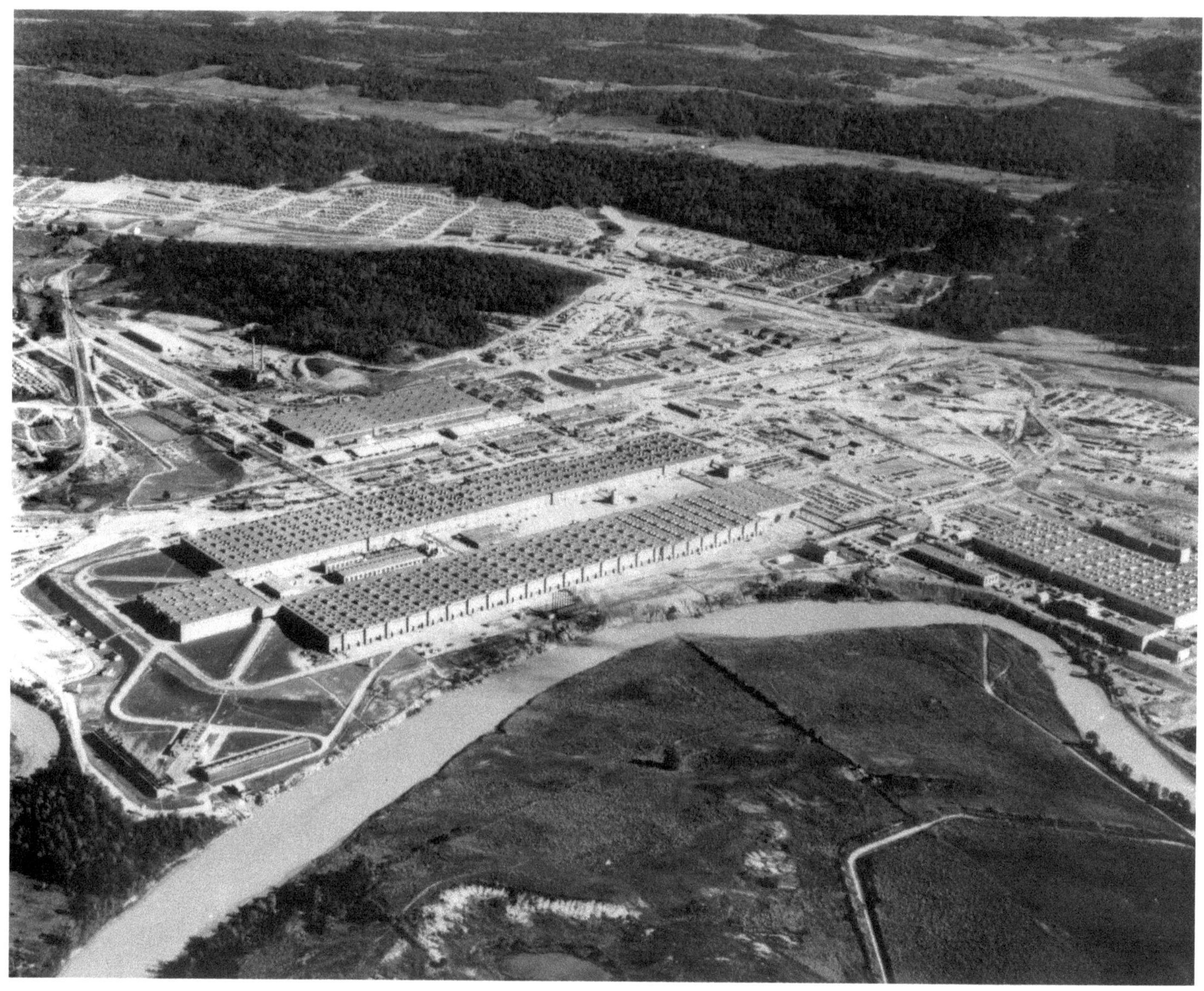

An aerial photo of the enormous gaseous diffusion building at K-25, nearly a mile long. Construction began in 1943, in advance of the final design of the process it was to use, and was completed in early 1945, employing 12,000 workers. Employees inside the building relied on bicycles. In the background is the residential area called Happy Valley.

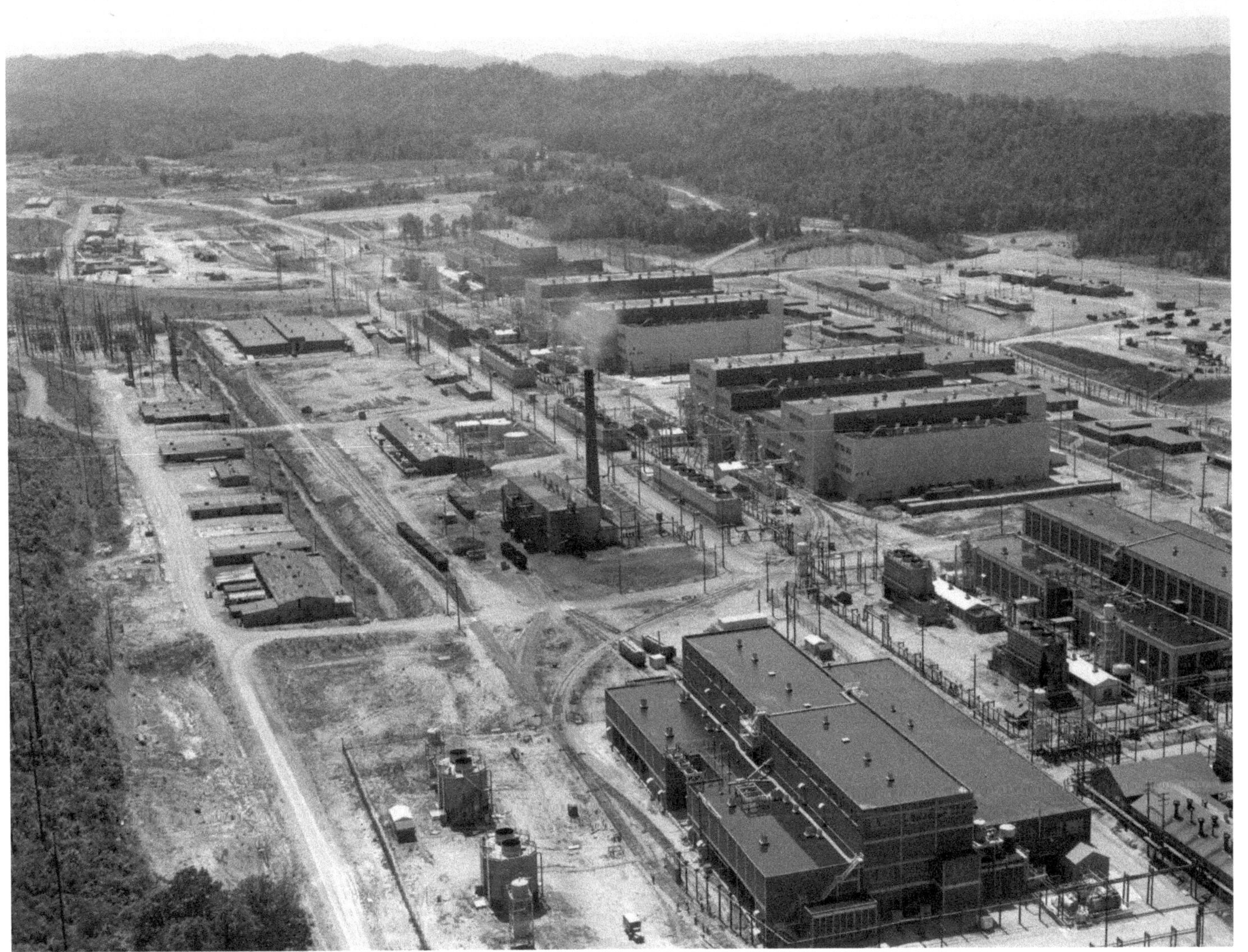

A separate facility in the next valley over from K-25 was being built to house an electromagnetic separation process. This process used huge electromagnets and devices called calutrons, which sent a stream of charged particles through the magnetic field, deflecting lighter isotopes from heavier ones and collecting them in separate Alpha and Beta tracks. This 1947 photo of Y-12 faces west toward the Alpha buildings.

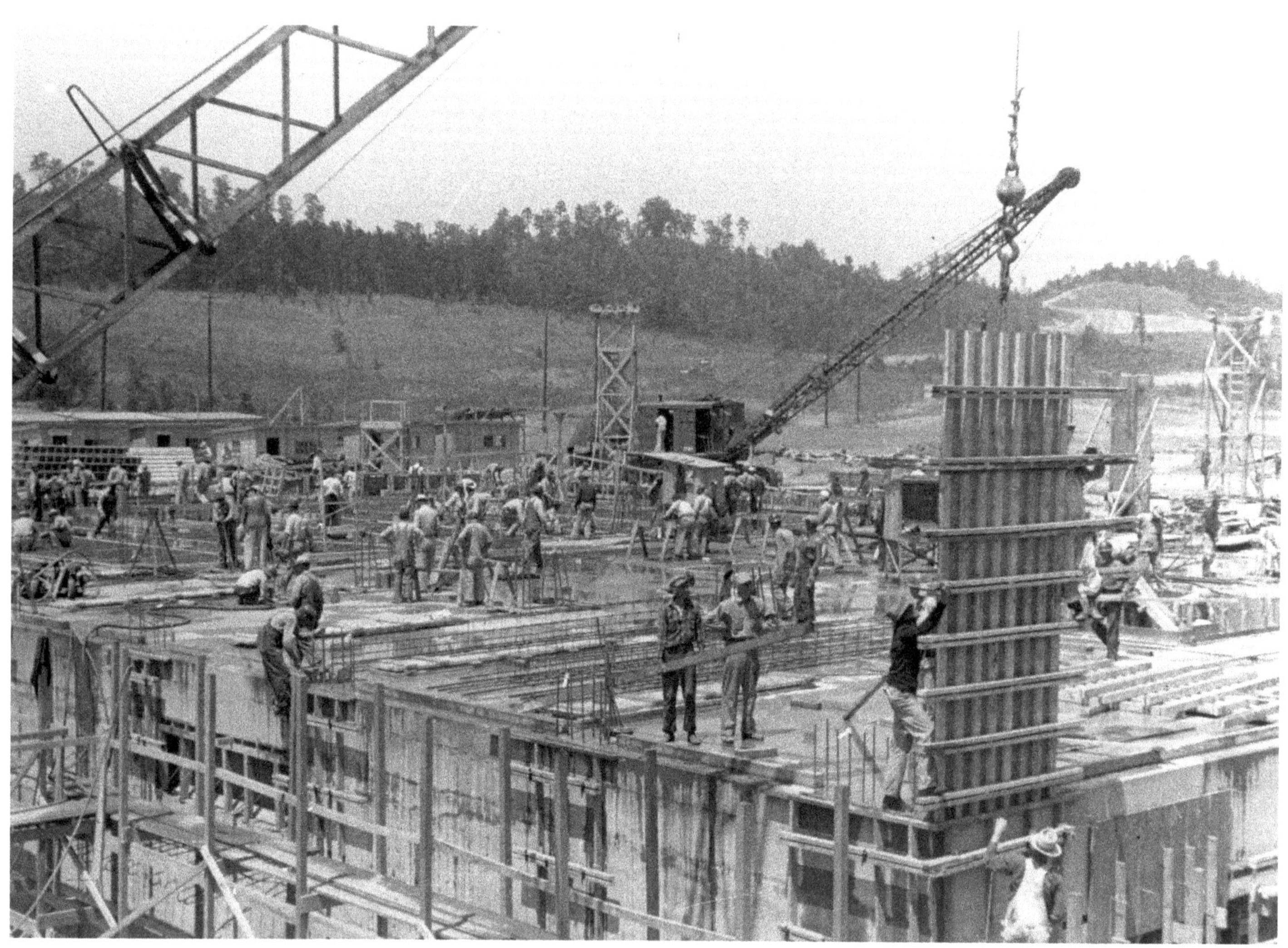

Thousands of construction workers were working on hundreds of buildings at the same time at the three major sites in Oak Ridge. Here construction workers are installing forms and rebar of Building 9731 at the Y-12 site.

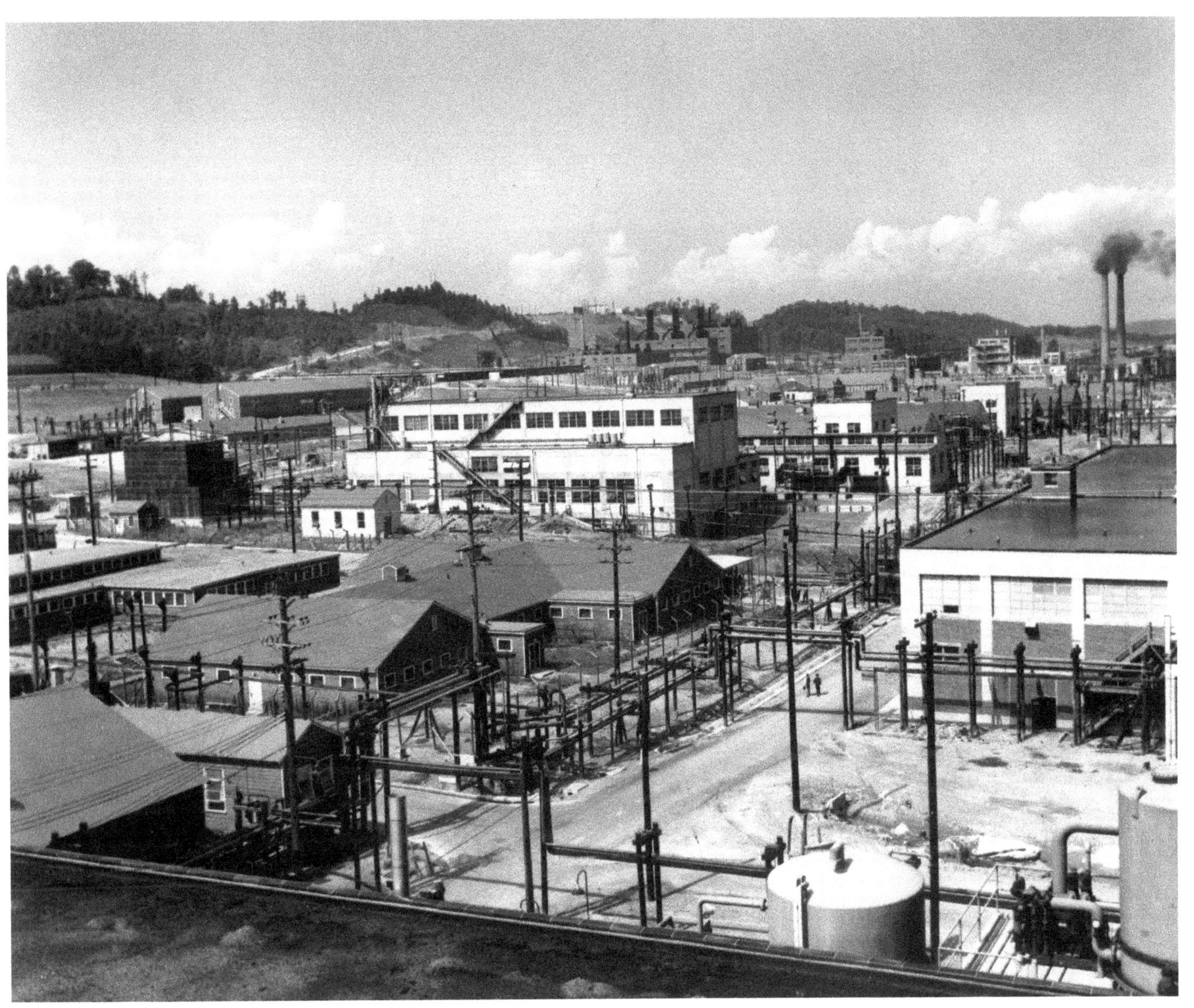

This 1945 photo of Y-12 faces east showing the many buildings and complexity of the facility.

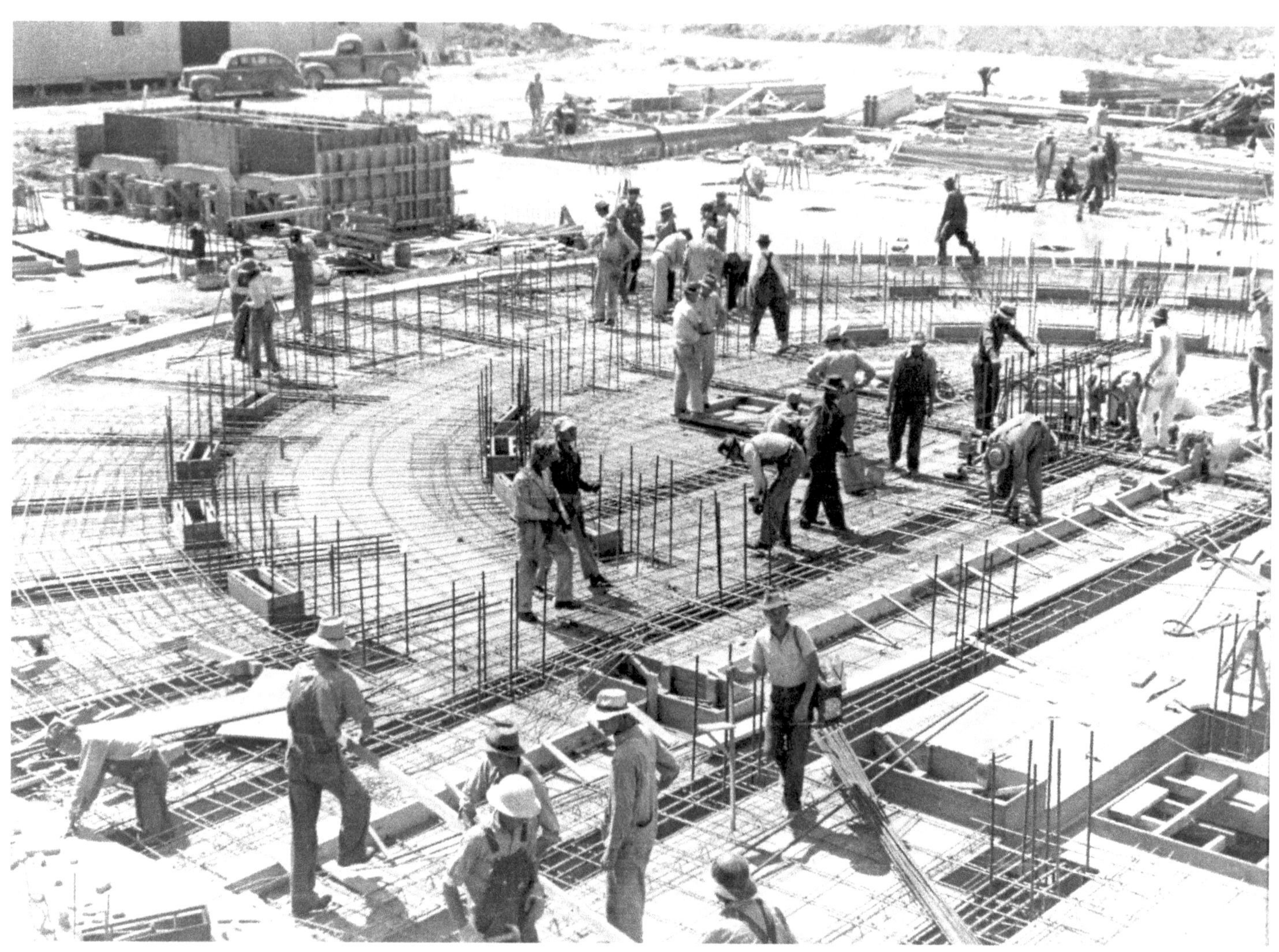

In this image, the foundation for the Alpha Racetrack is being constructed at Y-12. The Alpha and Beta racetracks were huge electromagnets. The Alpha Racetrack was more than 120 feet long, 75 feet wide, and 15 feet tall. Because copper was needed for the war effort, the project borrowed 15,000 tons of silver bullion from the United States Treasury to construct the coils for the magnets. A stream of charged particles was sent through a gap in the magnet, which had a strong magnetic field. This deflected atoms differently depending on their isotopic weight and charge. The two isotopic streams were collected in tanks.

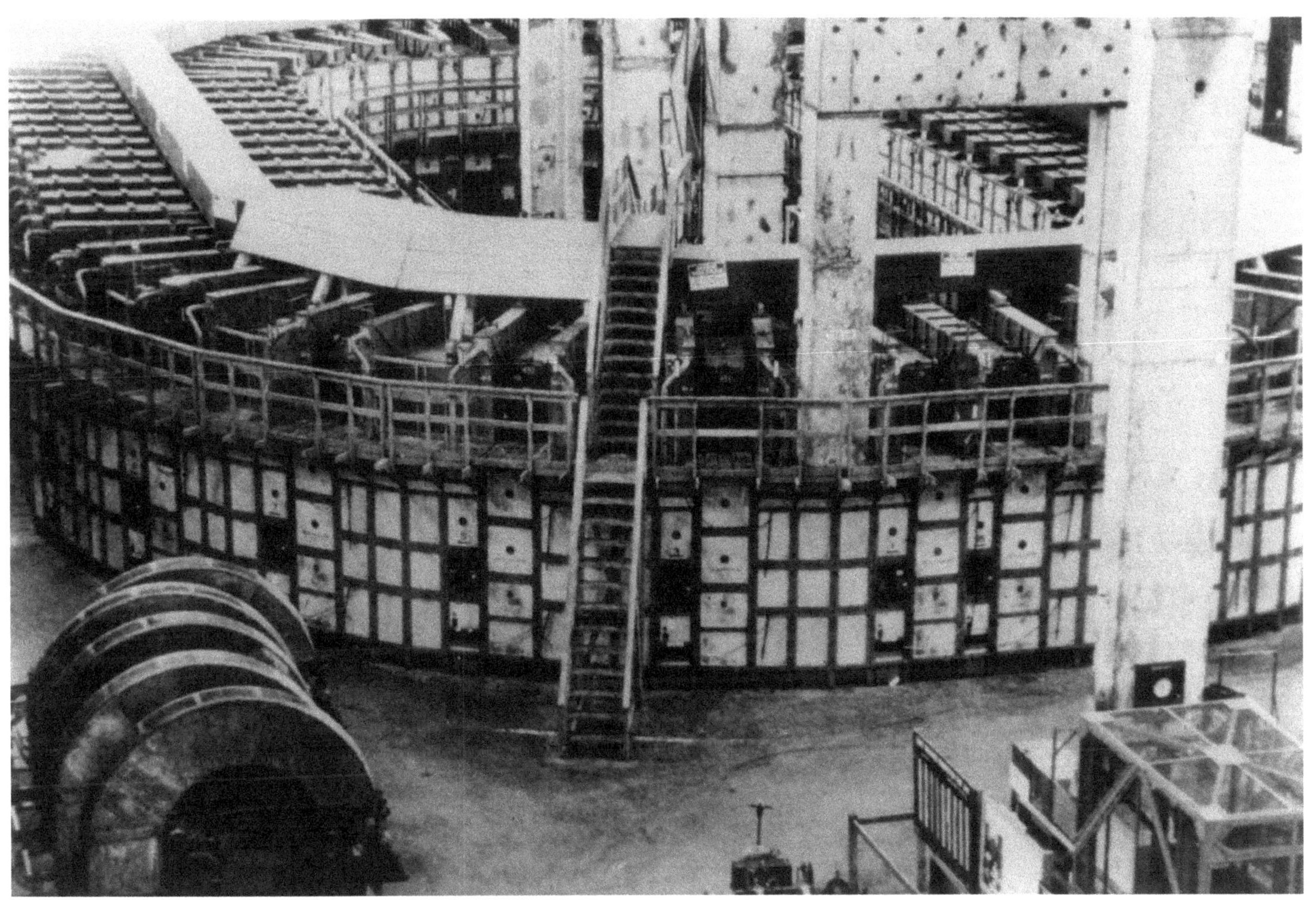

In 1943 the Alpha Racetrack began operation. In the left foreground are parts of the calutrons, the key component of the electromagnetic separation process. Problems forced the first racetrack to shut down, and the second began operation in January 1944. Uranium-235 was produced in quantities measured only in grams.

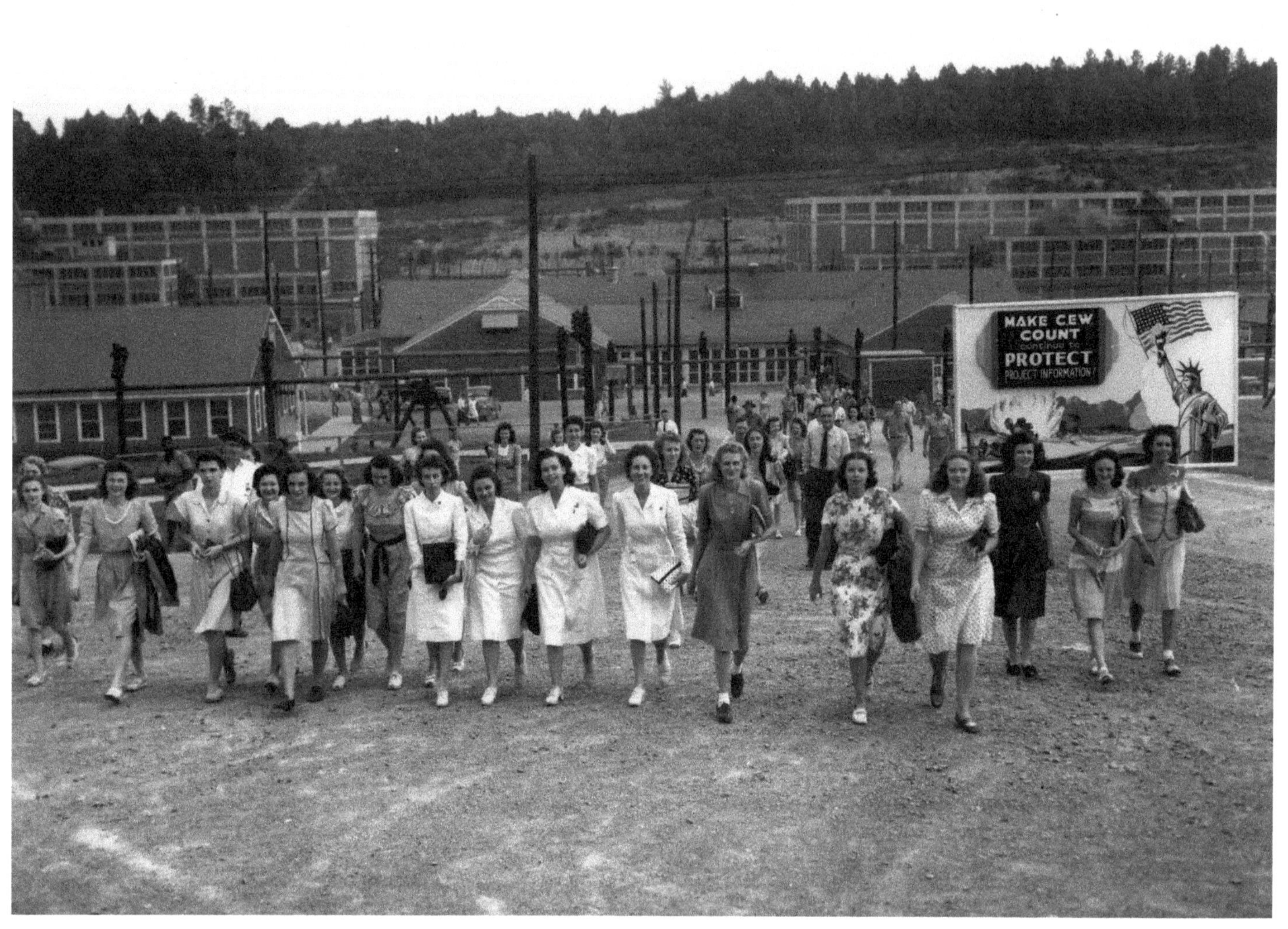

Work for the more than 24,000 workers went on 24 hours a day 7 days a week with three shifts that rotated every 7 days. This is a shift change at Y-12. Women played an important role at the plants in many capacities.

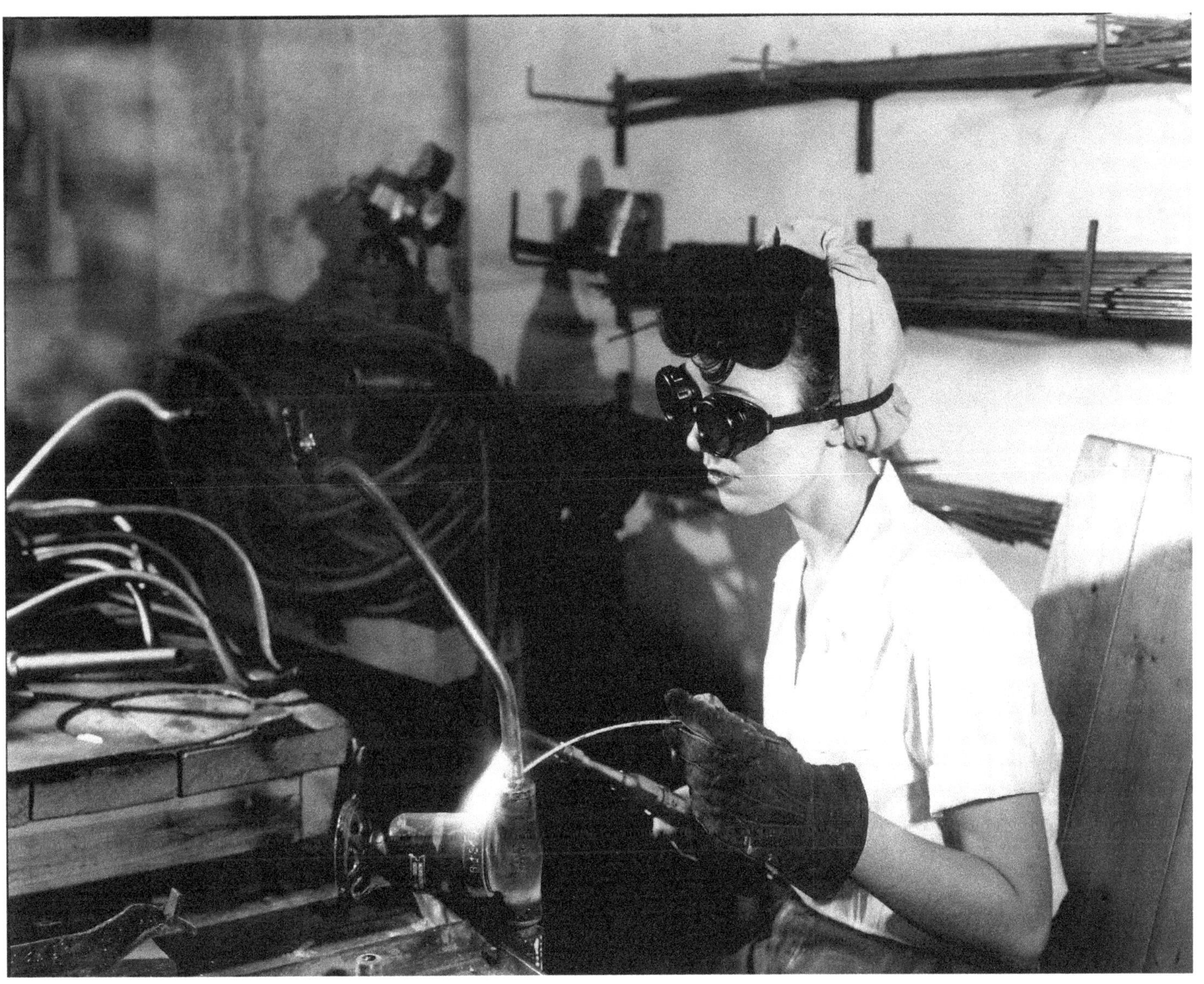

Women filled many roles on the Manhattan Project, including fabrication and welding. This Y-12 worker is making a specific piece of equipment over and over again for the hundreds and hundreds of identical units the project required.

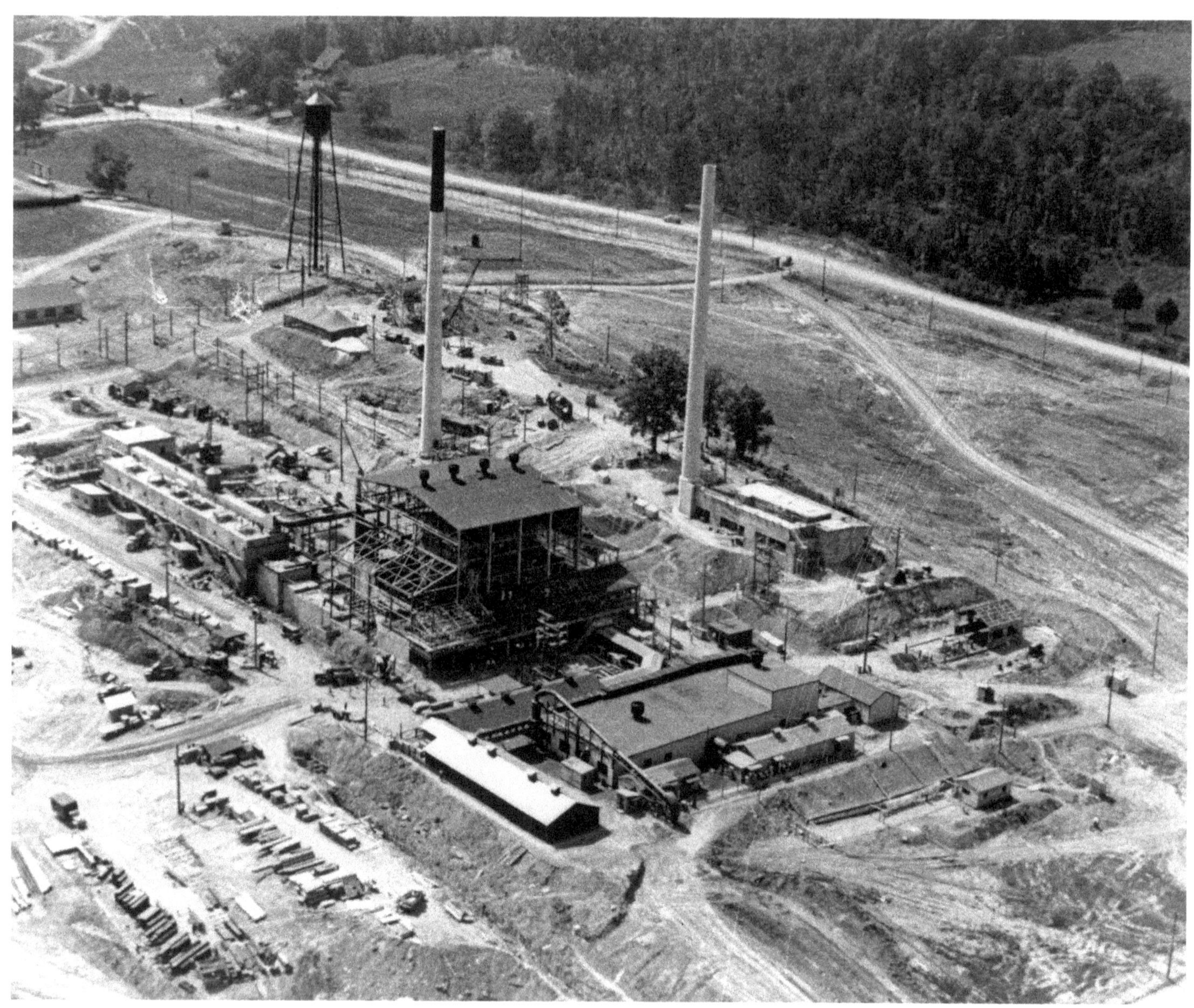

A third site in Oak Ridge, located along the Clinch River in a different valley from those of Y-12 and K-25, became home to the X-10 facility and the world's second nuclear reactor. Called the Graphite Reactor, the second reactor was based on CP-1 in Chicago, the world's first reactor. It was built in only ten months and went into operation on November 4, 1943, using neutrons produced by the fission of uranium to convert uranium into plutonium.

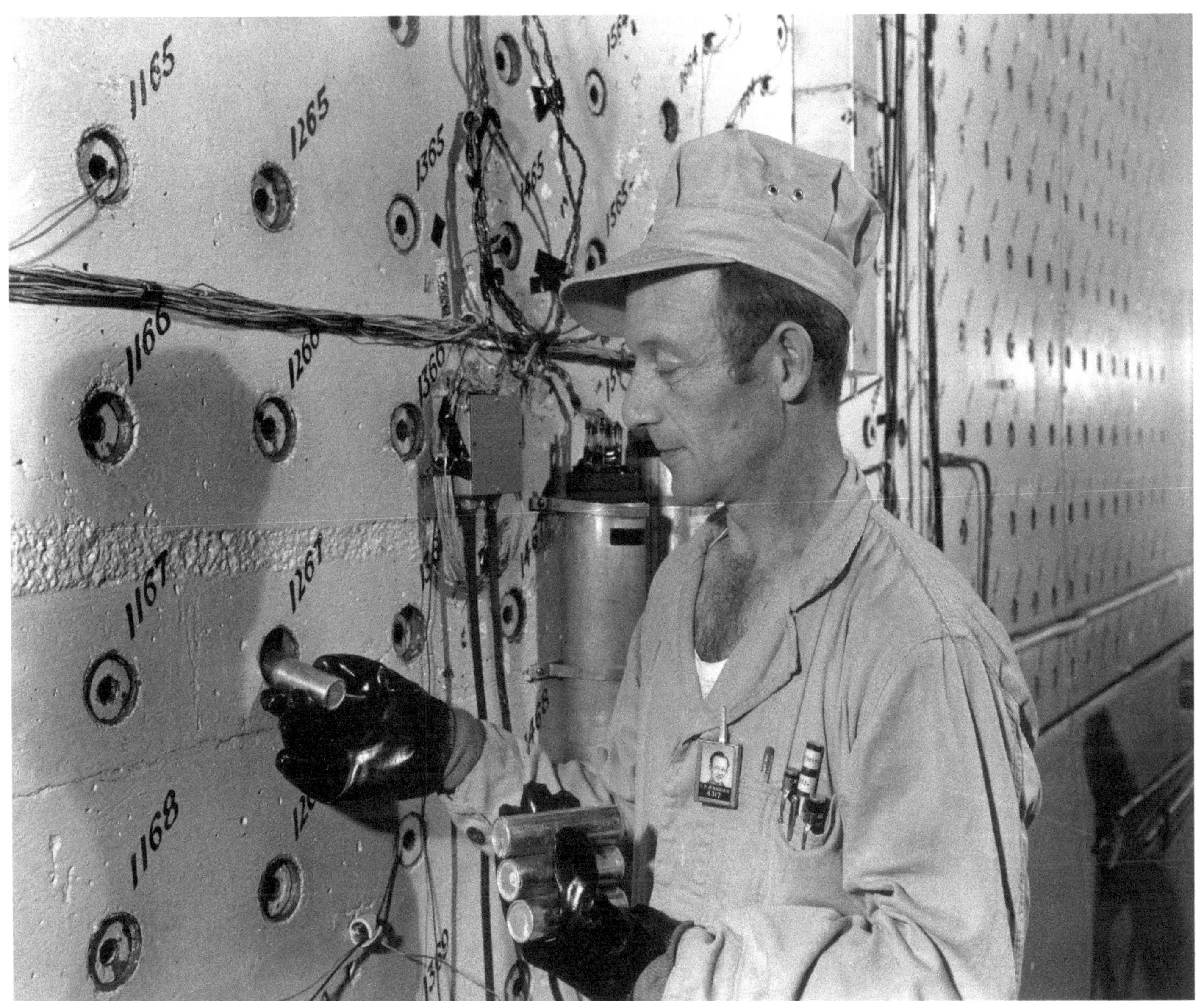

A worker holds a handful of heavy uranium slugs and is placing one into tube 1267 on the face of the Graphite Reactor to be irradiated. Uranium is extremely heavy. For comparison, a gallon of milk weighs about 8 pounds, but a gallon of uranium would weigh about 150 pounds. A small cube of uranium a foot to a side would be rather difficult to tote around—it would weigh 1,165 pounds.

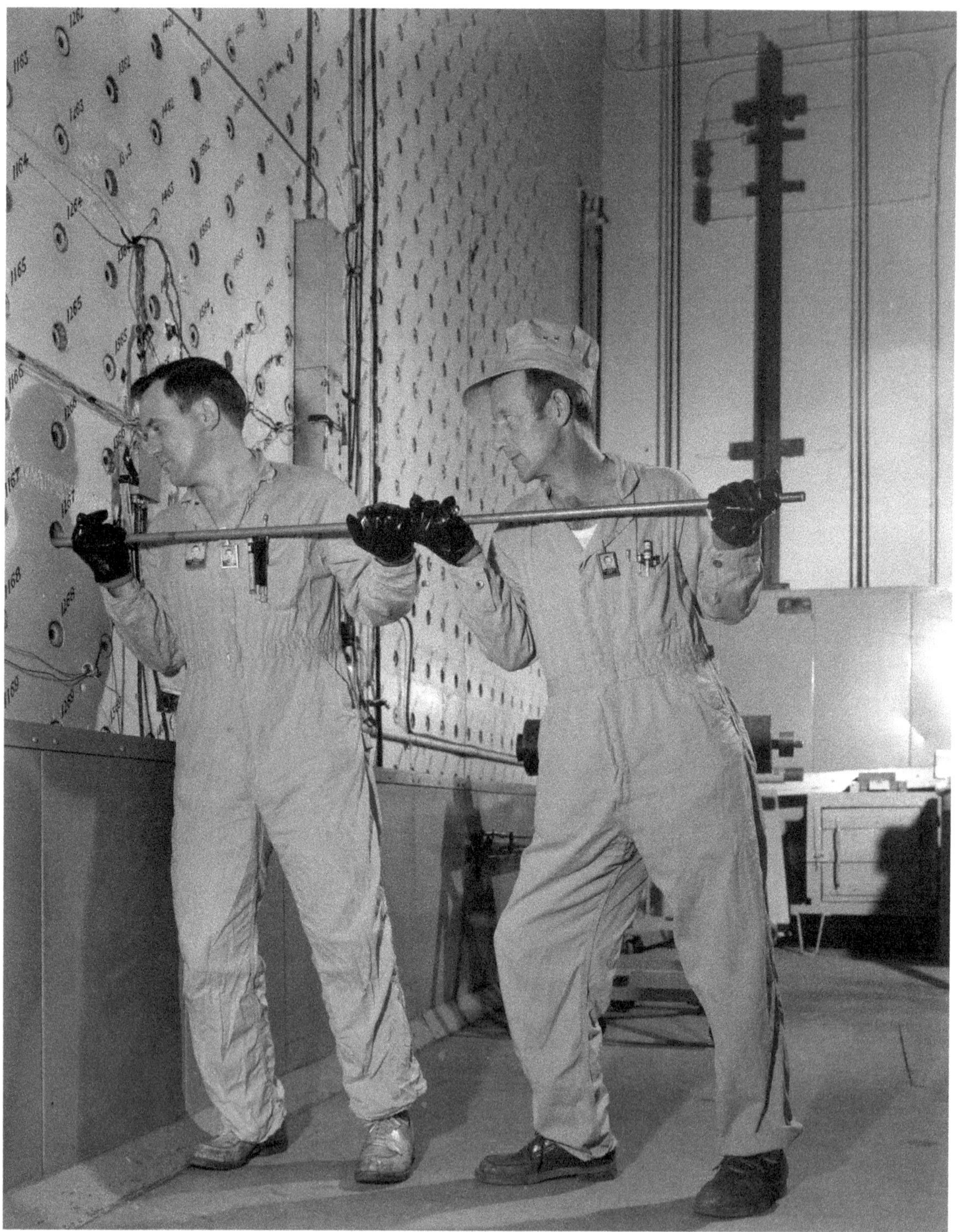

At the X-10 facility, two men use long rods to push fresh uranium slugs into a channel on the face of the Graphite Reactor. As they push fresh slugs in, highly radioactive irradiated slugs are in turn forced out the back of the reactor into a chute that drops them into water. After weeks of storage underwater to decay, the slugs are removed for chemical separation of the plutonium.

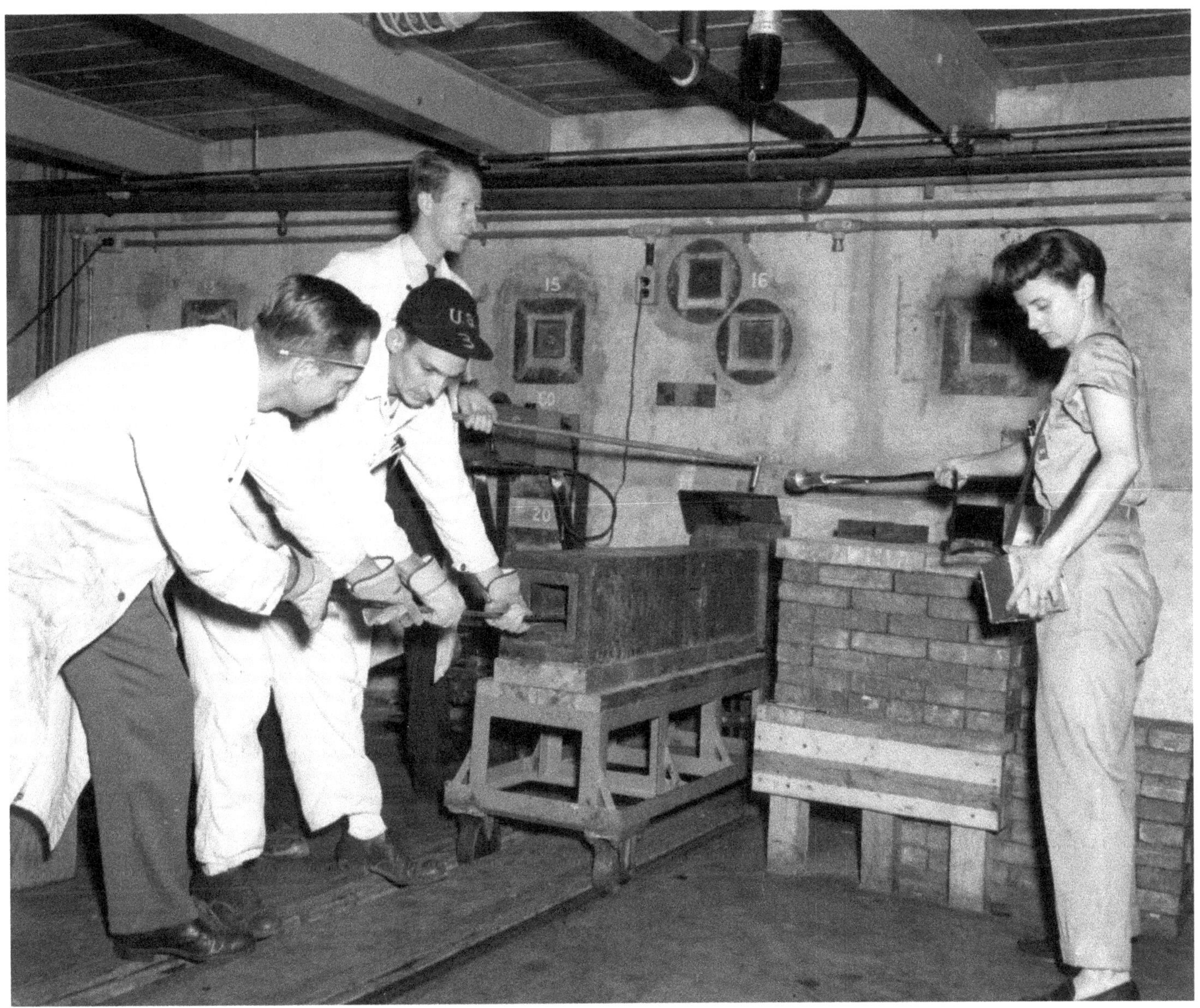

Dr. Ralph Overman extracts radioactive slugs from the Graphite Reactor, which are then pulled into a protective shield made of lead. Mrs. Webber measures the radioactivity during handling.

The entire platform these men are standing on moved up and down along the face of the Graphite Reactor at X-10 to allow insertion and removal of the uranium slugs into the reactor core. Hanging on the wall in front of the men are steel push-rods 10 feet long. When one was pushed in, another was threaded to it to increase its length, enabling it to pass entirely through the fuel channel in the core and push the older slugs out the back into a reservoir of water to shield the radiation.

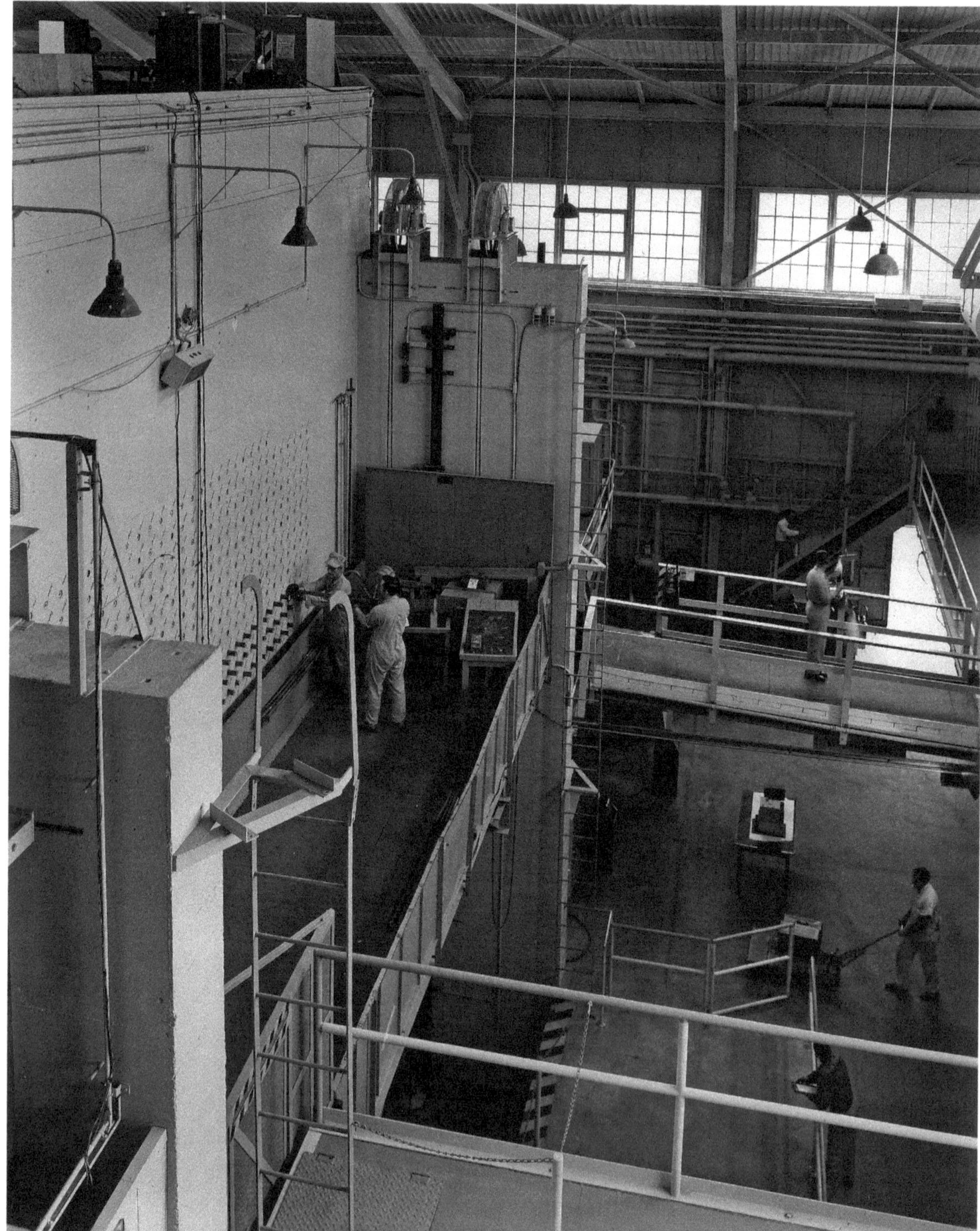

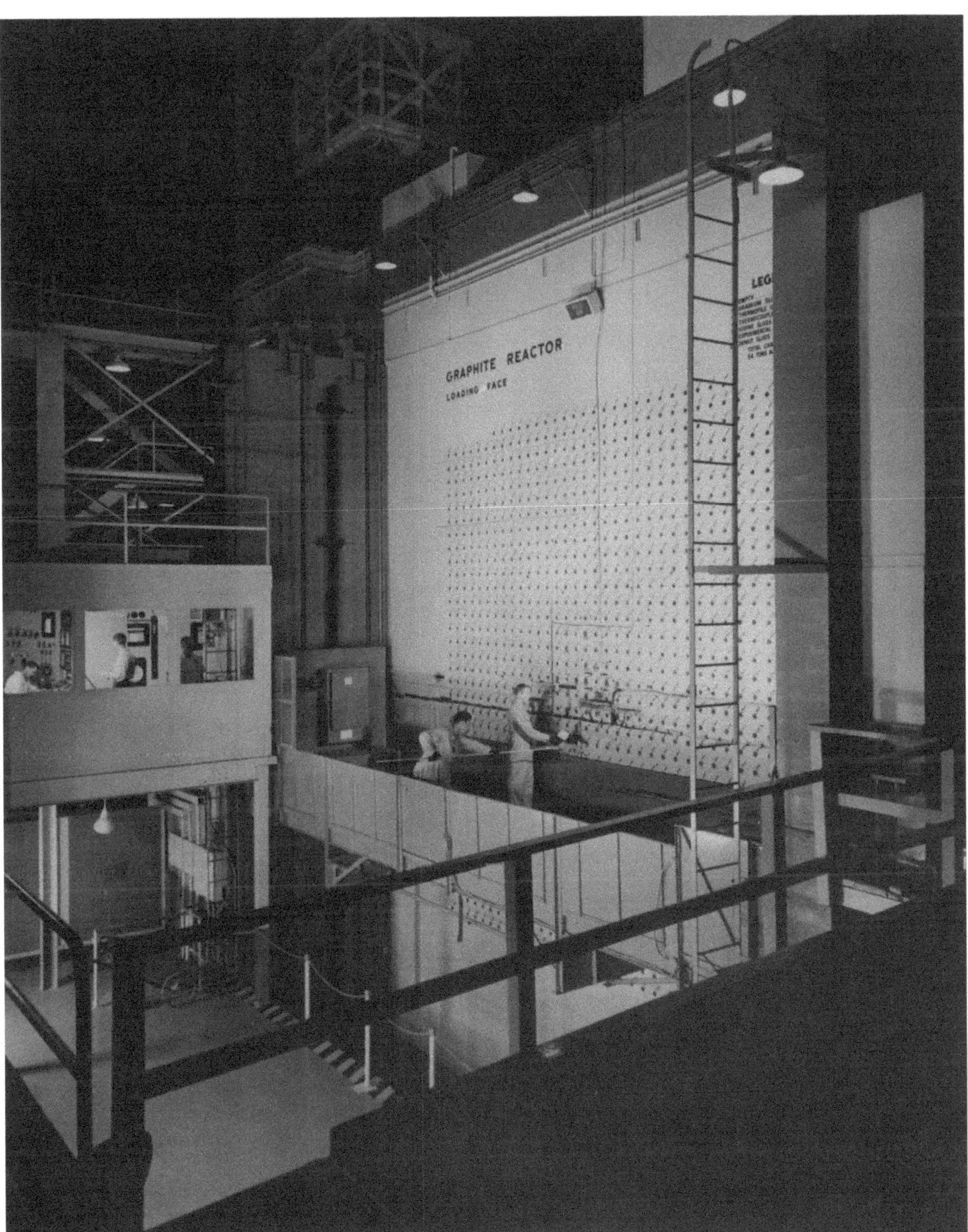

Another view of operations at the reactor.

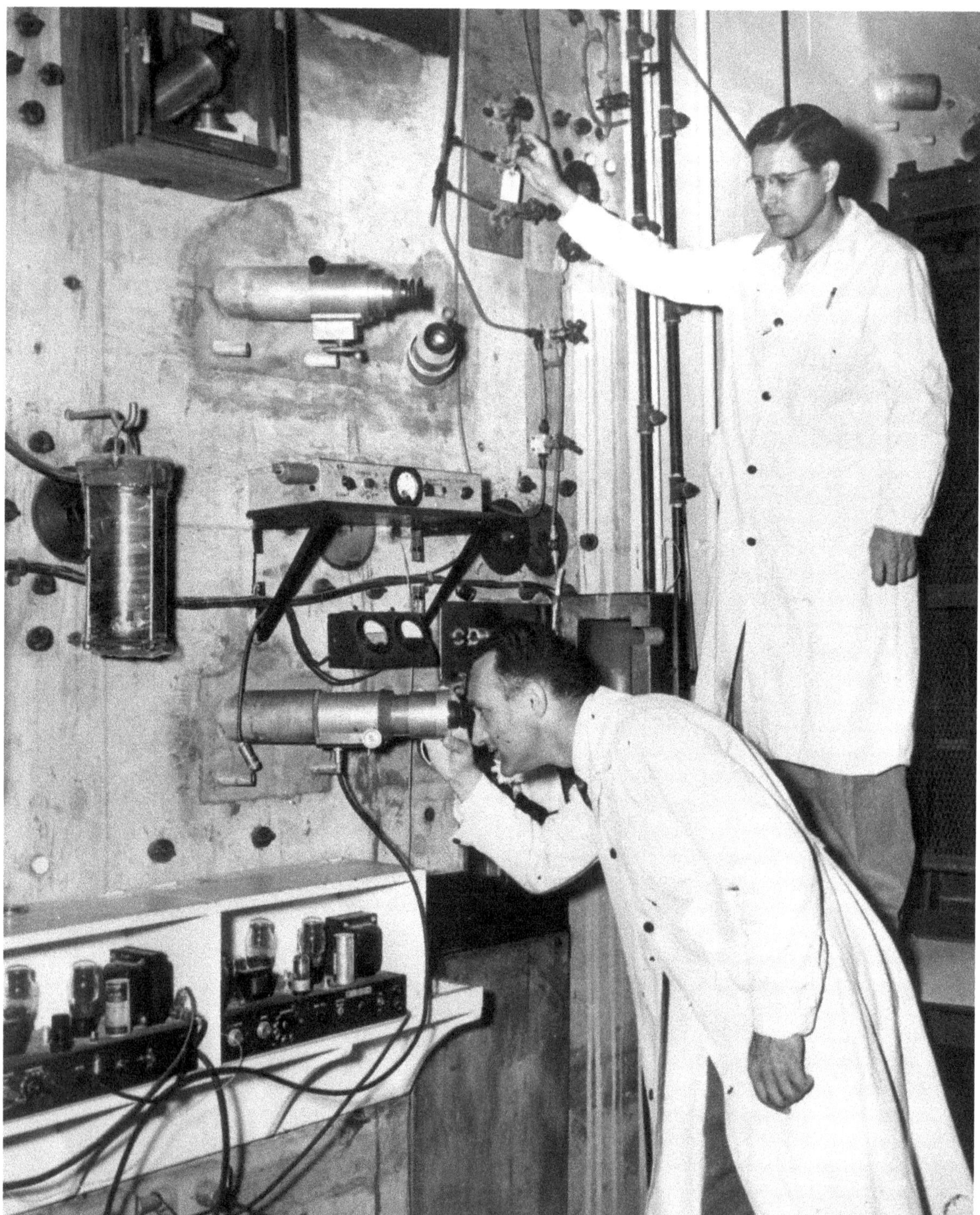

Dr. Edward Tompkins works a remote control apparatus while Dr. Waldo Cohn observes through a periscope to watch the reaction take place inside the reactor cubicle. Radioactive isotope preparation was also used for medical purposes.

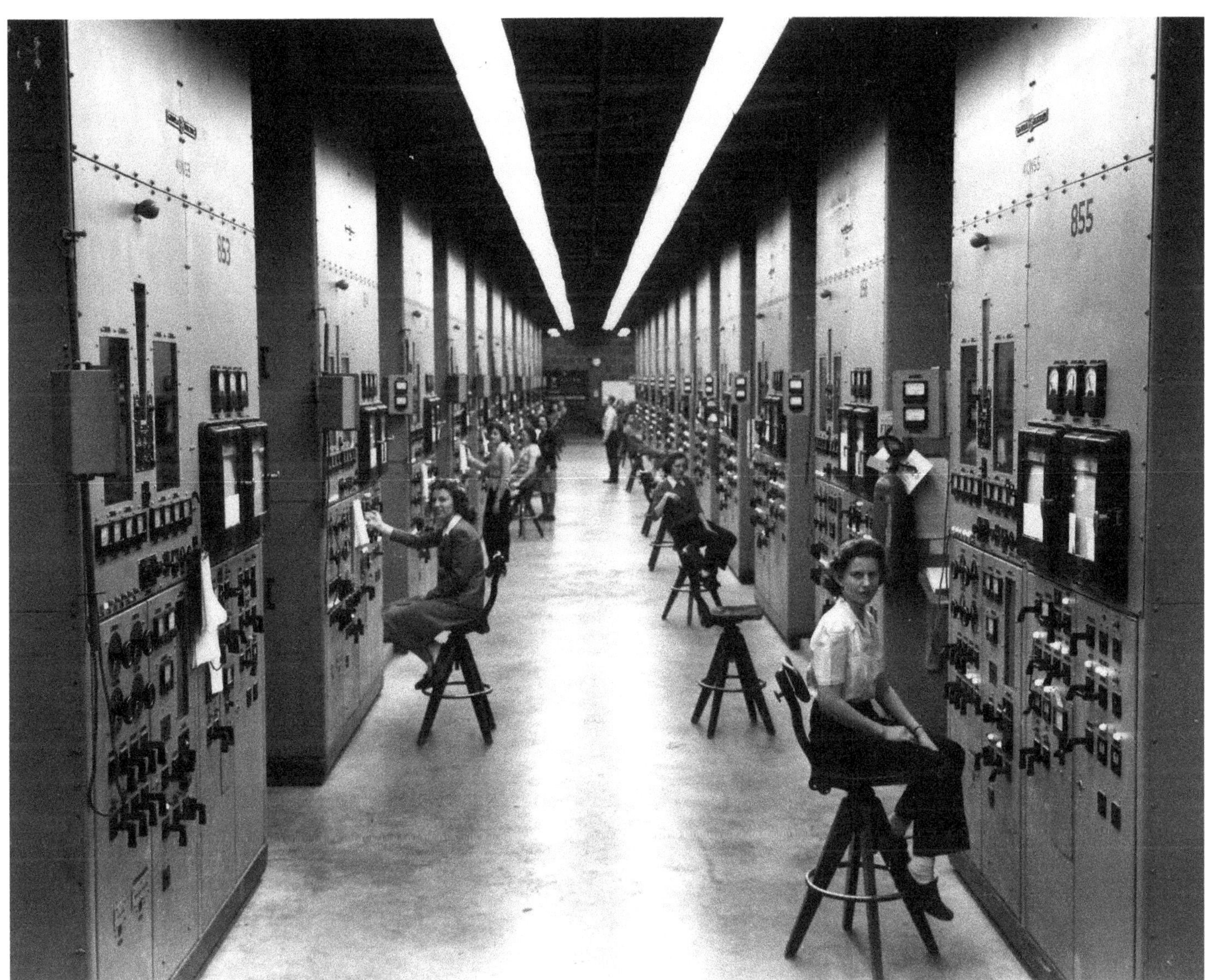

Gladys Owens sits on the first stool on the right, one of the many women staffing the Y-12 gaseous diffusion plant in 1944. These women monitored the dials, gauges, and paper recorders of the electromagnetic calutron process seven days a week, turning various control knobs to keep the needles pointed within a specific range. If something went wrong they would call supervisor Connie Bolling, the man standing in the background. At 100 years of age, Mr. Bolling still lives in Oak Ridge.

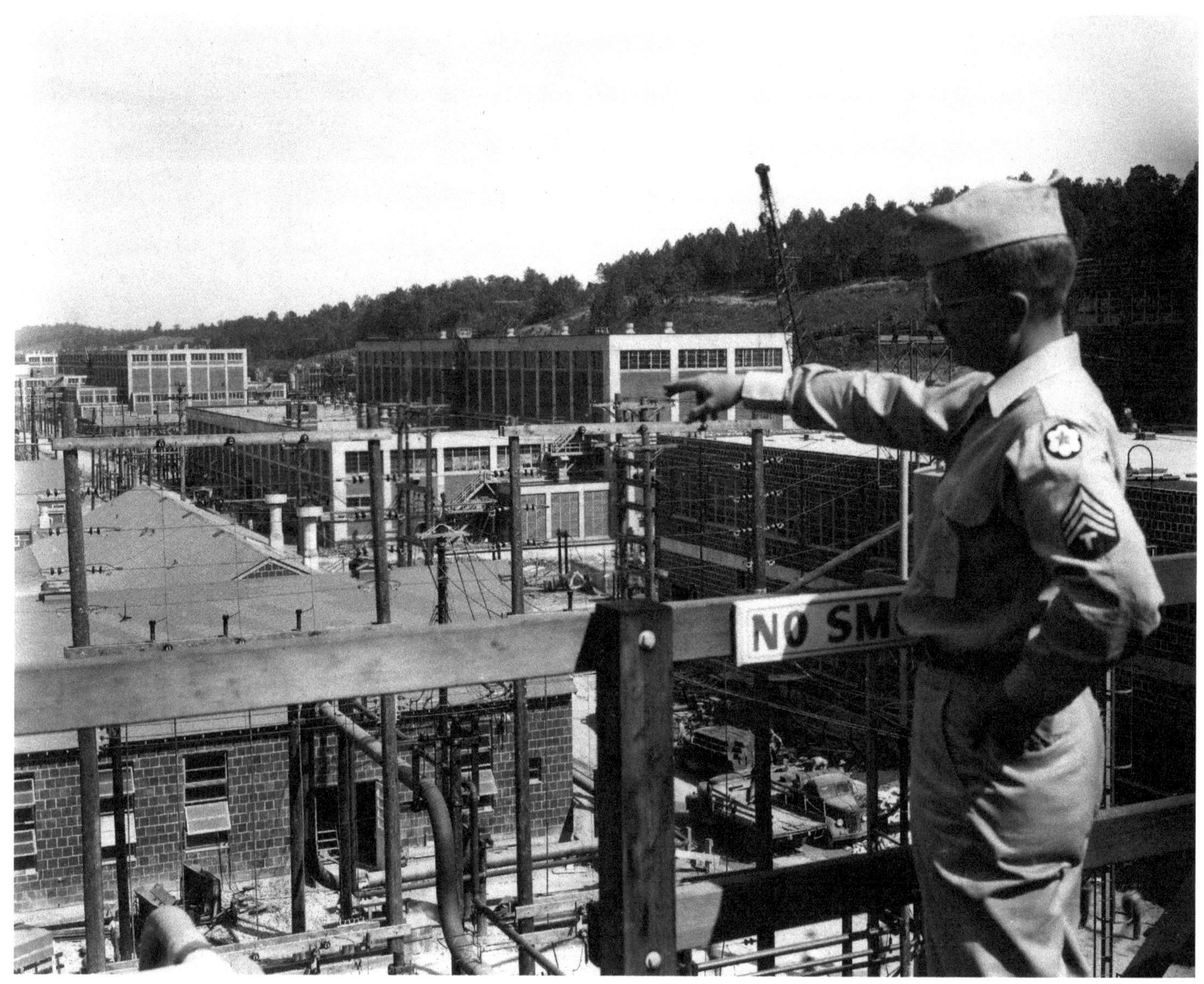

A military security guard looks out over the Y-12 complex in September 1944. The upper buildings contain the "racetracks," the electromagnetic process using calutrons.

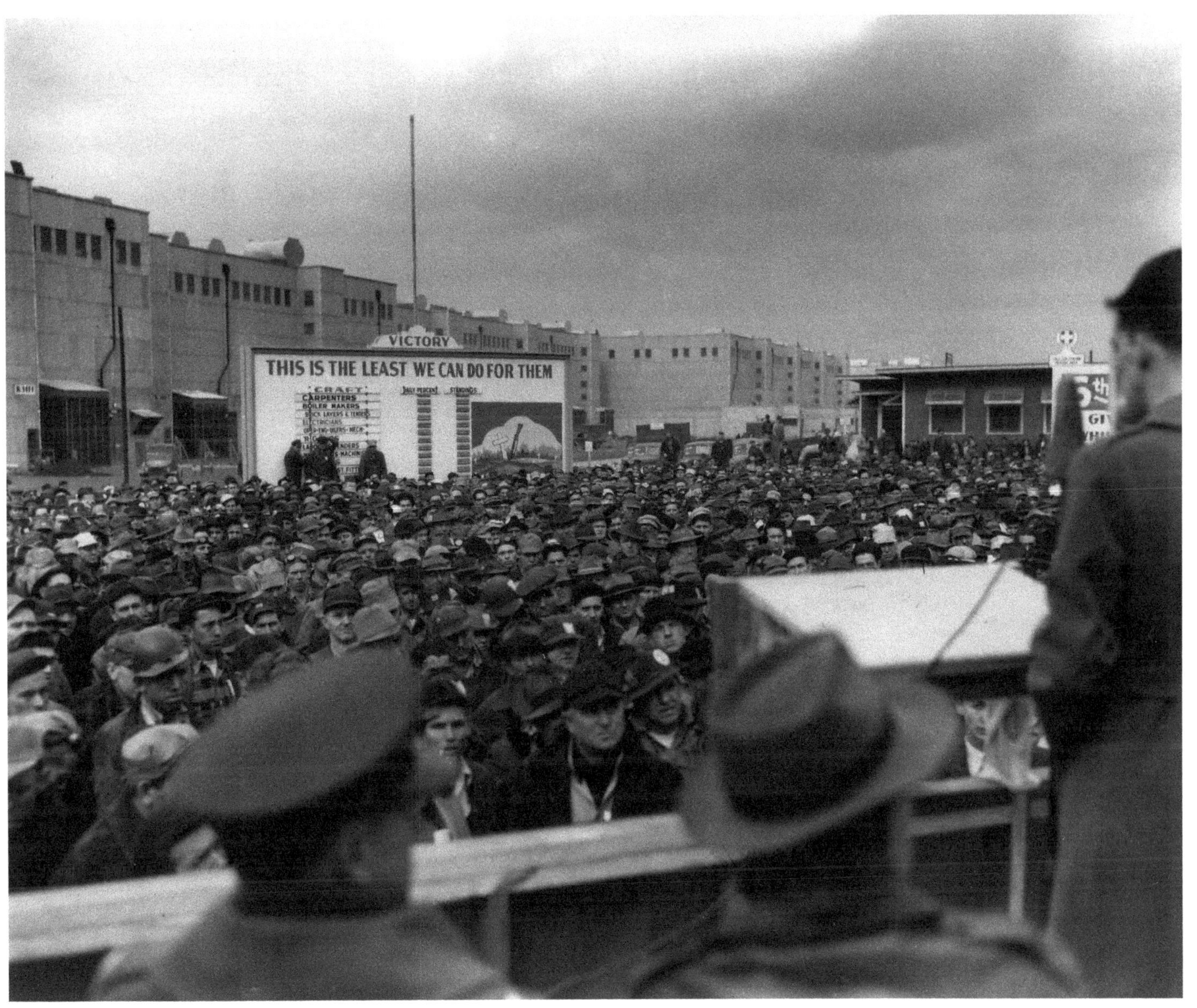

On December 13, 1944, war veteran Sergeant Mike Miller, who had lost an arm, spoke to the K-25 workers at a rally to instill the importance of what they were doing, and how critical it was to the war effort. The billboard says it all: "This Is the Least We Can Do for Them."

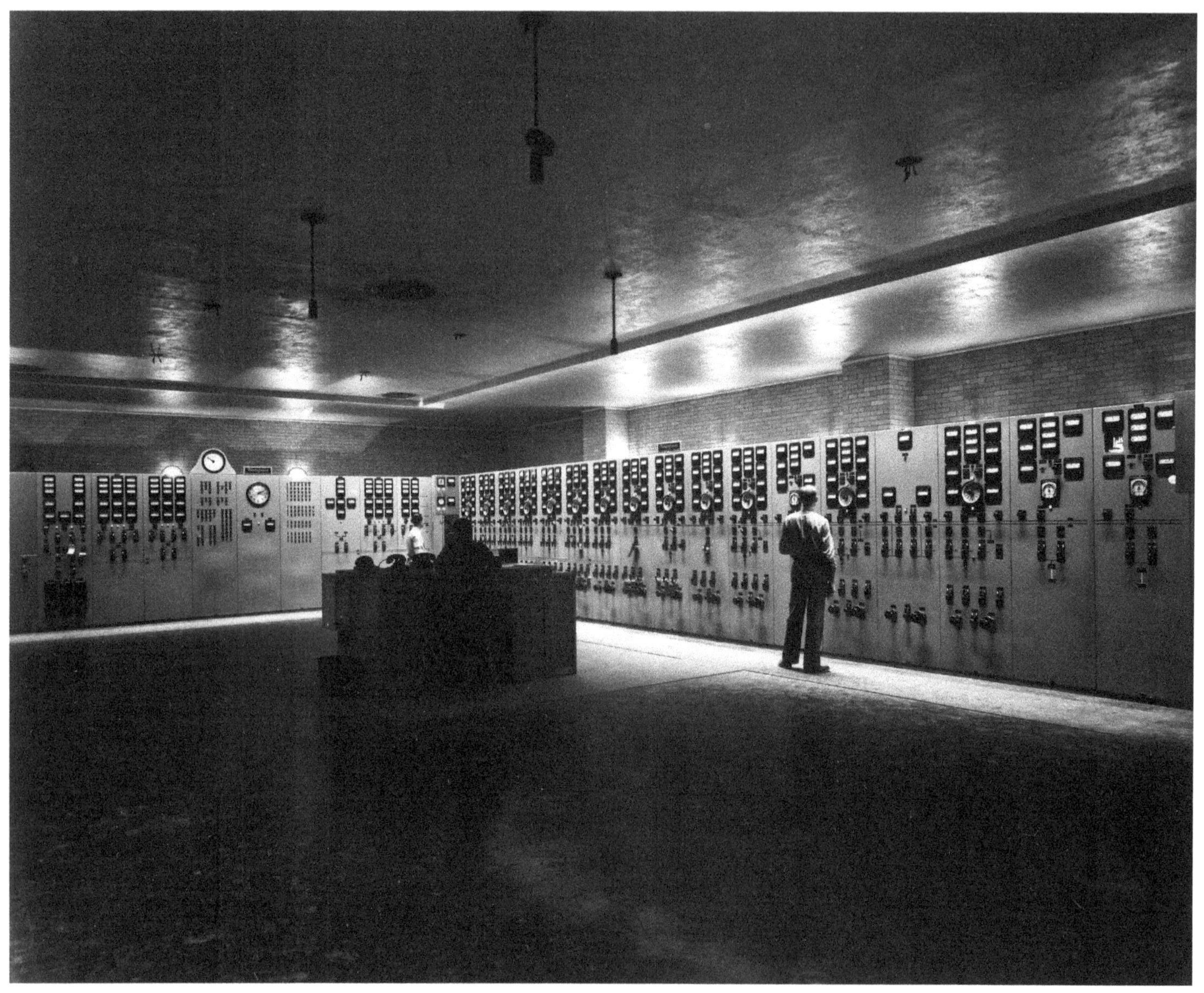

These workers are monitoring the hundreds of dials and meters in the K-704 Main Switch House control room at K-25.

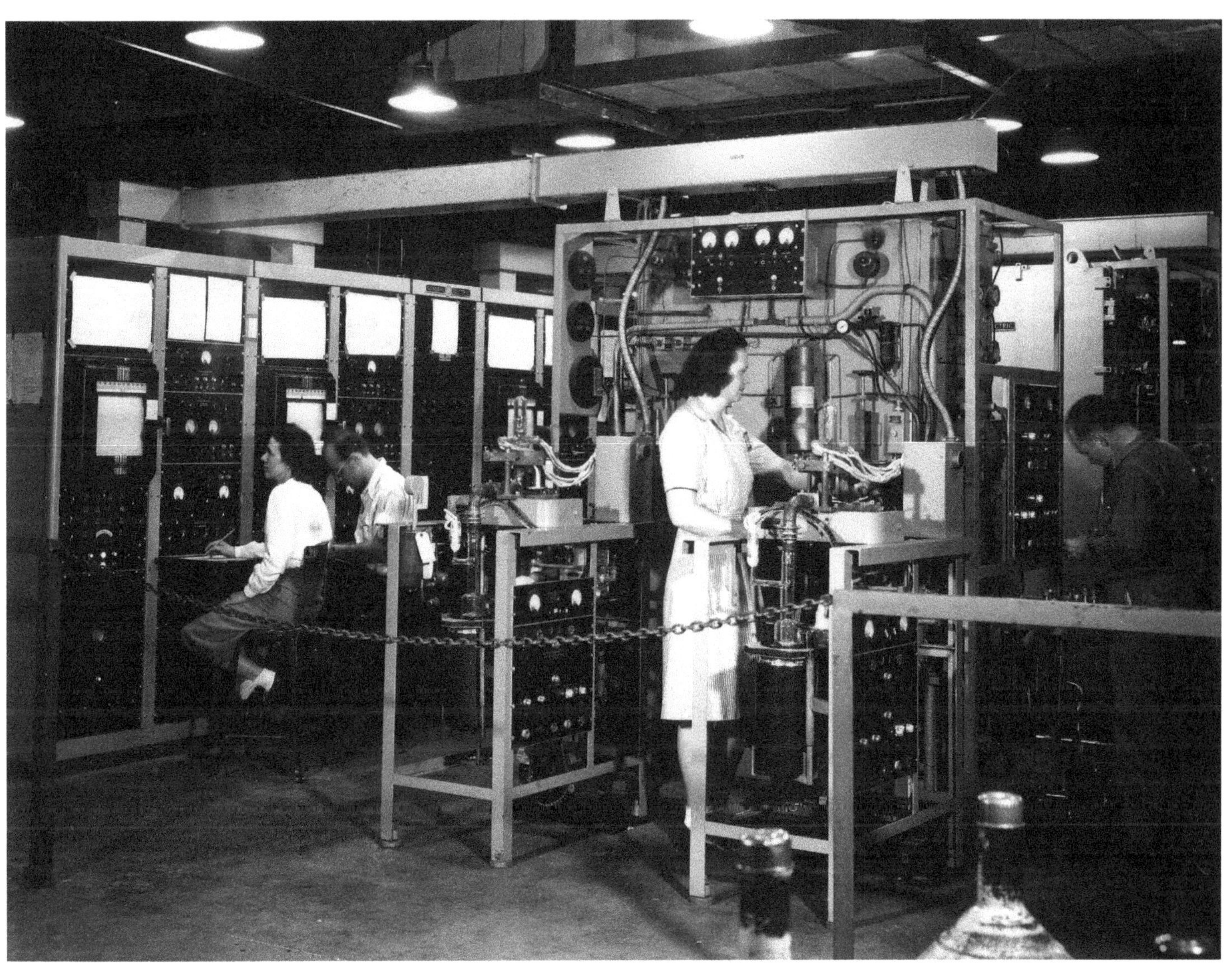

Shown here in 1945 is one of the K-25 monitoring and control areas. This woman is operating a spectrometer to determine gas quality in the separation process while other individuals monitor and log readings at control stations. There were many of these throughout the plant, and process monitoring was continuous.

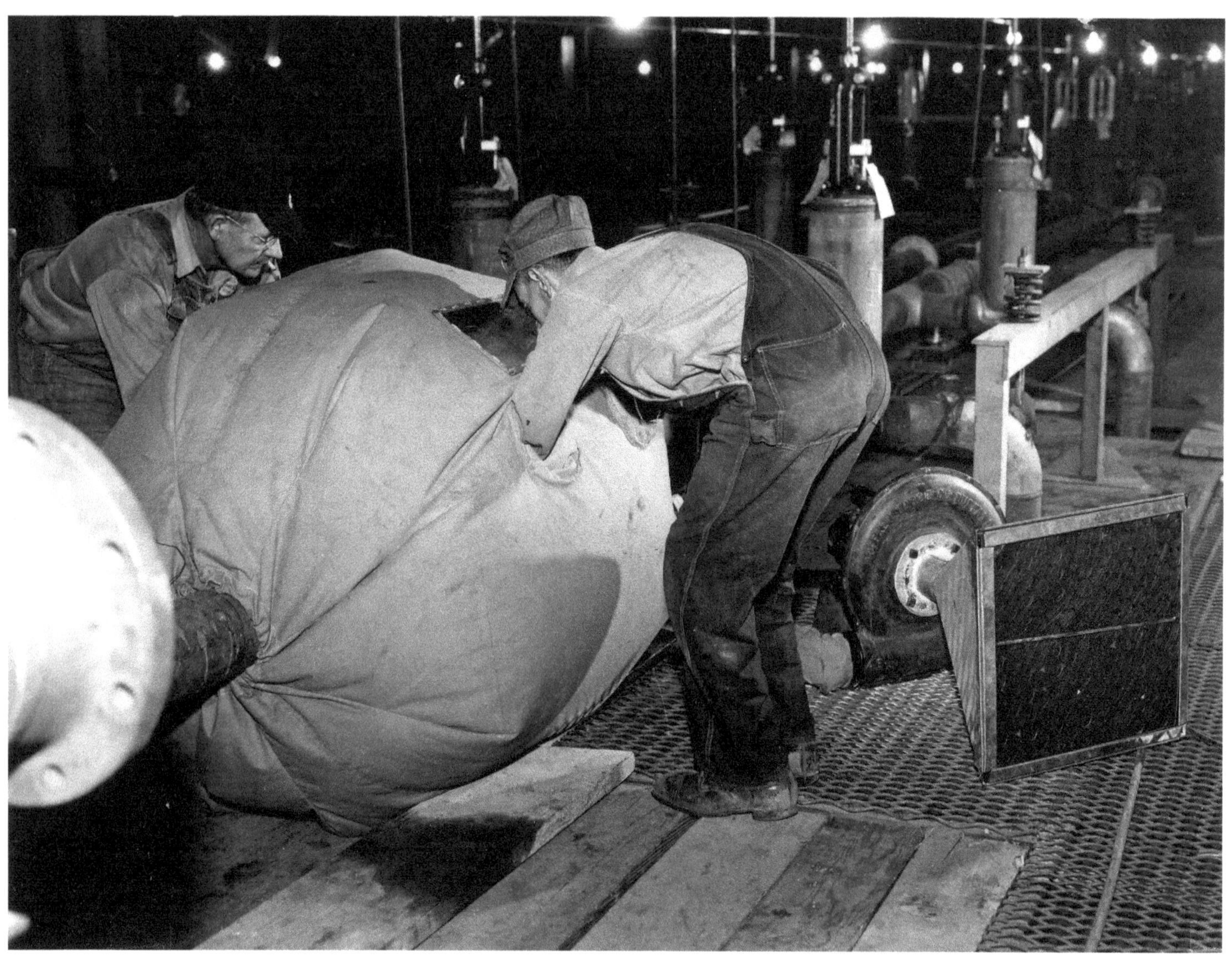

These two K-25 workmen have their arms in a protective shroud, which acts as a portable glove box. They were repairing or replacing a valve on a pipe which contained something hazardous. The bubble glove box would contain any leaking gas, which would be removed in filtration. The shroud would then be removed to the next needed location.

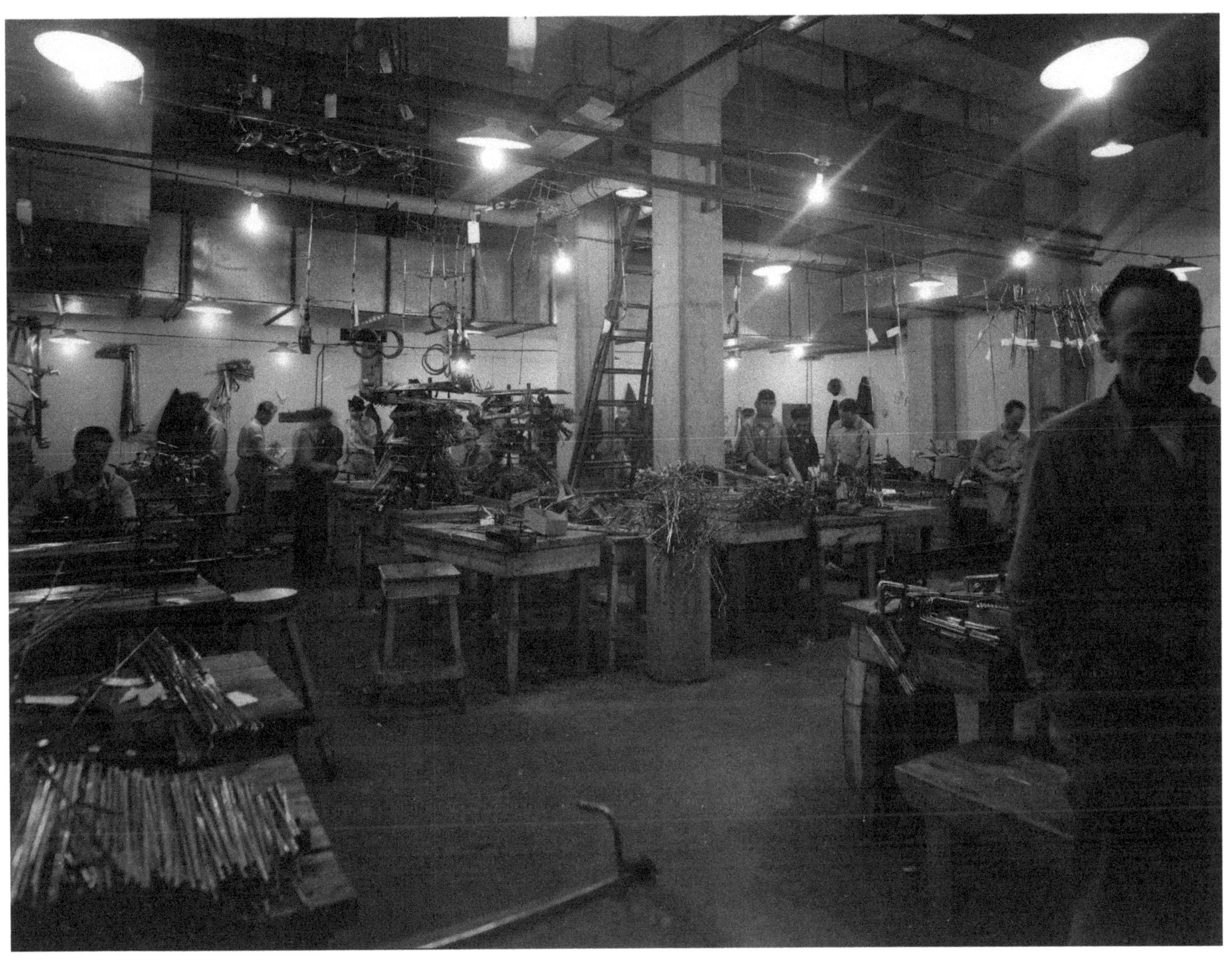

Machined parts had to be duplicated sometimes thousands of times owing to the large number of identical processing units needed. Prefabrication shops played key roles and were very busy places. Machinists are hard at work on May 1, 1945, in this shop located in building K-303-8 at K-25.

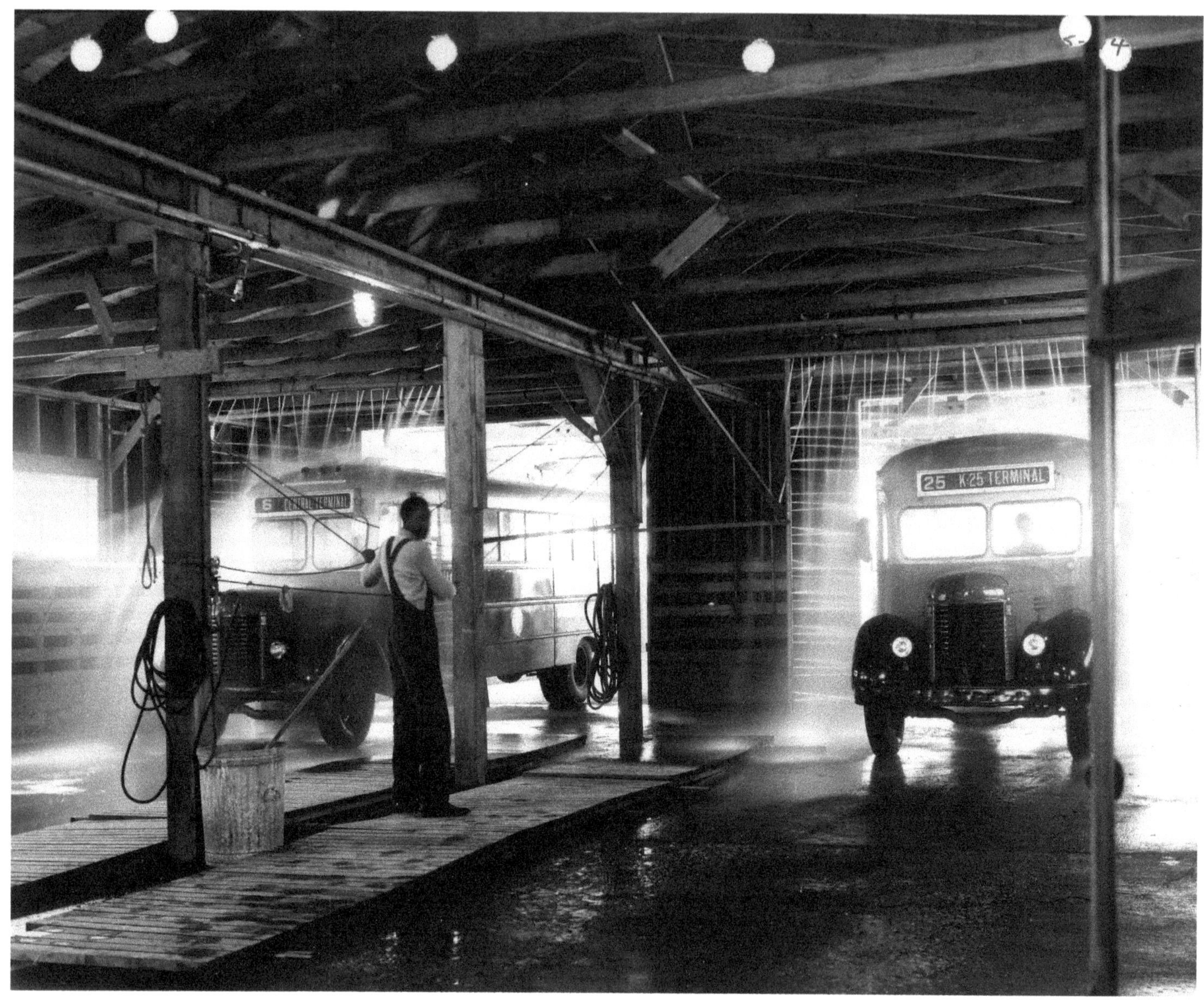

Hundreds of buses transported workers to and from their jobs at the various facilities. Cleaning and maintenance were continuous. This is a wash station at the K-25 bus terminal as it appeared in 1945.

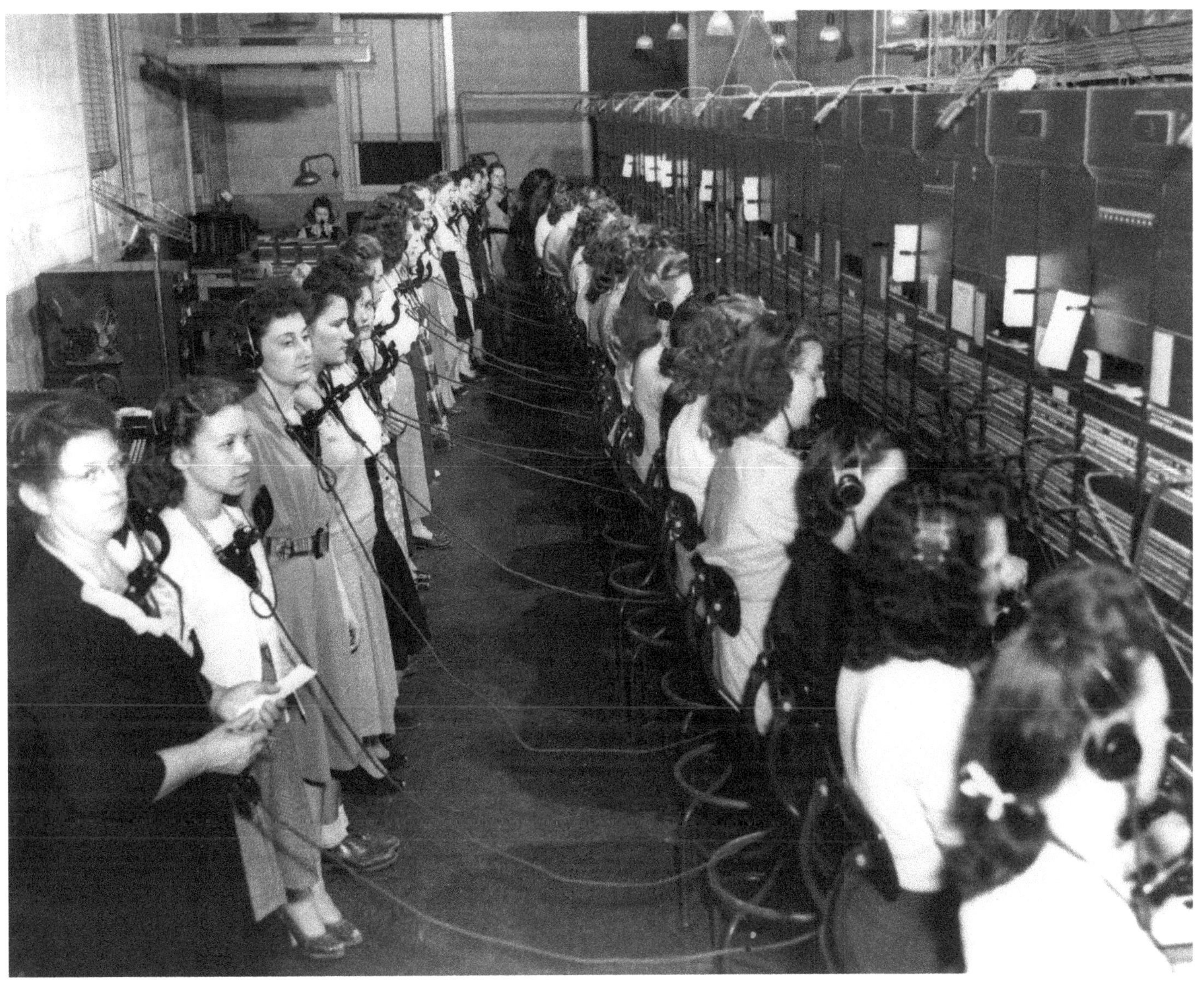

All calls into and out of the facilities were routed to this main switchboard. Outgoing calls were dialed by the operators. Preparing for a shift change, new operators are positioned to replace those at the station. Each operator wore headphones and talked into a receiver resting on her chest and held by a strap around the neck.

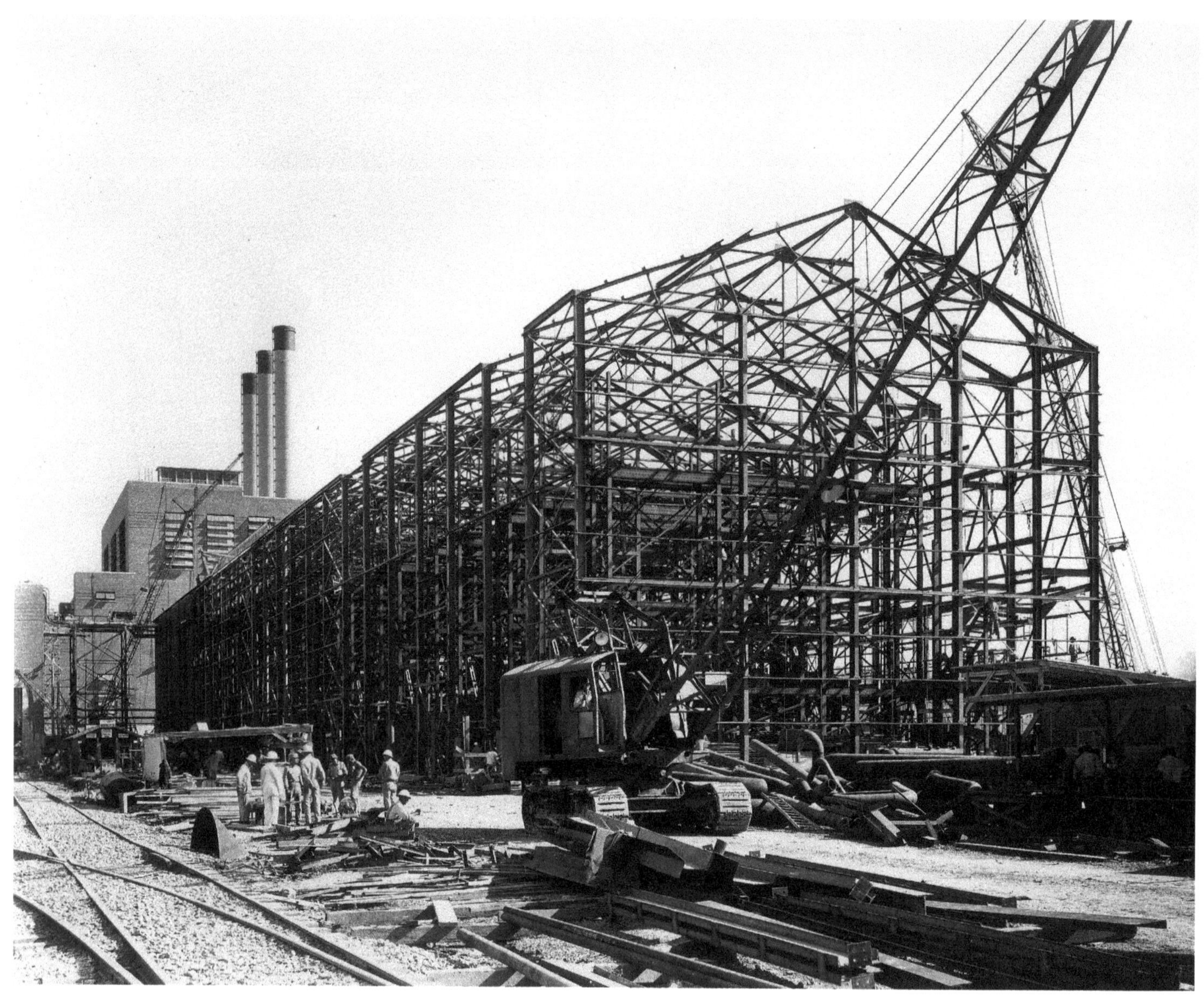

Shown here in 1944, the S-50 plant was built on the Clinch River down from K-25. It enriched uranium by means of a liquid thermal diffusion process. The building under construction was completed in 90 days. Steam was provided by the adjacent K-25 power plant.

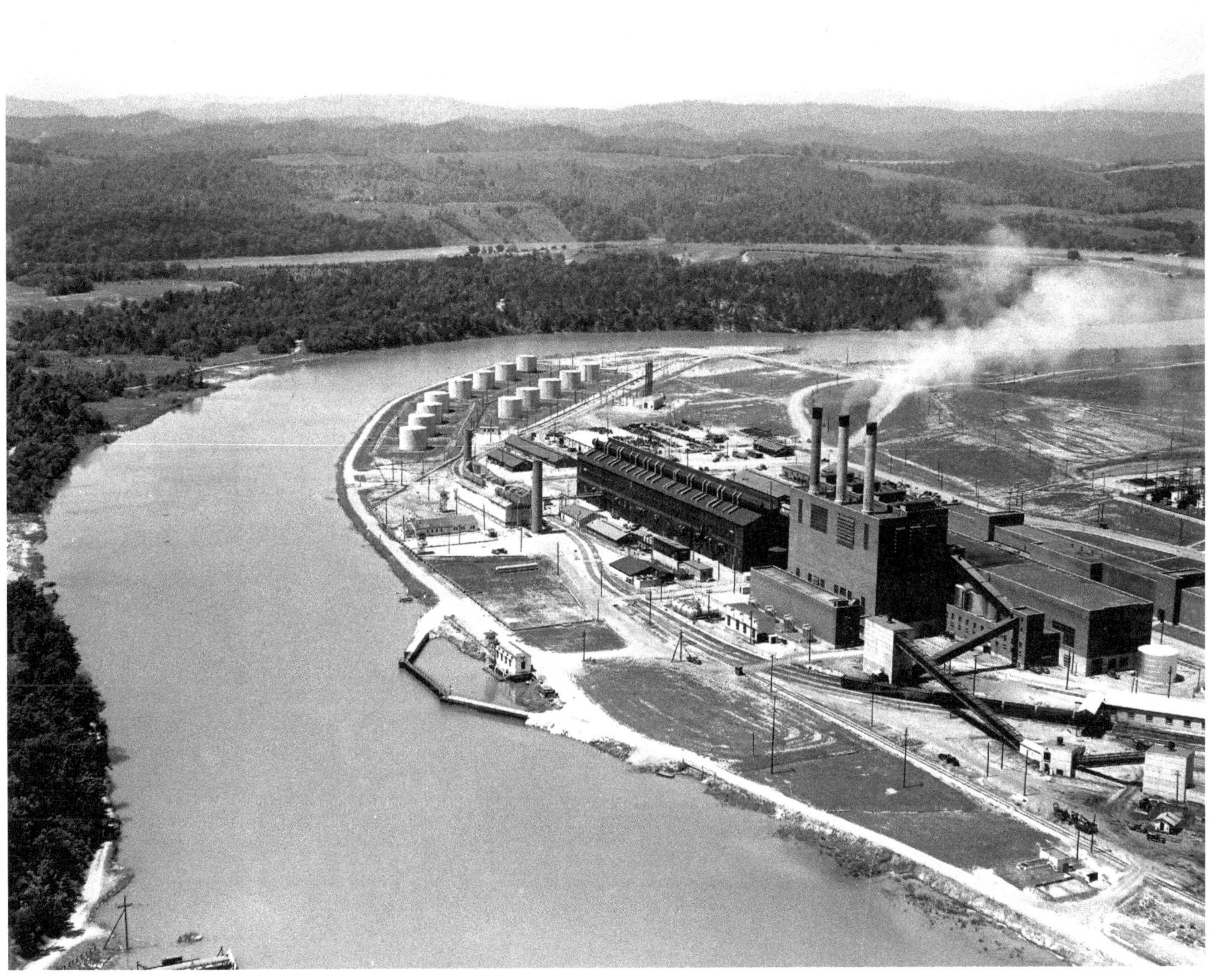

The S-50 plant was located near a power plant constructed to provide some of the electric power to K-25. In January 1945 it began production of uranium but its many problems forced it to shut down on September 9, 1945, less than a year after it began operating.

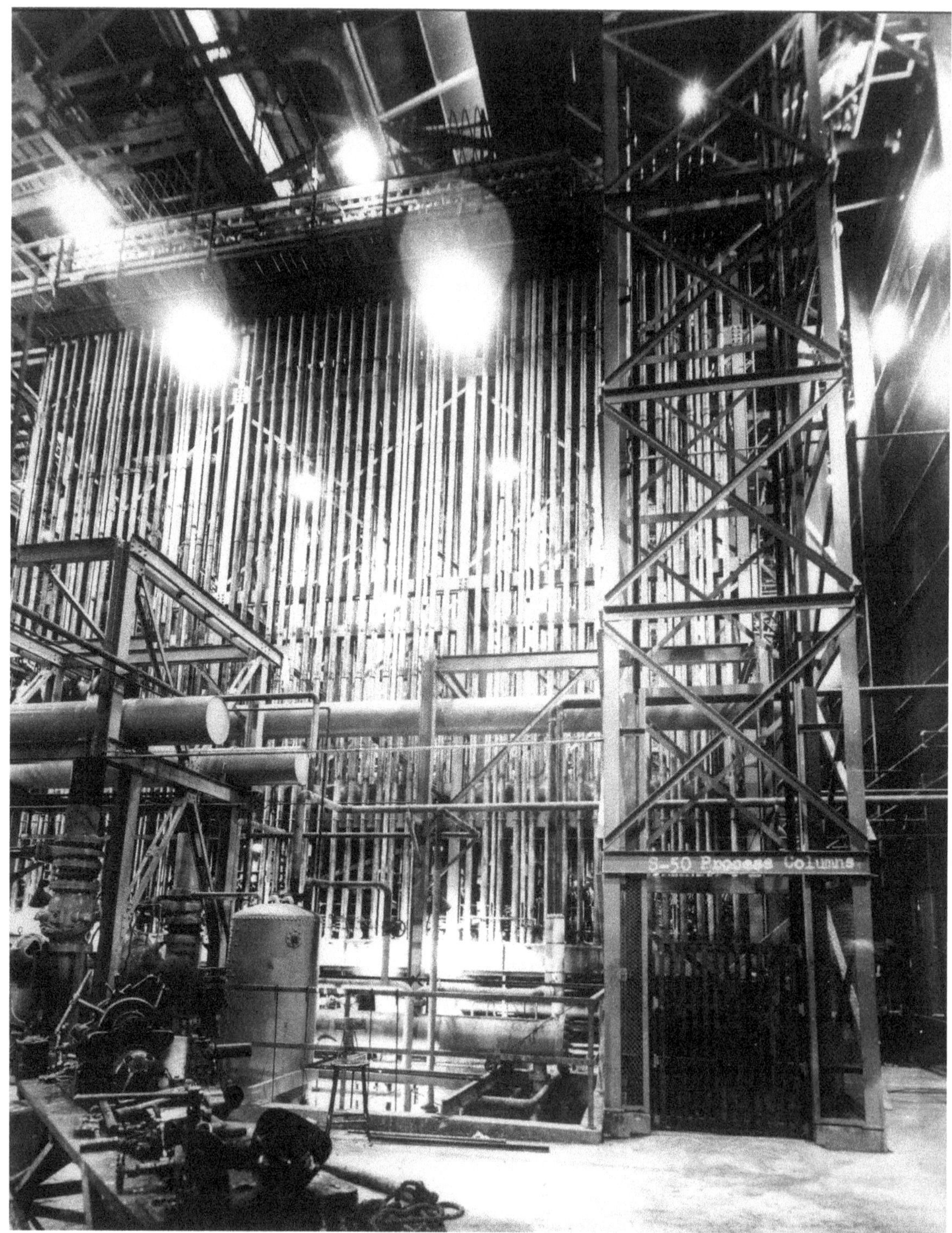

These tall banks of columns filled the S-50 plant. There were 2,142 copper and nickel diffusion columns 48 feet tall. The first stage of enrichment took place here, before the product was fed to the huge gaseous diffusion process at K-25, which enriched it further. The product was then fed into the calutrons at Y-12 to increase the concentration of U-235 for the Little Boy atomic bomb.

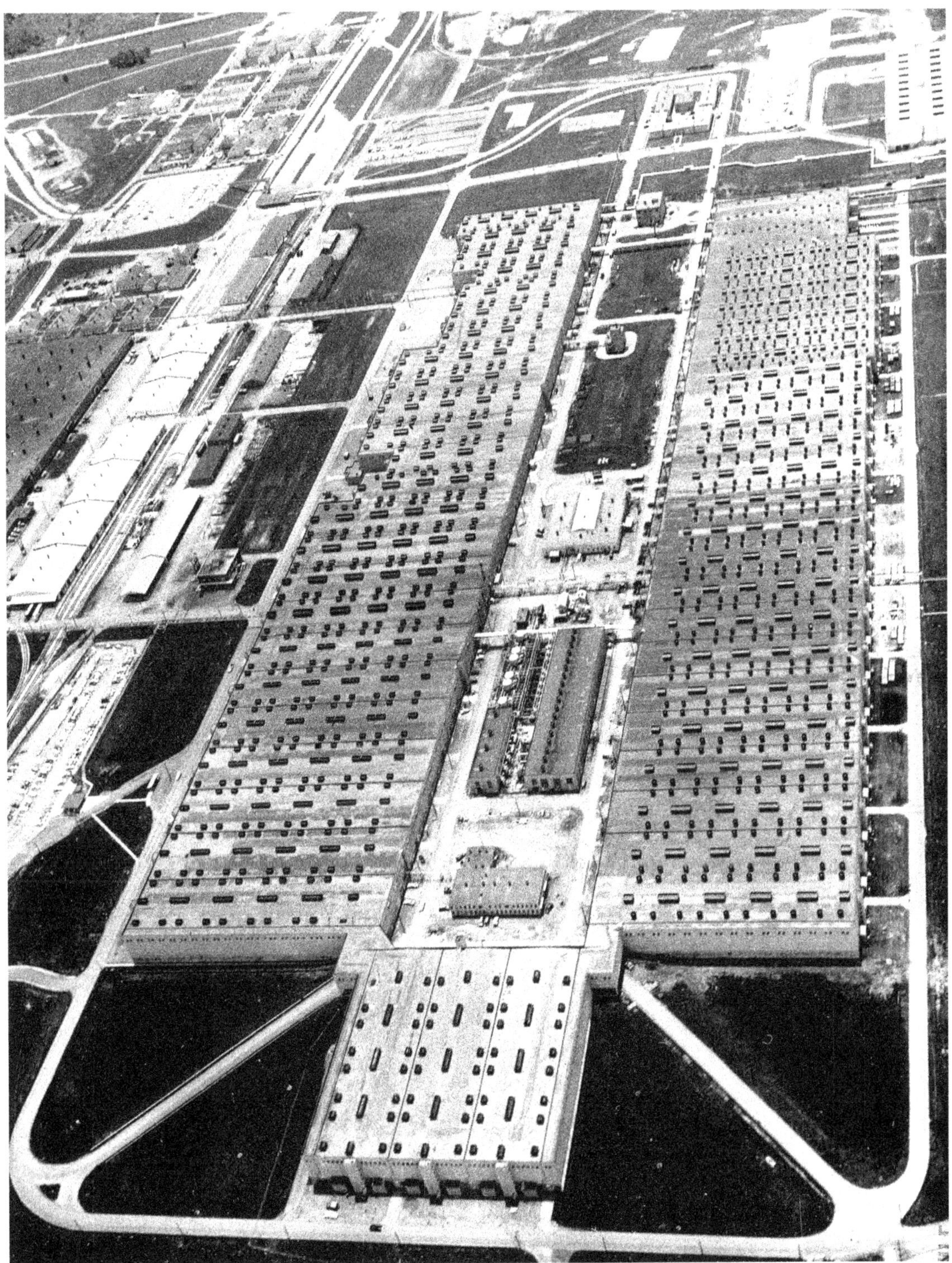

This is an aerial view of the enormous K-25 gaseous diffusion building, which housed the cascades. It is easy to see why the structure was deemed the largest single building in the United States at the time. It is paradoxical that a structure of immense size should be required to separate infinitesimal atoms of uranium from one another.

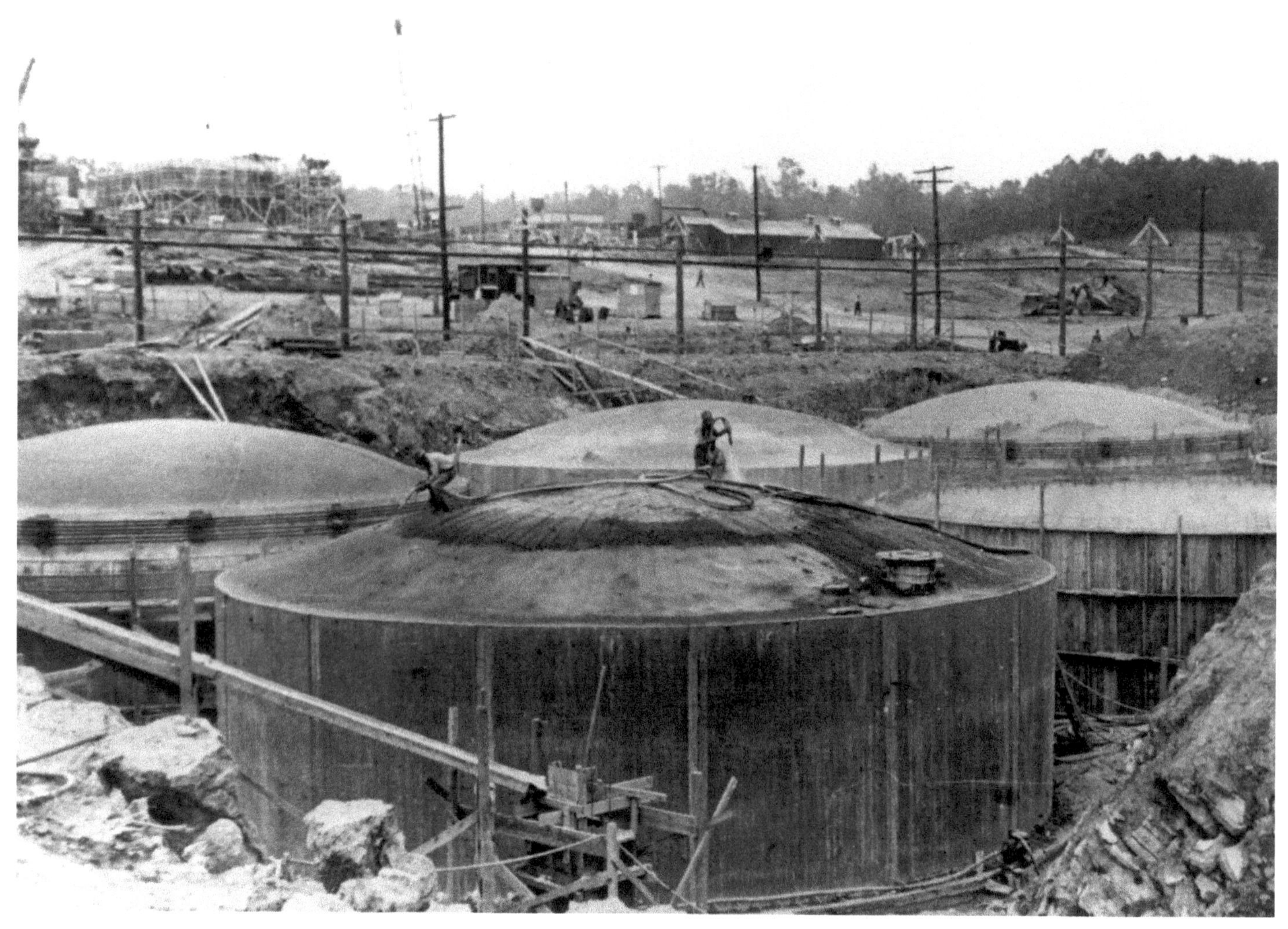

Highly radioactive liquid waste was produced at X-10 and stored in these thick-walled underground tanks made of a special concretelike substance called gunite. Shown here in 1943, each tank held 170,000 gallons of waste and sludge.

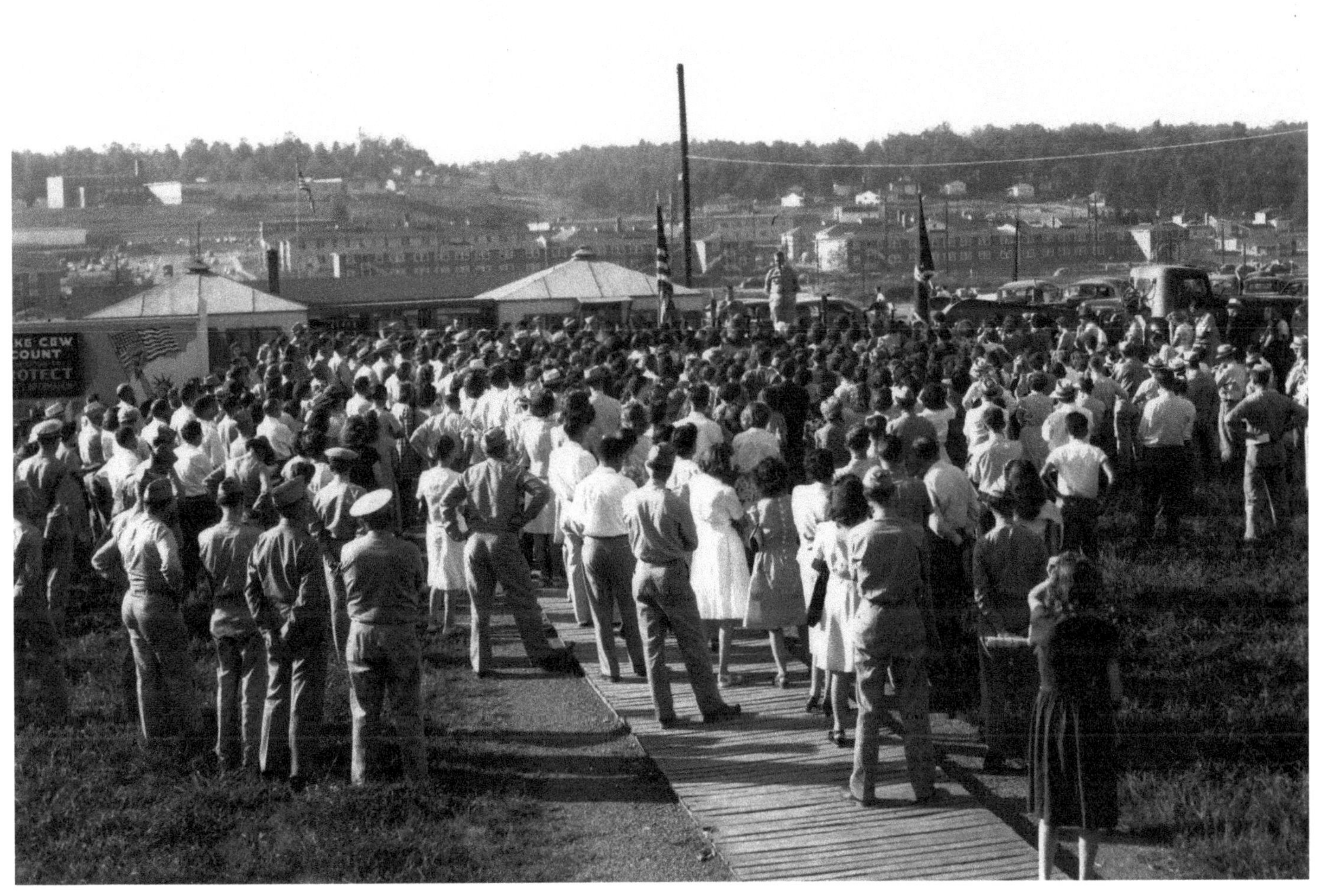

General Groves often took the opportunity to speak to workers to remind them of the importance of their contribution to the war effort. Here he speaks to a gathering in 1945 at the Oak Ridge federal building. The building in the background at left is the Oak Ridge High School. Dormitories are visible in the foreground.

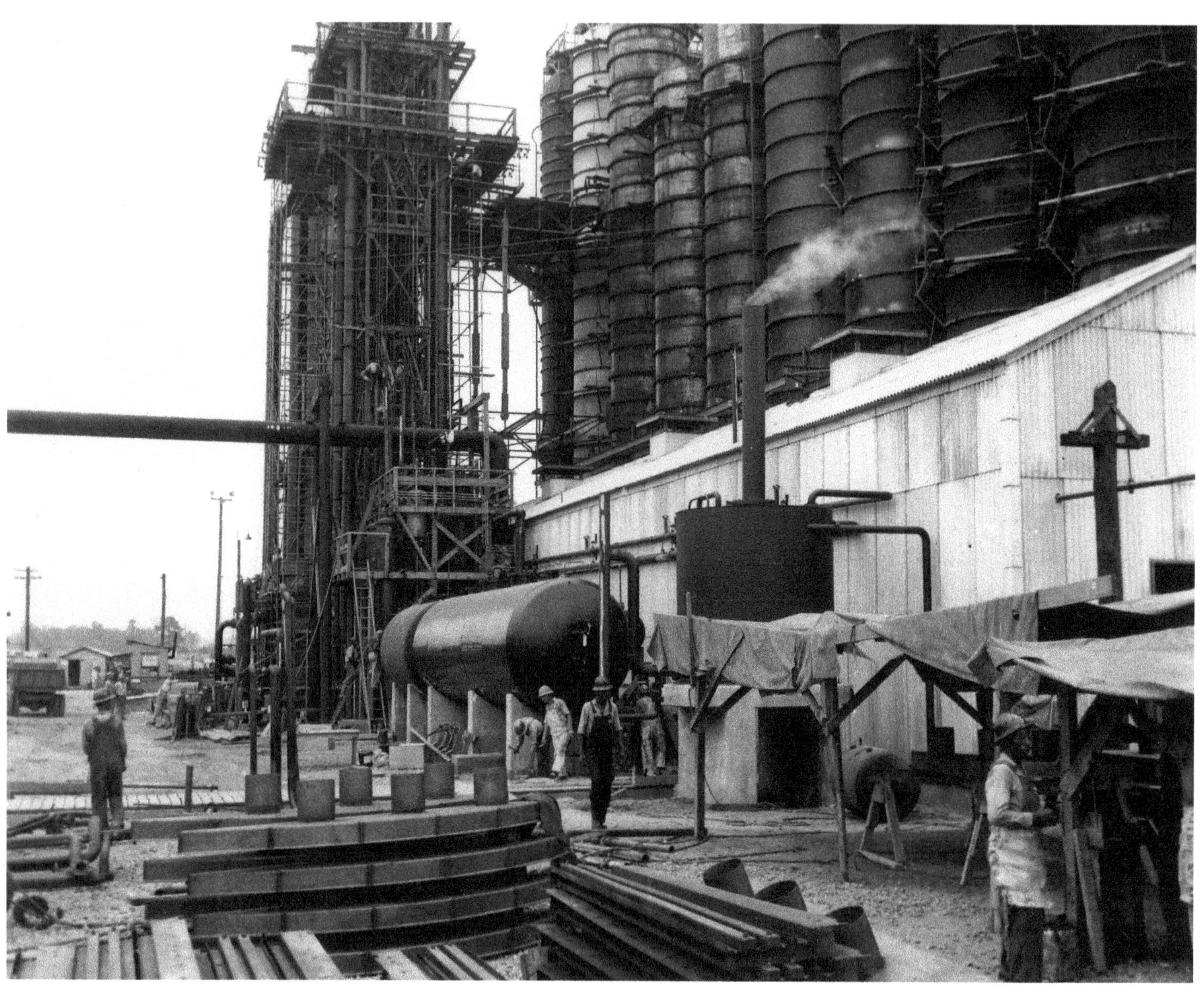

The Alabama Ordnance works in Childersburg, Alabama, shown here in July 1943, produced five million pounds of TNT a month during the war, but it also housed a top-secret operation. Thought to be an ammonia plant in a fenced-off area, it actually produced heavy water (D_2O) used in the Manhattan Project. D_2O contains deuterium, an isotope of hydrogen with more neutrons in its nucleus.

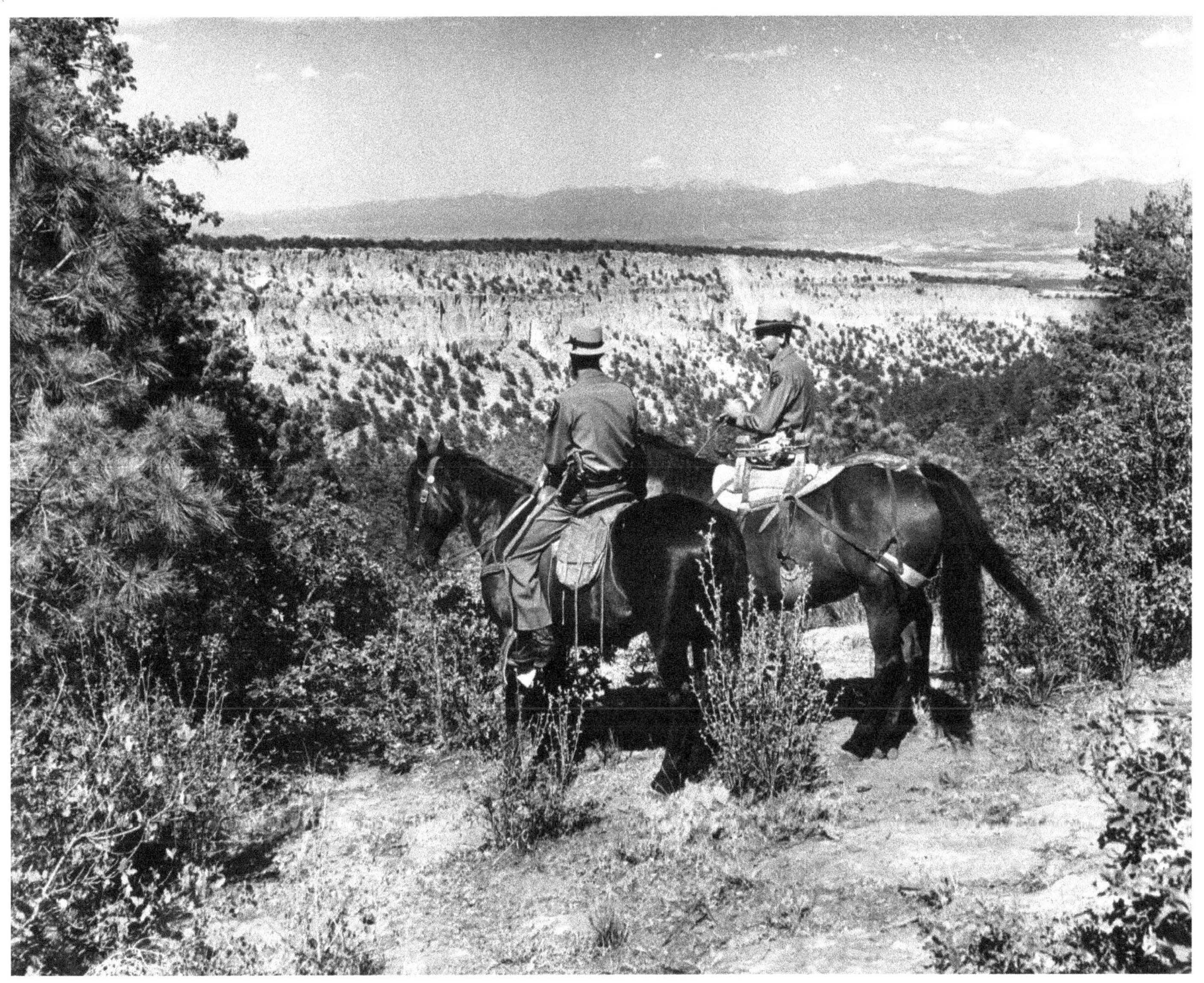

Los Alamos, New Mexico, provided the isolation needed for another secret facility. Only a few homesteaders were in the area when it was purchased by the government. Here a security patrol checks the area for unwanted visitors.

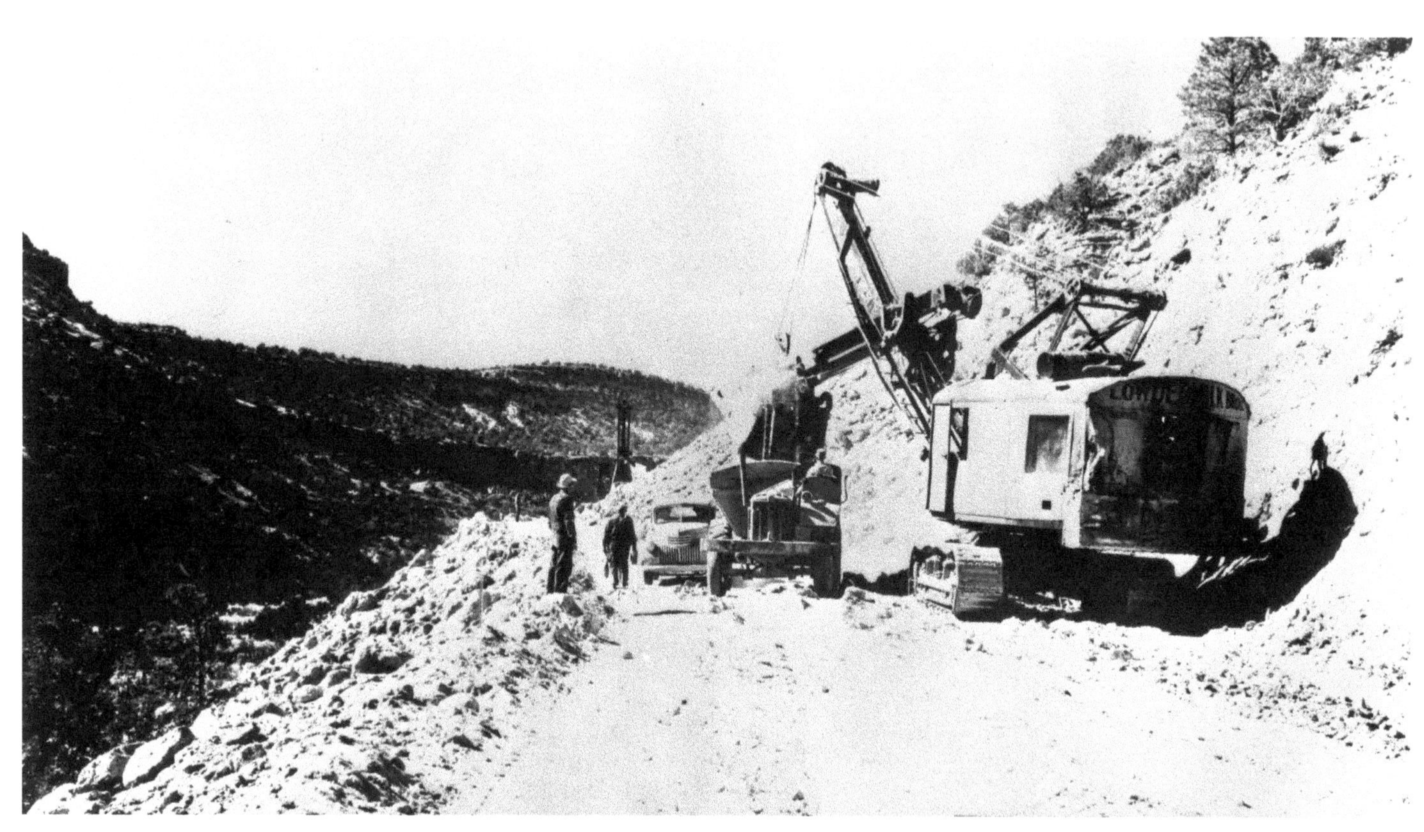

In this view, the highway to Los Alamos is under construction.

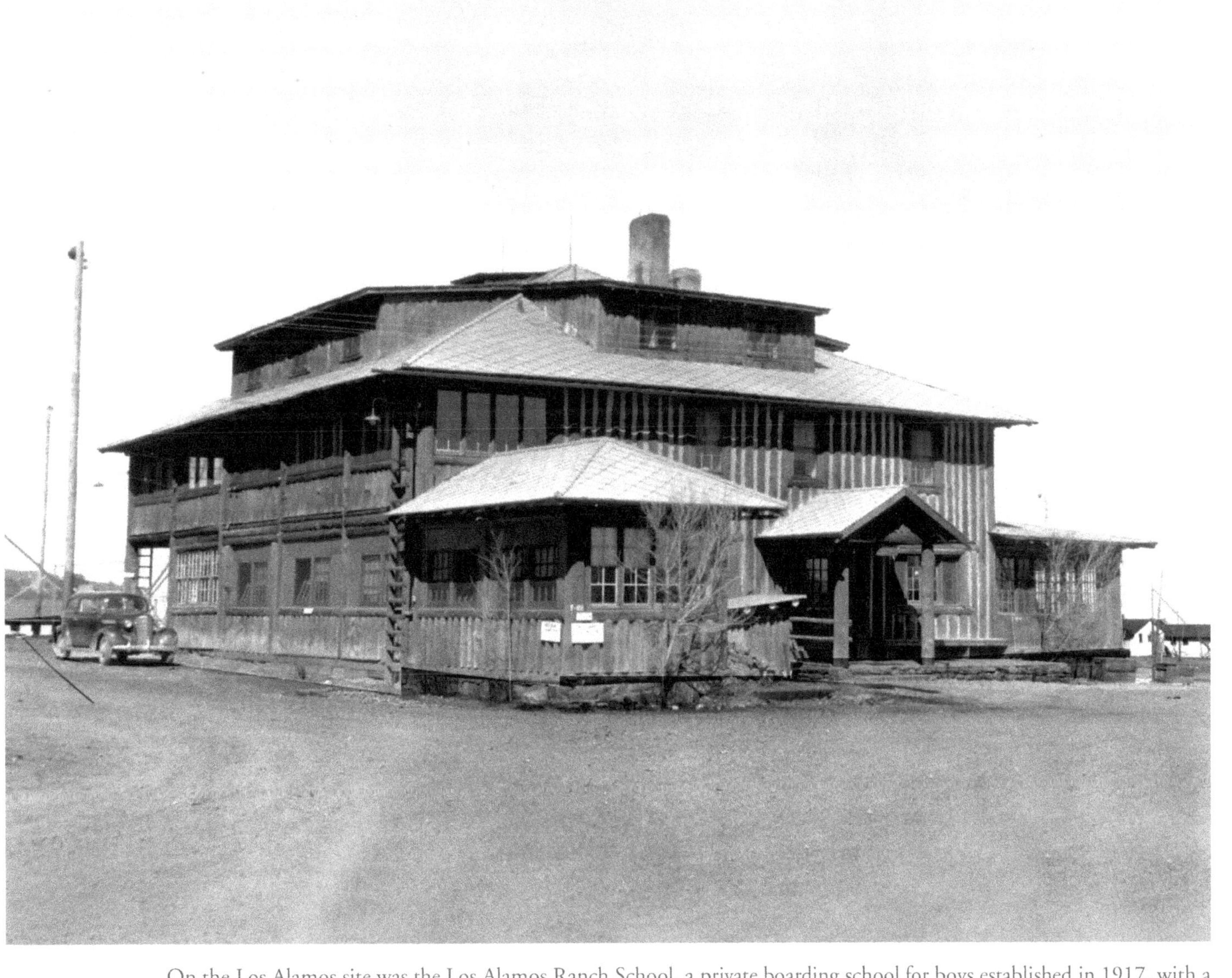

On the Los Alamos site was the Los Alamos Ranch School, a private boarding school for boys established in 1917, with a college preparatory curriculum and outdoor training. It was purchased in November 1942 for the Manhattan Project and is shown here in 1943. Originally called Site-Y, it was later known as Los Alamos Scientific Laboratory. This is the "Big House," formally classrooms, but used to house the first scientists.

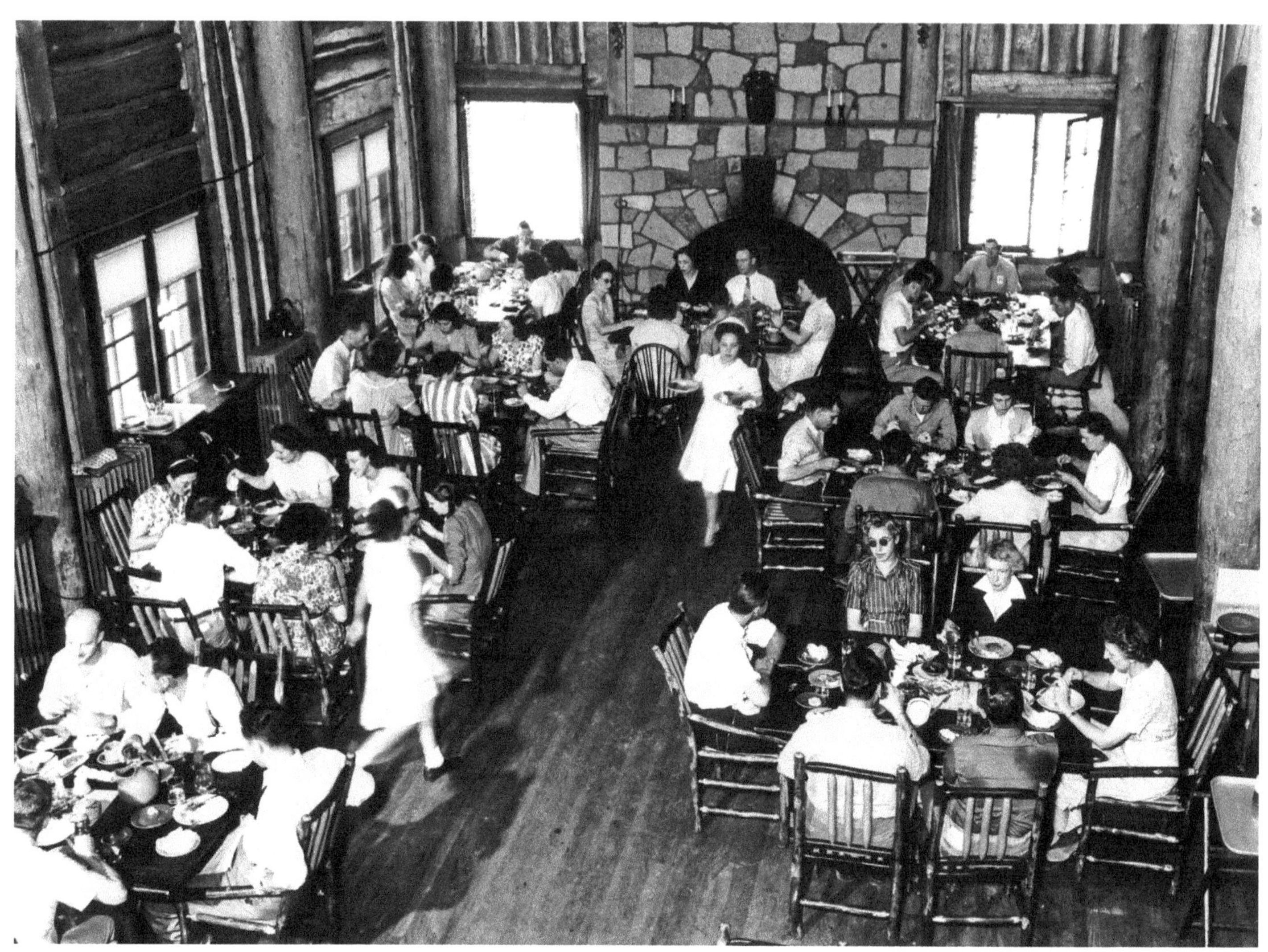

This photo was taken inside the Fuller Lodge in 1946, the main cafeteria of the Los Alamos Ranch School, where scientists and staff enjoy a meal. It was a popular place.

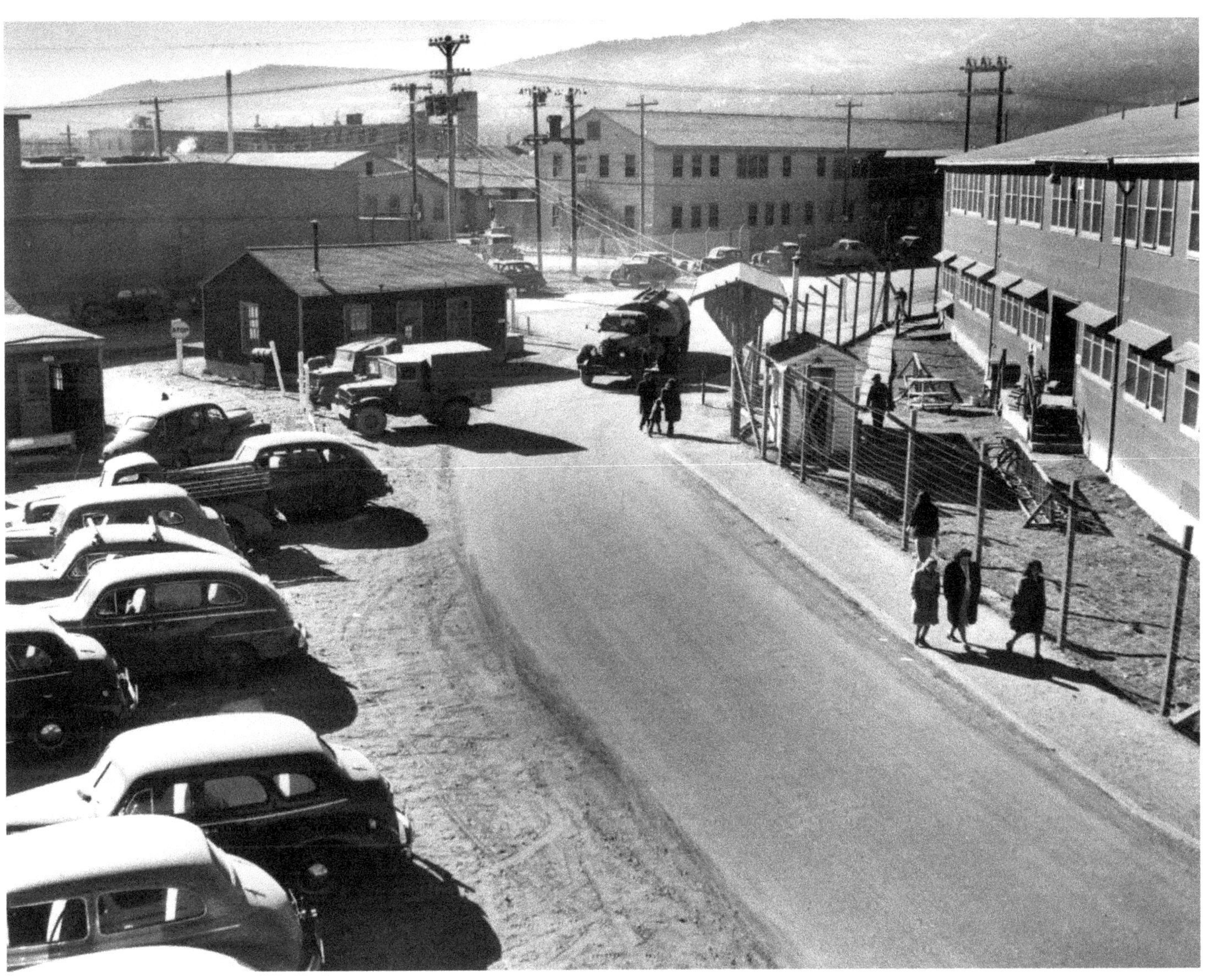

After entering Site-Y's main gate, workers were required to pass through another checkpoint before being allowed to enter this top-secret laboratory in Technical Area-1.

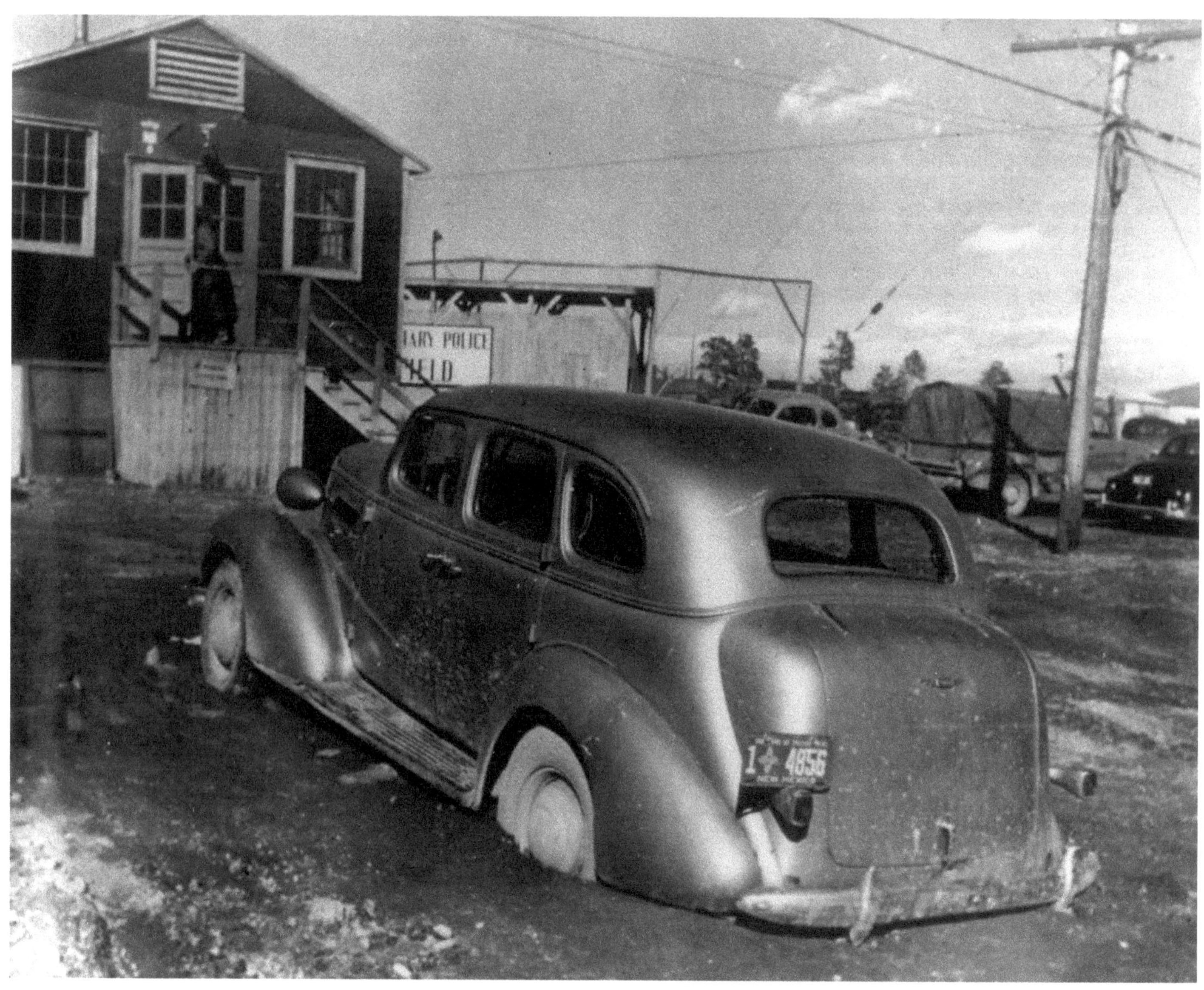

Parking at Los Alamos. When dry, roads were all dirt—when it rained, they became mud. This vehicle looks as though it could use a little nuclear power under the hood. July 1945.

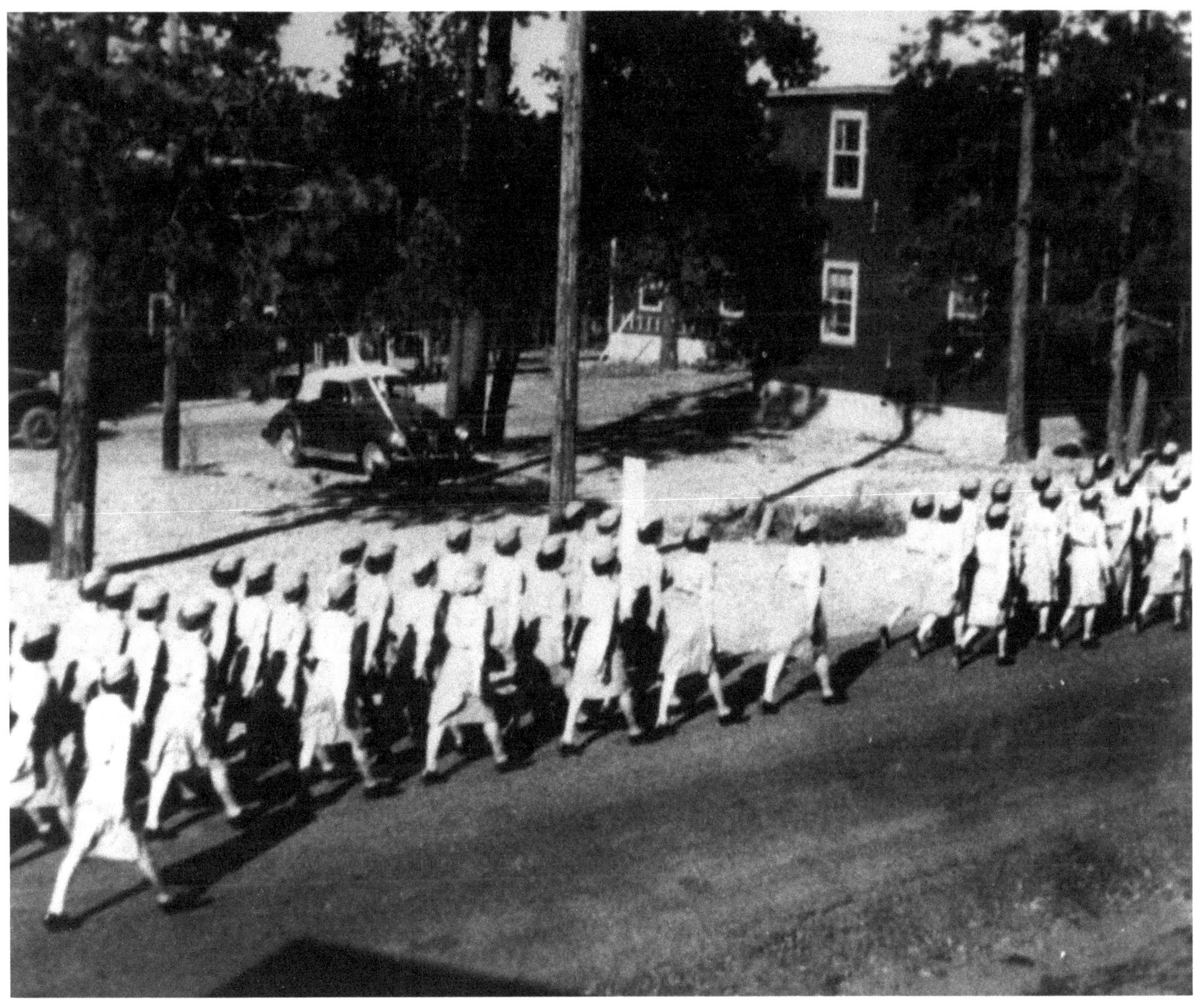

Throughout the Manhattan Project as well as in the war generally, women played important roles. Here in 1945, a unit of the Women's Auxiliary Corps is marching in formation at the Los Alamos, New Mexico, facility.

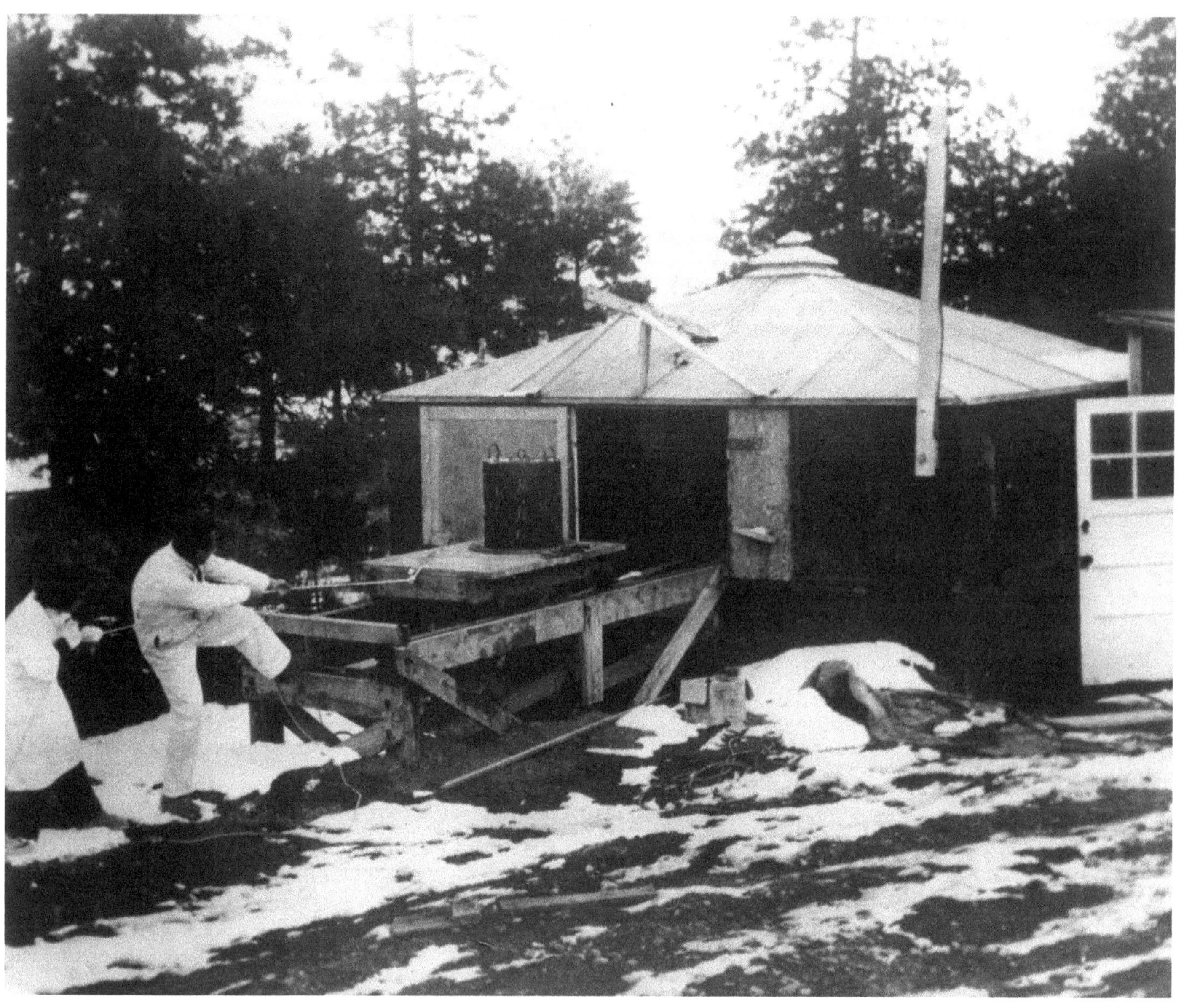

Technicians pull a radioactive source from one of the storage buildings. The crude methods used in those early years would be unacceptable today, let alone storing the source in such an insecure wooden building.

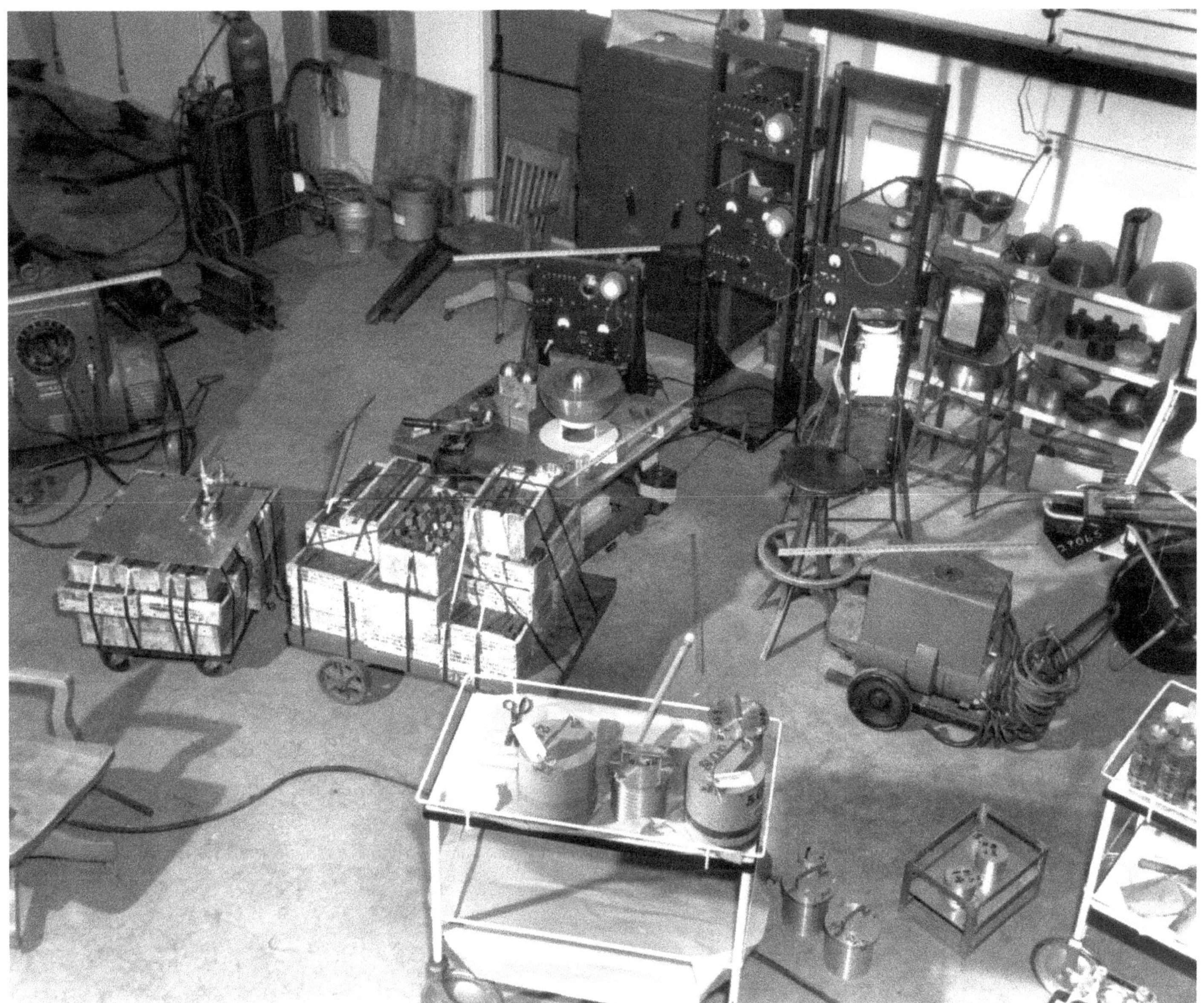

On May 21, 1946, Louis Slotin accidentally triggered a fission reaction with a burst of heavy radiation in this Los Alamos laboratory. When the fission took place he knew exactly what had happened and reacted immediately to prevent exposure to his colleagues. He was rushed to the hospital and treated for radiation poisoning, but there was little that could be done for him. He died nine days later, becoming the second victim of a criticality accident.

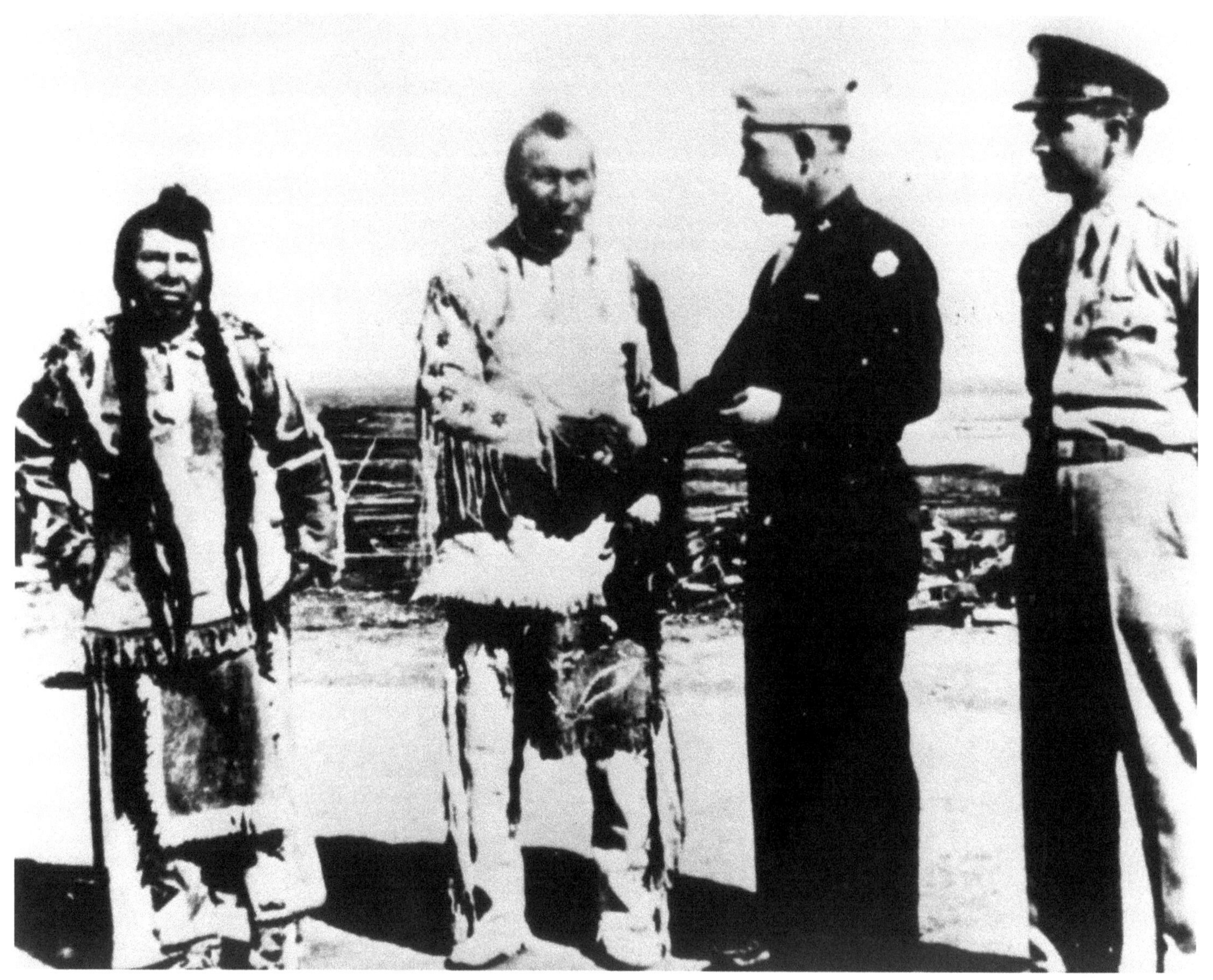

In this 1943 photo, Corps of Engineers Officers meet with the Wanapum Indians in Priest Rapids Valley, the area that was to become the Hanford Site. Indian assistance was requested in the war effort and they were told that they could no longer enter this part of the land.

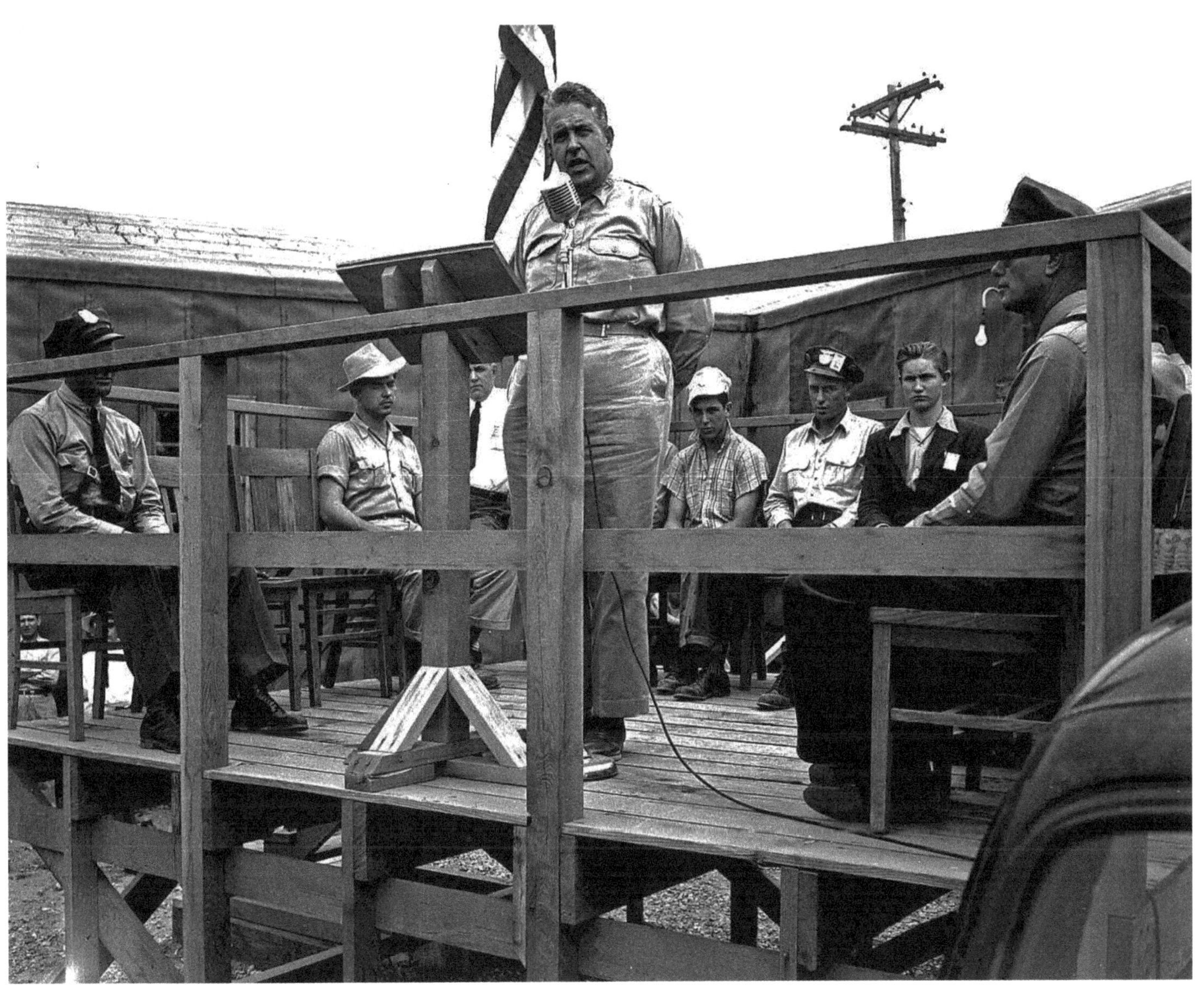

General Groves visited Hanford in early 1944 to speak with the workers about the importance of their work, the need for safety, and the secrecy required.

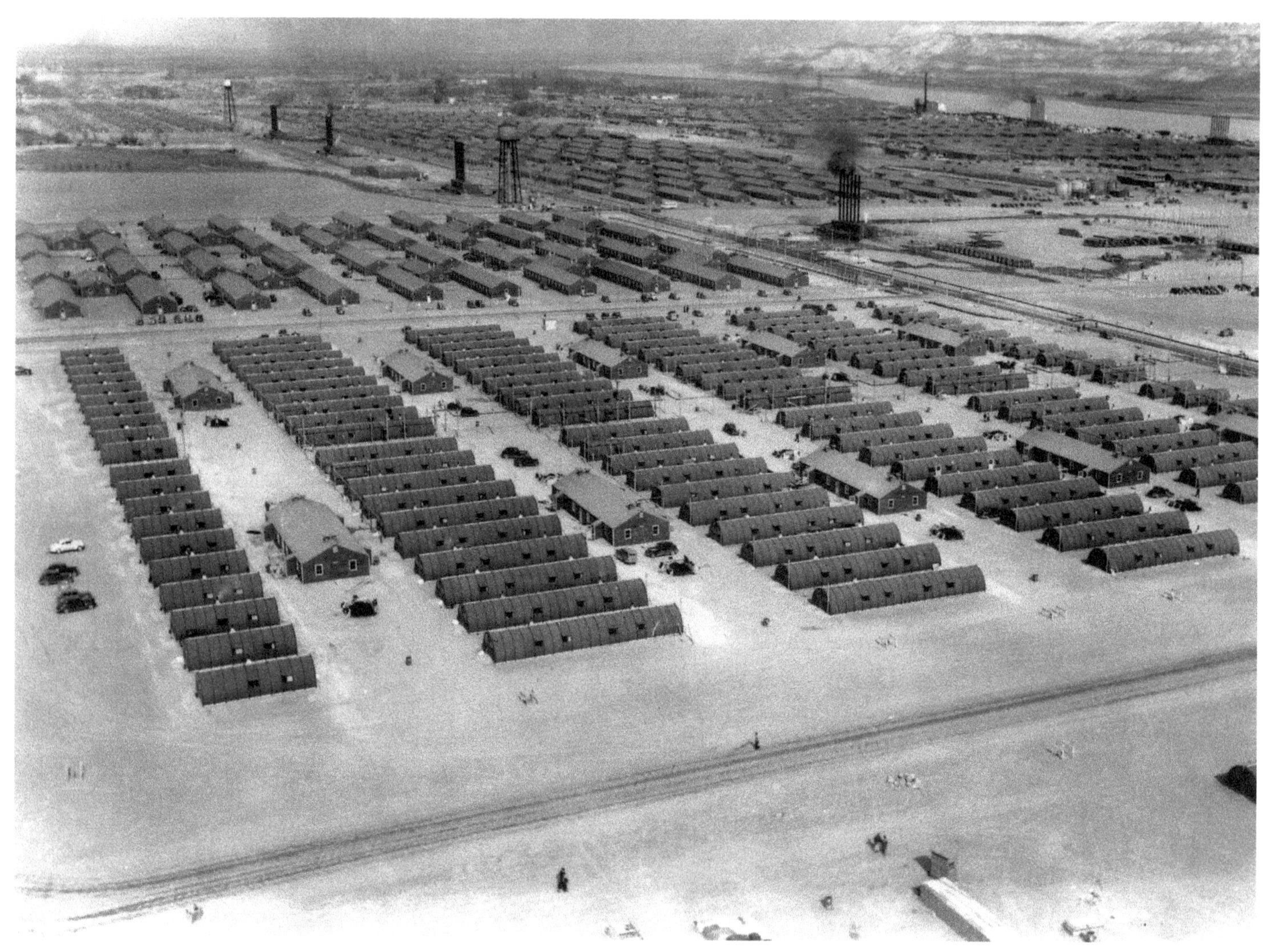

Overnight Hanford went from barren scrub and sagebrush land to 50,000 people. This photo shows many of the 880 housing units built. In the foreground are hutments, 16 by 40 feet, each housing ten workers. Both men and women lived in them. Bathroom, showers, and laundry facilities were located between and central to the rows of hutments.

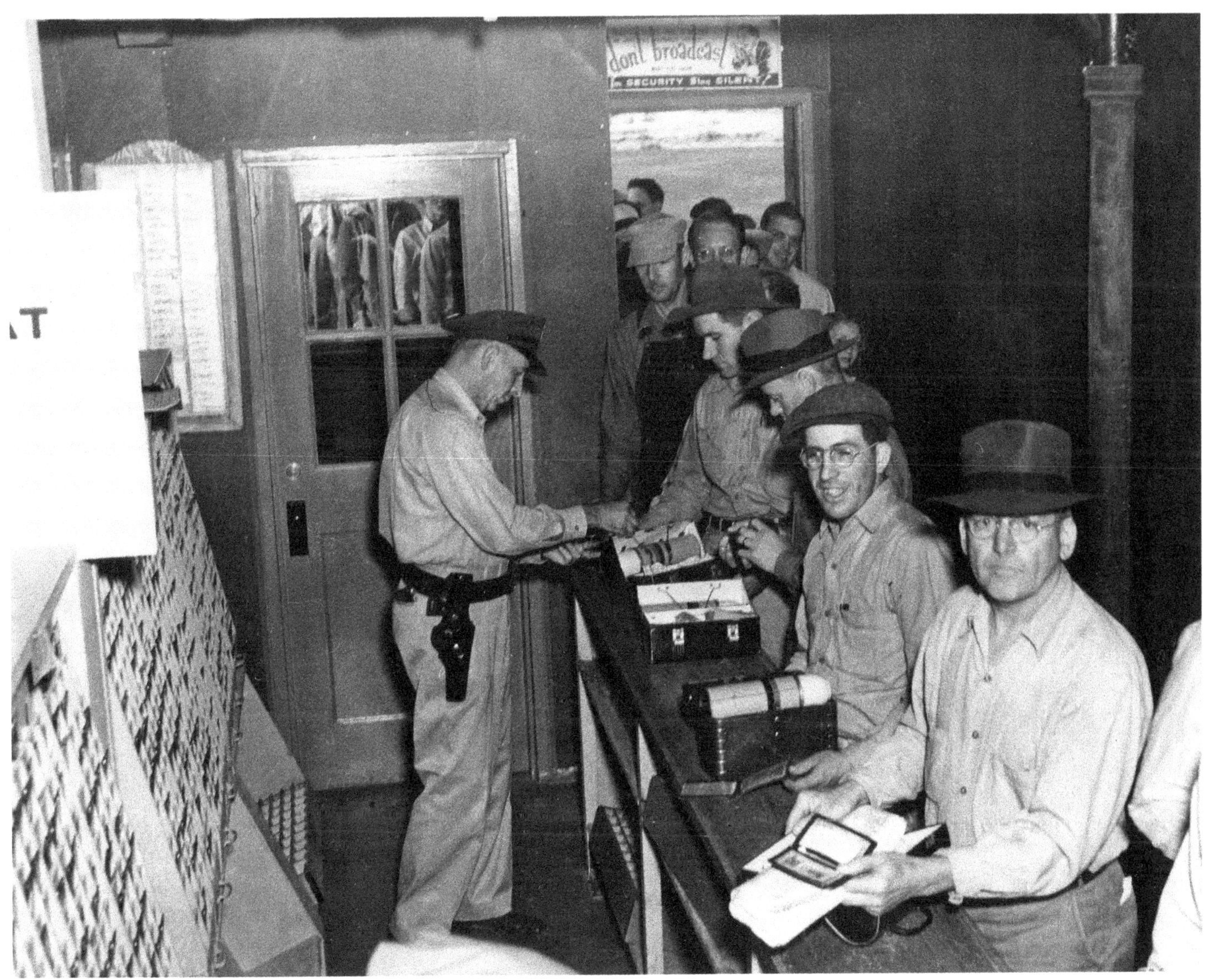

All workers wore security badges while on site. Everything carried into the site was thoroughly inspected by security guards, including lunch boxes as seen here at a Hanford security check station in 1945.

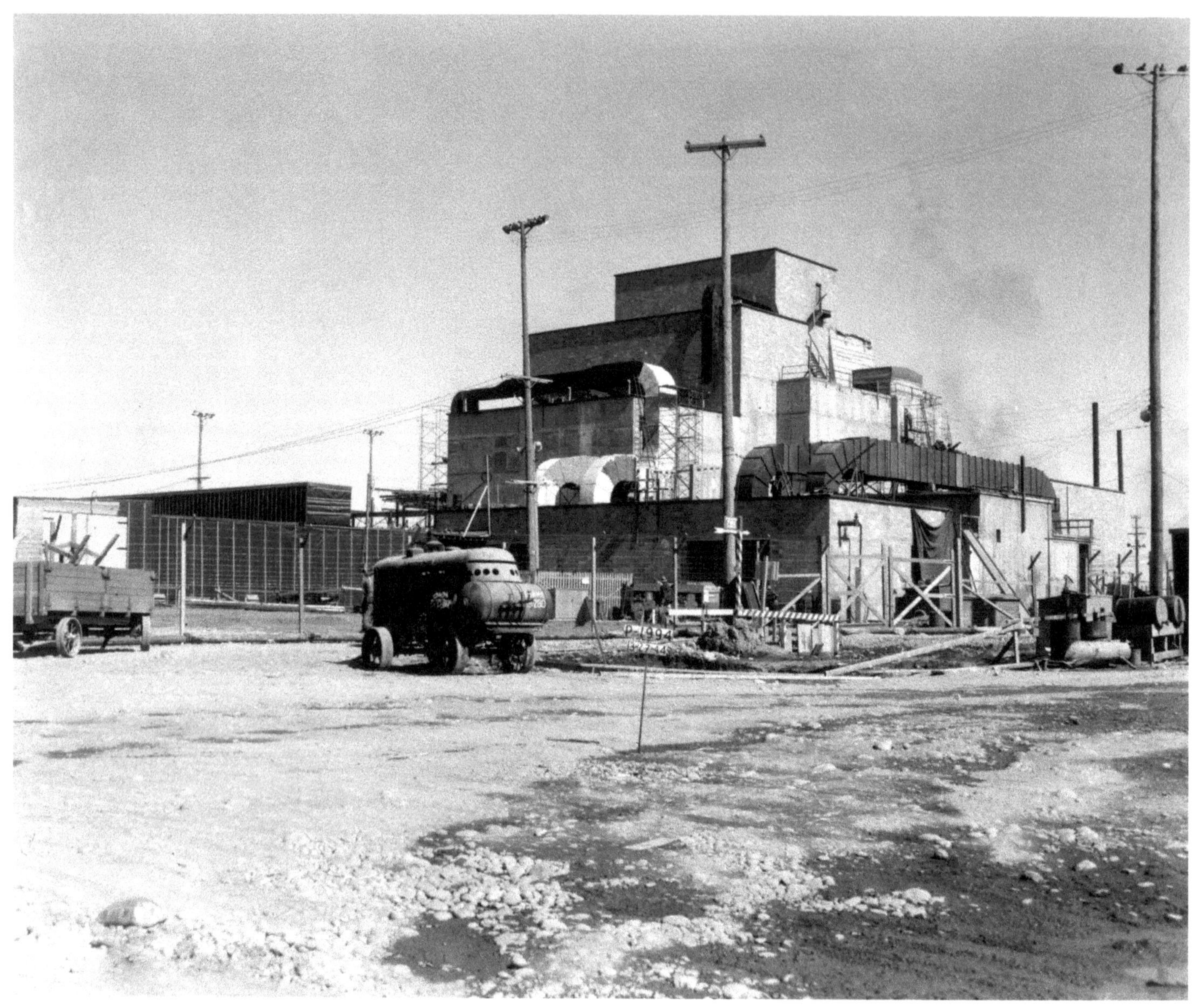

Everything but the tall ventilation stacks has been constructed at the first reactor on the Hanford site, the B-Reactor, in this image.

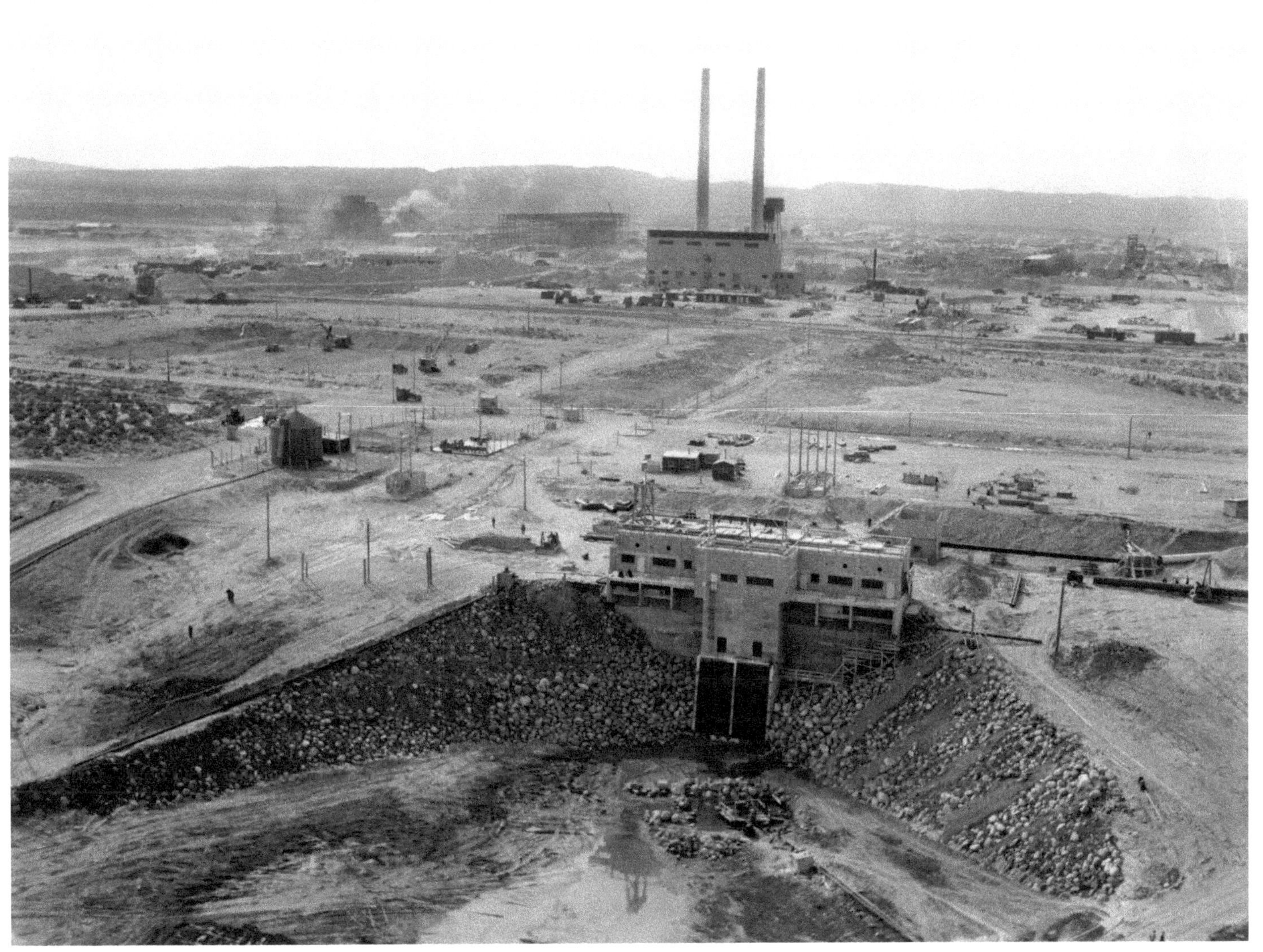

In the foreground shown here is the 181-8 Pump House under construction. The large openings are the intakes for Columbia River water. The 184-B Power Plant rises in the background. Like the facilities at Oak Ridge, the Hanford facilities required an immense amount of power. Power House 184-B was built to provide the B-Reactor and support facilities with steam for heating and processing.

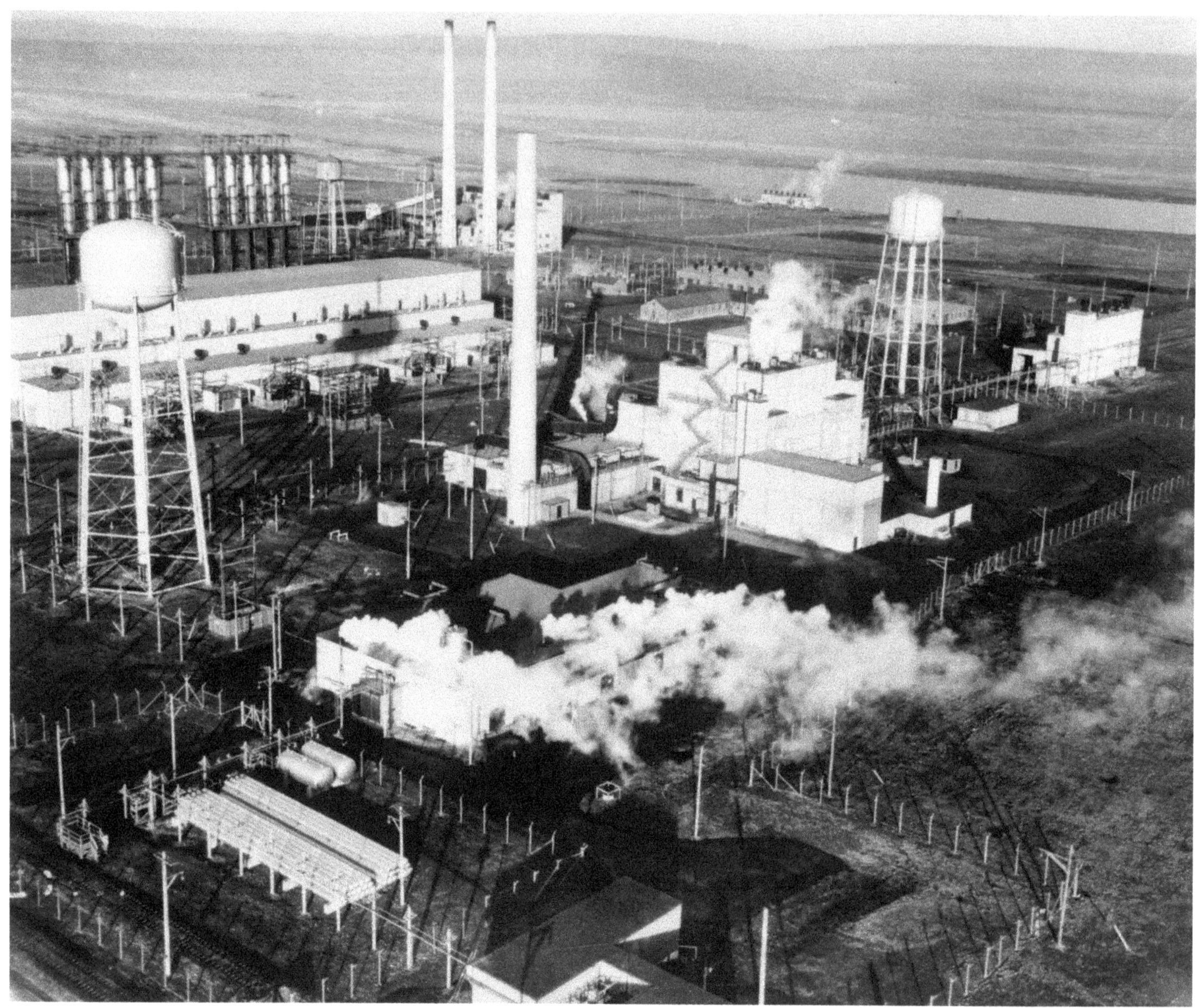

Facing northwest toward the Columbia River this is an aerial shot of the B-Reactor, the first of nine plutonium production reactors at the Hanford Site, and the world's first full-scale nuclear facility. It was constructed in only 11 months and went critical on September 26, 1944.

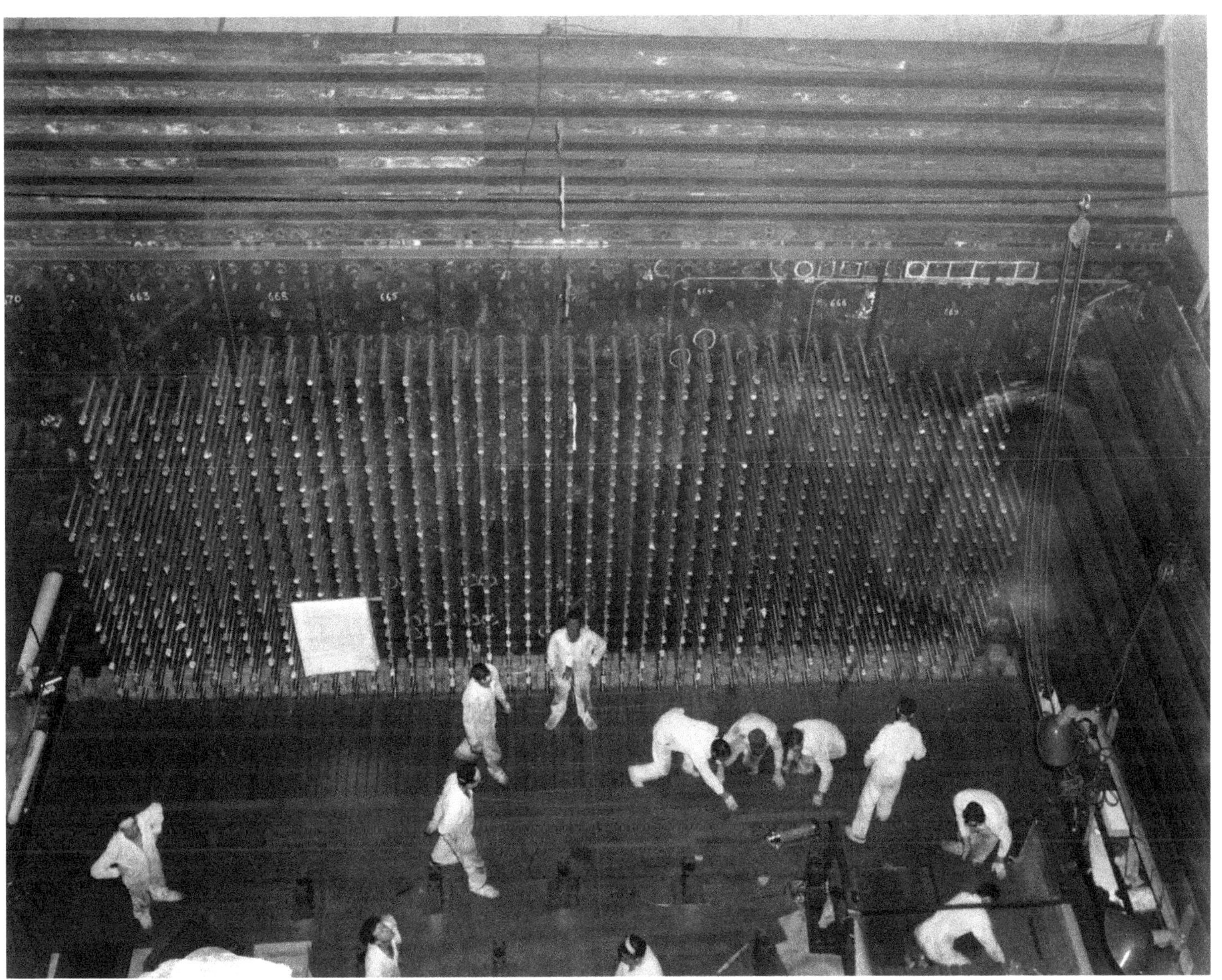

These workers are in front of the "gun barrels" protruding into the Hanford 105-B pile. There were 2,004 tubes, which ran from the front face to the rear of the reactor. They were made of very pure aluminum and coated with a zinc alloy. The inside diameter was a little over an inch and a half. Workers used truckloads of Kotex pads to swab the insides of every tube for they had to be completely free of all contaminants.

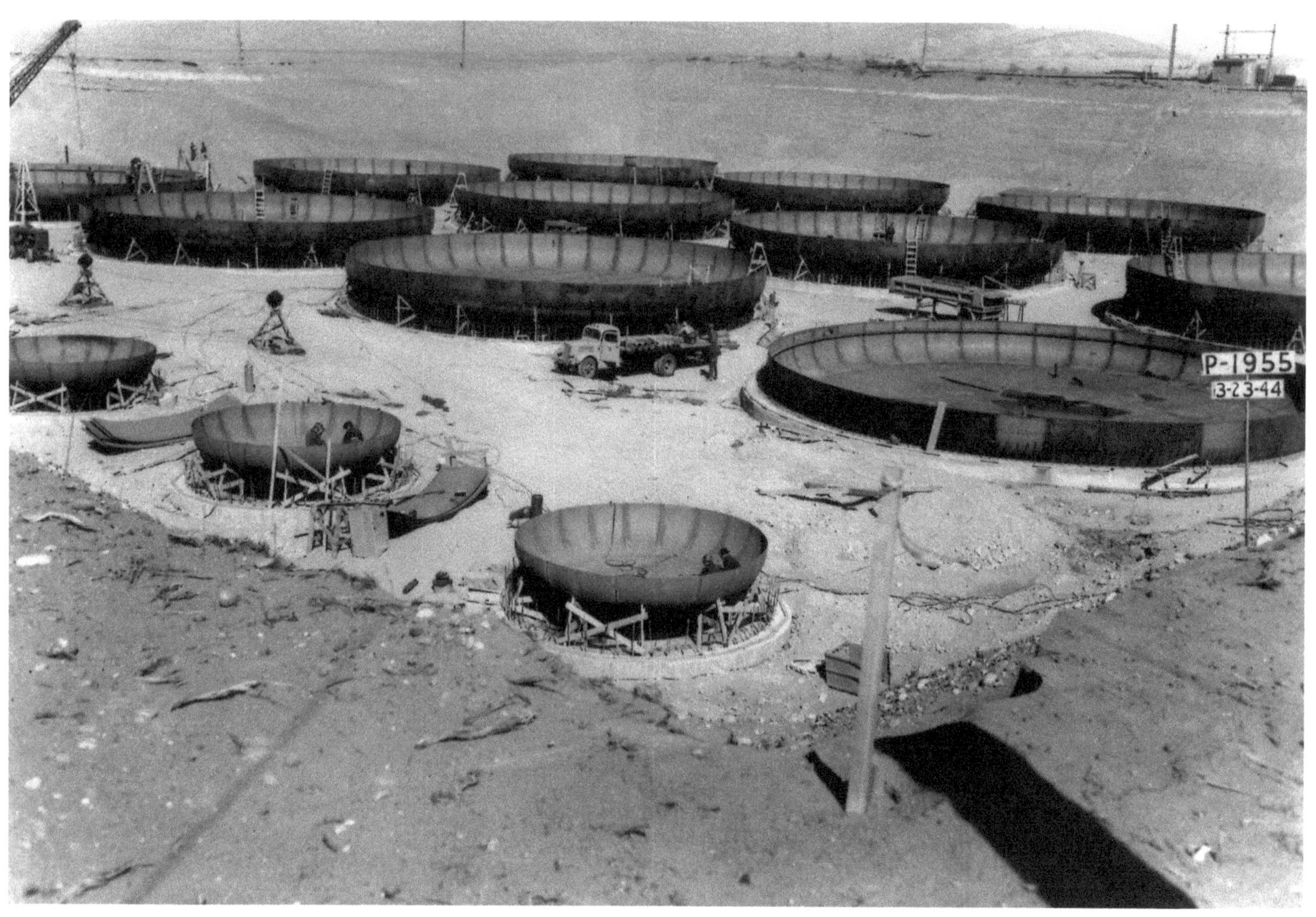

The reactors at Hanford produced highly radioactive wastes that had to be stored. Here in 1944, the 241-T tank farm is under construction, the first of many waste-storage tanks.

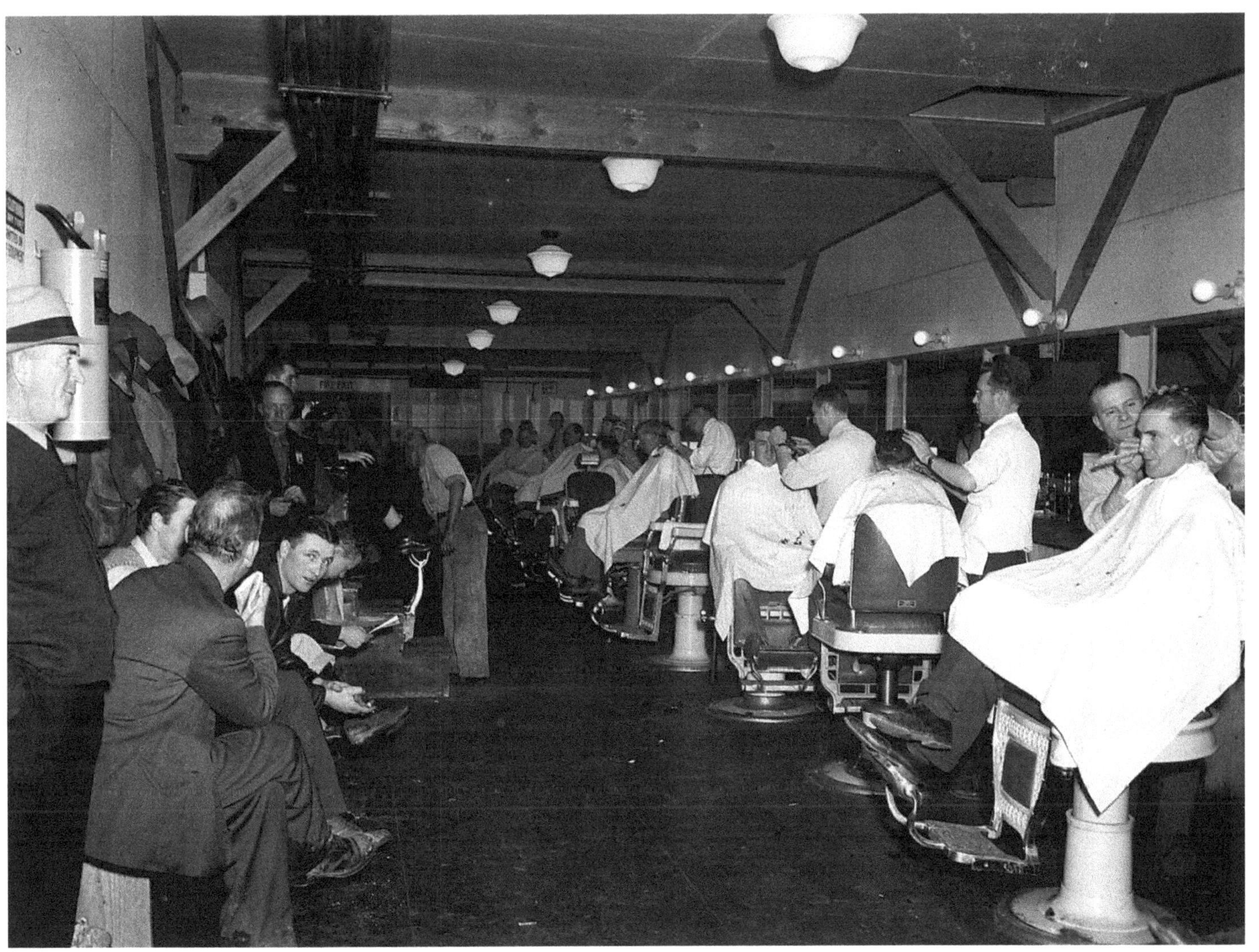

Like other Americans, workers and family members needed to shop for clothing and shoes, not to mention services like haircuts. The barbershop was a place to chat and catch up with friends. This family-owned shop remains in business today.

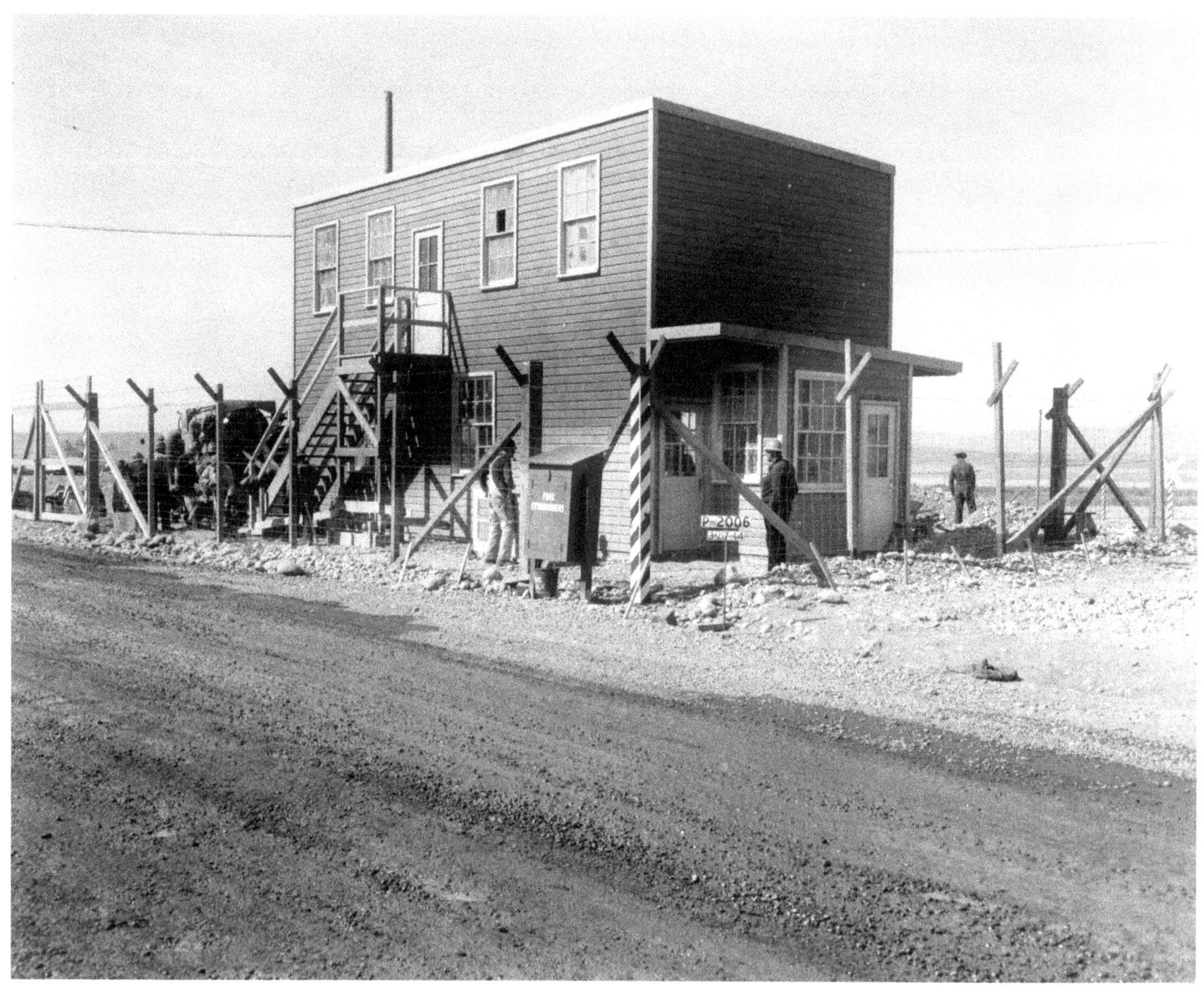

This 1944 photo is the 1701-B Main Gate Guardhouse at the Hanford facility, which gave access to the 100-B area. On the second floor, radiation detection dosimeters and film badges worn by workers were read and exchanged.

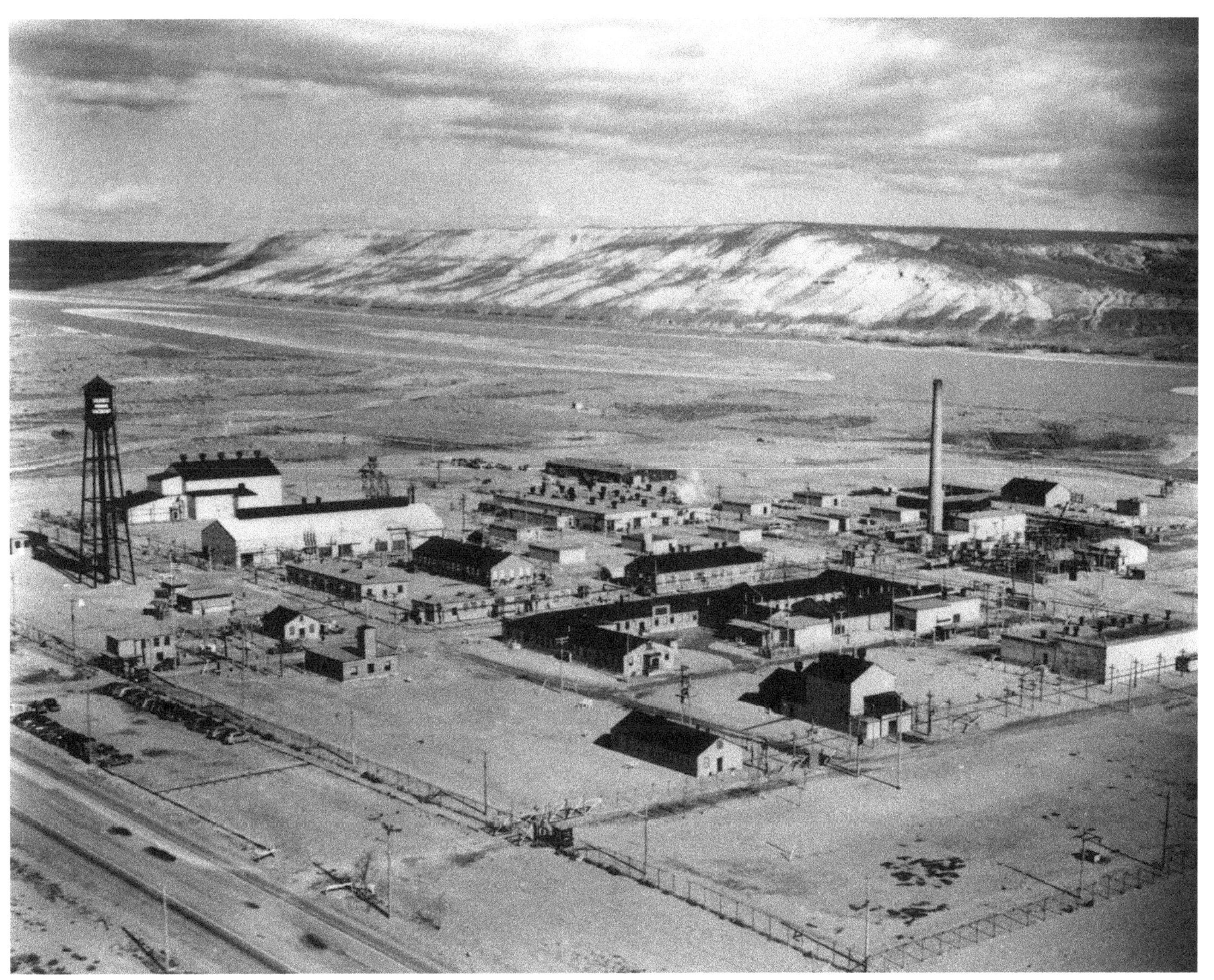

This is an aerial view of the 300-Area of the Hanford facility recorded after the war in 1949.

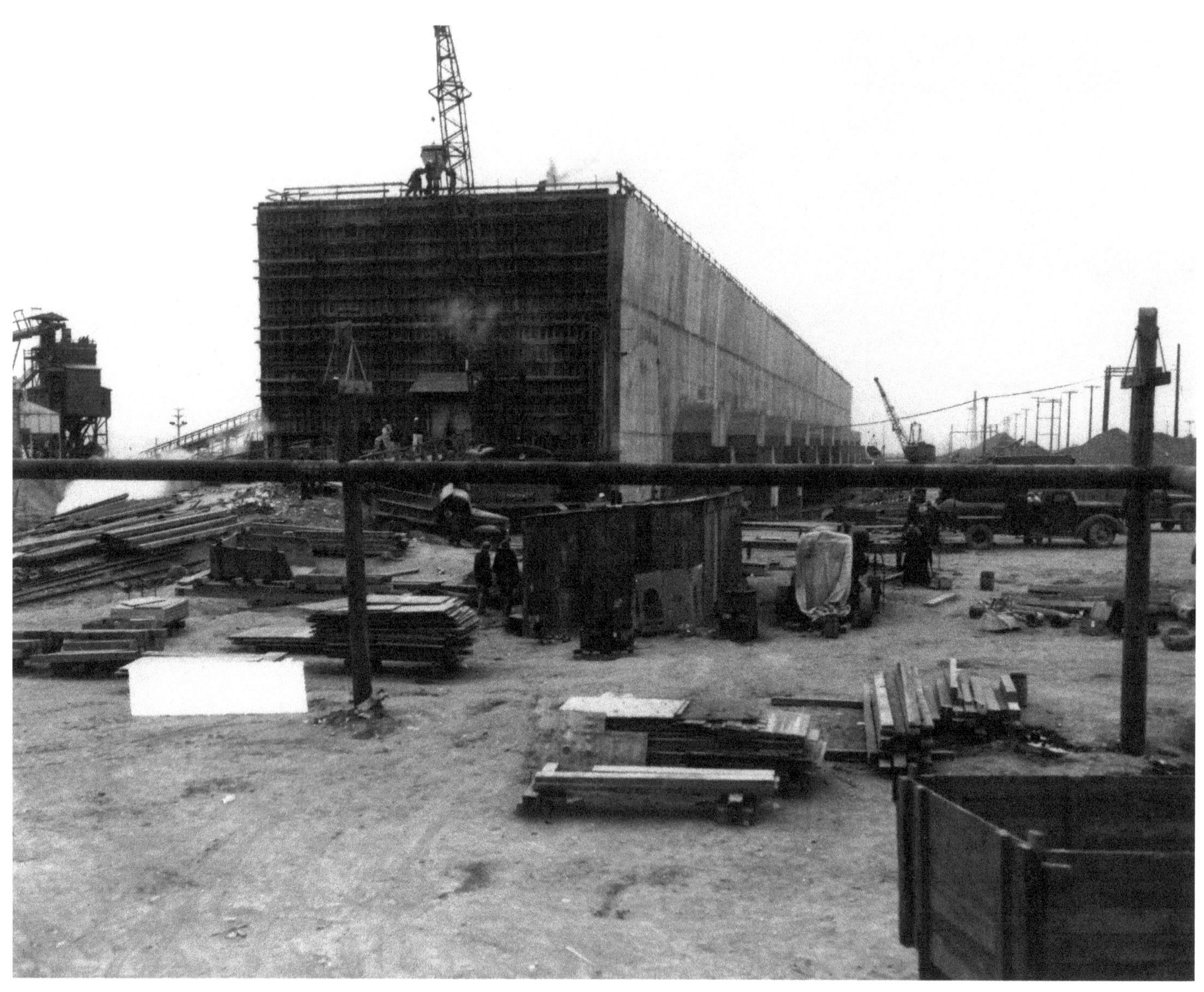

In the 200-West complex of the Hanford Site were the 221-T and 221-U chemical separation buildings called the "Queen Marys" because they resembled an ocean liner being built. When completed in December 1944, they were 800 feet long, 65 feet wide, and 80 feet tall and contained 40 process pools. The 221-T and 221-U are shown here under construction in 1943. The "Queen Marys" were the world's first large-scale facilities built to separate isotopes of highly radioactive plutonium.

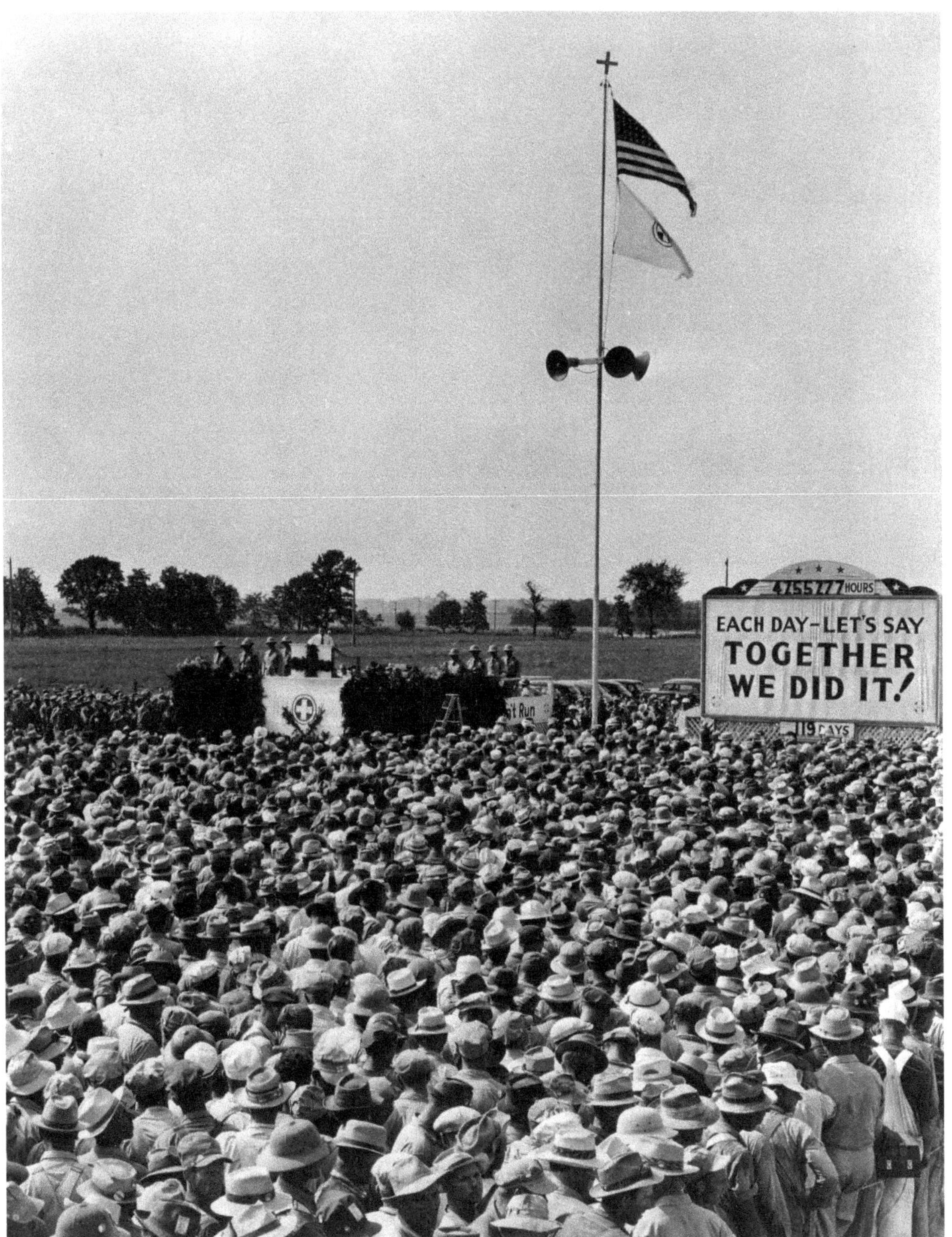

Until recent times, hats were standard wearing apparel among most Americans. Workers attending this Hanford rally in 1945 sport everything from pith helmets to fedoras. Finding one hatless person in the crowd would be quite a challenge.

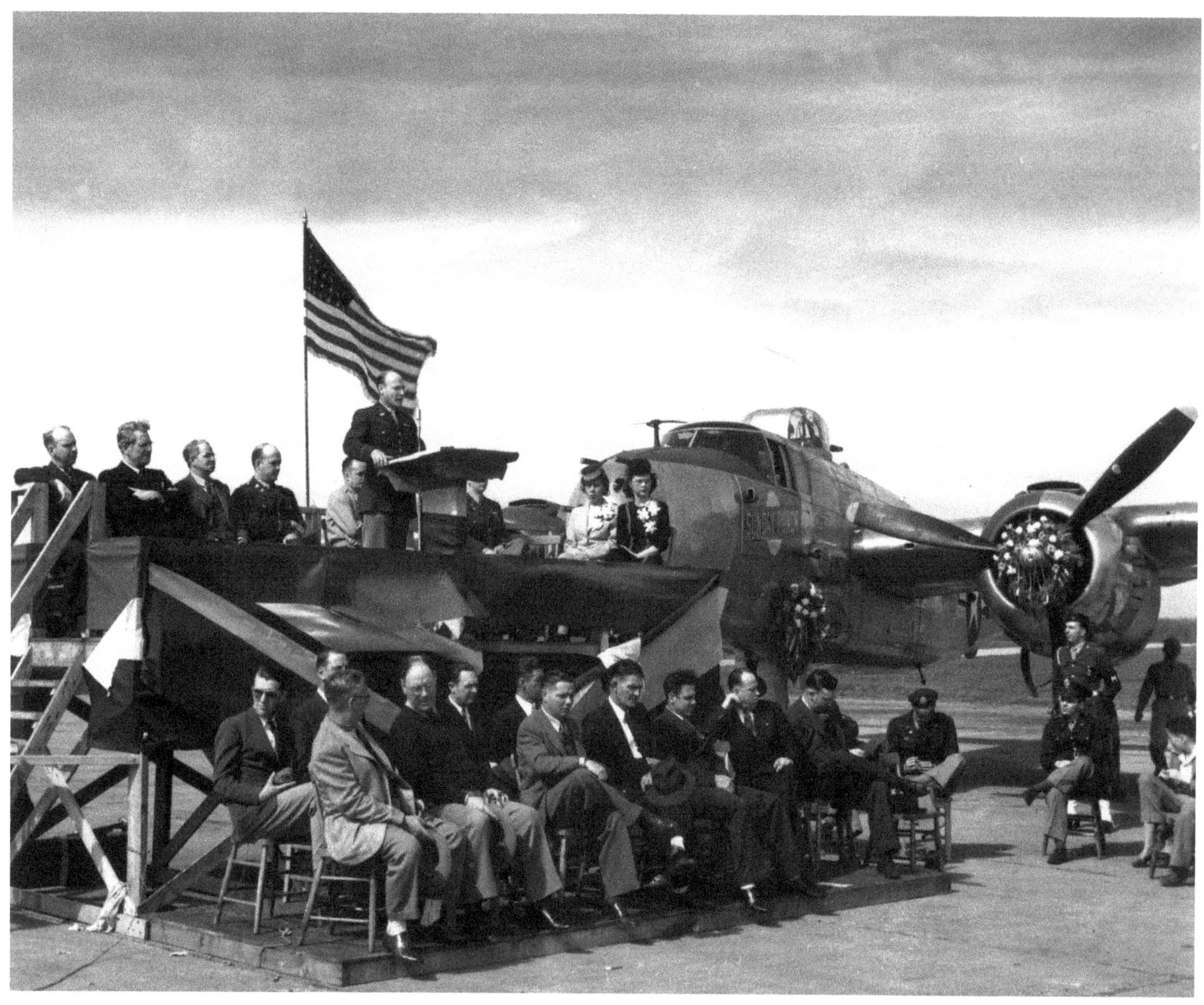

The workers at the K-25 site in Oak Ridge donated a Sunday workday to commission this Mitchell B-25 Bomber. They presented it to the Army Air Force in 1945, naming it *Sunday Punch.*

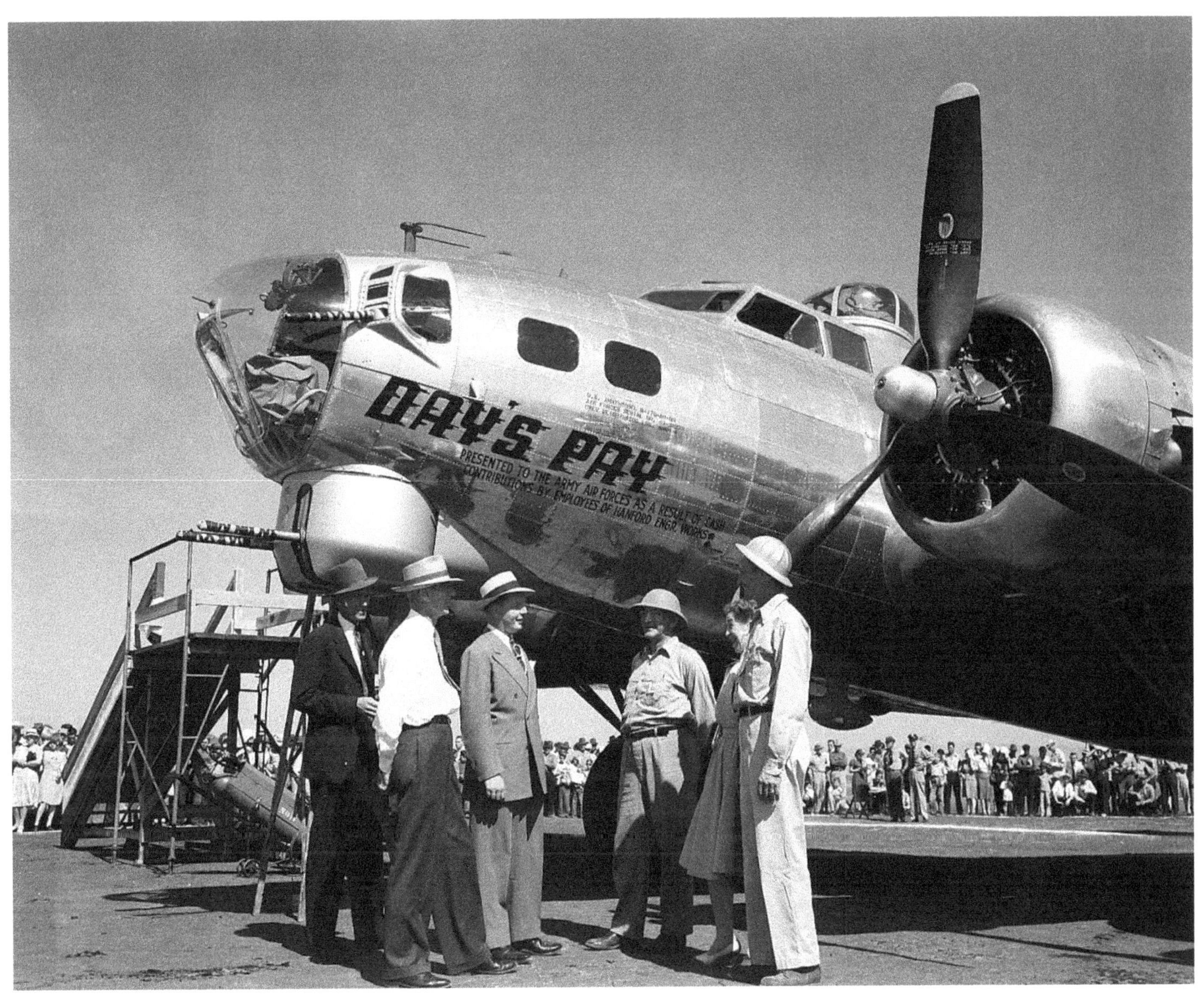

Dignitaries gather around the newly built B-17 named *Day's Pay* purchased by the Hanford workers and presented during this ceremony. Although Boeing's B-17 Flying Fortress became prized as a workhorse during the war, the B-29 Superfortress would be called upon to deliver the atom bomb to Japan.

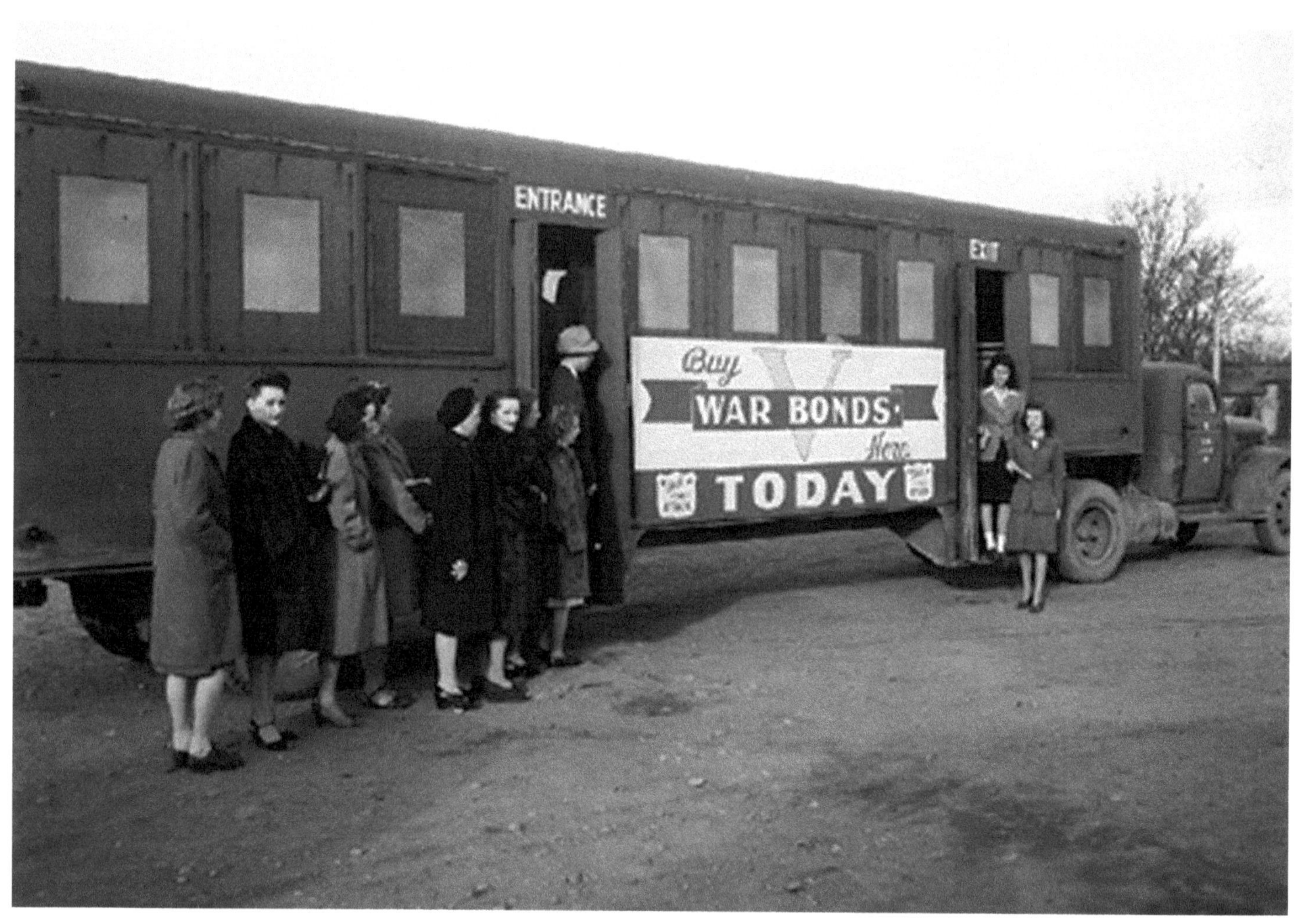

During the war effort, war bonds were an important way to support the troops. Hanford residents line up to purchase bonds from this mobile semitrailer, which made its rounds to the many facilities on site so that all would have a chance to help.

Work and Family Life

THE DEDICATED AMERICANS WHO MADE IT ALL POSSIBLE

Tens of thousands of individual workers were needed to carry out the mission of the Manhattan Project. Some Americans contributed to the cause by forfeiting their land, being given only weeks to leave their homes and farms far from metropolitan areas. Overnight huge tracts of land were purchased, without approval by the landowners, to construct the gargantuan facilities. Armies of construction workers and equipment were brought in to begin clearing the properties for the various facilities and for infrastructure and housing for workers and their families. Tens of thousands of prefabricated houses, small trailers, tiny hutments, and dormitories were erected as living quarters. Within or adjacent to the various construction sites, small cities quickly sprouted and grew to substantial size, with their own cafeterias, laundry houses, post offices, base exchanges, shopping areas, as well as schools, theaters, recreational centers, swimming pools, ball diamonds, and more. And it happened in three states.

Most workers put in ten-hour shifts, six days a week, and construction went on with three shifts a day, usually every day. Only a few select people knew what was being built or what the final goal was, but everyone knew that what he or she was doing was for the war effort and hard work meant bringing our soldiers home. There were reminders everywhere of the importance of the work and the serious need for secrecy about what was being done. It was clear to every worker that he not share the details of his particular job, and thus, no one talked about what he or she did. Everyone understood that the subject was simply forbidden and didn't ask for or offer information.

Women played a key role in the Manhattan Project. World War II required the military service of the majority of the young men of many nations, and women were needed to fill the roles at home ordinarily undertaken by men. Their work became crucial to the war effort, in particular the operation of the various facilities. These facilities incorporated utterly new, highly complex sciences, with thousands of large and small dials and gauges, and as many knobs and handles to adjust. Women could excel at roles that required close attention to detail, and working with all the bells and whistles of these new facilities was one such role. Segregation prohibited blacks and whites from eating, shopping, or living side-by-side, but all self-sacrificing Americans, of every race, worked together for a cause bigger than themselves. It was said that inside the fences of the secret cities few truly cared about the color of a person's skin. Most shared a language and a heritage, all shared a nation, and all shared a single, motivating purpose.

Children were ever present, so schools, clinics, and recreation facilities were an important part of life on the reservations. Though most living facilities were small and left much to be desired, everyone seemed to understand that it was just the way of things and families made the best of what they had. Life was not easy for adults or for children, but complaints were few. Americans of every stripe understood that what they were doing was to help end a horrible war.

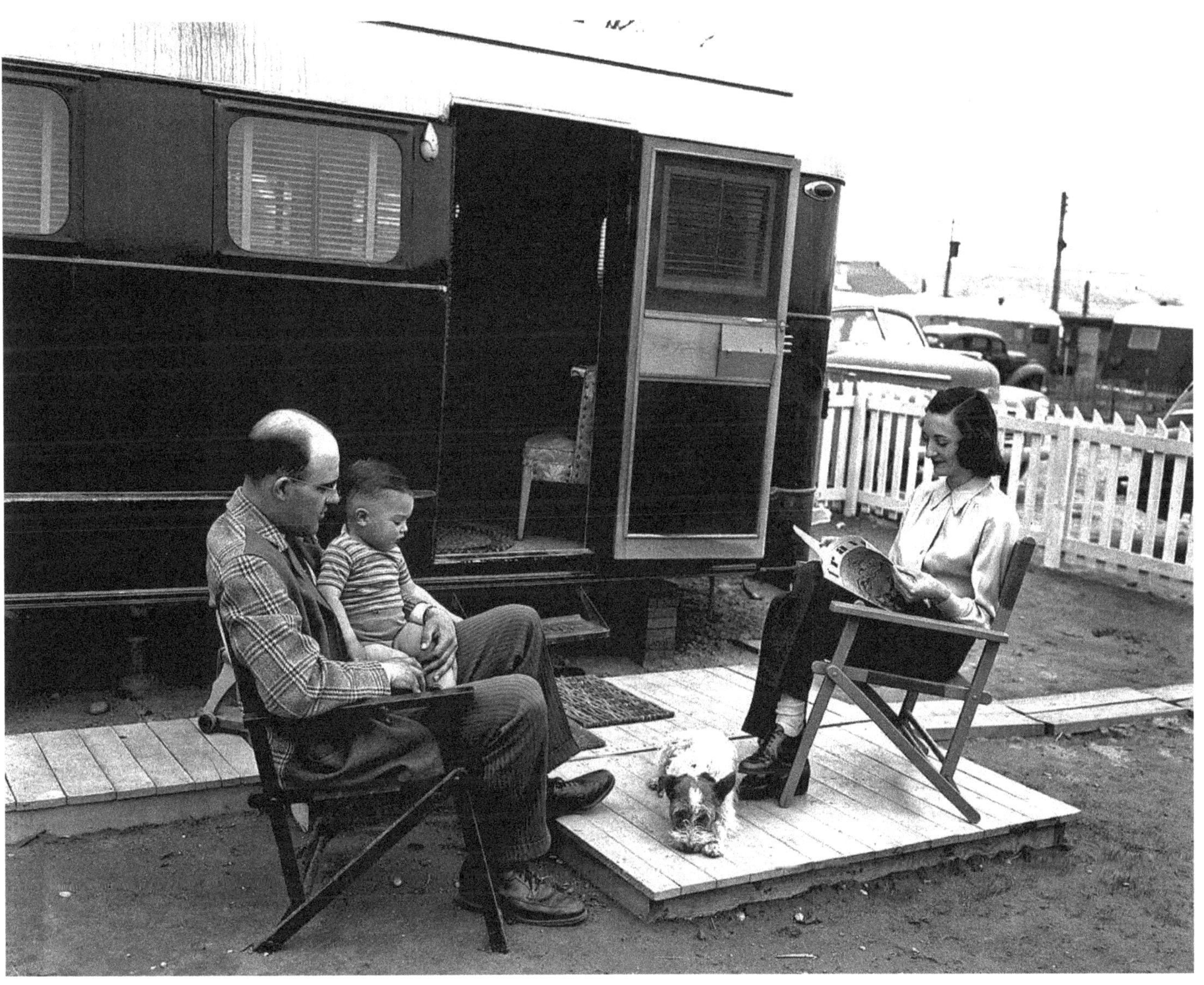

The wife and dog get the patio while the family enjoys the comforts of home inside their picket fence. The constant construction and excavation in the fine, ashy soil created blowing dust and sand that made lawns and gardens nearly impossible to cultivate on the Hanford reservation. Boardwalks were essential, for when it rained, everything turned to mud.

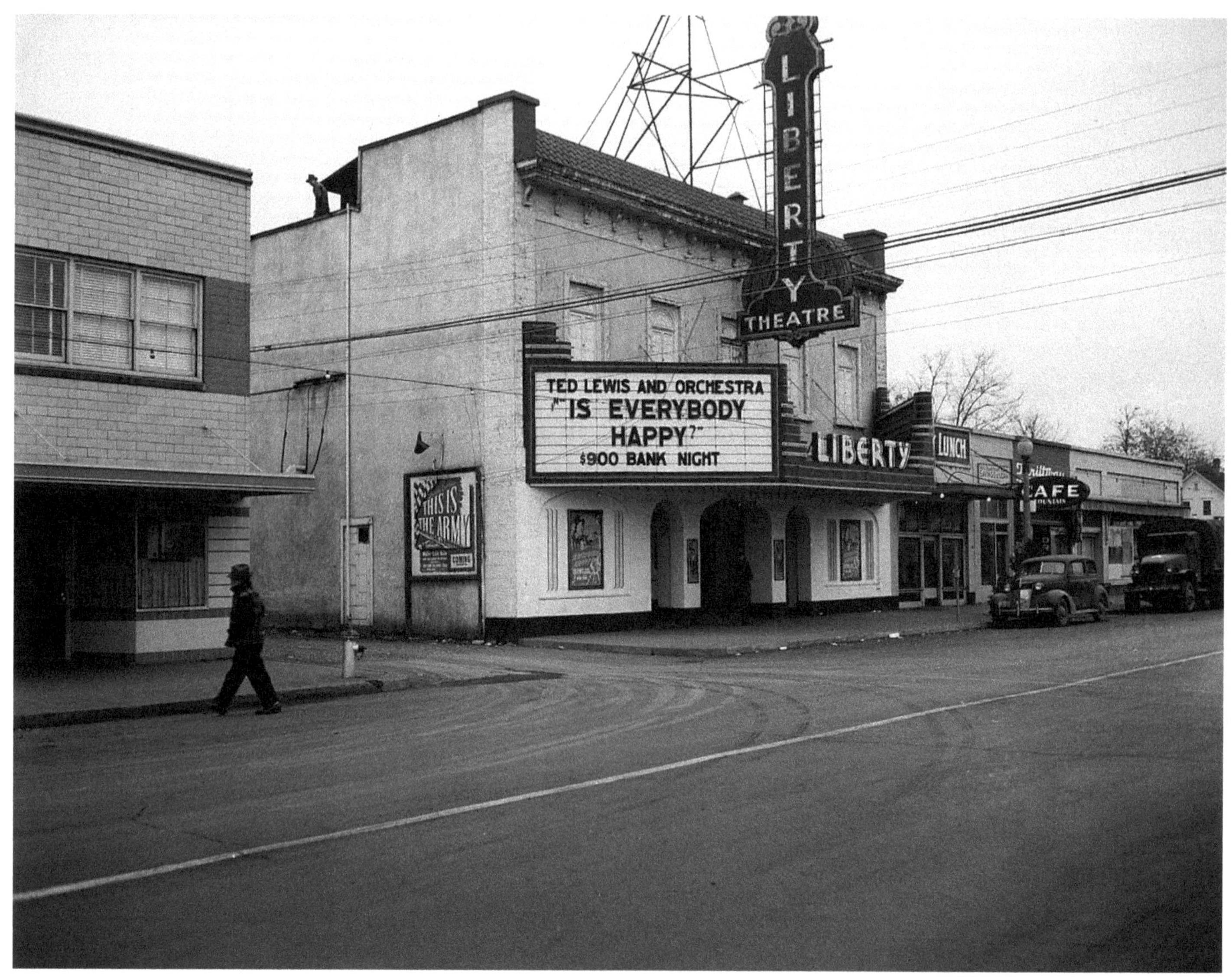

One of the oldest communities near the Hanford site was Pasco. The Liberty Theatre provided live entertainment onstage and had a full basement for dance bands that played often. Ted Lewis's "Is Everybody Happy" was being performed when this image was recorded.

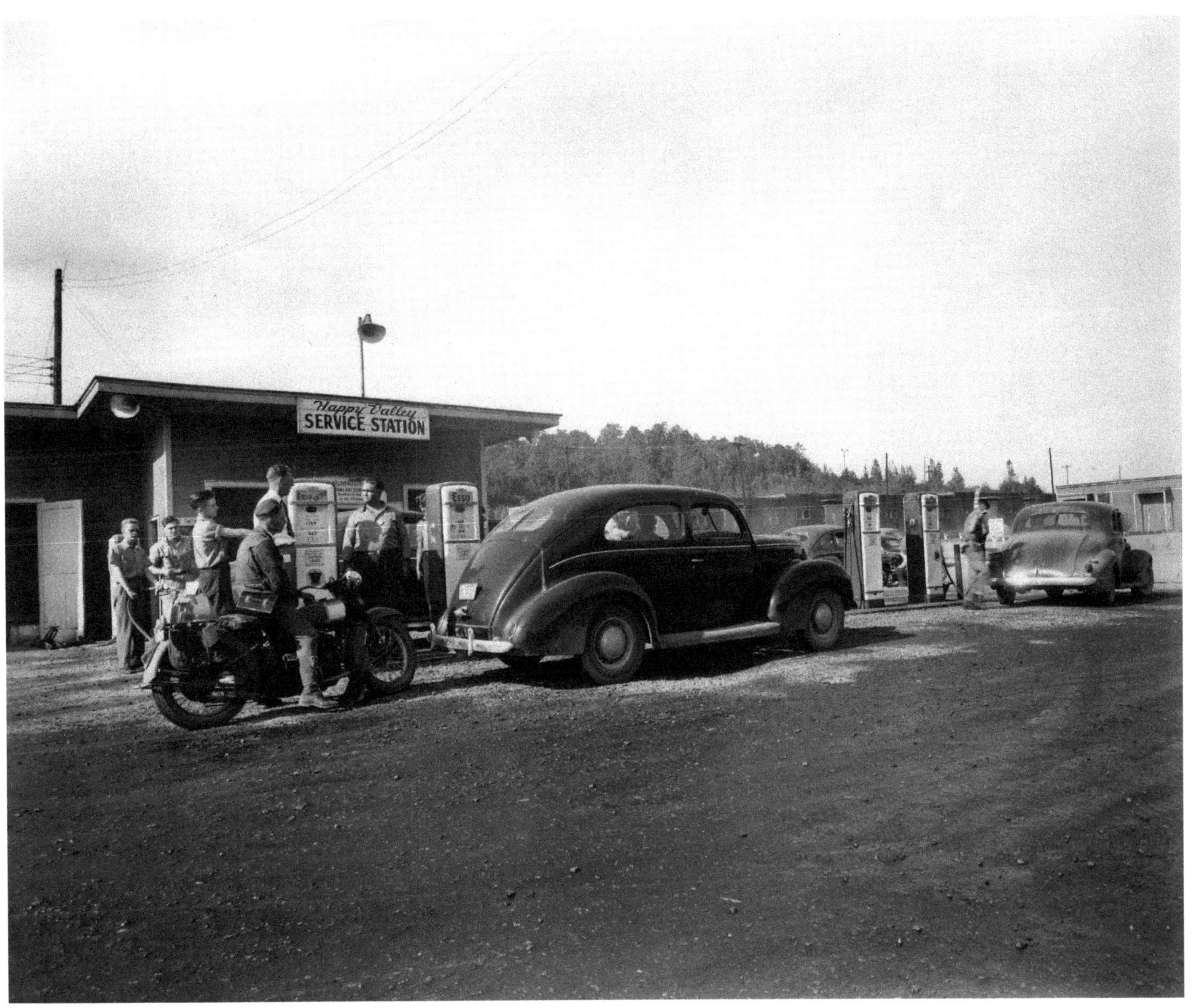

Shown here in 1943, this Esso service station was located in a large residential area called Happy Valley. A mini-city with everything needed for residents and workers, Happy Valley was built adjacent K-25 and was home to about 15,000 workers and their families.

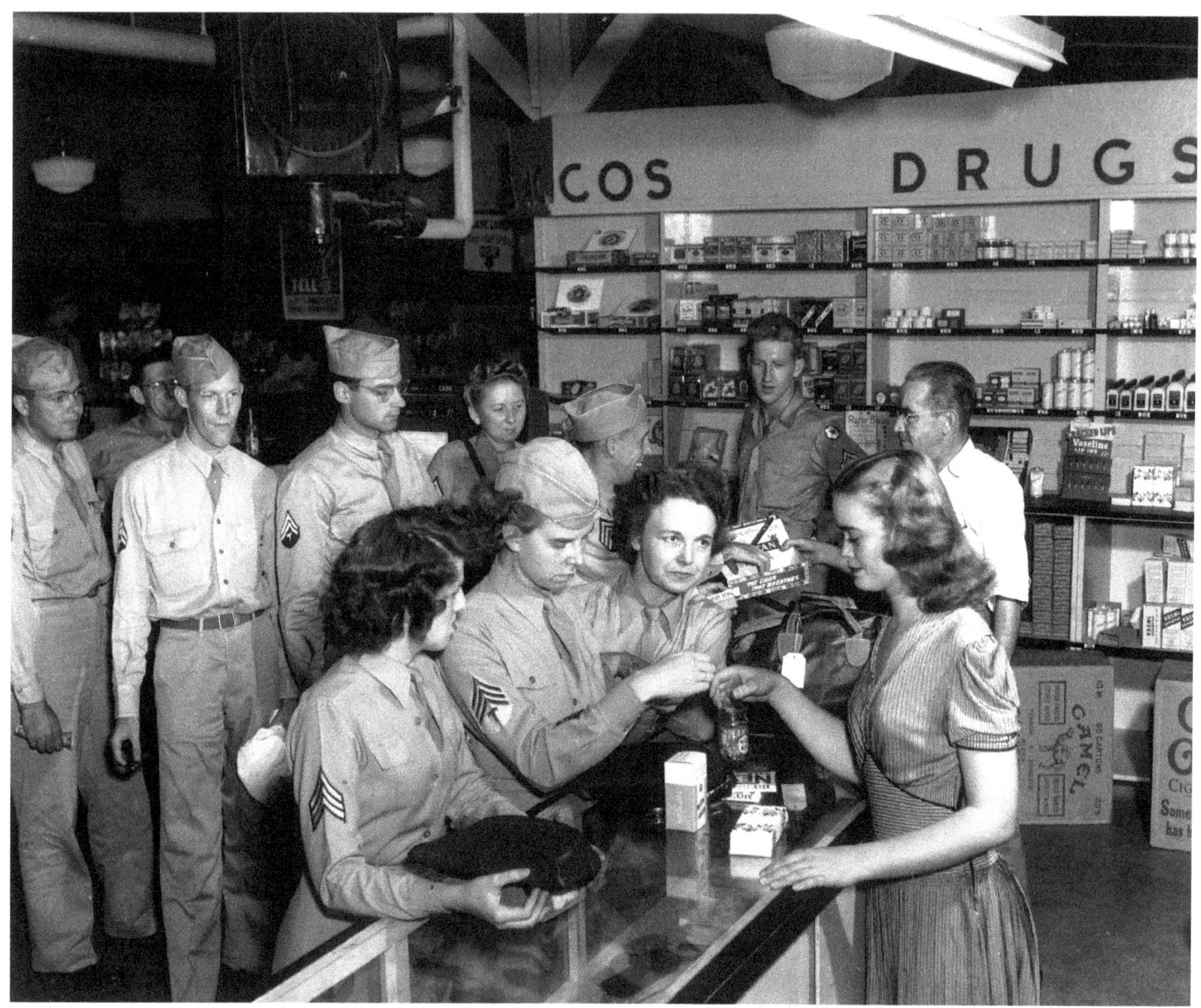

During the war cigarettes were rationed, along with sugar and other staples. The Army Post Exchange was a busy place that often ran out of supplies. Workers and family members were accustomed to waiting in long lines to purchase provisions.

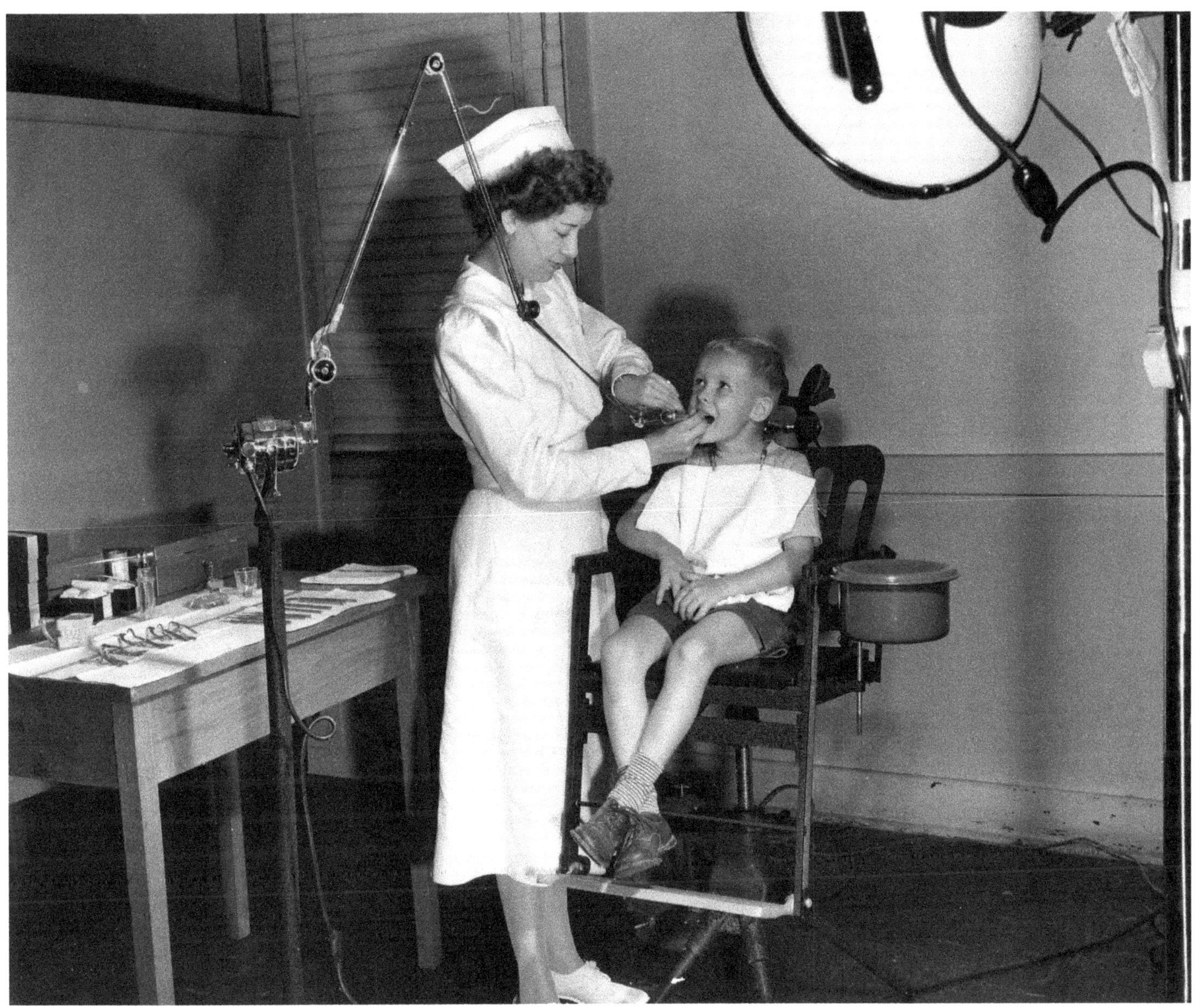

Using an old-fashioned dental drill, a nurse works on the teeth of a young boy in the Oak Ridge medical center. This youngster seems to be in reasonably good spirits despite the gravity of his situation.

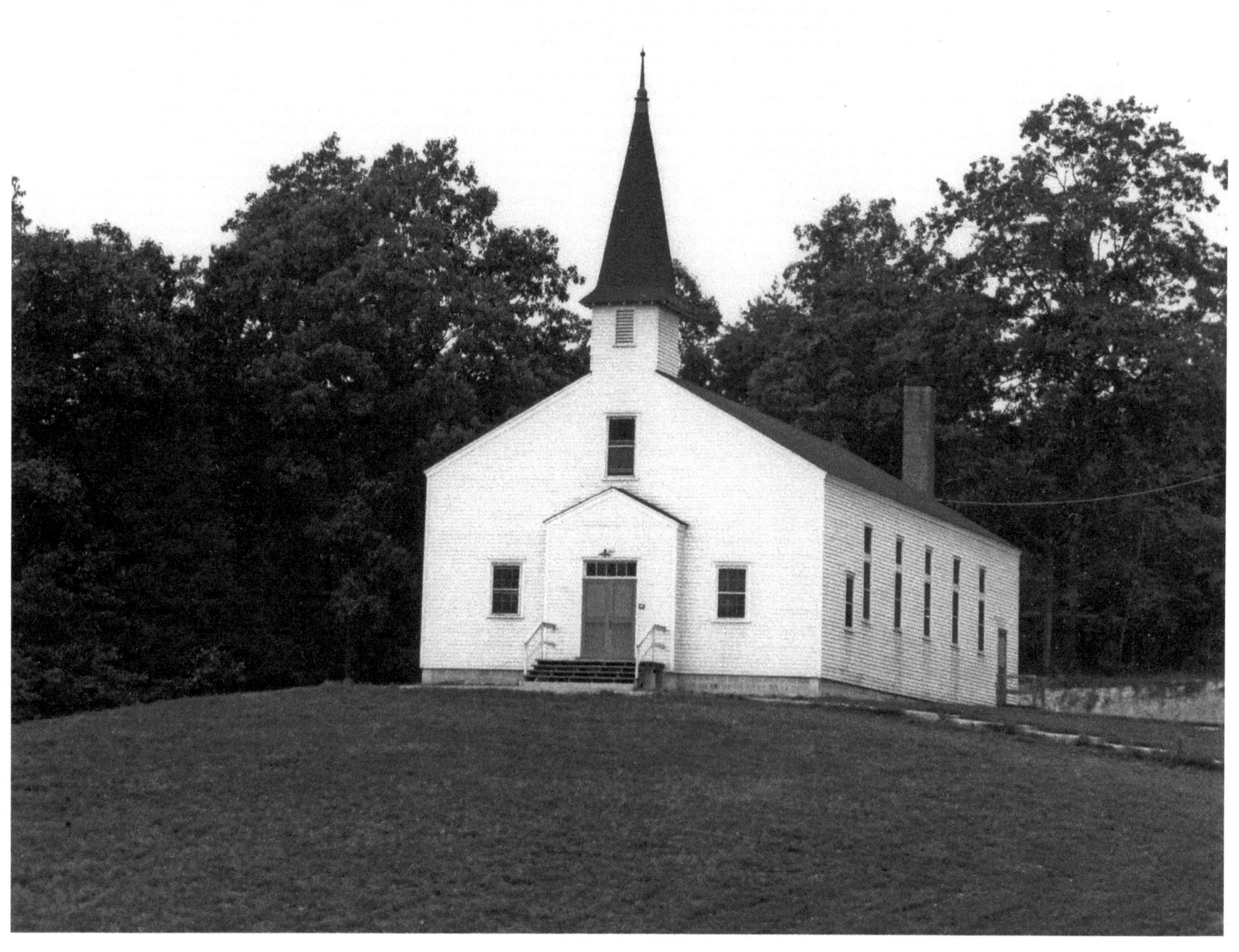

Chapel-on-the-Hill was built in 1943 for workers and their families and used for multi-denominational services. The church is still in use in Oak Ridge today.

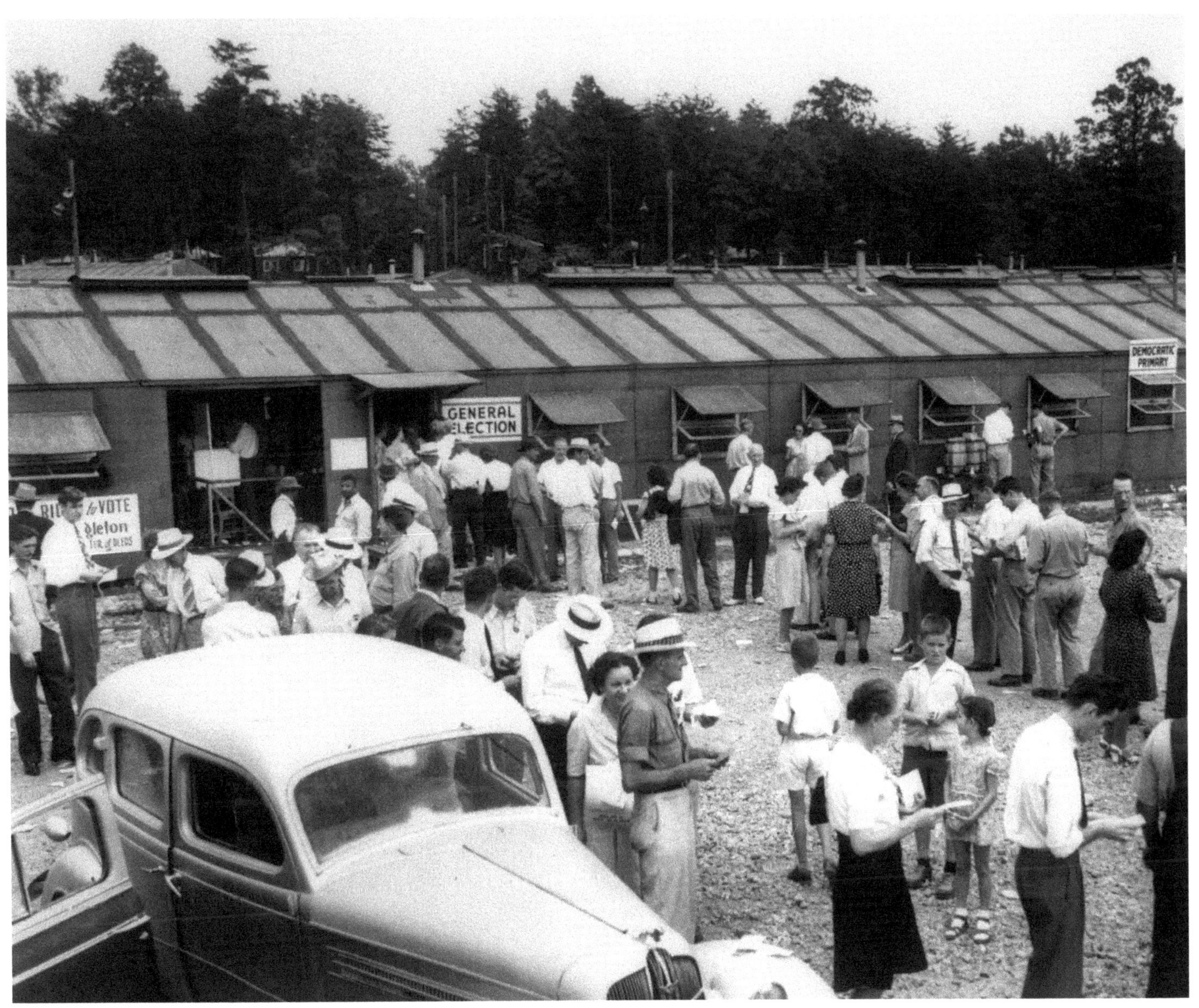

People are milling around to register and vote in the first election held in Oak Ridge. There were 1,441 ballots cast.

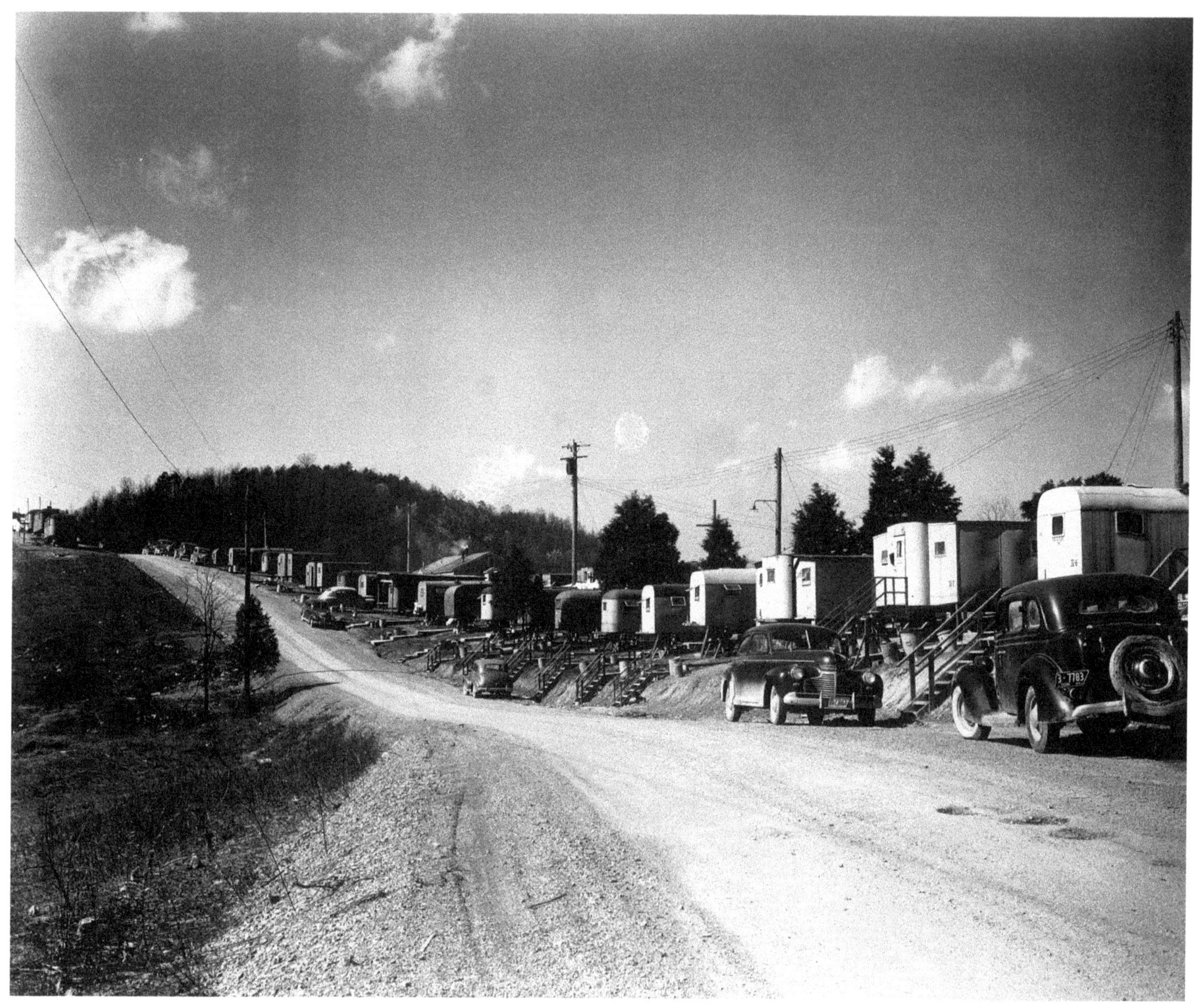

The Federal Public Housing Authority provided hundreds of trailers for workers. Even more government trailers were moved in as well as privately owned units as the number of workers and families increased.

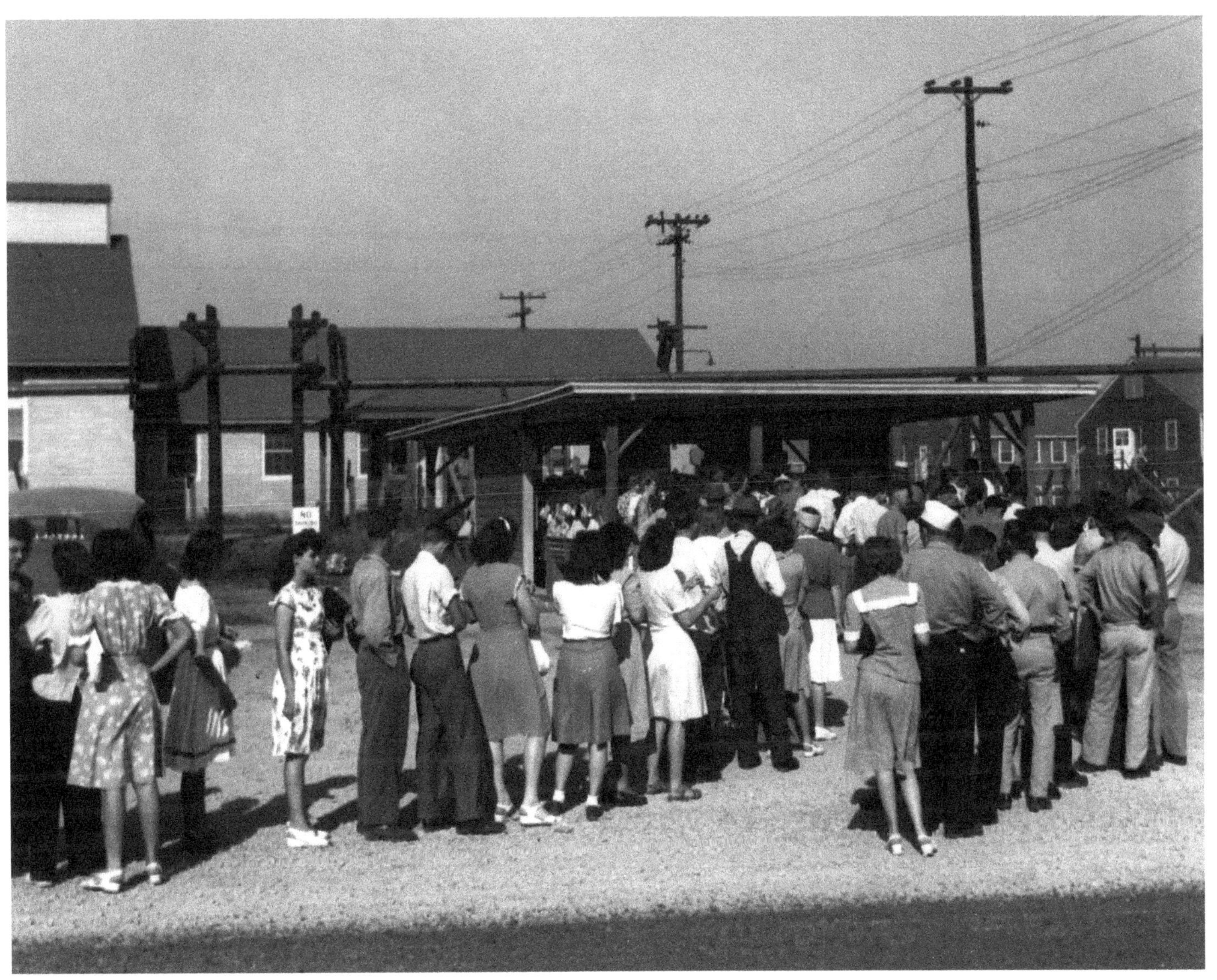

In 1945, Tennessee Eastman employees wait to pass through a guard check station to enter the Y-12 facility.

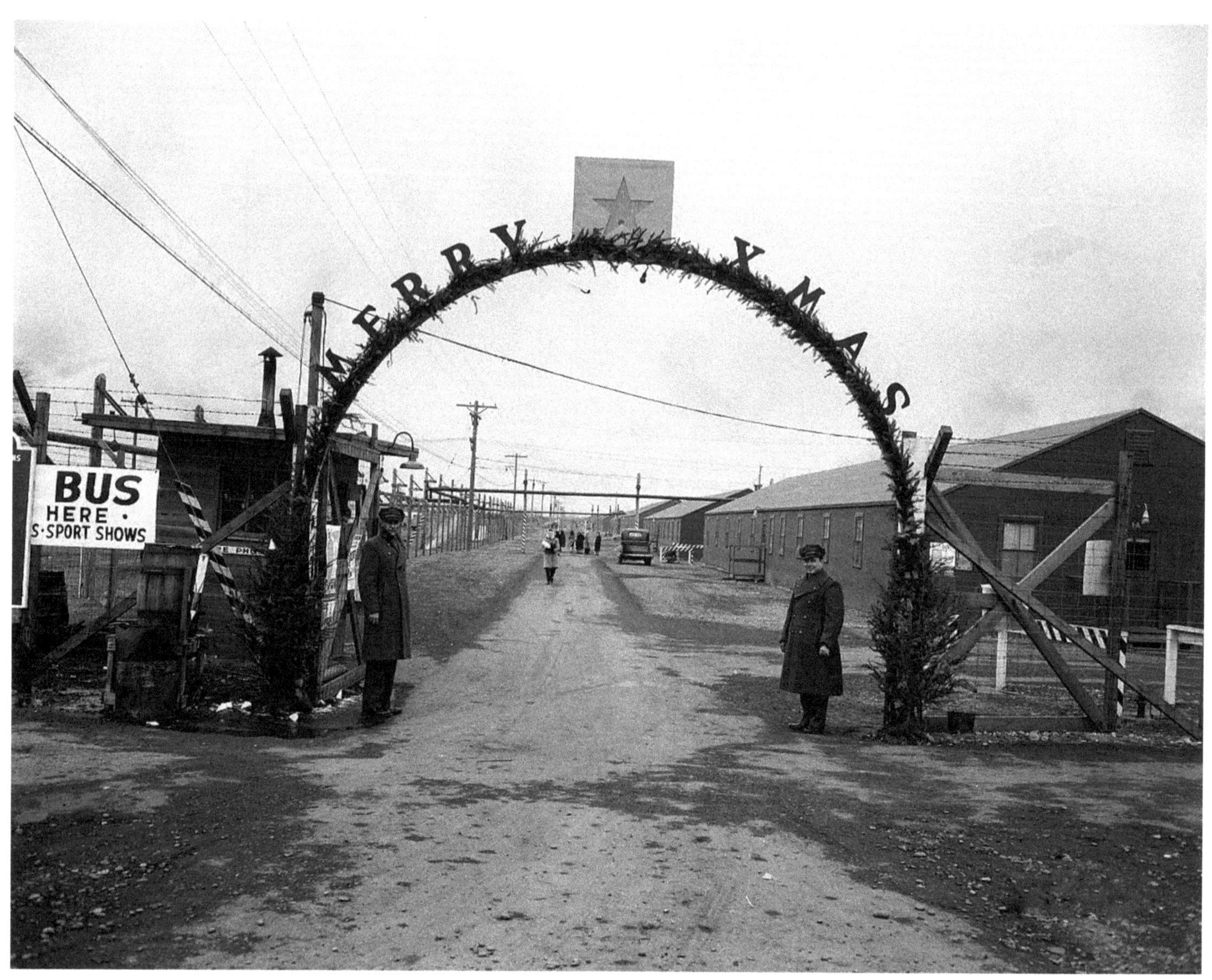

Shown here around Christmas 1943, the Hanford guards did their part to bring a Merry Christmas to all who entered through the guard gate.

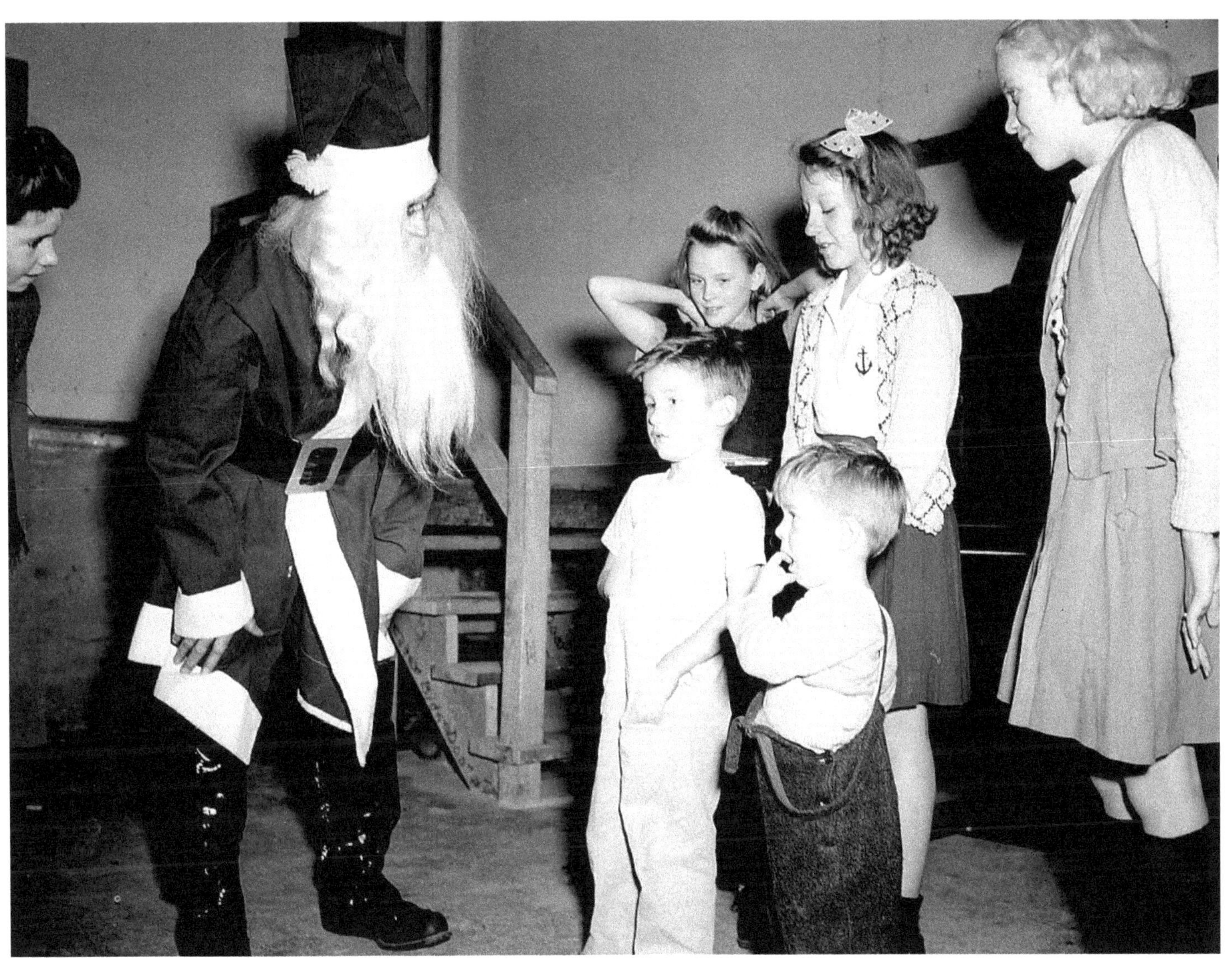

A not-so-rotund Santa pays a visit to the children of Hanford during Chrsitmas 1943. One young lad gazes up at him inquisitively, perhaps thinking, "He sure seems skinny, must be the war effort."

Security was a serious matter and even Santa Claus was subject to a full search. In 1944, two security guards check Santa's gift bag before he enters Oak Ridge through the Elza Gate checkpoint.

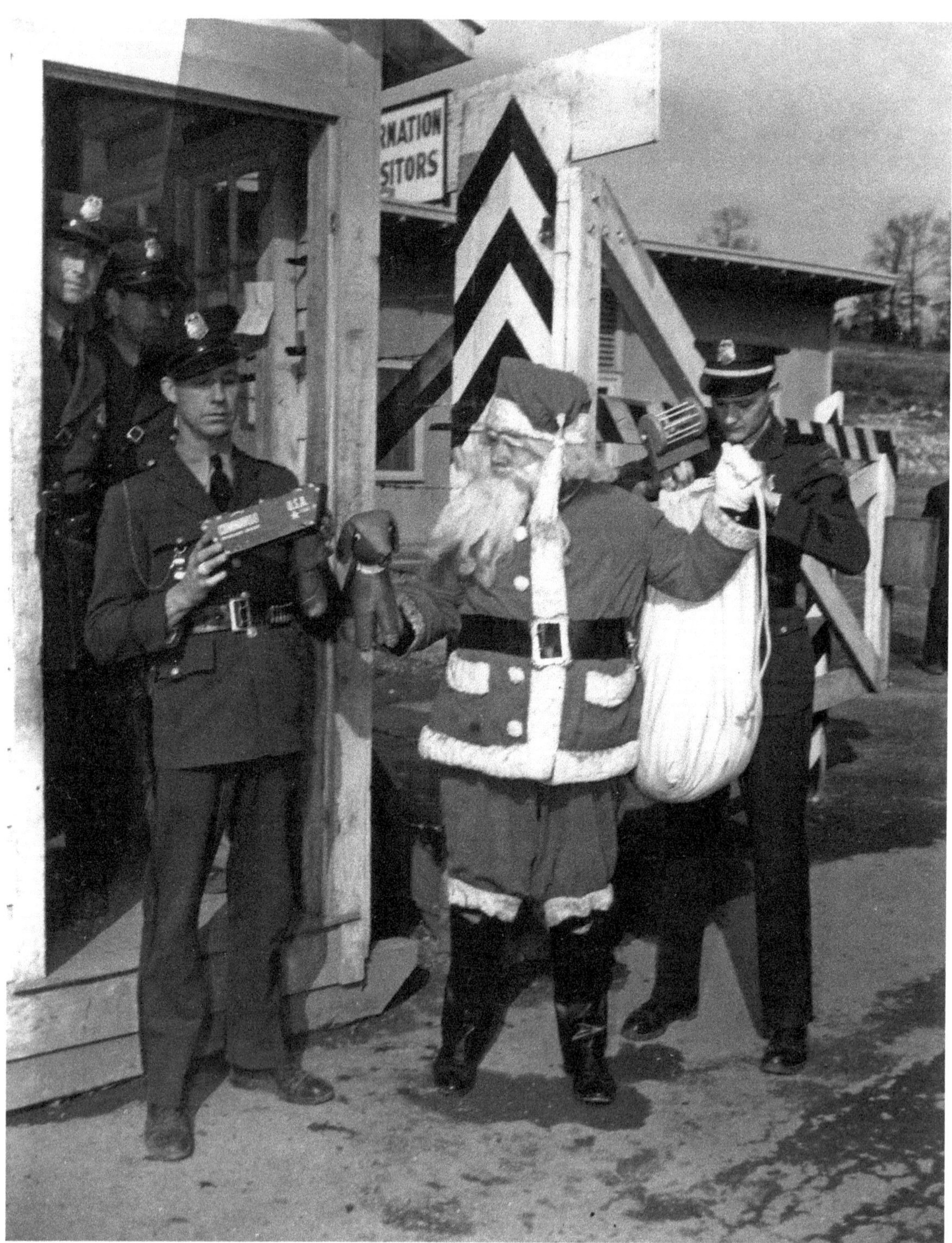

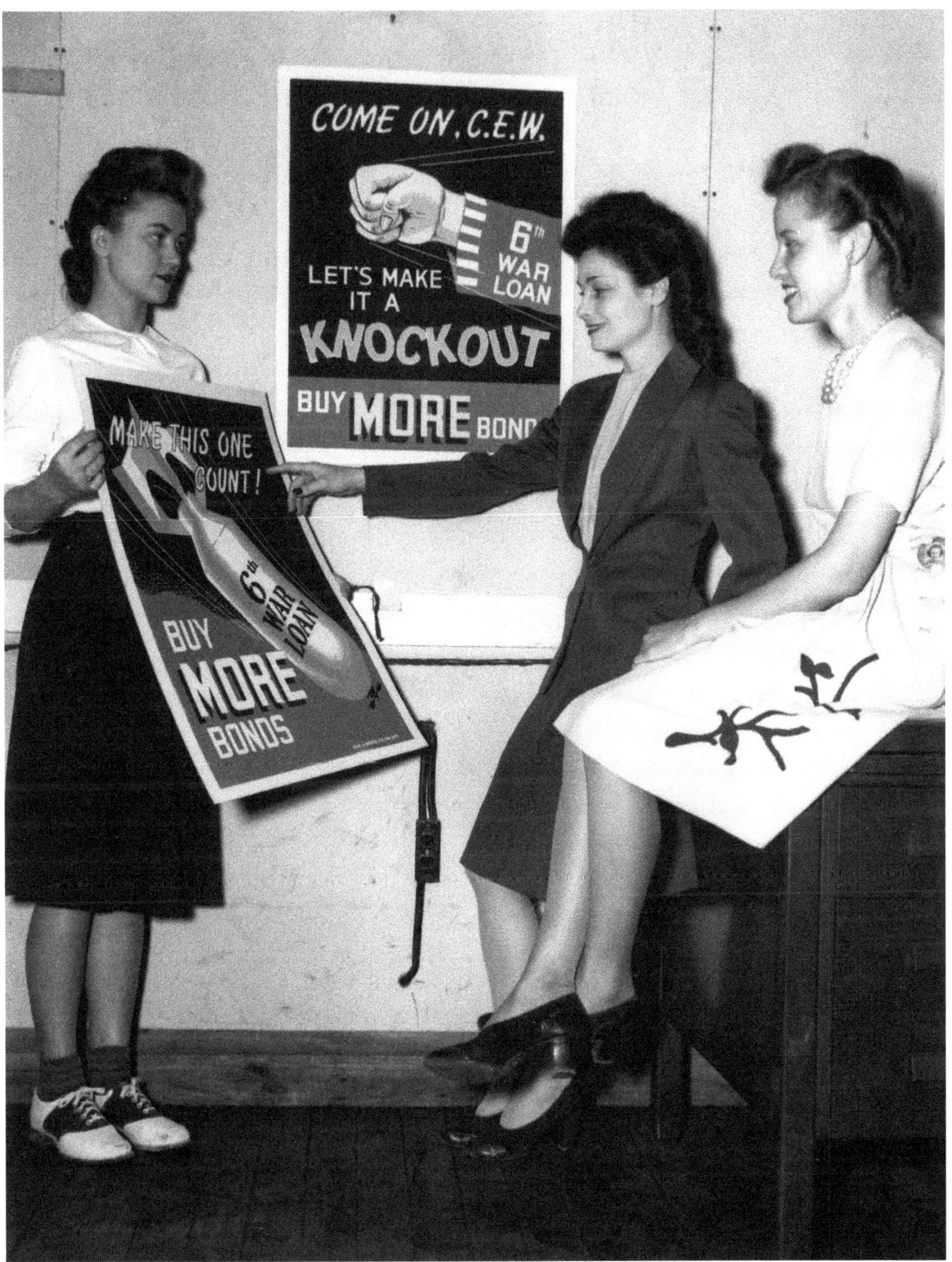

One of the many bond drives to help the war effort, this drive is under way in November 1944. Workers knew their hard work and dedication was to help bring the war to an end, but they did not know it was to build a nuclear bomb. In hindsight, it seems odd that a bond drive poster would picture a bomb when only the scientists and military managers knew this was the purpose of the Manhattan Project.

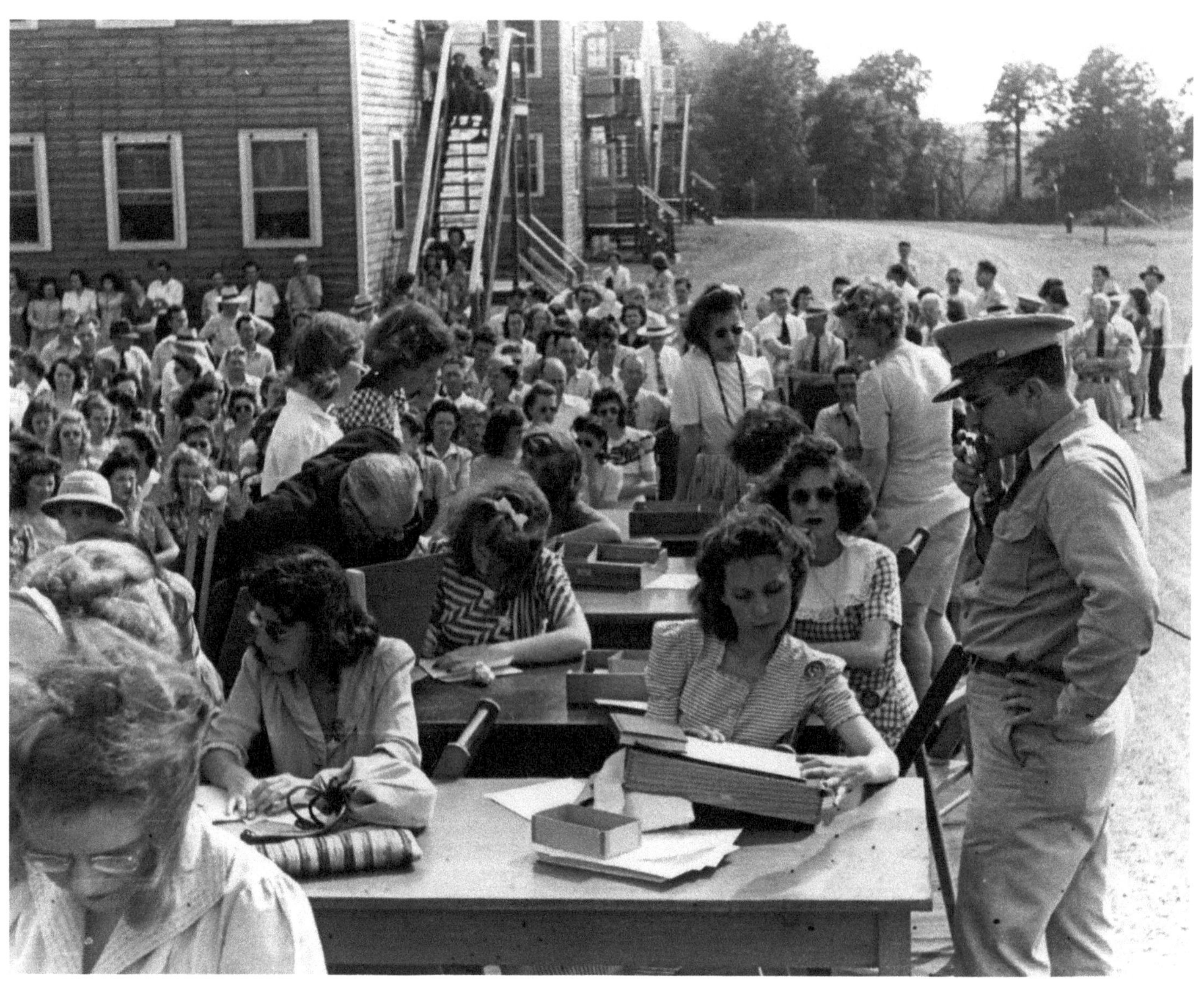

This bond-drive rally is being held at the federal building medical headquarters in downtown Oak Ridge in June 1944. Everyone was eager to help the war effort.

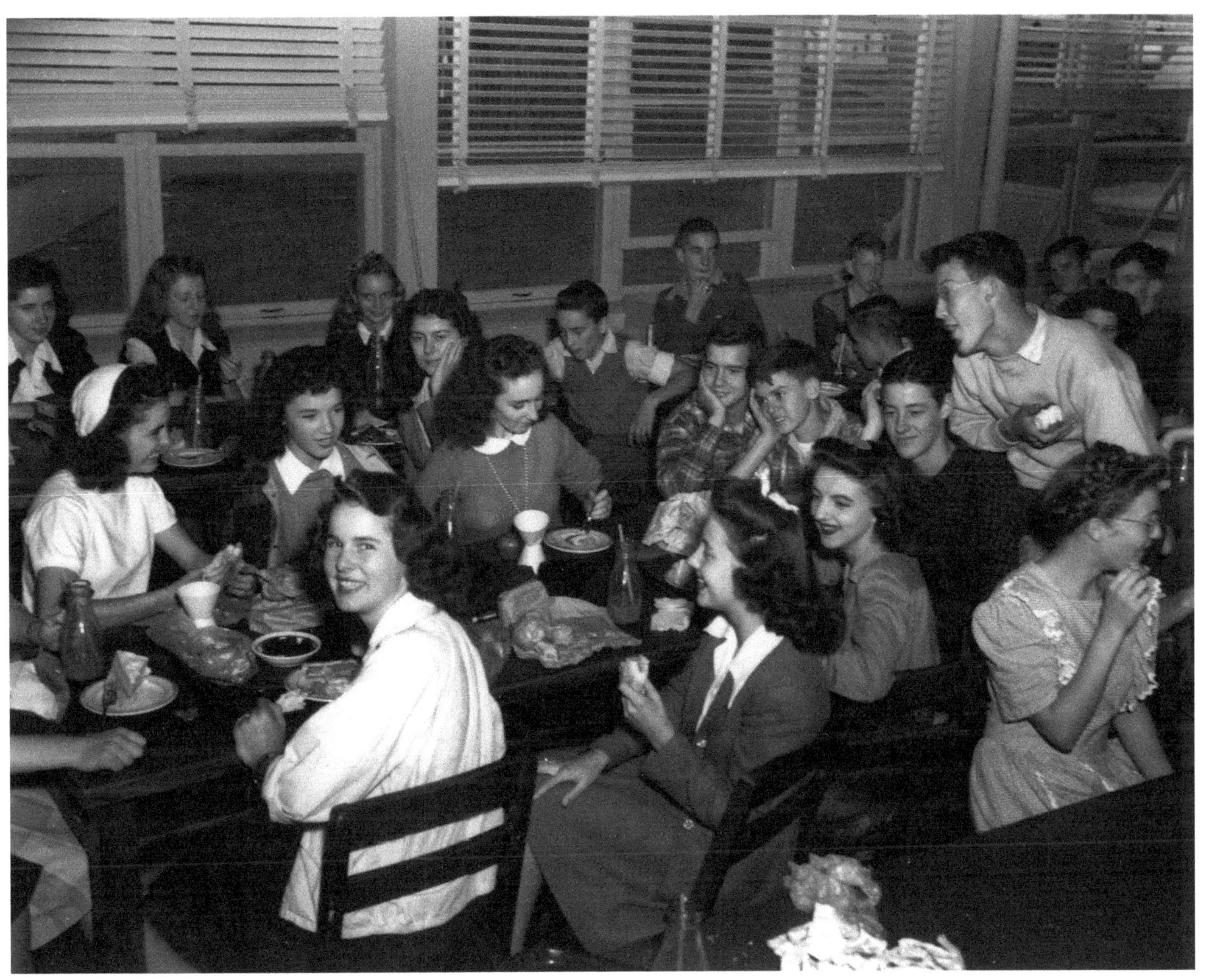

This photo was taken on October 19, 1944, in the Oak Ridge High School cafeteria. The boys are paying close attention to the girls, but of course the girls pretend not to notice.

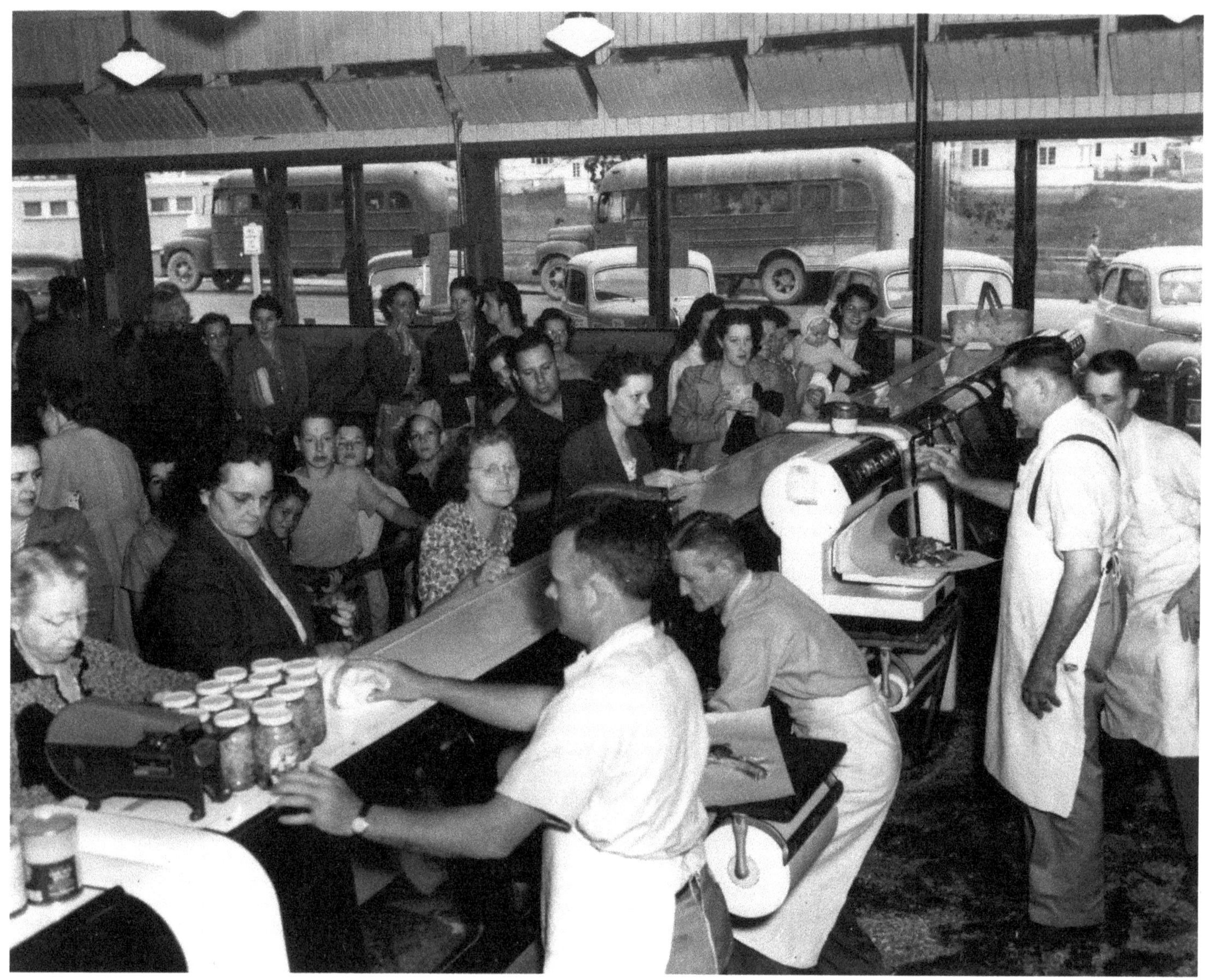

The Elm Grove Grocery Store or City Market on Tennessee Avenue was a very popular place. Residents were accustomed to standing in line to get meat and other staples, and shoppers often found empty shelves. This image was recorded in 1943.

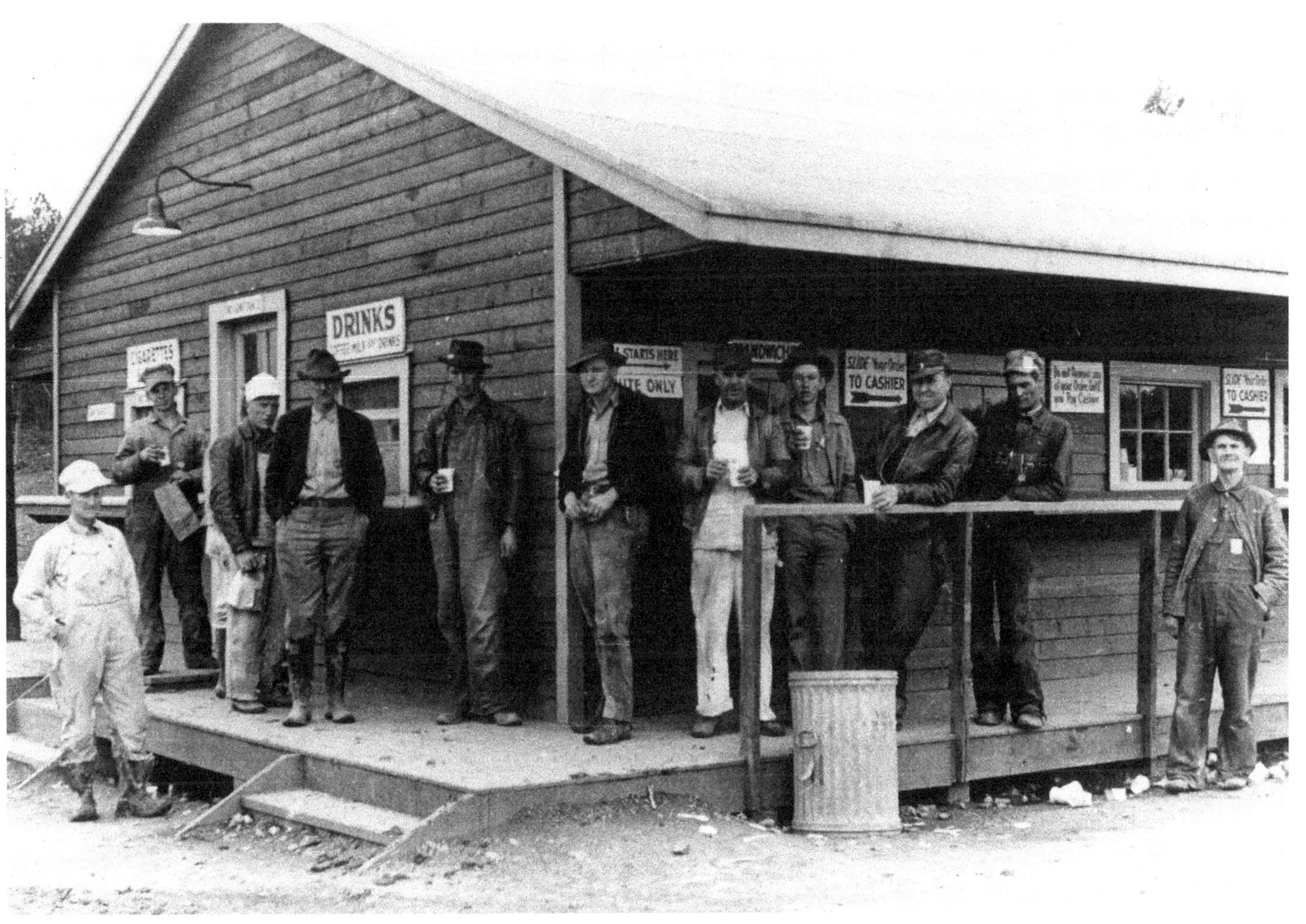

Snack bars were located in the work areas, and during lunch or breaks they were popular places. The different windows provided different items such as drinks, sandwiches, or cigarettes. Before the computer era, signage was hand-lettered, a skill that required considerable effort and aptitude to acquire. Workers are lining up here in April 1944.

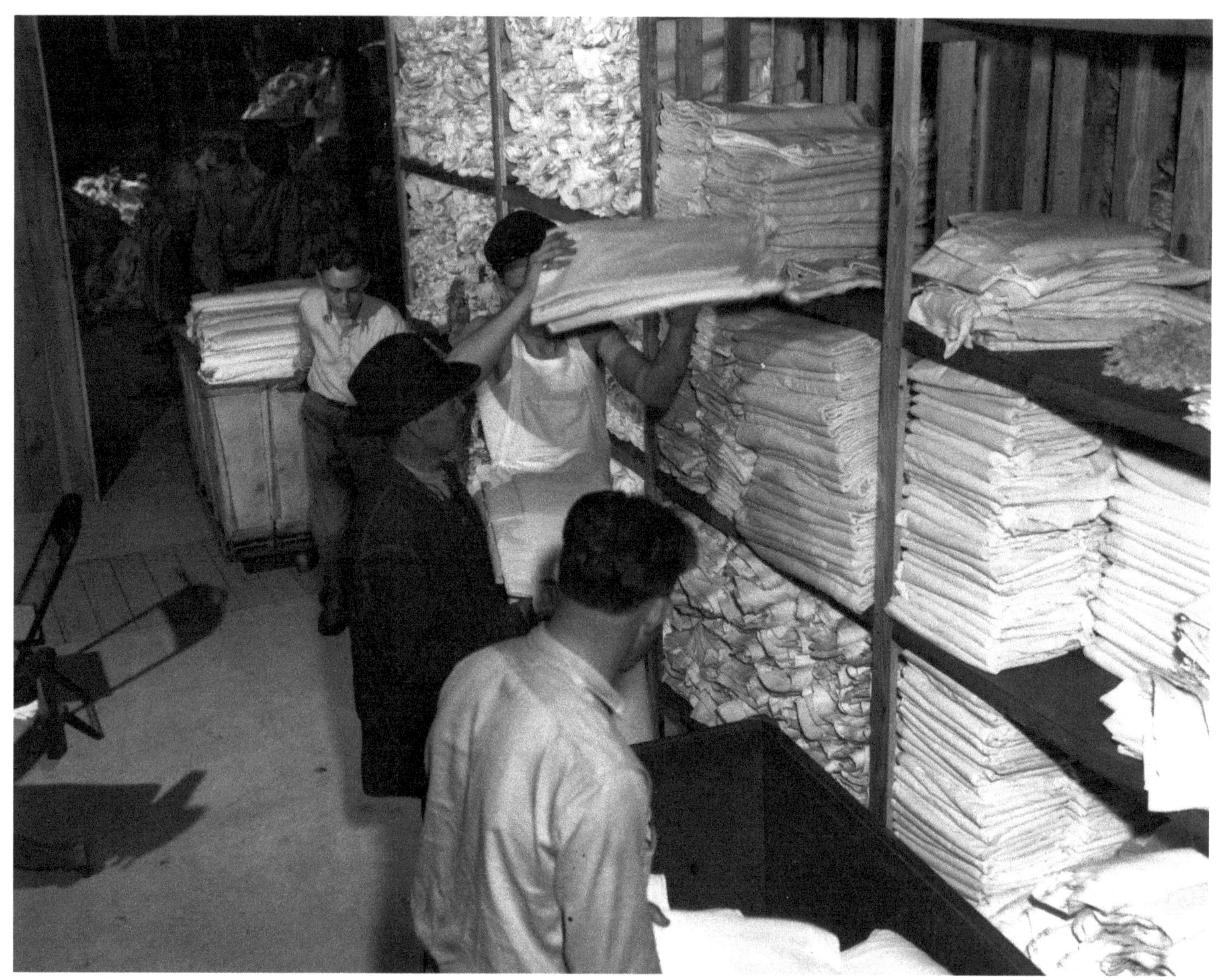

Thousands of workers lived in the many dormitories and barracks throughout the Oak Ridge Reservation. Piles of dirty linens wait in the back room to be laundered here in March 1945, while clean sheets are brought in from the laundry facilities and stacked in a dormitory linen room.

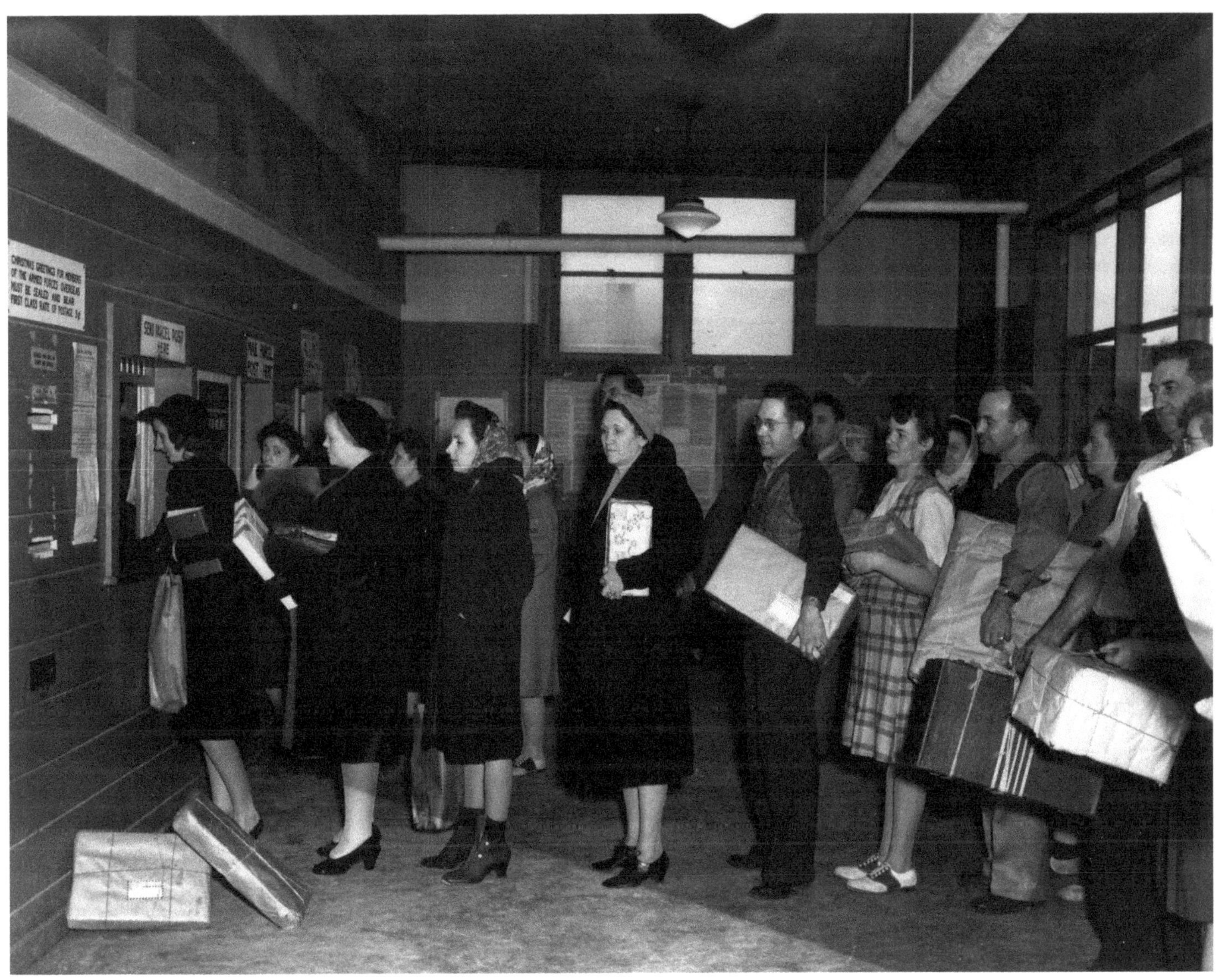

People line up during the 1944 Christmas season to mail packages at the Grove Center Post Office in downtown Oak Ridge. The sign at far-left announces, "Christmas Greetings for Members of the Armed Forces Overseas Must Be Sealed and Bear First Class Rate of Postage 3¢."

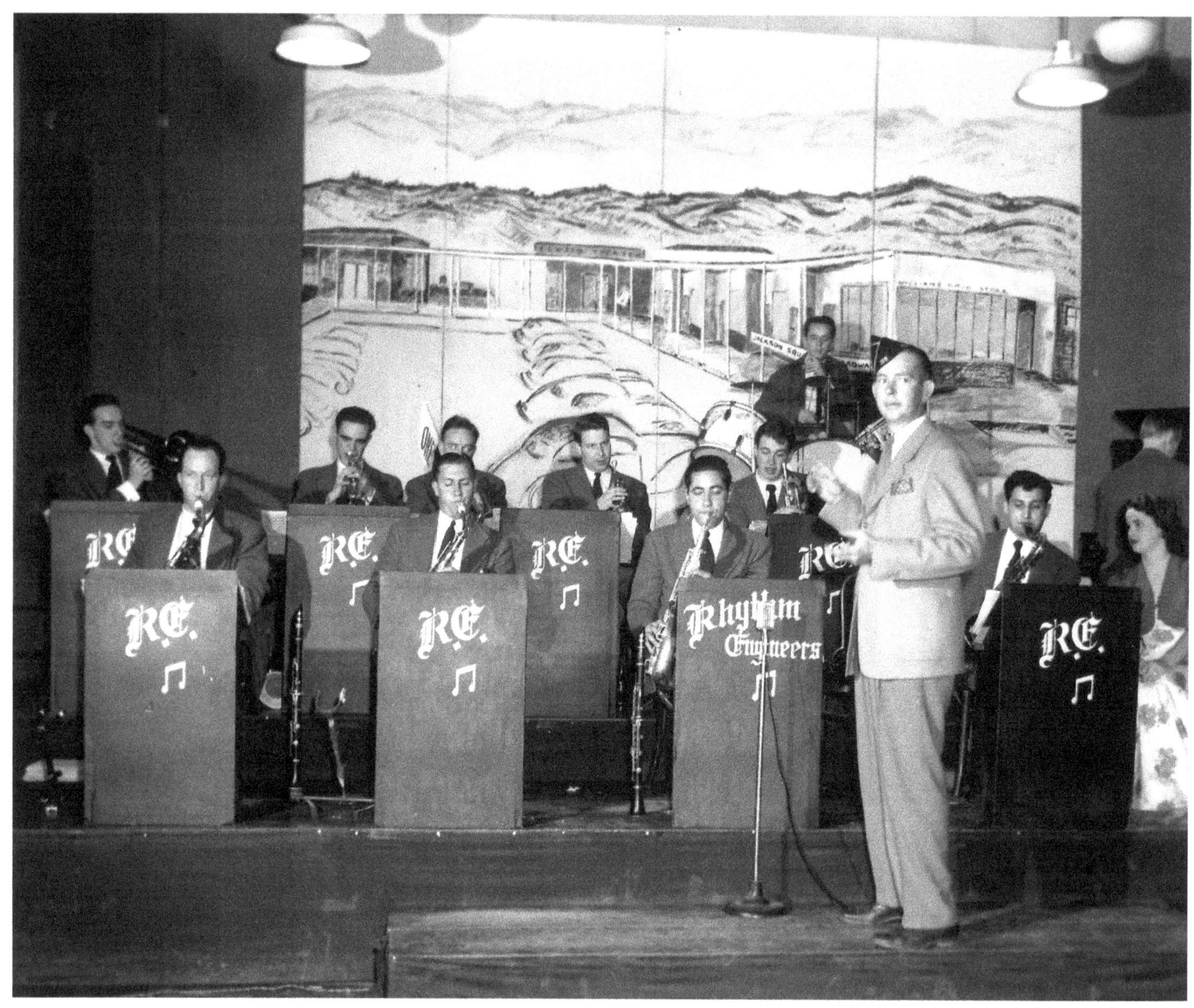

A group of musically talented engineers got together to form the "Rhythm Engineers." They performed at various functions in Oak Ridge, here at a dance with a mural of Jackson Square painted on the back wall.

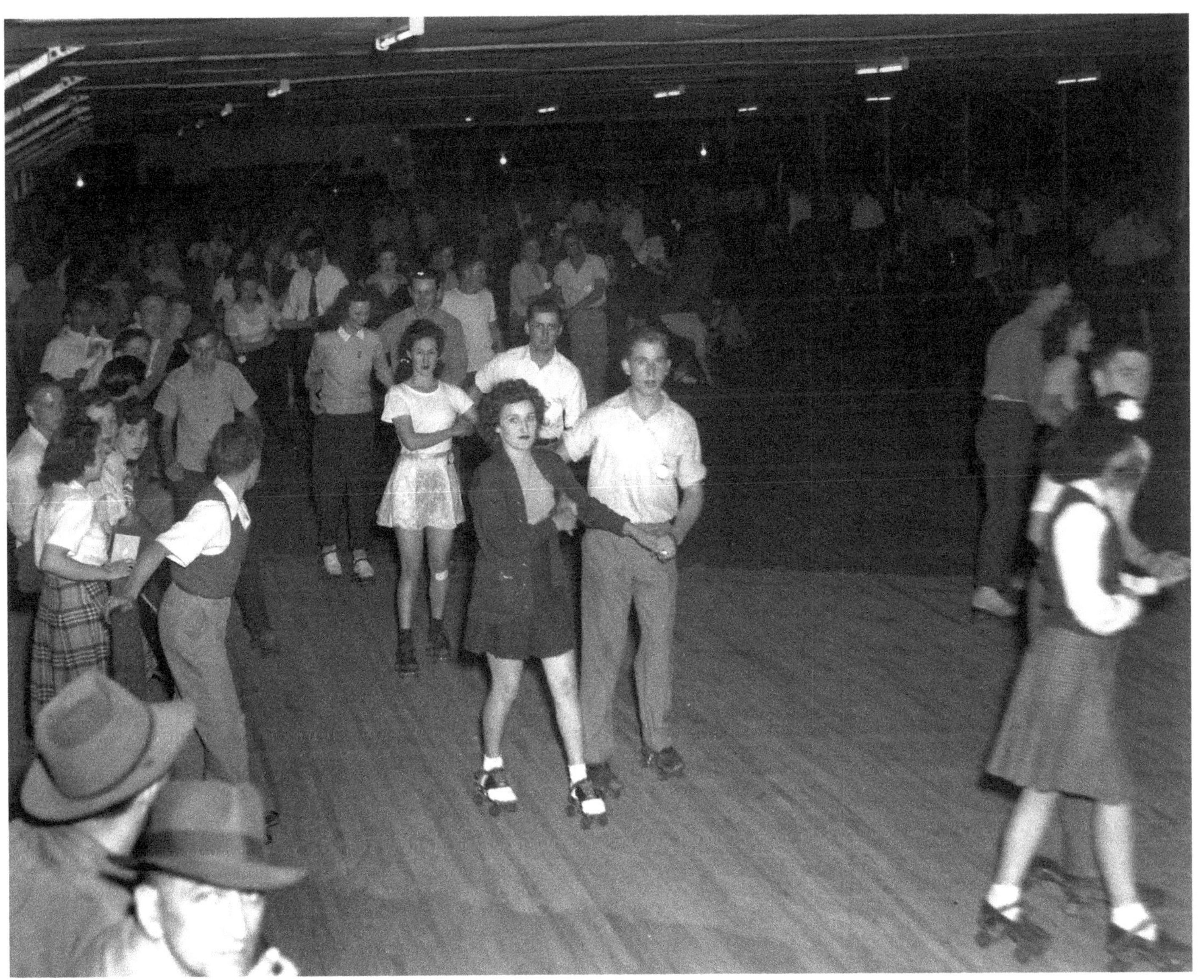

Oak Ridge residents hit the wood floor at the Meyers Brothers skating rink shod in roller skates that attached to their shoes with a skate-key. The Oak Ridge Recreation and Welfare Association organized many social activities including music, art, drama, dancing, and skating.

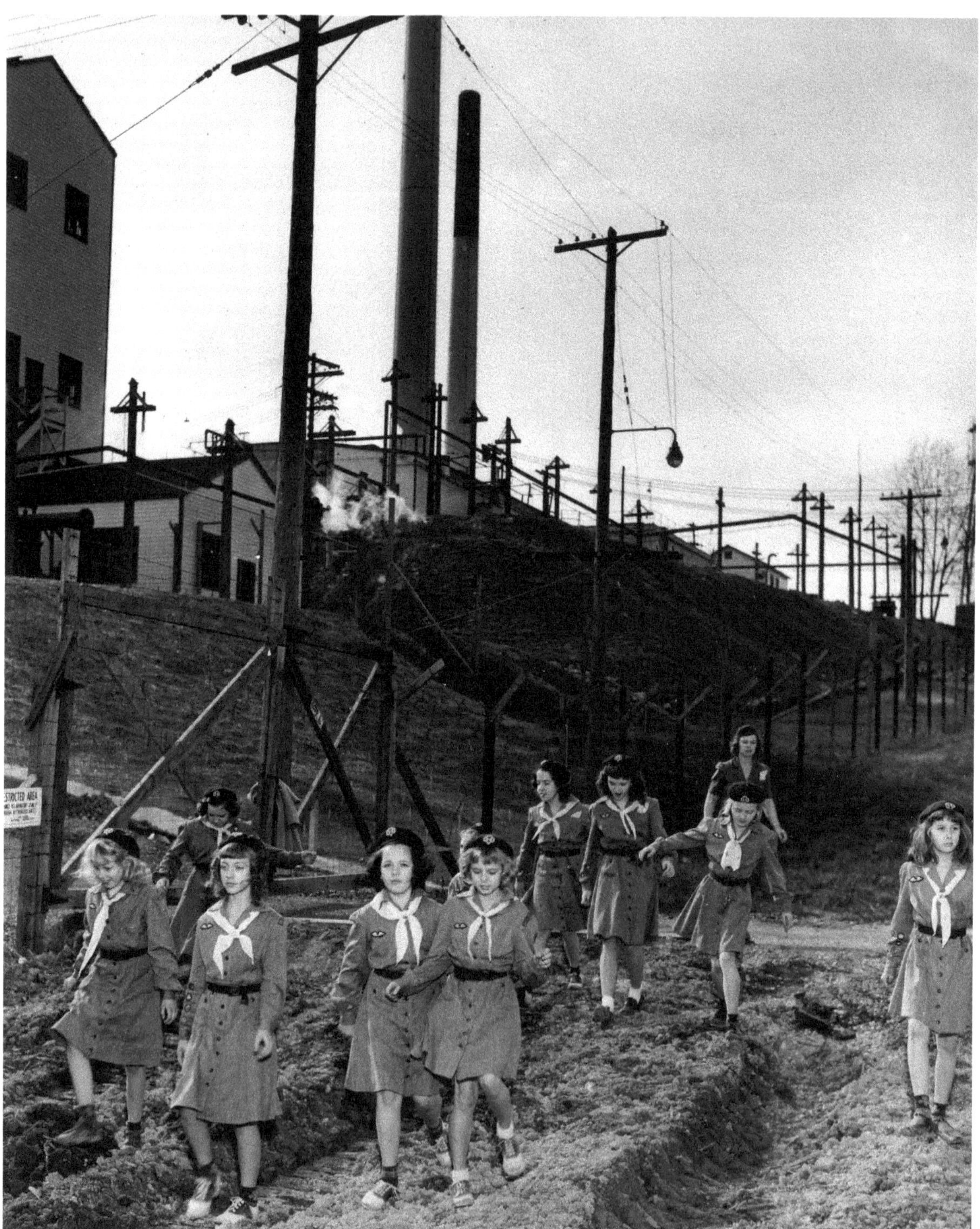

Behind the fence, top-secret activities were taking place at the Graphite Reactor, while girl scouts enjoyed an outing to see what was being done for the war effort in Oak Ridge.

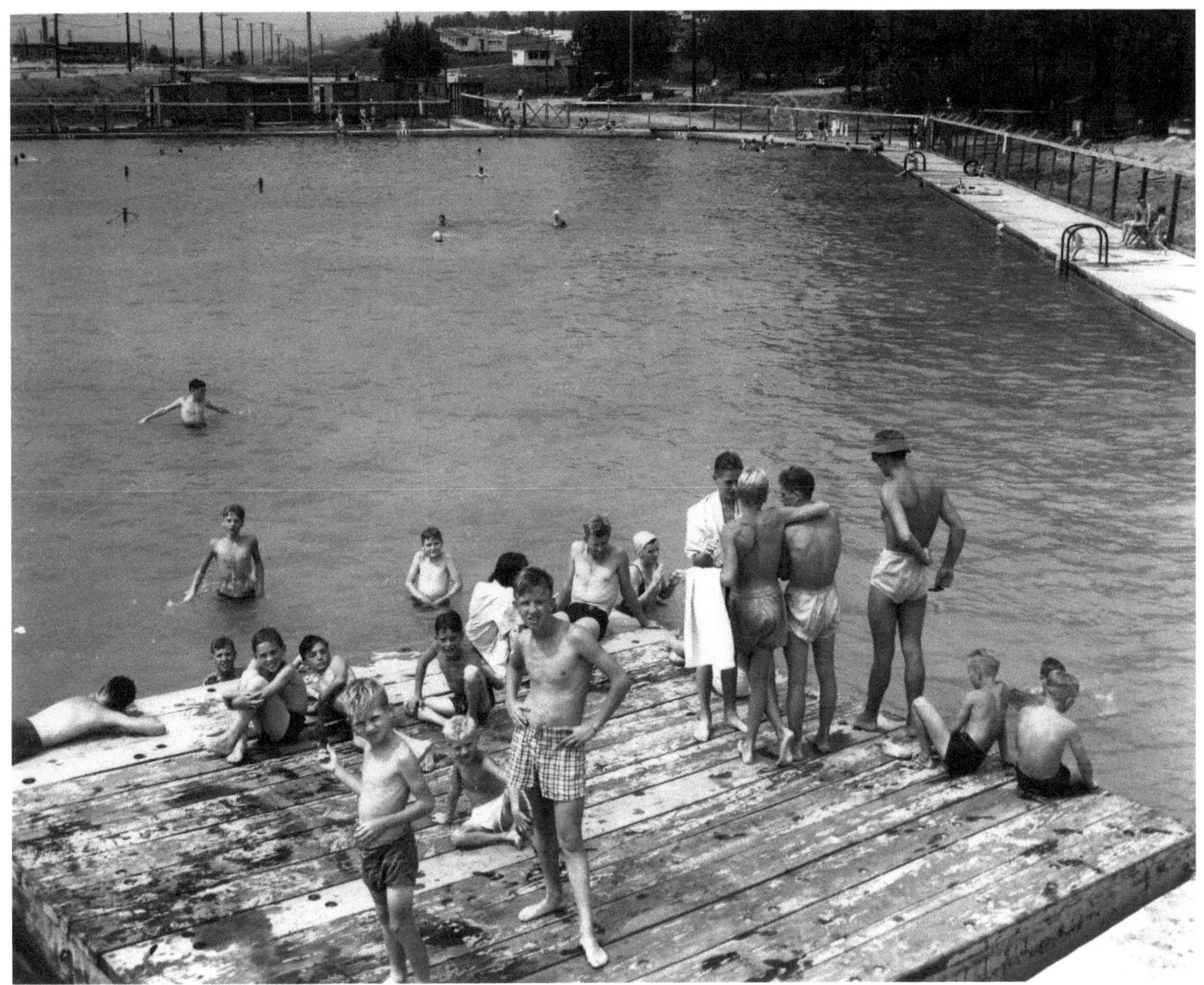

A huge swimming pool was built at Grove Center for Oak Ridge families. The pool was two feet deep at the shallow end and twelve feet deep at the deep end. It was spring fed, and is still in use today. The boy in the checkered swimsuit is Jessee Bernard; the others are not identified.

A typical office setting, October 1944. A worker with family photos on his desk makes a call on one of the first phones to be installed in the facility. The sign on the wall makes it clear that the phone was only to be used for official calls. All calls in and out went through an operator.

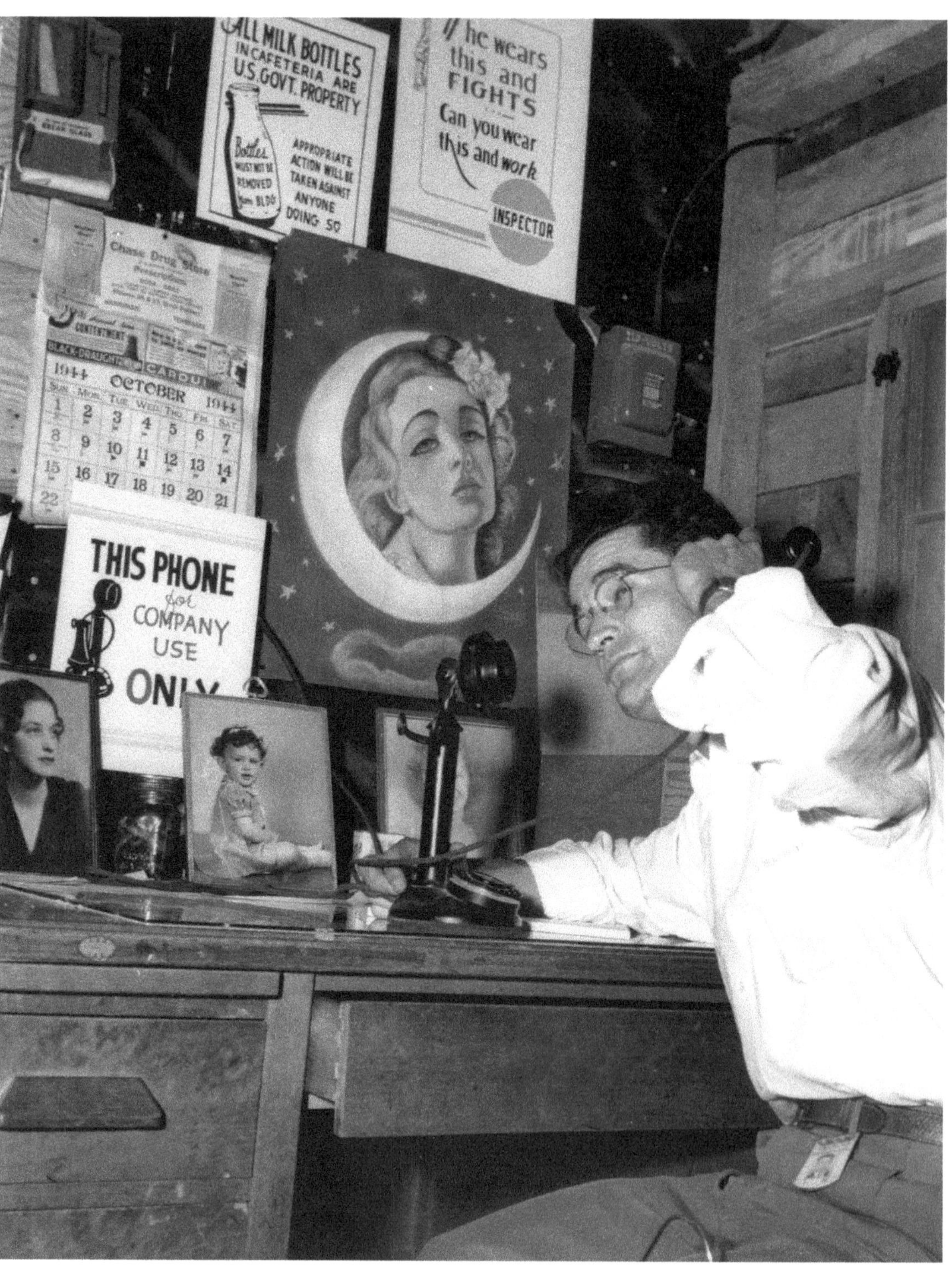

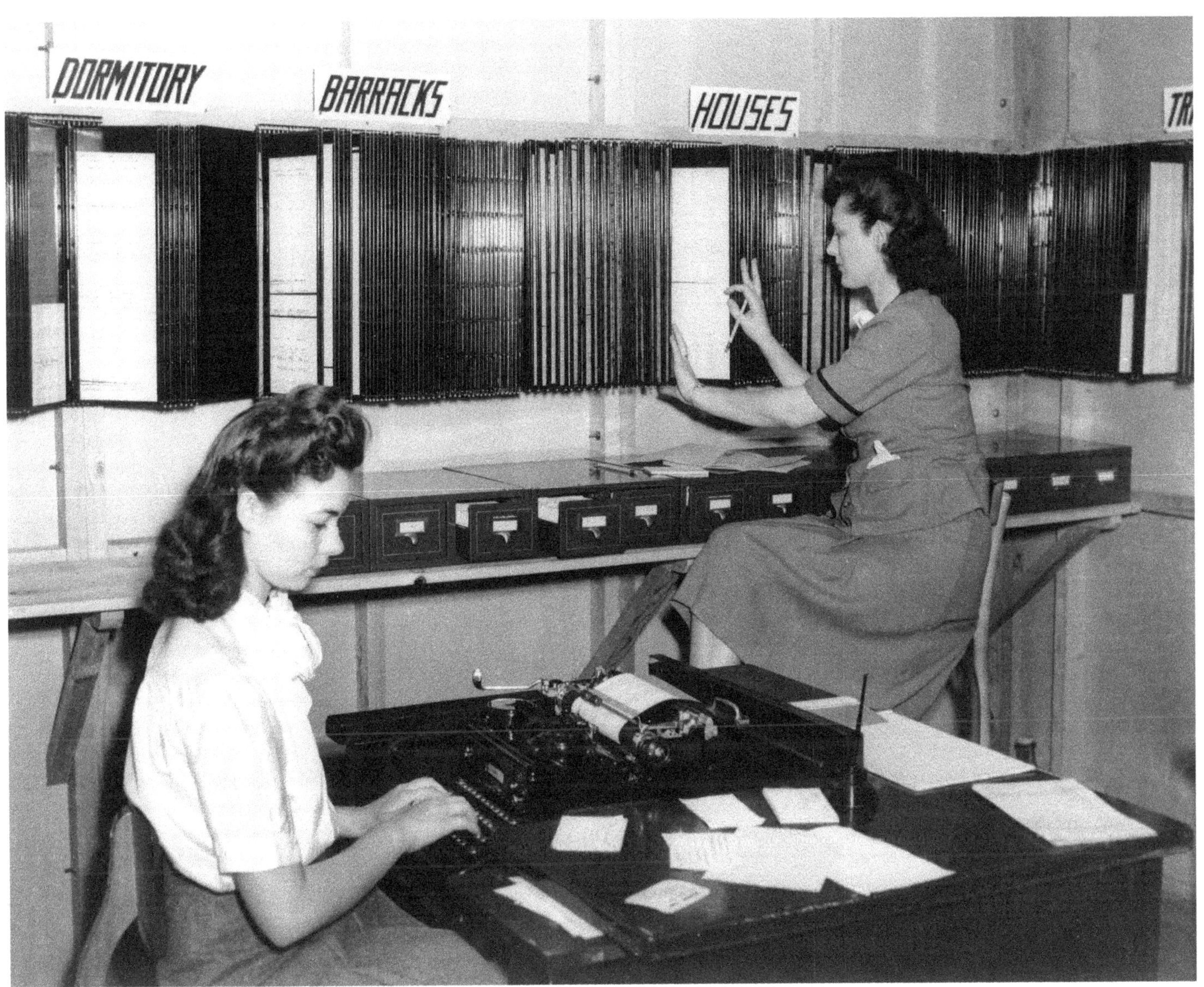

Shirley Davis on the right looks up a name in the Oak Ridge city directory to keep it up-to-date. Every resident in the dormitories, apartments, houses, trailers, barracks, and hutments was listed in the directories hanging on the wall. It was a full-time job keeping these lists of thousands of residents accurate. September 1944.

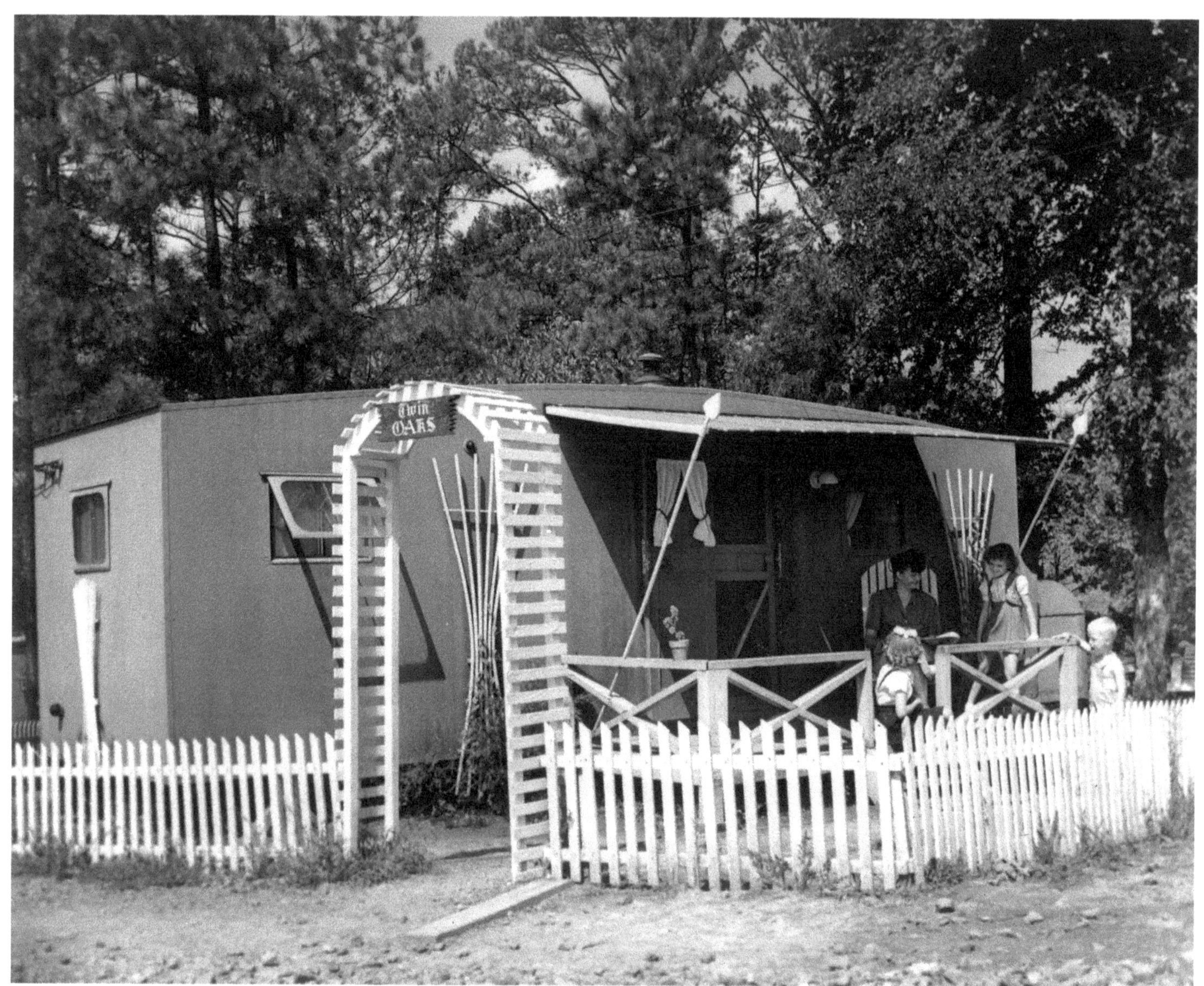

Though living conditions were anything but ideal, workers and their families went out of their way to make their homes as nice as possible. Here Mrs. Rebecca Marlin sits on a small deck while her three children play in the tiny yard inside the picket fence. Photographed in September 1944, this trailer sits in the Oak Ridge community of Middletown, home to the first trailer camp in Oak Ridge.

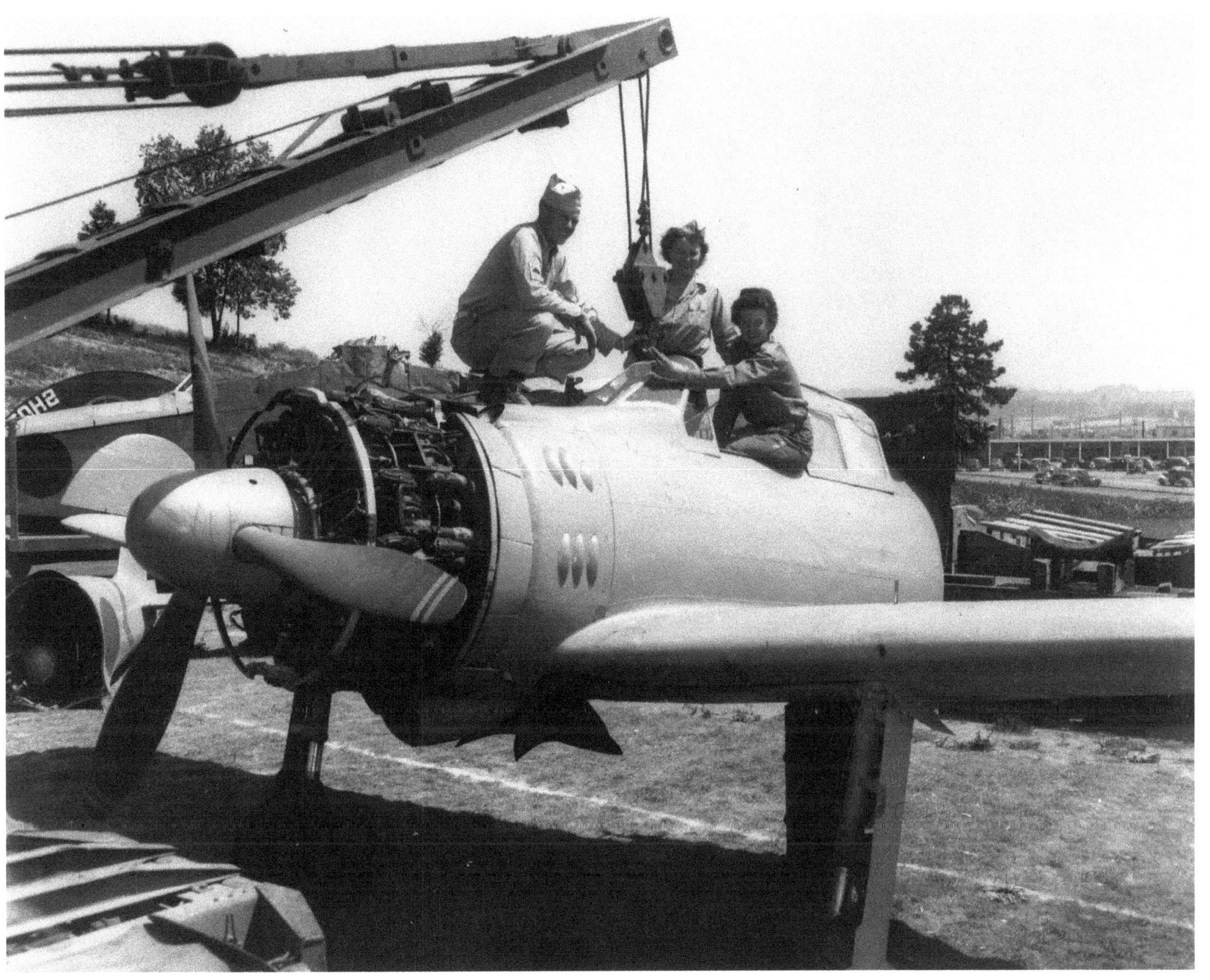

Two women (WACs) and a soldier check out the cockpit of an enemy plane shot down in the war. The plane was set up in the city to remind everyone of the importance of their work in the war effort. August 1945.

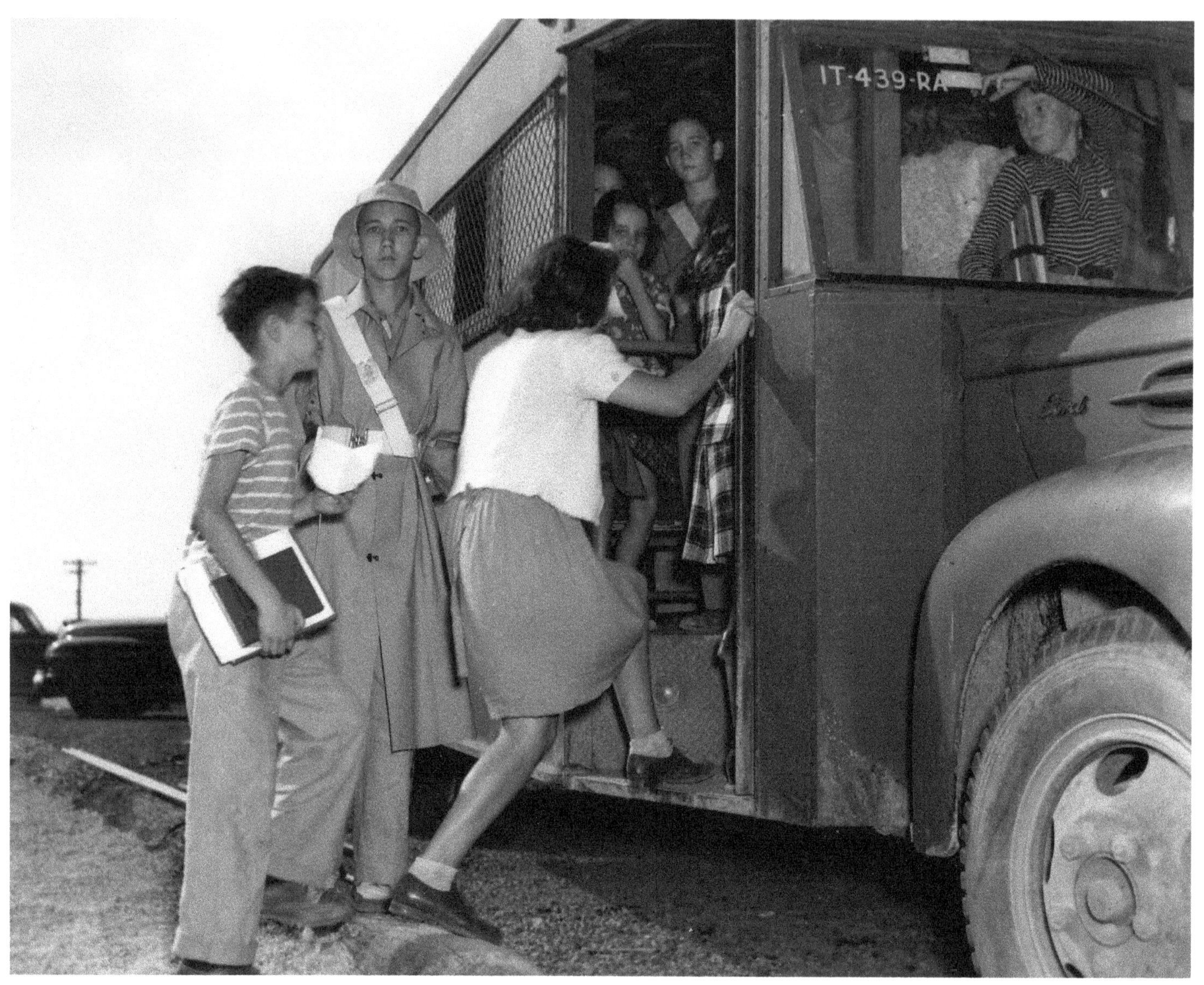

A young Safety Patrol officer takes his job seriously watching and helping children safely enter the school bus at the Highland School in Oak Ridge in September 1944.

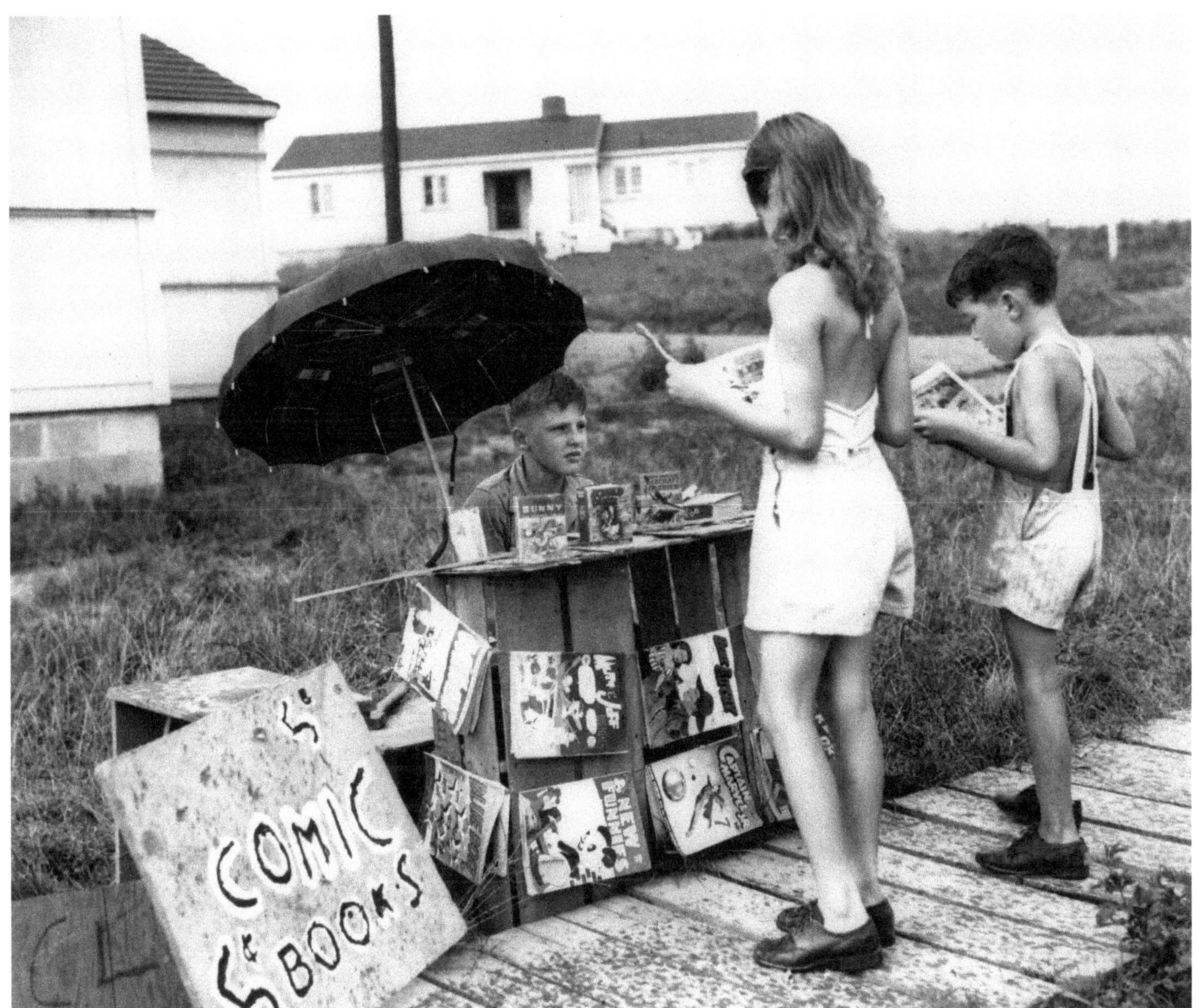

An enterprising young man, Wayne Kinser, decided to make some money by selling his extra books, including many comic books for a nickel. He built his little stand, and shaded by an umbrella set up shop. Ruth Hayes and George Flack check out their choices on the boardwalk. Comics collectors of later years would pay far more than a nickel for these issues. August 1945.

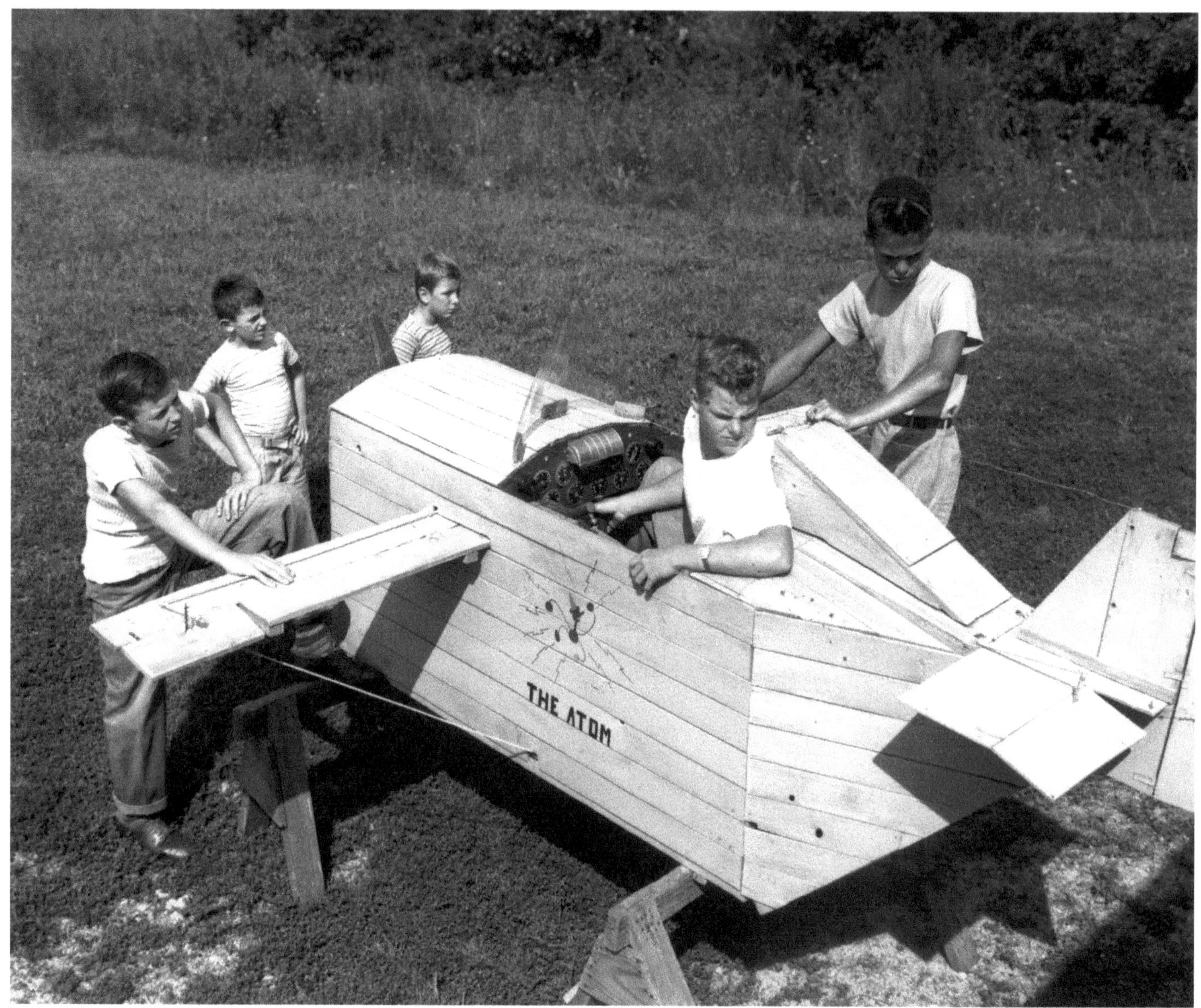

Boys will be boys. Leave it to five industrious young men to use their spare time to build their own plane for the war effort. Here they check out the control systems of their plane, appropriately named *The Atom,* prior to delivery to the Air Force.

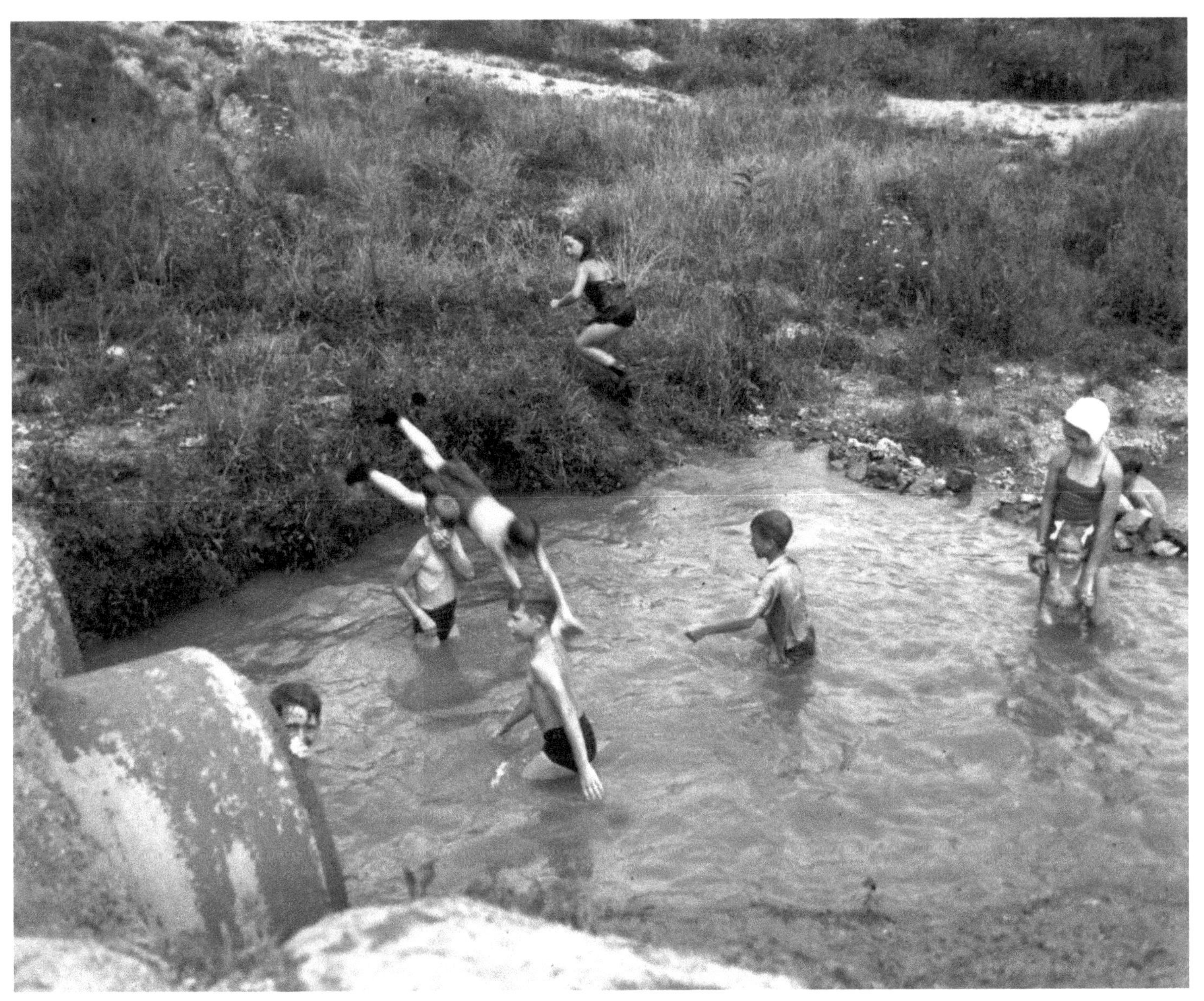

Children will always find new places to play and enjoy. Here they turn a culvert ditch located on East Drive in Oak Ridge into a swimming hole.

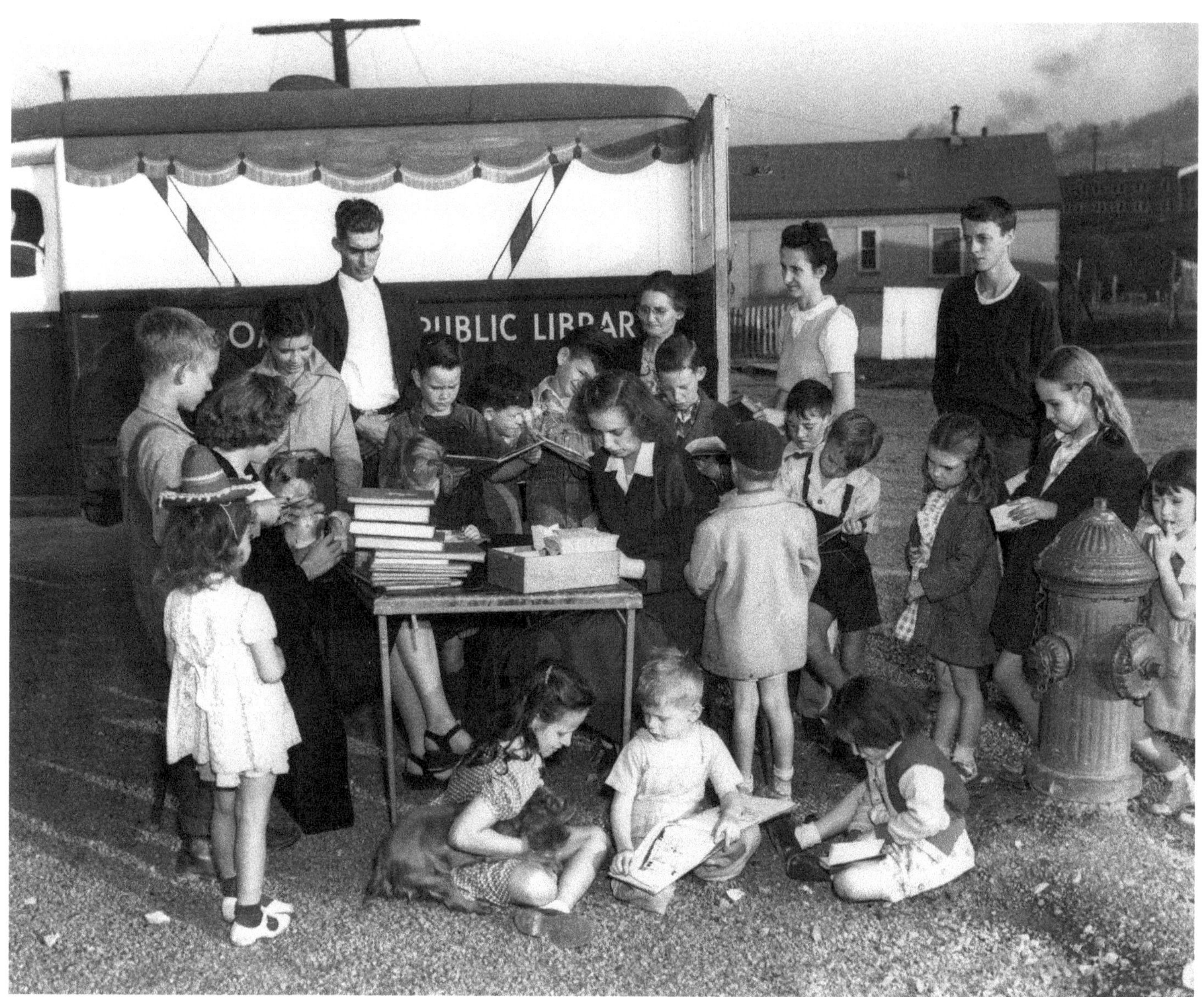

Bookmobiles were extremely important to the children. This one periodically made its way to all the residential areas, where children picked out their books from about 1,000 choices onboard. Rubye Steakley, left, and Mary Lyons assist the children and fill out the check-out cards. During school months the bookmobile was on the road 263 days and covered 3,156 miles. Puppet shows were also performed.

Coal was brought into the Oak Ridge facilities by rail and unloaded into large piles. Workers would then fill collapsible buckets and place them in delivery trucks. When the truck was full, it would deliver the buckets to the residential areas for the coal stoves that provided heating and pick up the empty buckets.

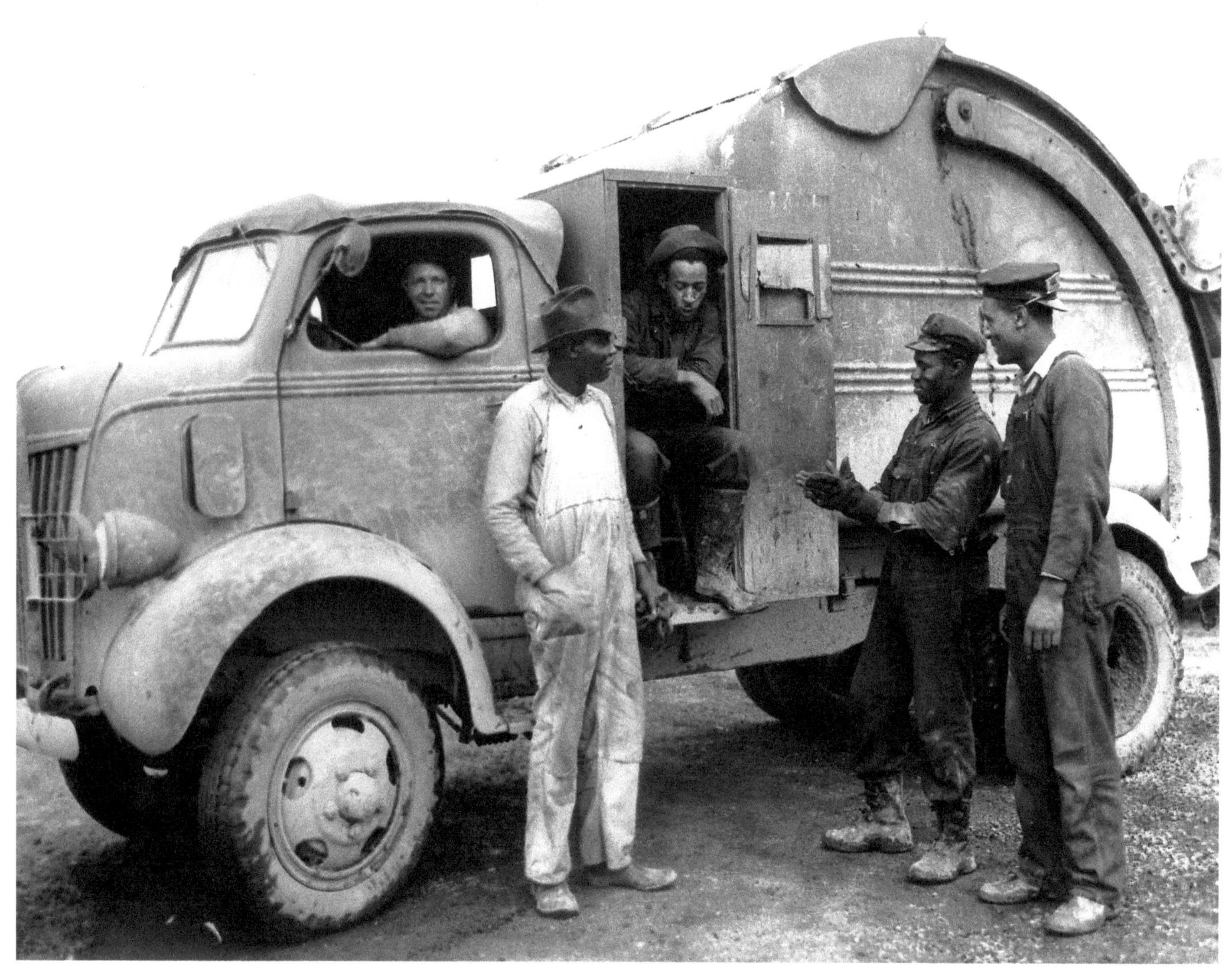

Trash pickup from the thousands of residents was a full-time job. The refuse was taken to an on-site landfill located in Gamble Valley.

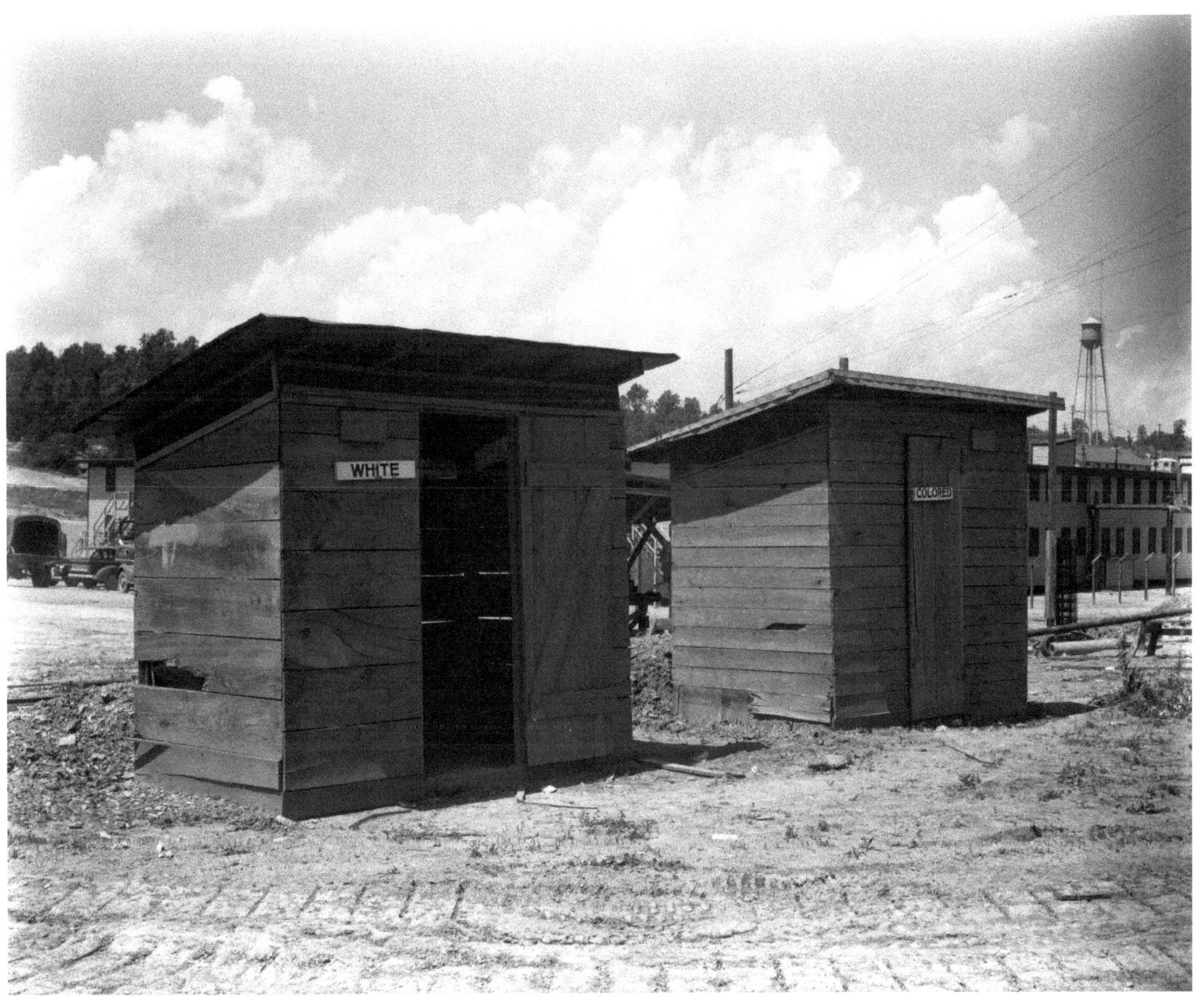

Shown here in 1943, these not-so-modern outdoor privies could be seen throughout the Oak Ridge Reservation where work was under way. Owing to segregation laws, they were generally found in pairs.

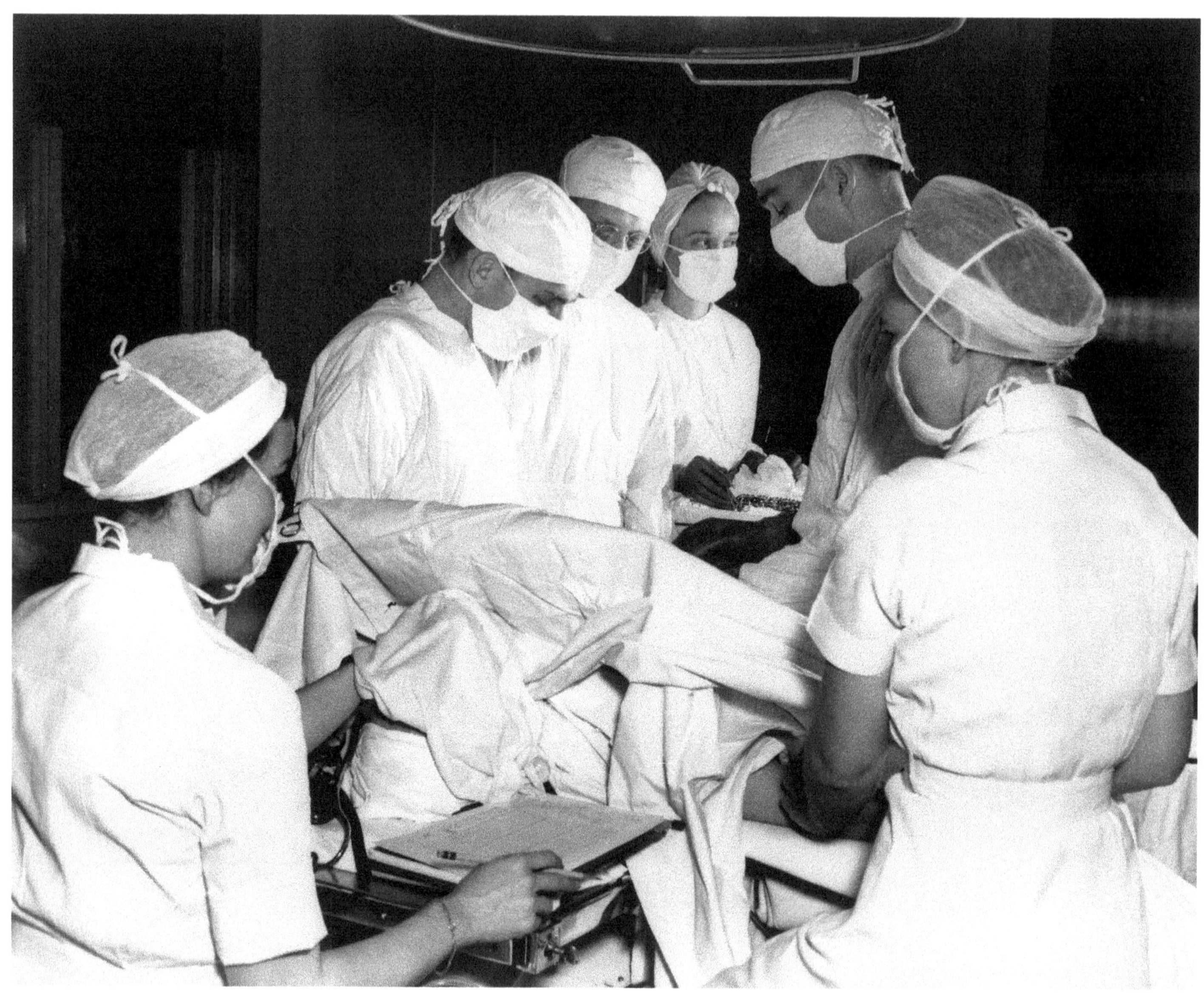

Surgery is under way in November 1944 at the Oak Ridge Hospital with Dr. Rea, Dr. Clark, Dr. Kallestead, and Nurse Burks and two others carefully doing their jobs.

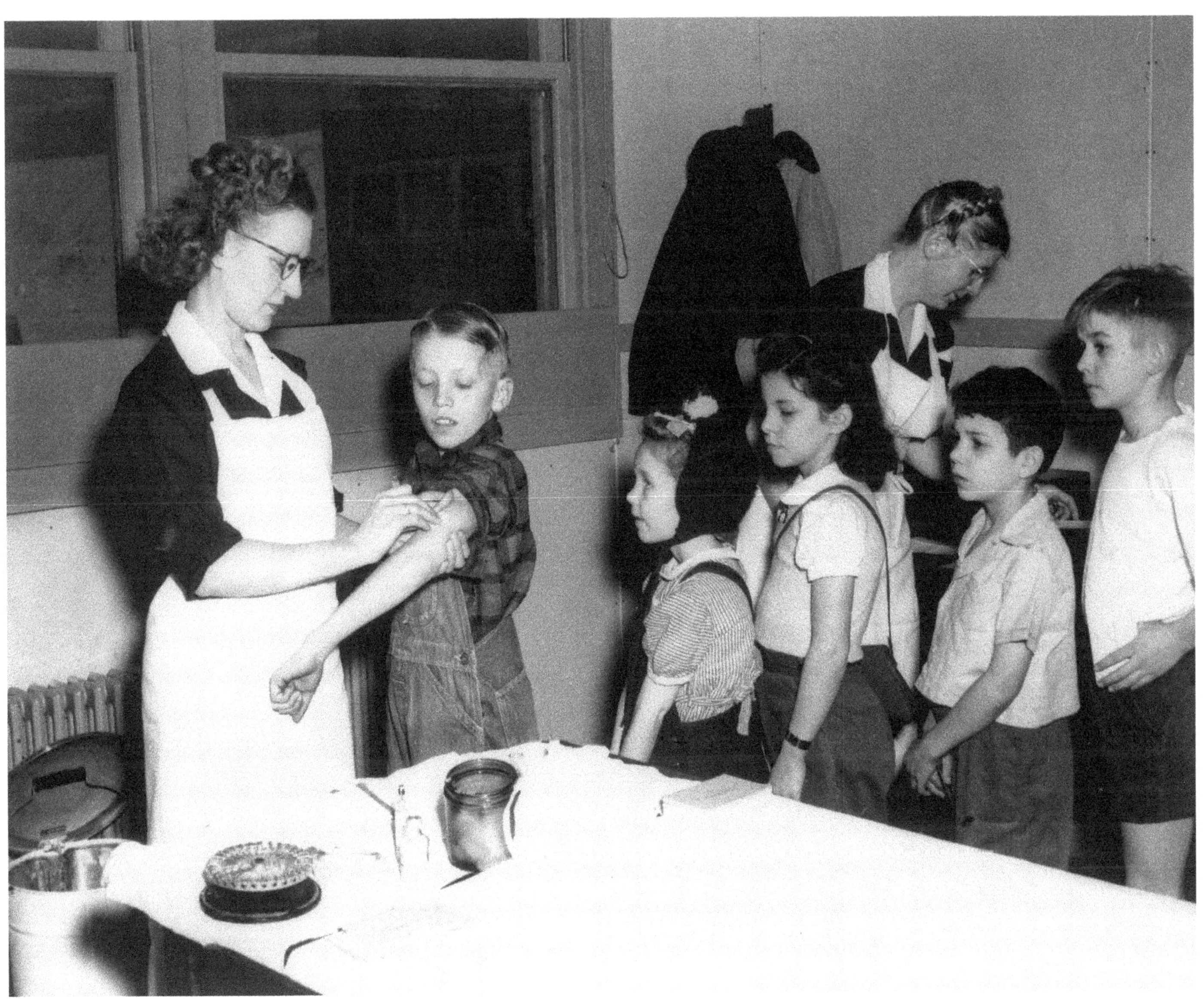

Public Health nurse Gladys Johnson gives Glen Wisecarver a shot while other students stand in line and wait their turn.

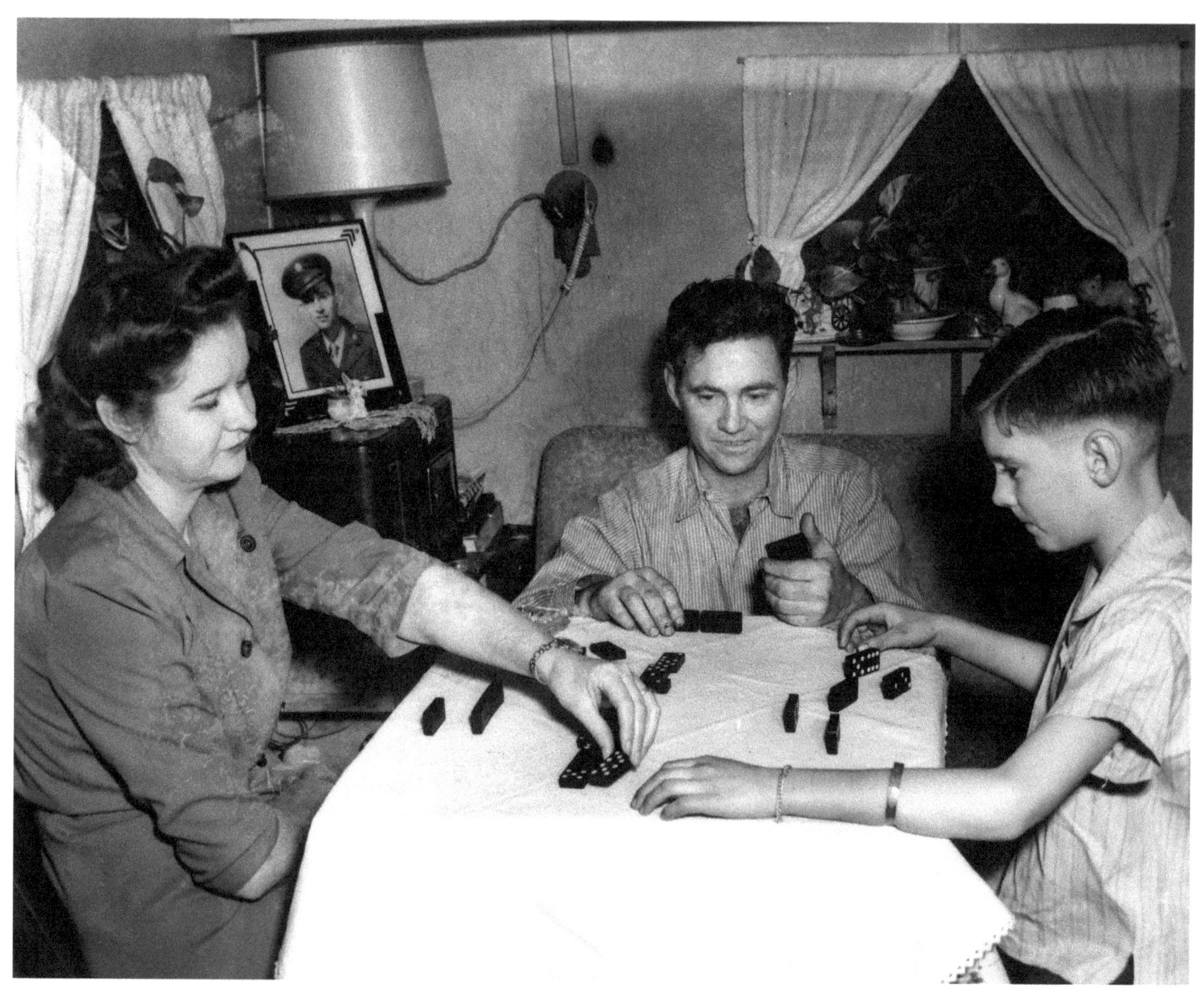

Mr. and Mrs. William Christopher and their son Bill play dominoes together in their tiny trailer while listening to the radio.

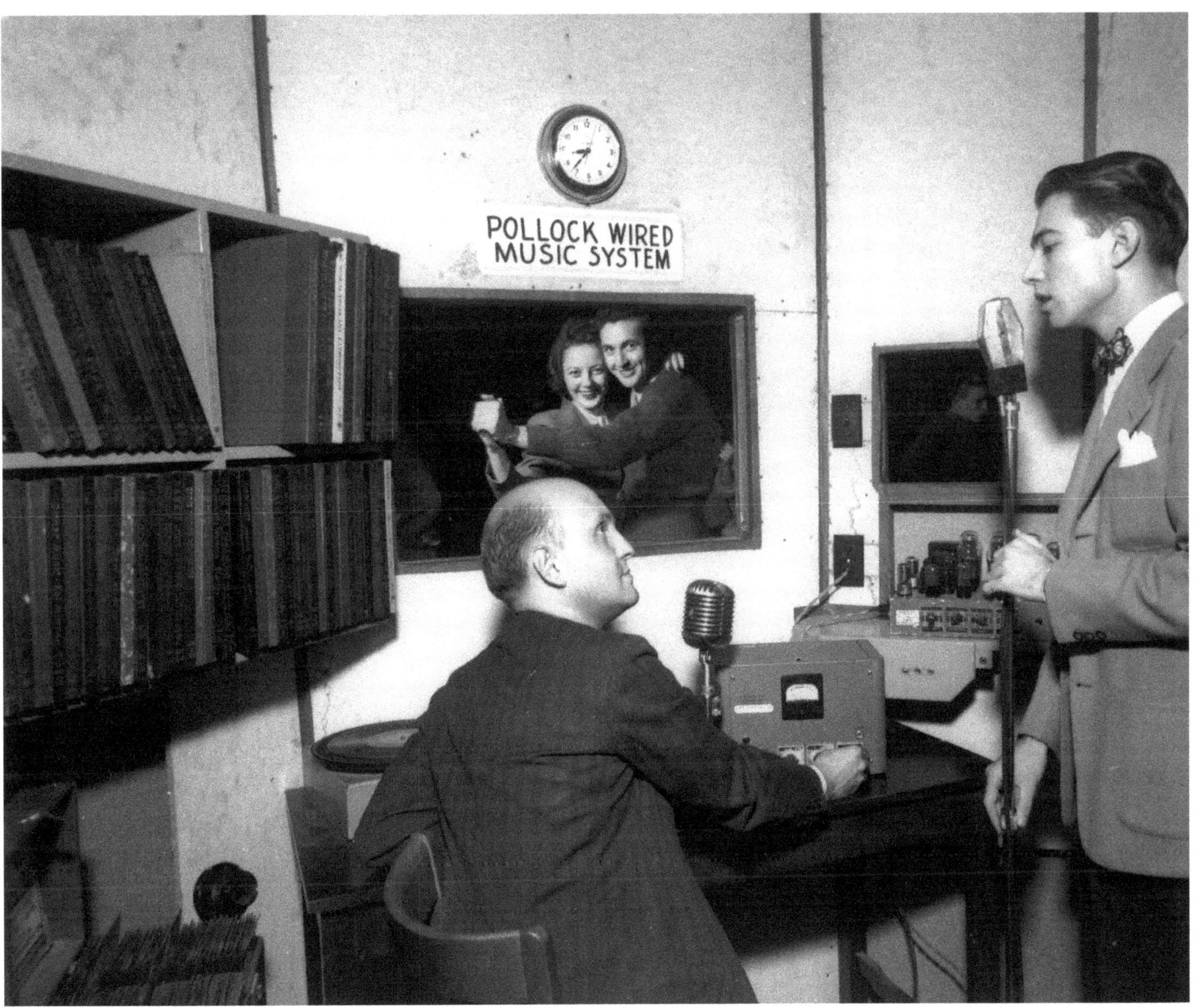

The local radio station was an important way to deliver music and messages to residents. Here in 1945, Bill Pollock operates the controls and Berl Henry sings, while couples dance outside the radio station's booth.

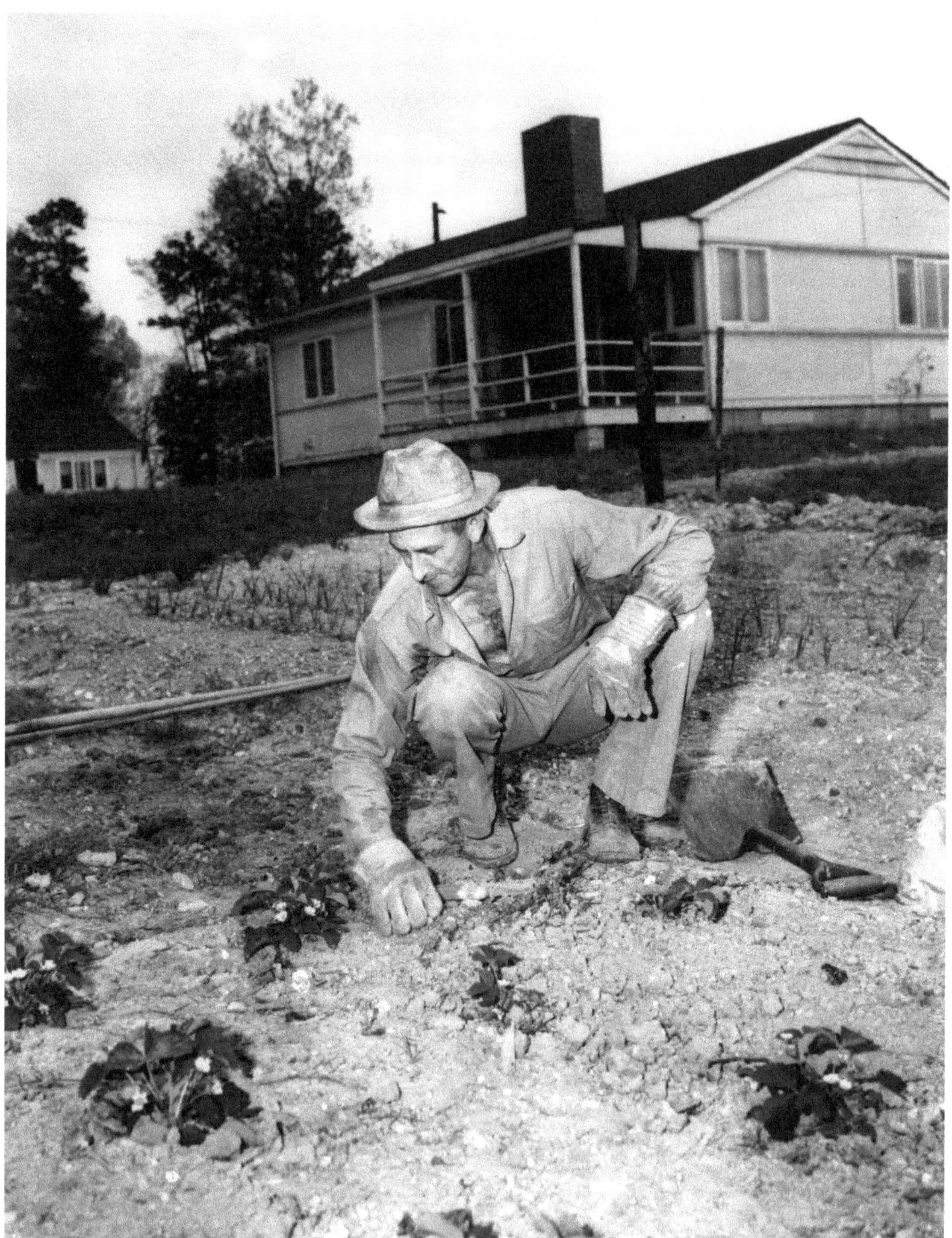

A worker takes care of the strawberry plants growing in his Victory garden. Americans far and wide planted Victory gardens, an effective way to support the war effort and an activity almost everyone could participate in.

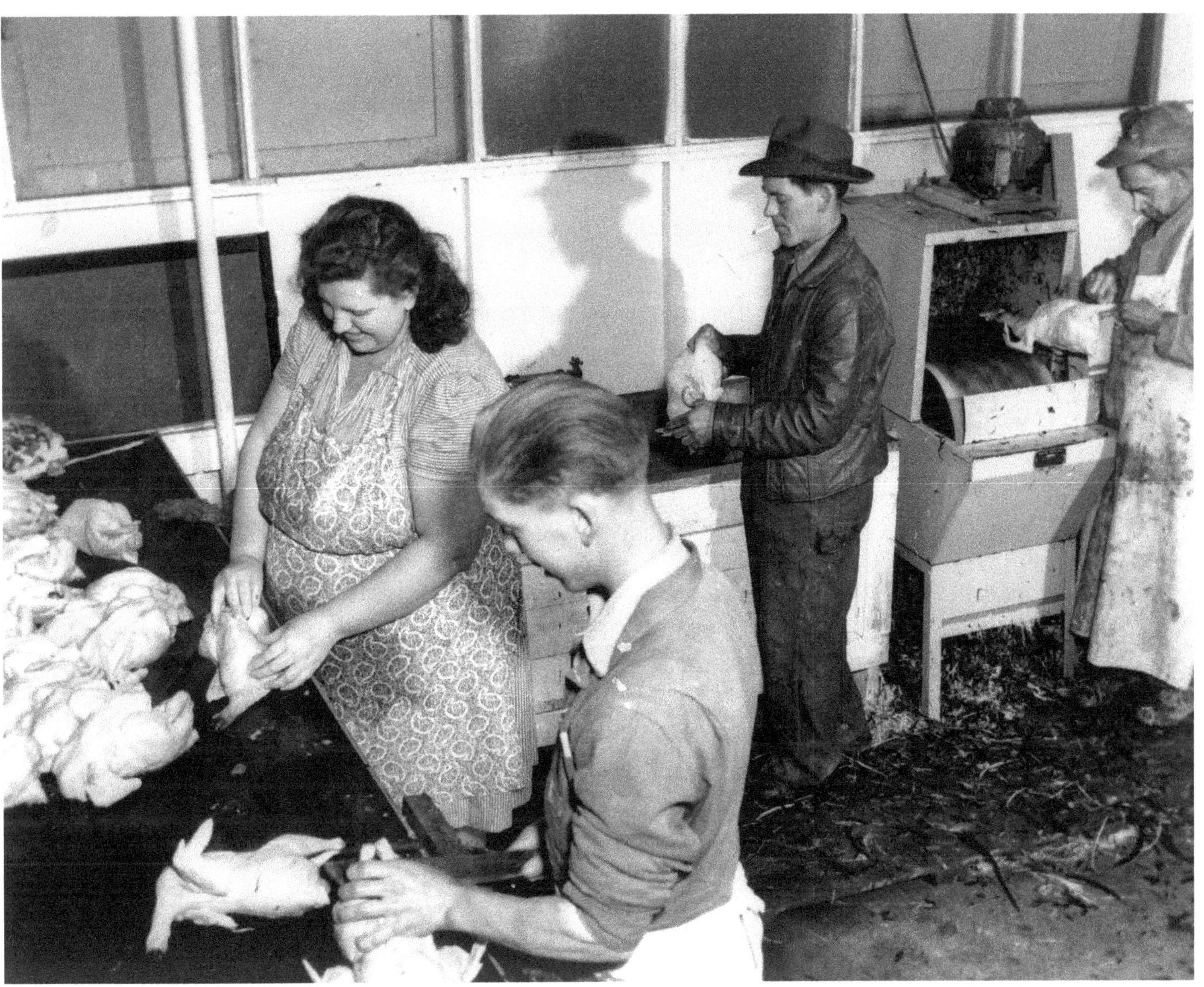

The Central Cafeteria was a popular and busy place, feeding hundreds of workers daily. A chicken farm provided fresh poultry. The individual on the right puts the chicken into the chicken plucker where a spinning drum with large rubber fingers removes the feathers. The next worker then burns off the pin feathers, and the women finish the cleaning and preparation for cooking. Clearly, smoking on the job was of no concern in the 1940s.

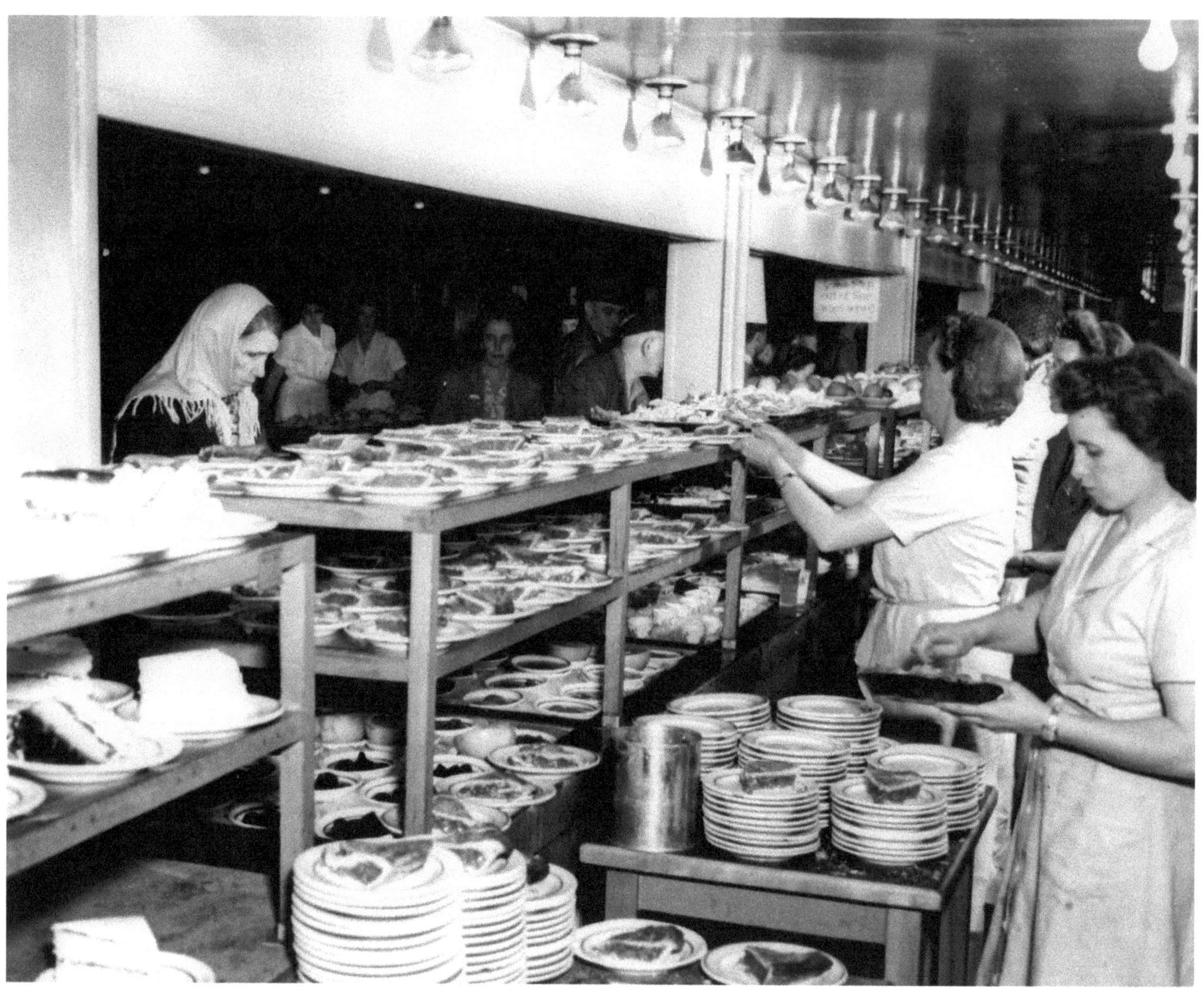

Hundreds of dessert plates with pieces of pie and cake fill three shelves for selection by workers at the Central Cafeteria dessert area. The cafeteria was one of the busiest places on site. May 1945.

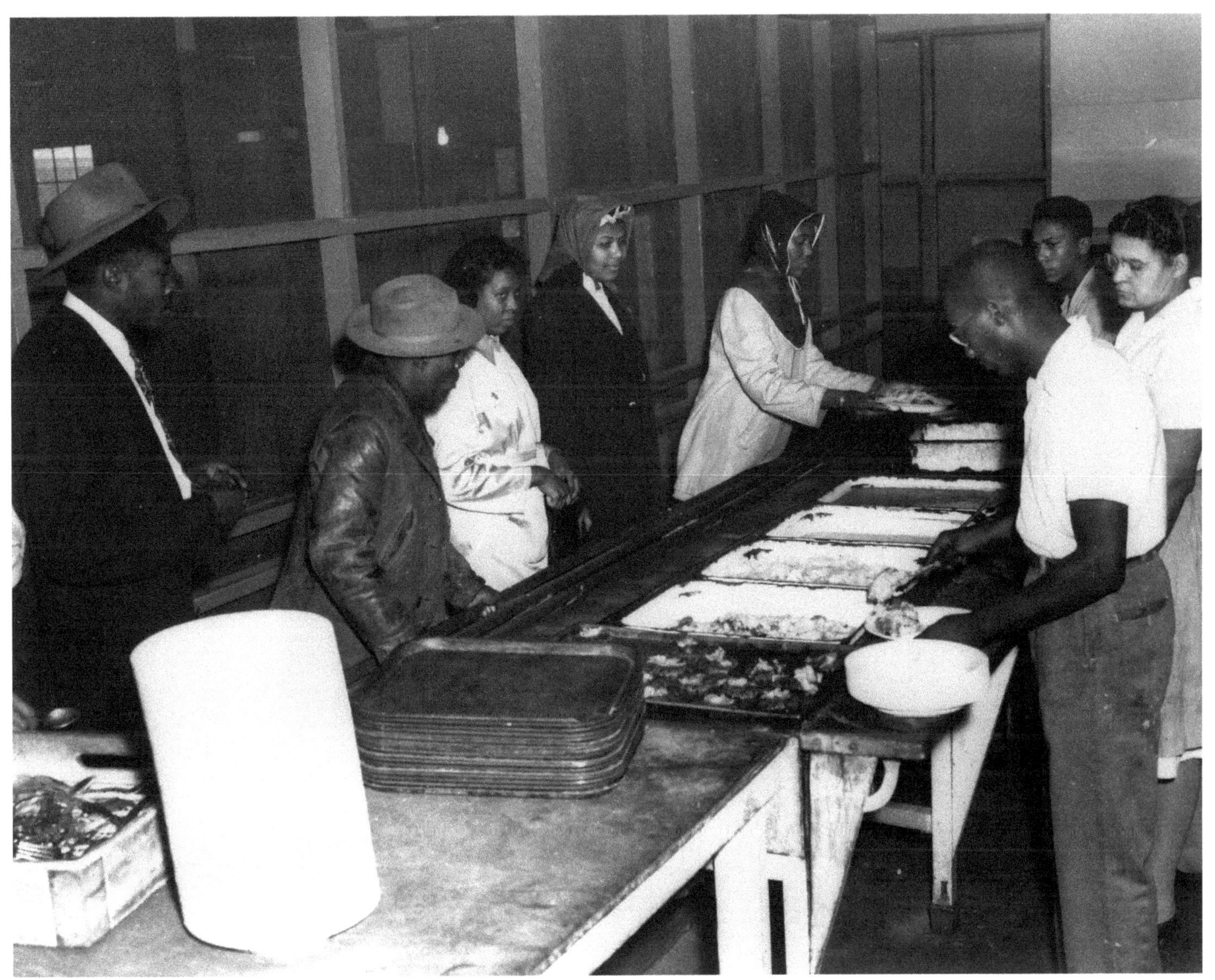

Though whites and blacks worked closely side-by-side, segregation prescribed a separate cafeteria for black workers. The food was just as good and often included items not typically found in the Central Cafeteria.

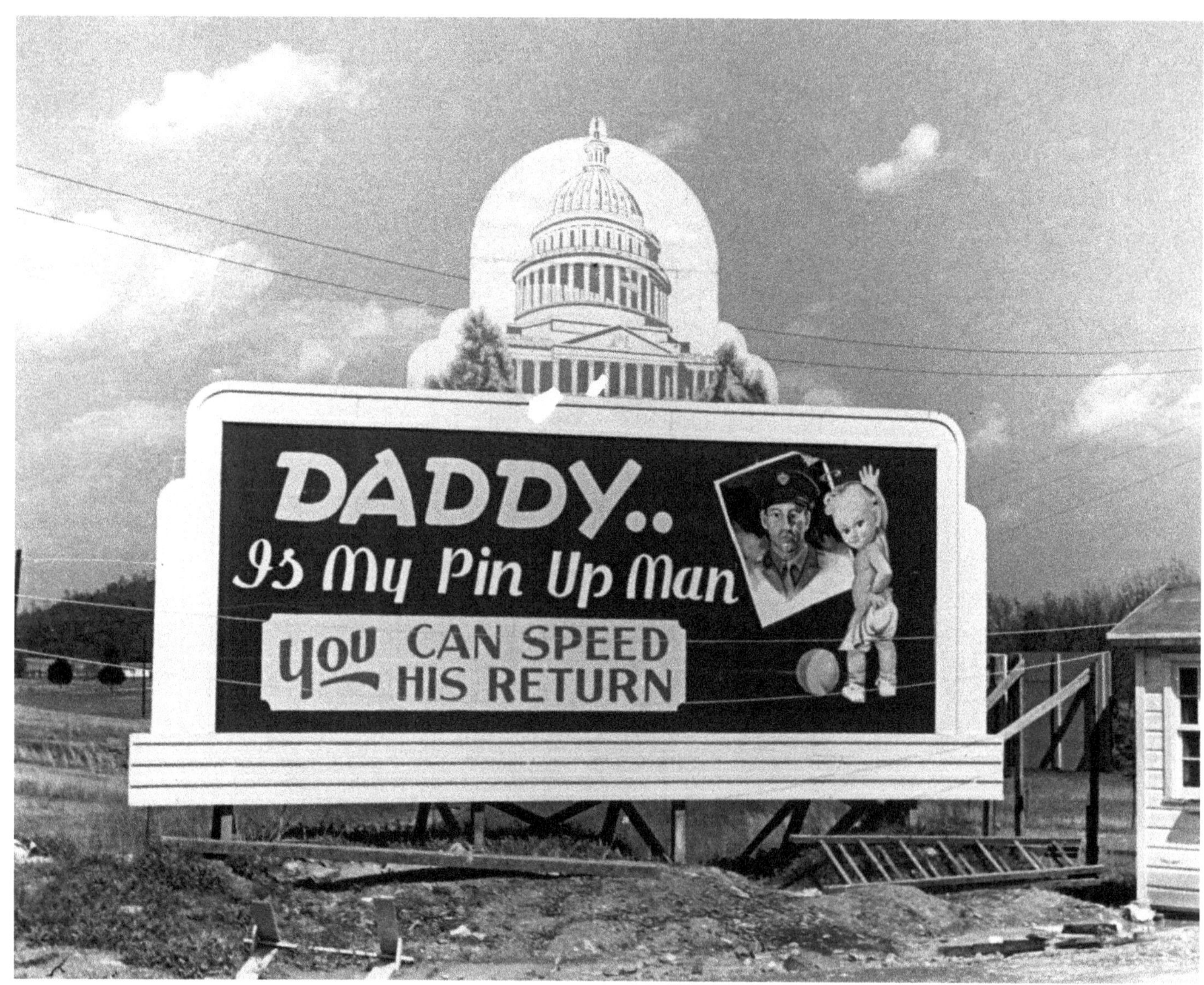

Throughout the Oak Ridge Reservation there were many large billboards with usually one of two messages: Do your job and bring our soldiers home quickly, or remember the need for secrecy and do *not* talk about your job. This billboard depicts a toddler asking workers to work hard and bring Daddy home.

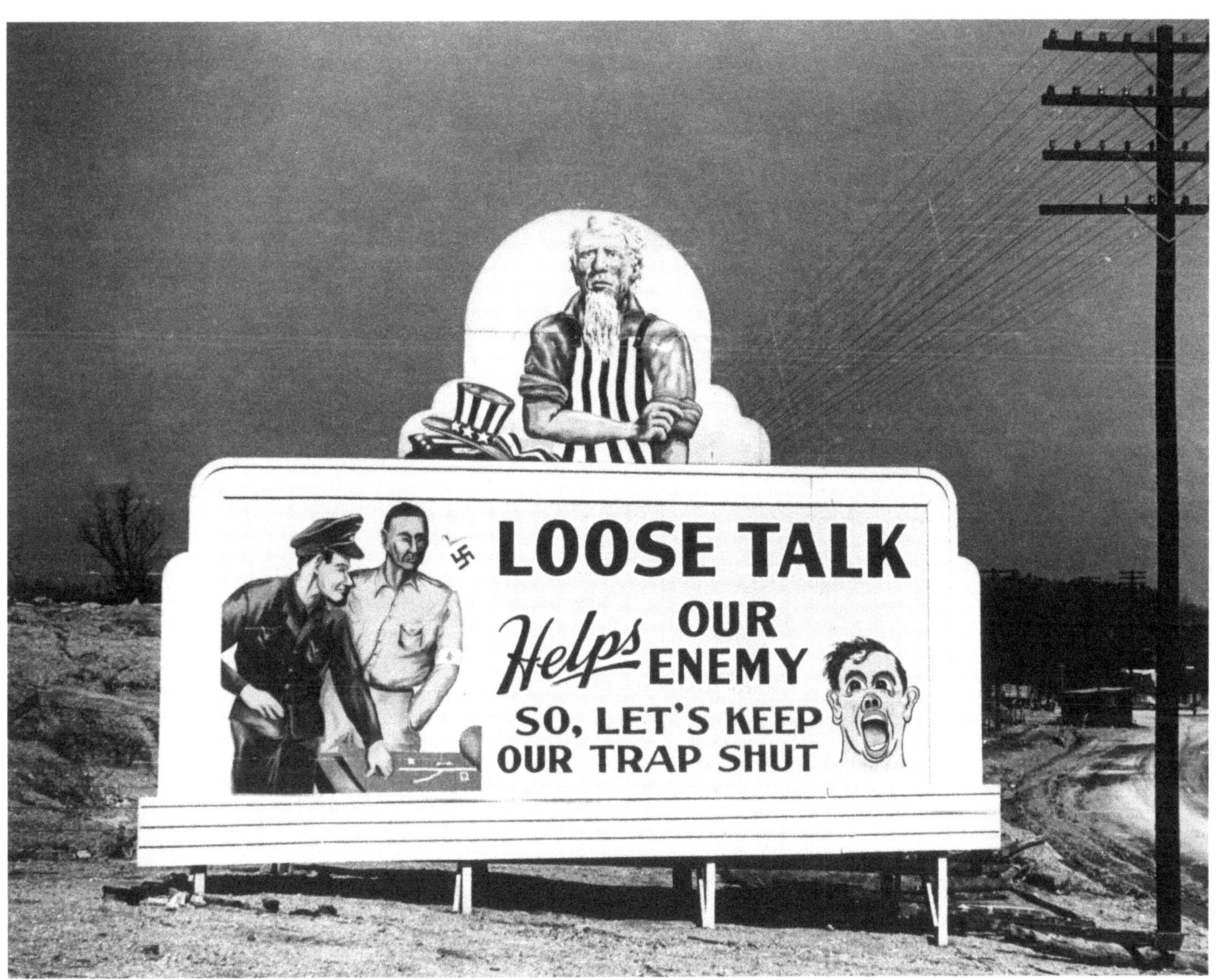

On this billboard the message is clear: Don't talk about your particular job—keep your mouth zipped. Billboards dotted the landscape all around the sites.

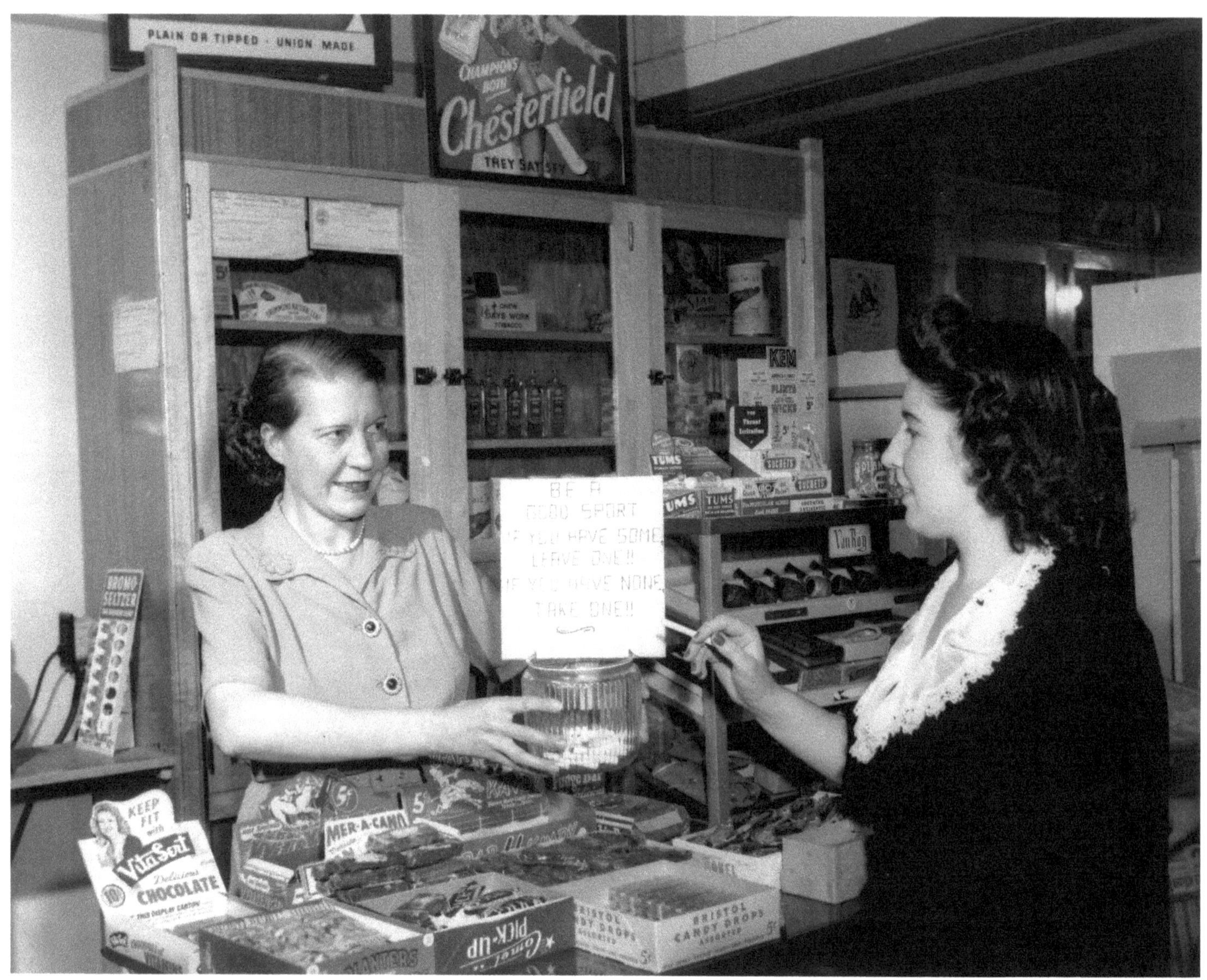

Lorrane Yance holds a bowl out to R. L. Bennette. Smoking was not considered a health risk in the 1940s. On the counter at this store was a bowl with a sign that read, "Be a good sport. If you have some, leave one! If you have none, take one!" If you were out of cigarettes you simply reached in and helped yourself, a gift from those who had plenty.

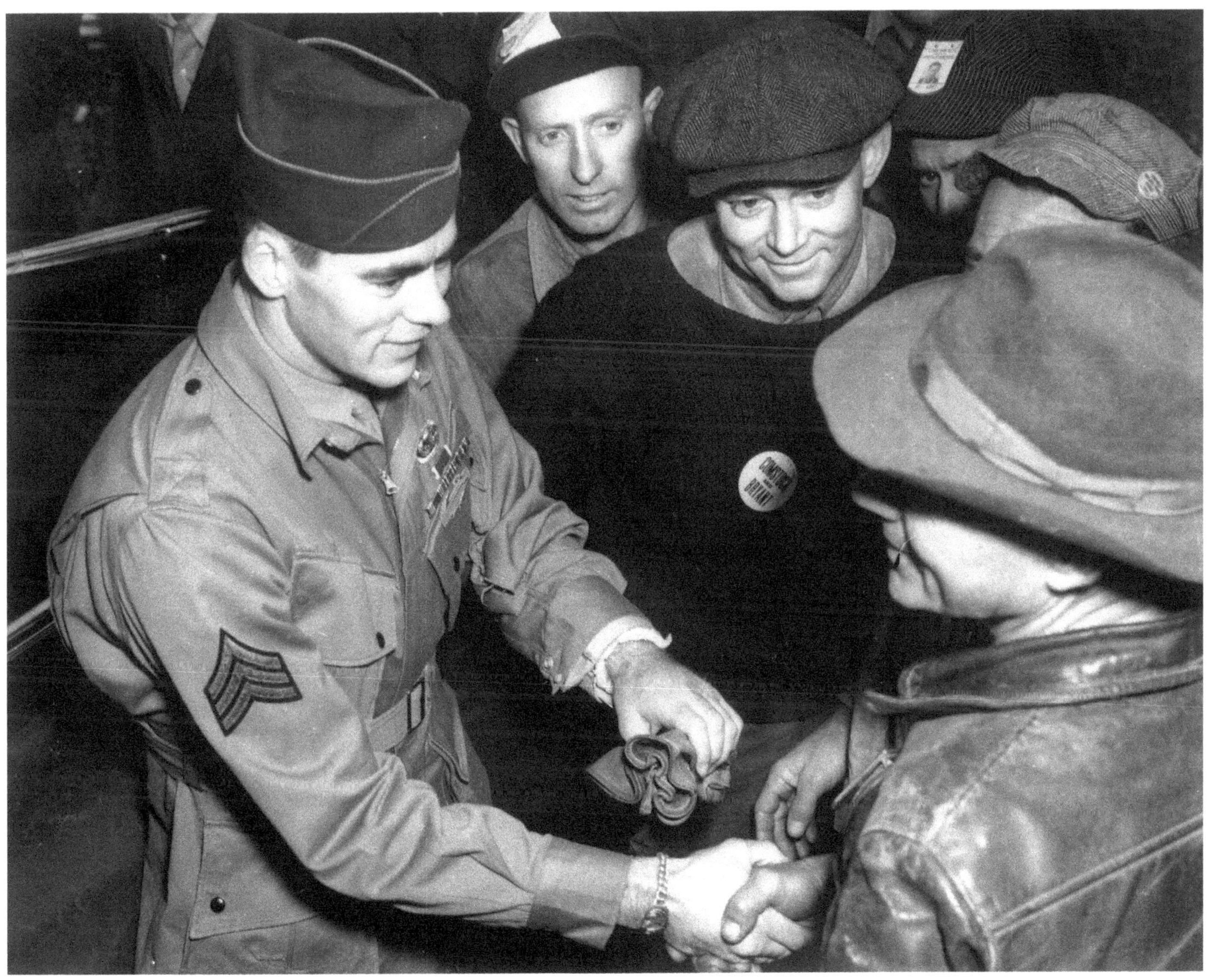

A war combat veteran greets and chats with Oak Ridge workers, thanking them for their hard work and reminding them of the importance of what they are doing.

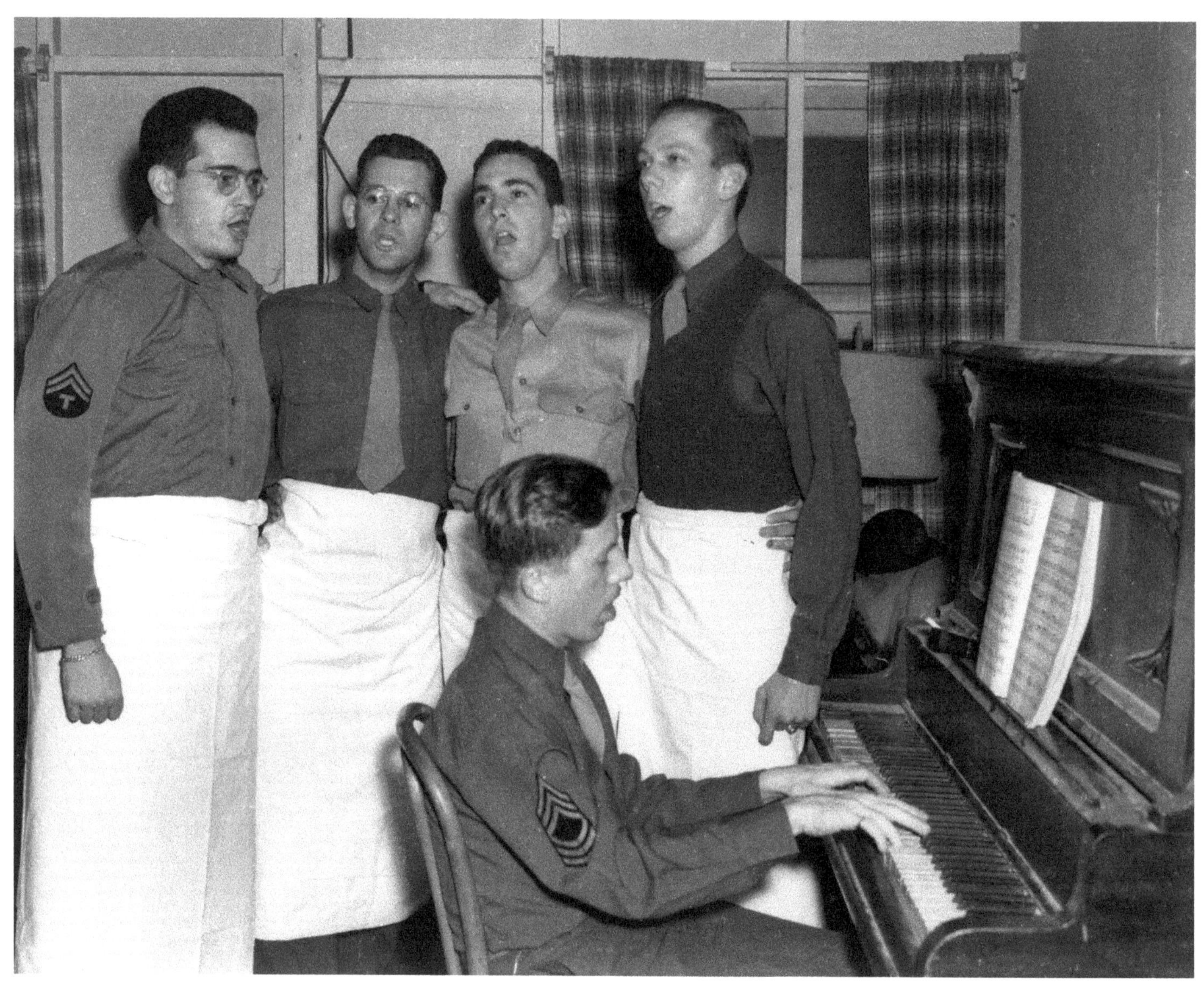

Soldiers Bob Blaubach, Jim Ord, Cliff Weill, Bill Walters, and Bob Goetle at the piano rehearse for a play at one of the barracks in December 1944.

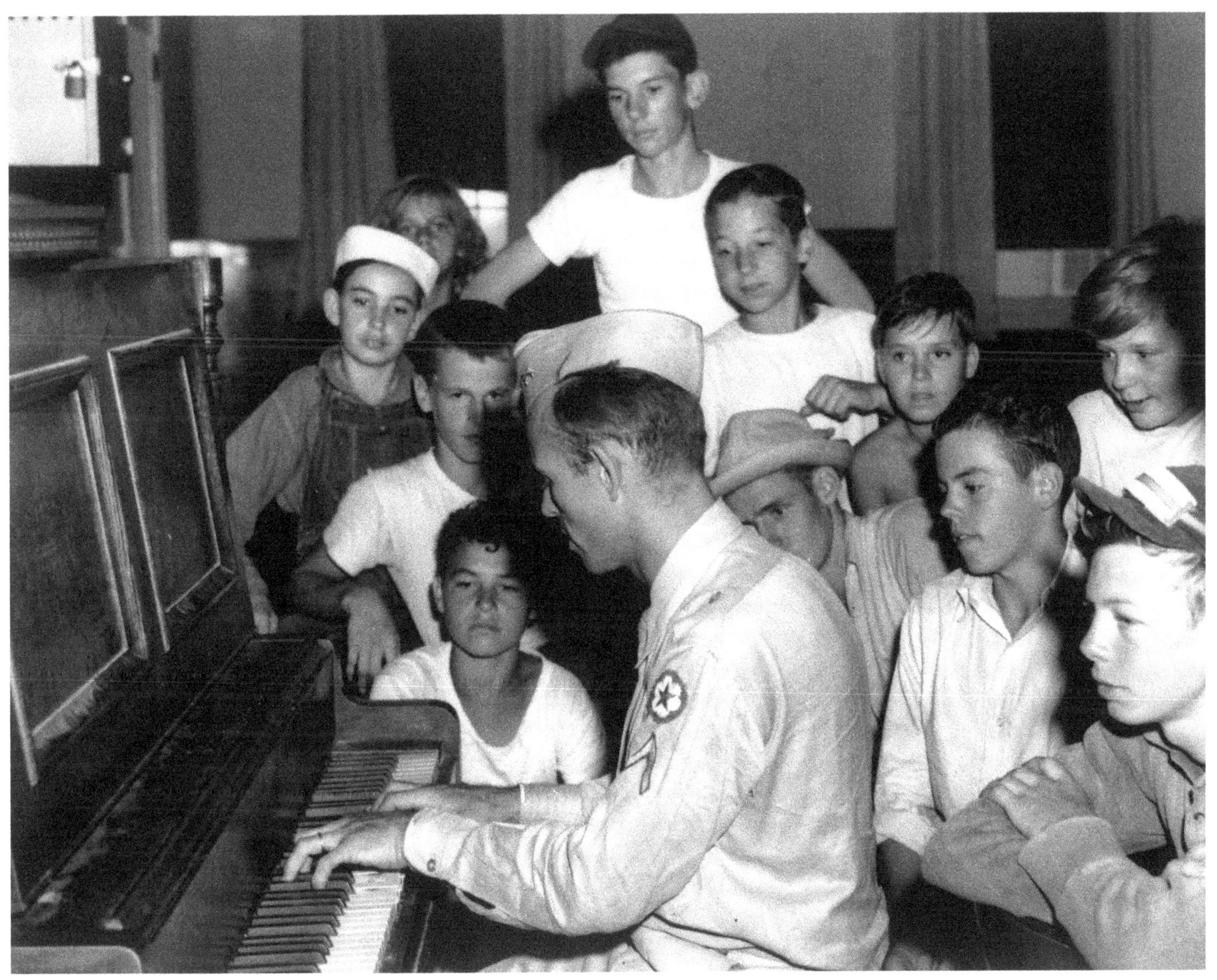

In July 1945, Private Cullie B. Woodall at the piano entertains children in the Gamble Valley community center, one of the residential areas inside the secret city of Oak Ridge.

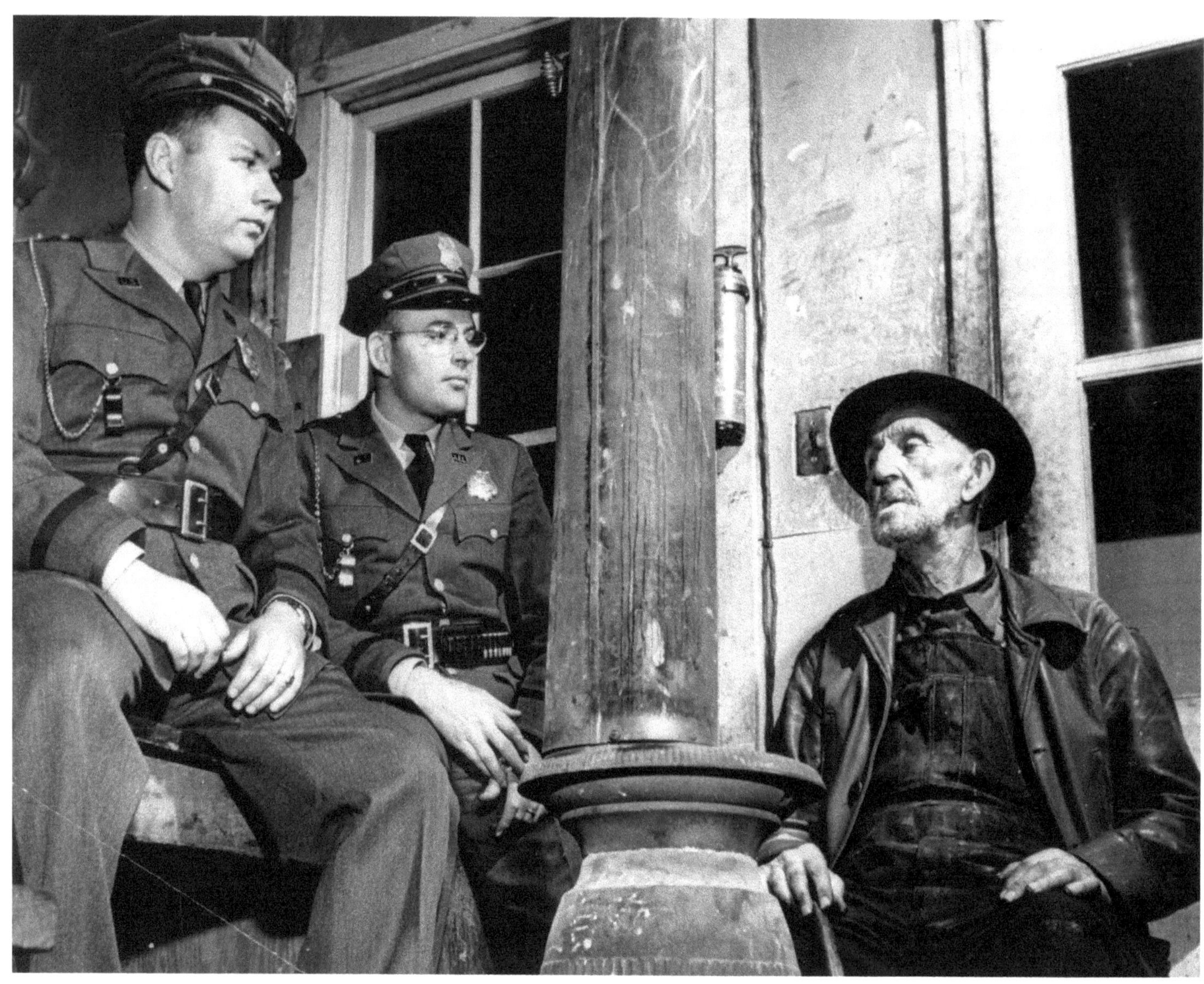

Just outside the Blair security gate lived 82-year-old William Henry Alonzo. He became a common fixture in the guardhouse, sitting near the old wood stove, where he'd tell stories to the guards about the old days.

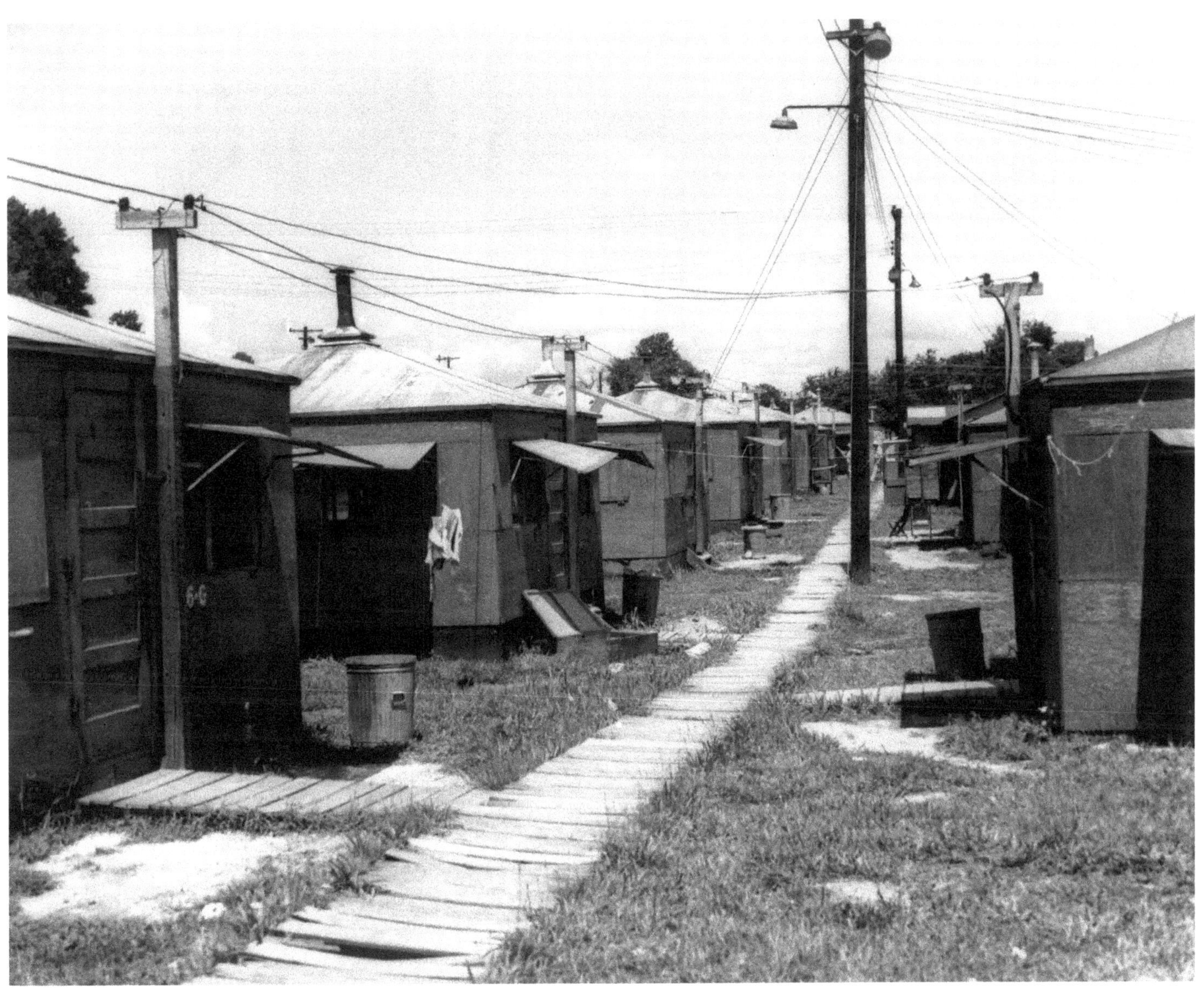

Many workers and their families lived in the hutments, which had electric lighting and were heated with a coal stove. Communal restroom and shower facilities were centrally located down the long boardwalk. There were few complaints among workers about living conditions at the facilities. Everyone understood the demands of the war effort and simply took everything in stride.

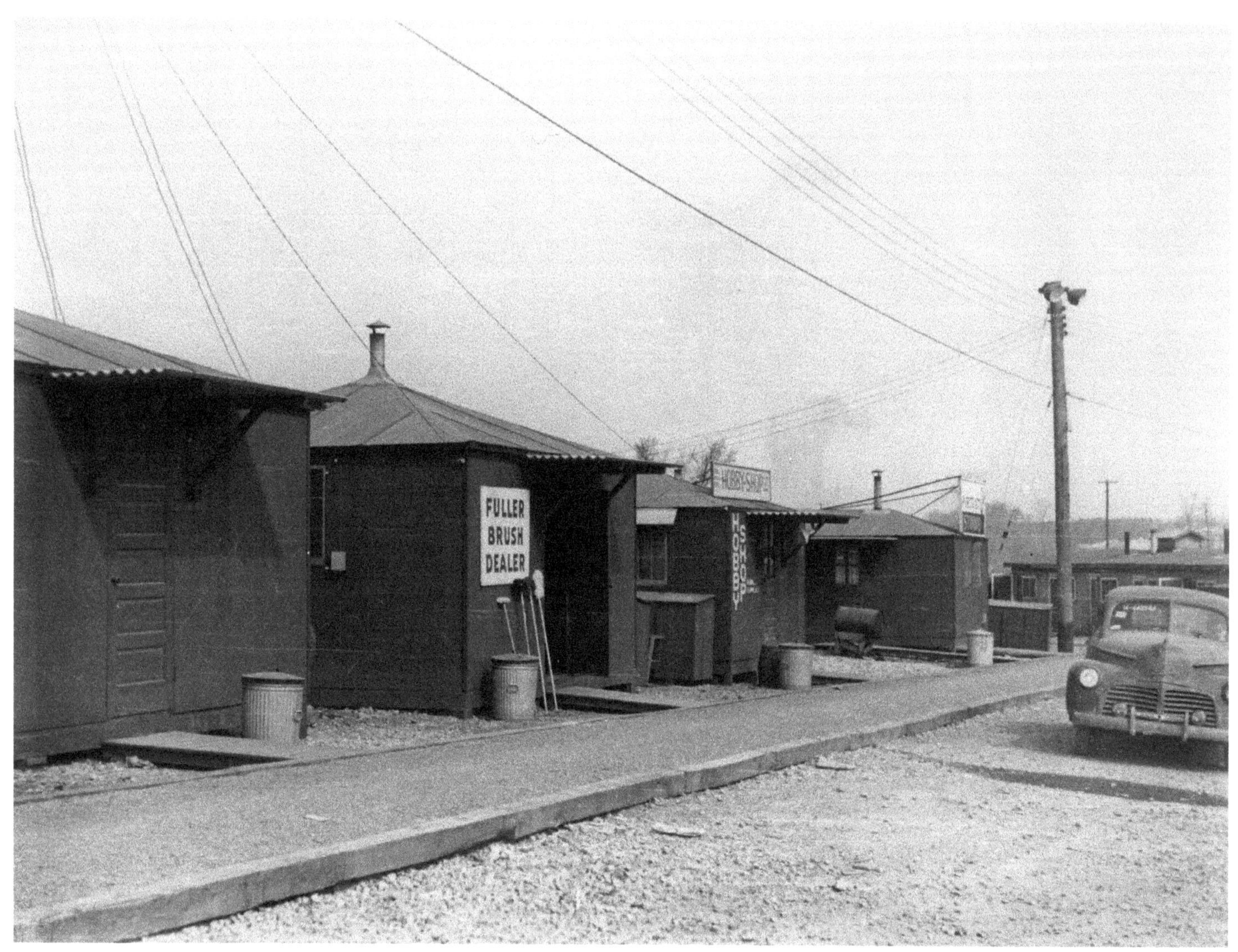

Not quite the shopping mall of today, these stores along the boardwalk were important to local residents. Shown here in March 1945 are the Fuller Brush store, a hobby shop, and a portrait studio. This small strip mall was located on the corner of Oak Ridge Turnpike and Illinois Avenue.

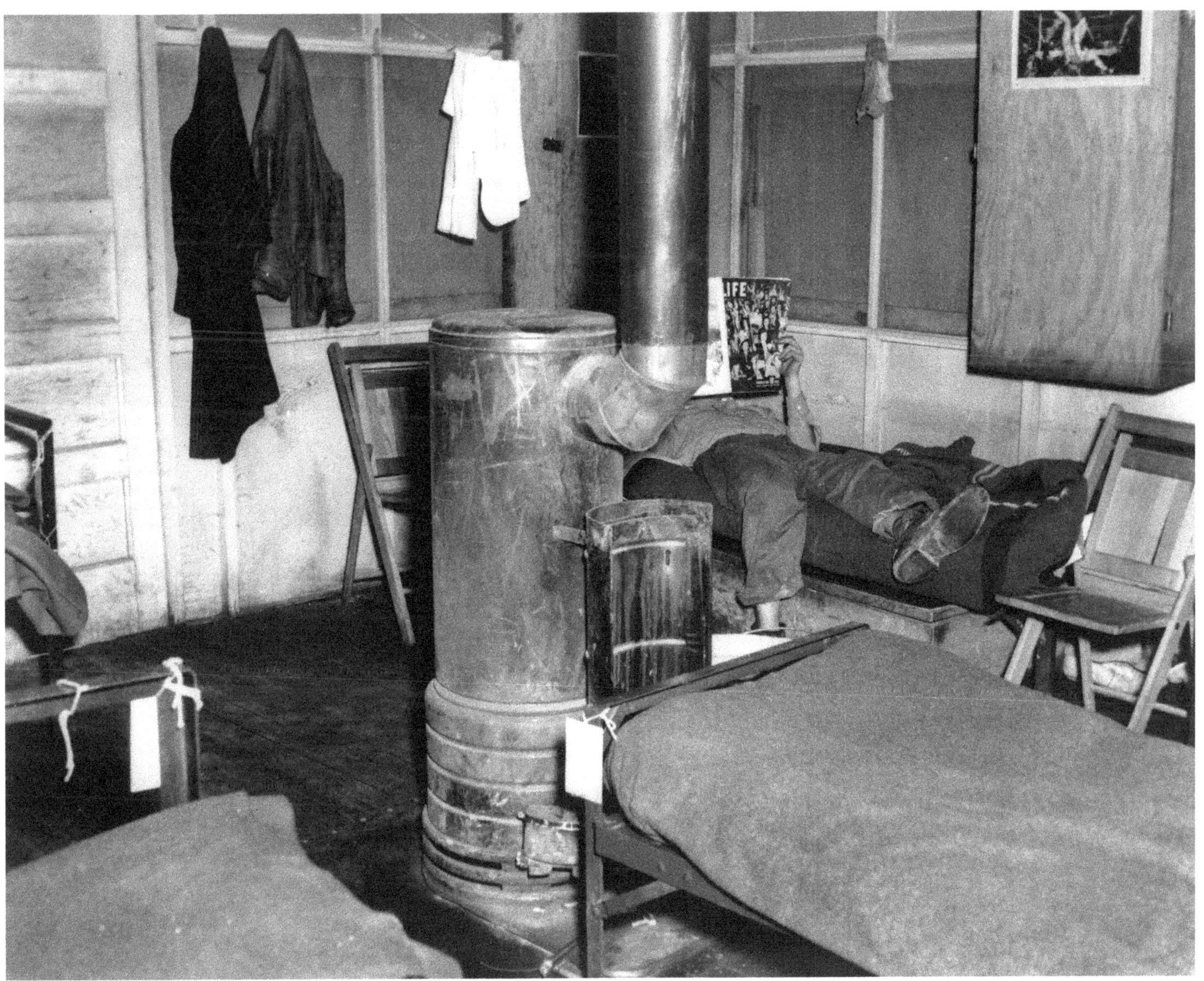

All the comforts of home—well almost anyway. This is the interior of a typical hutment where a worker relaxes and reads a magazine on his bed. Two other beds fill the foreground with a coal stove in the middle. There was no insulation in the walls, no water, and no toilet, yet this was the living unit for thousands of workers, black and white.

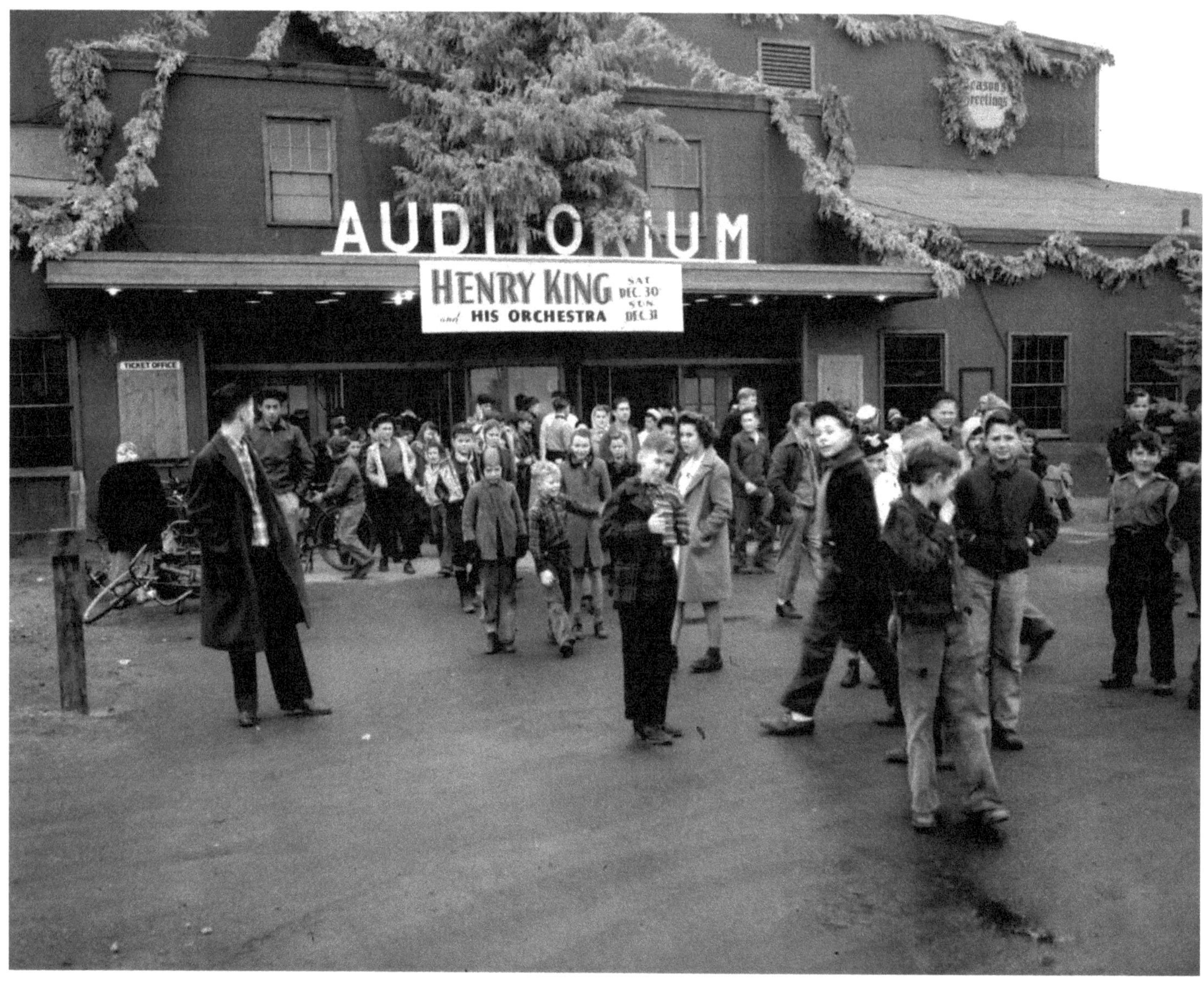

Children at the Hanford facility gather outside the auditorium at Christmas to see a play. The birthrate at Hanford during the Manhattan Project was one of the highest in the nation, burdening the medical facility and raising the concern of General Groves. One unidentified worker with a taste for poetry said it this way:

The General's in a stew
He trusted you and you
He thought you'd be scientific
Instead you're just prolific
And what is he to do?

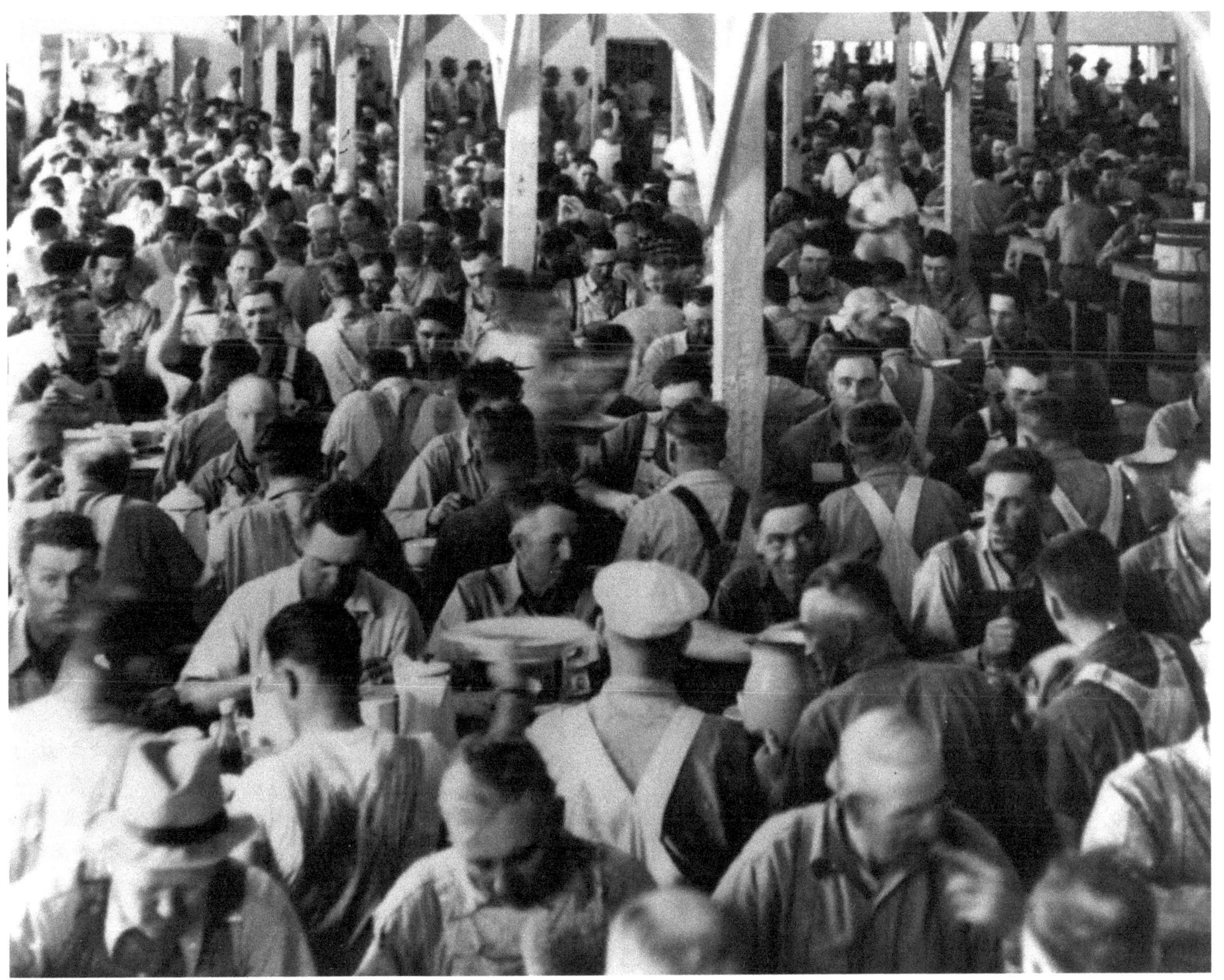

As always lunch was a popular time of day and the cafeterias were bustling places. In 1943, these Hanford workers eat and take a break from their hard work and challenging day to relax and catch up with co-workers.

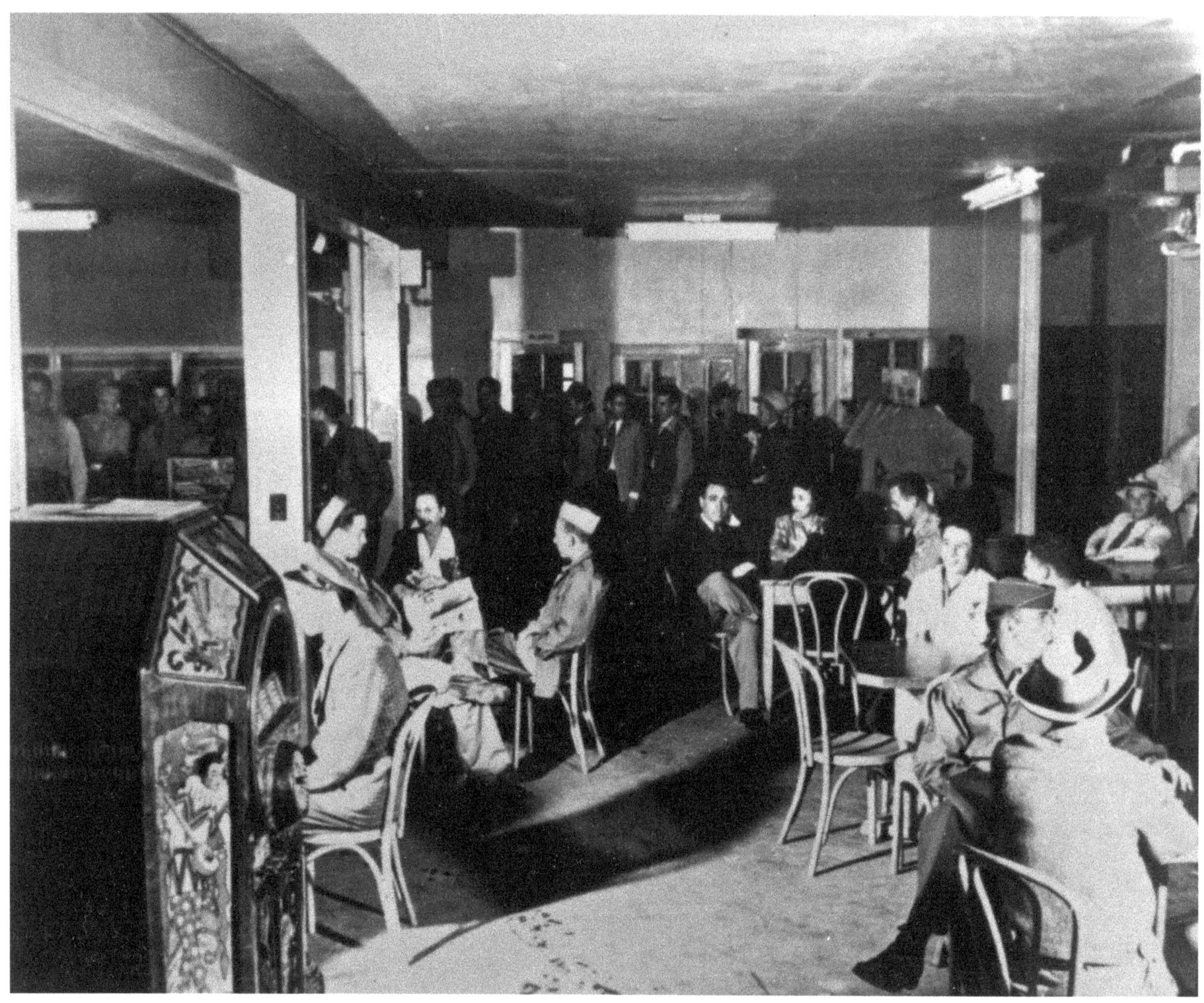

Inside the Army Post Exchange at Los Alamos in 1945, soldiers and workers enjoy their time off, relaxing to the music of a jukebox. These people did not know what was being done at the facility. Rumor had it that some sort of military death-ray was being devised.

Turning Theoretical Physics into Nuclear Bombs

Proof of the Devastation and Sorrow Ahead

During the early days of the Manhattan Project, it quickly became clear how difficult and slow it would be to conduct the needed bomb-making research at universities scattered throughout the nation. The decision was made to bring the greatest minds together in one secret research laboratory. Groves, Oppenheimer, and Lawrence selected a remote mesa in New Mexico and purchased the 54,000 acres. On the property was the Los Alamos Ranch School, a large boarding school for boys that included more than 50 buildings. All the buildings were refitted for the project, and soon the site became a bustling town with hundreds of buildings, research facilities, schools, theaters, homes, trailers, hutments, and offices, along with extremely tight security.

No one knew if a bomb could actually be built, but the scientists understood that when an atom of uranium is struck by a neutron it can break into two new fission fragments and release three new neutrons and a large amount of energy. These newly released neutrons in turn can strike other uranium atoms causing many more fissions and neutron releases, ultimately creating a chain reaction. The trick to producing a bomb was to force enriched uranium or plutonium together in a fraction of a second to break all the atoms apart and release all the neutrons instantaneously, producing nuclear supercritical mass and the release of a colossal amount of energy. This was the practical application of Einstein's famous equation $E = MC^2$, where E equals energy, M equals mass, and C^2 equals the speed of light squared, or, energy equals mass multiplied by the square of the speed of light (186,282 miles a second times 186,282 miles a second). Stated simply, a very small amount of matter happens to be a very large amount of energy. By example, if all the nuclei of all the atoms of a Lincoln penny were ripped apart, the energy released could power New York City for two years.

We should remember that these physicists used only paper, pencils, and slide rules to calculate the number of neutrons (subatomic particles) that might or might not collide with other atomic nuclei to produce superexplosive energy. Furthermore, how enriched the uranium or plutonium needed to be was an unknown, and researchers had only just begun producing small quantities of either element. So much had to be determined, designed, and tested, the true genius of the people involved cannot be doubted. The Los Alamos site conducted the nuclear research, as well as advanced high-explosive research and development to determine exactly how to create the needed implosion to trigger nuclear criticality.

Early in 1943, Oppenheimer and other scientists designed a gun-type bomb to shoot one piece of uranium-235 (the bullet) down a barrel into a second piece. The principle behind the bomb was so certain (and the supply of uranium-235 was so small), no testing beyond laboratory investigations was needed. A bomb called "Little Boy" would be built and deployed, without a single test, over the Japanese city Hiroshima.

Because uranium was difficult to separate, a way to use plutonium was needed. It was soon learned that plutonium would not work in a gun-type bomb, for experiments by Emilio Segre (later the winner of a Nobel Prize) demonstrated that if used in a gun-type bomb, plutonium would fizzle. The chain reaction would begin prematurely, releasing enough energy to disperse the critical mass of plutonium before enough of it could undergo fission to yield a colossal explosion. To circumvent this hurdle, Seth Neddermeyer proposed creating a supersonic shock wave with high explosives to symmetrically crush and implode a ball of plutonium. Understanding the potential, Oppenheimer reorganized the laboratory to explore Neddermeyer's proposal, struggling to overcome the many problems of building a device precise enough and strong enough to create the needed implosion.

Testing was essential. The first plutonium device, called "the Gadget," was tested on July 16, 1945, at a location near Alamogordo, New Mexico, named the Trinity site (today known as White Sands Missile Range). At 05:29:45, the Gadget was detonated at the top of a tower 100 feet tall. The resulting flash was brighter than the sun. The explosion created a shock wave felt 100 miles away, a mushroom cloud reaching to a height of 7.5 miles, and a hole of radioactive glass in the desert 10 feet deep and 1,100 feet wide. The huge steel tower that held the bomb was completely vaporized. Upon witnessing the blast, the director of the test, Kenneth Bainbridge, looked at Oppenheimer and said, "Now we are all sons of bitches."

Work immediately began to design a plutonium implosion bomb. It would be called "Fat Man."

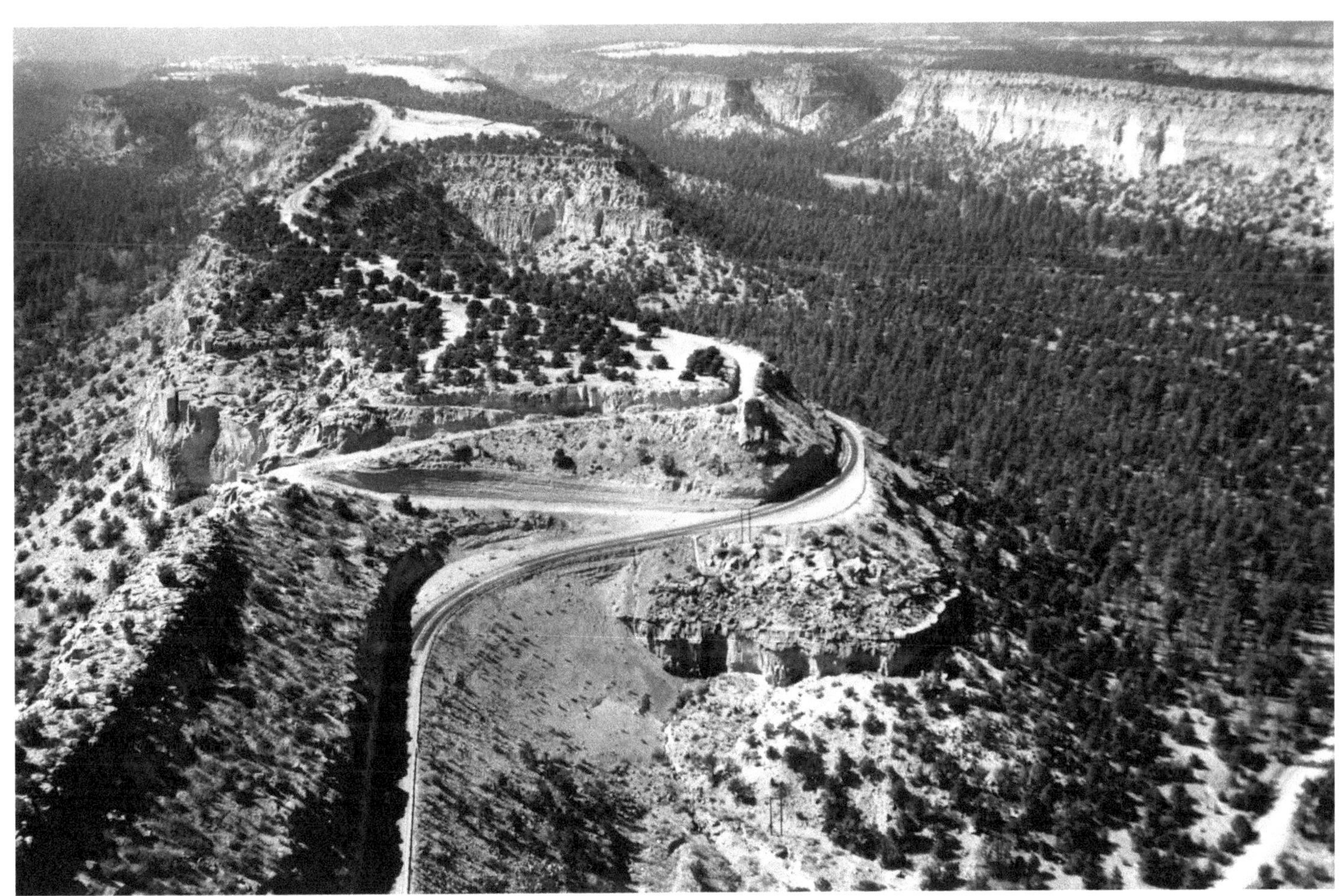

The highly secret Los Alamos facility was in the middle of nowhere, the ideal place to hide such a facility. This is the main Hill Road, facing west to the site. Residents and workers at the site enjoyed the beauty of the area but thought the drive to get there was scary and dangerous in many places.

Herb Lehr carries a critical part of "the Gadget," the first device to be tested at the Trinity site, into the McDonald Ranch House at Los Alamos in July 1945. The magnesium case Herb is carrying contains the initiators. Small aluminum cylinders would be inserted into the holes in the case.

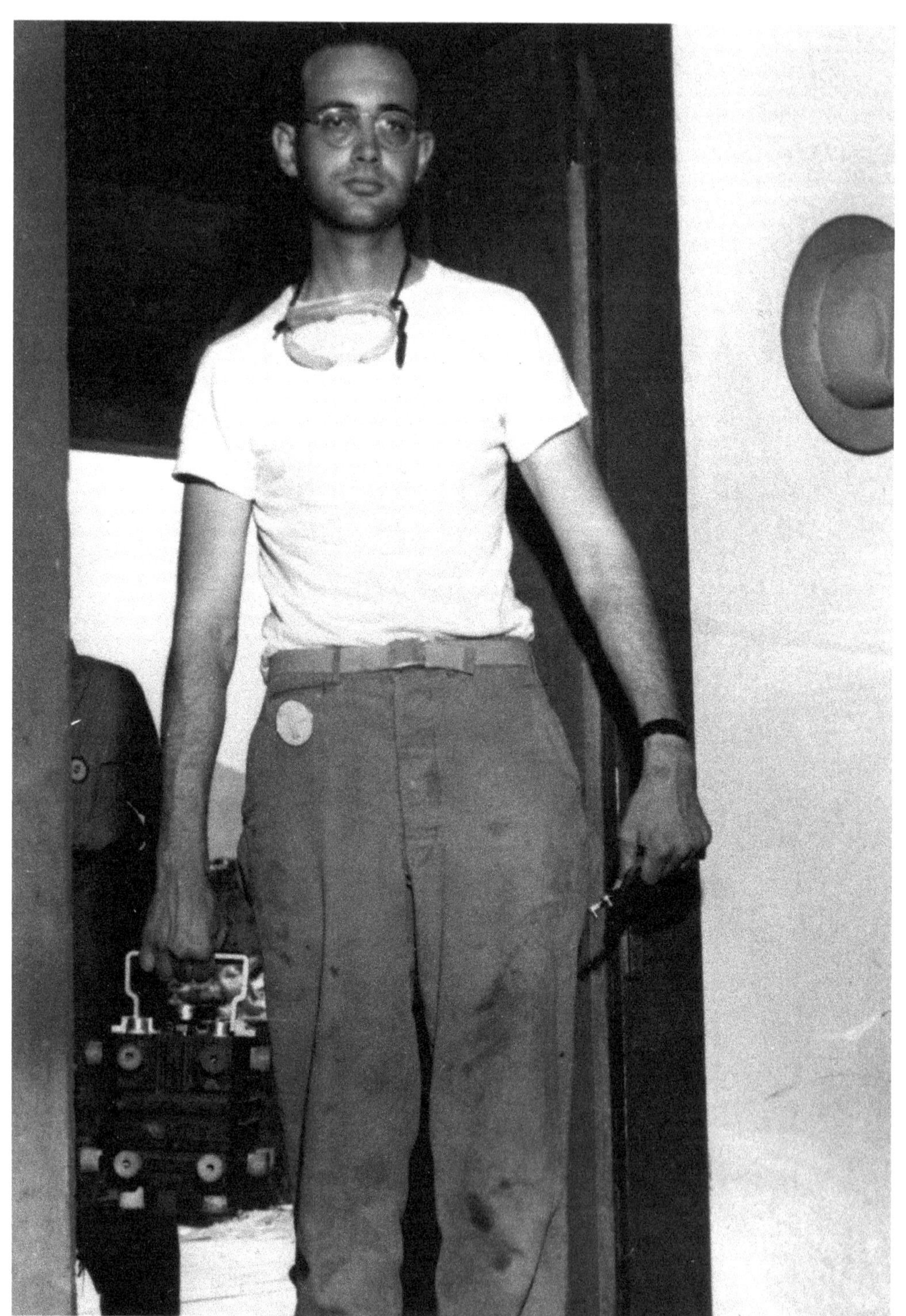

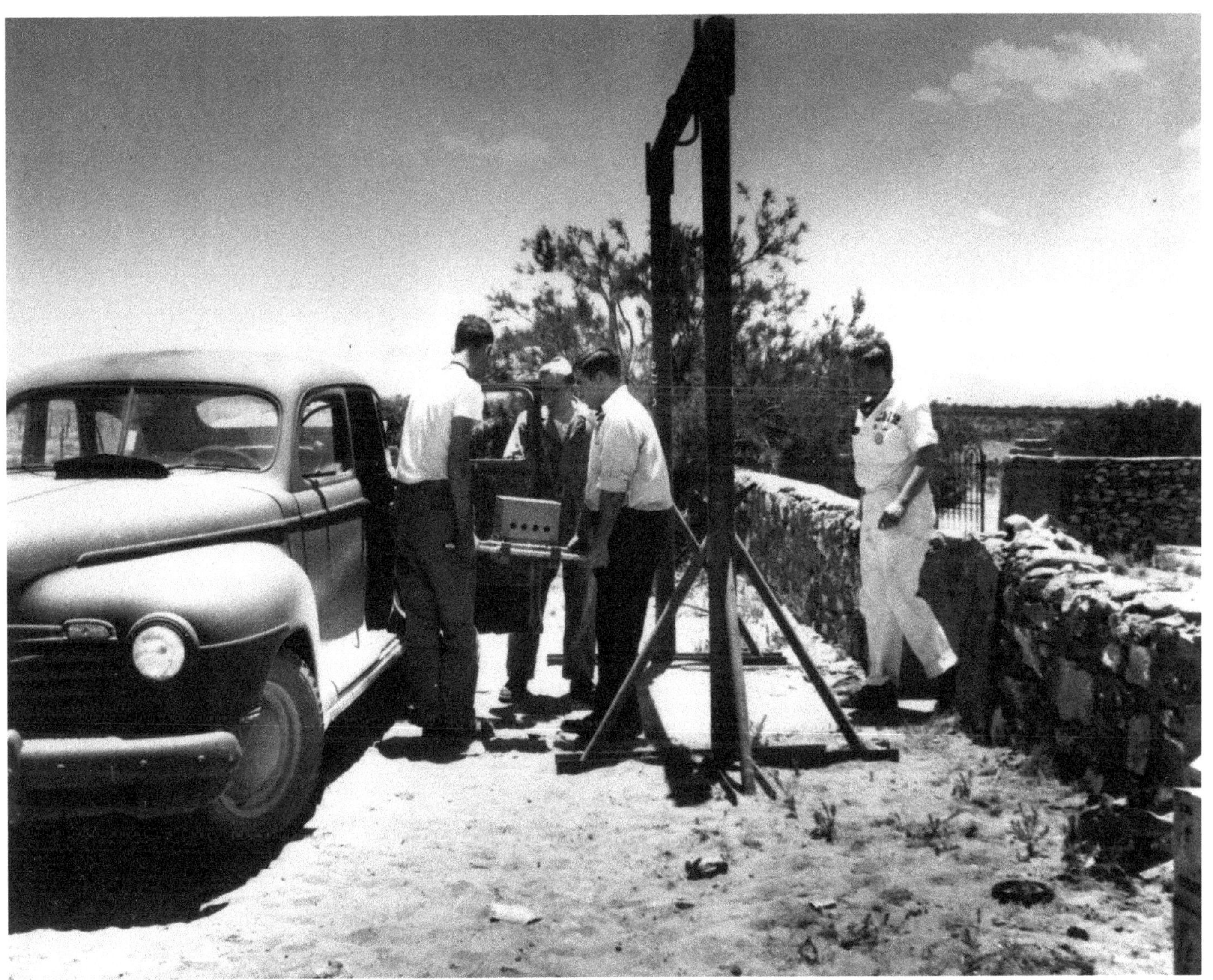

The most important component of the Gadget was the fragile plutonium core. Herb Lehr and Harry Daghlian are loading the completely assembled core into the backseat of this 1942 Plymouth on July 16, 1945. That anyone would consider loading the back of a car with a plutonium core and driving it anywhere is today considered unthinkable.

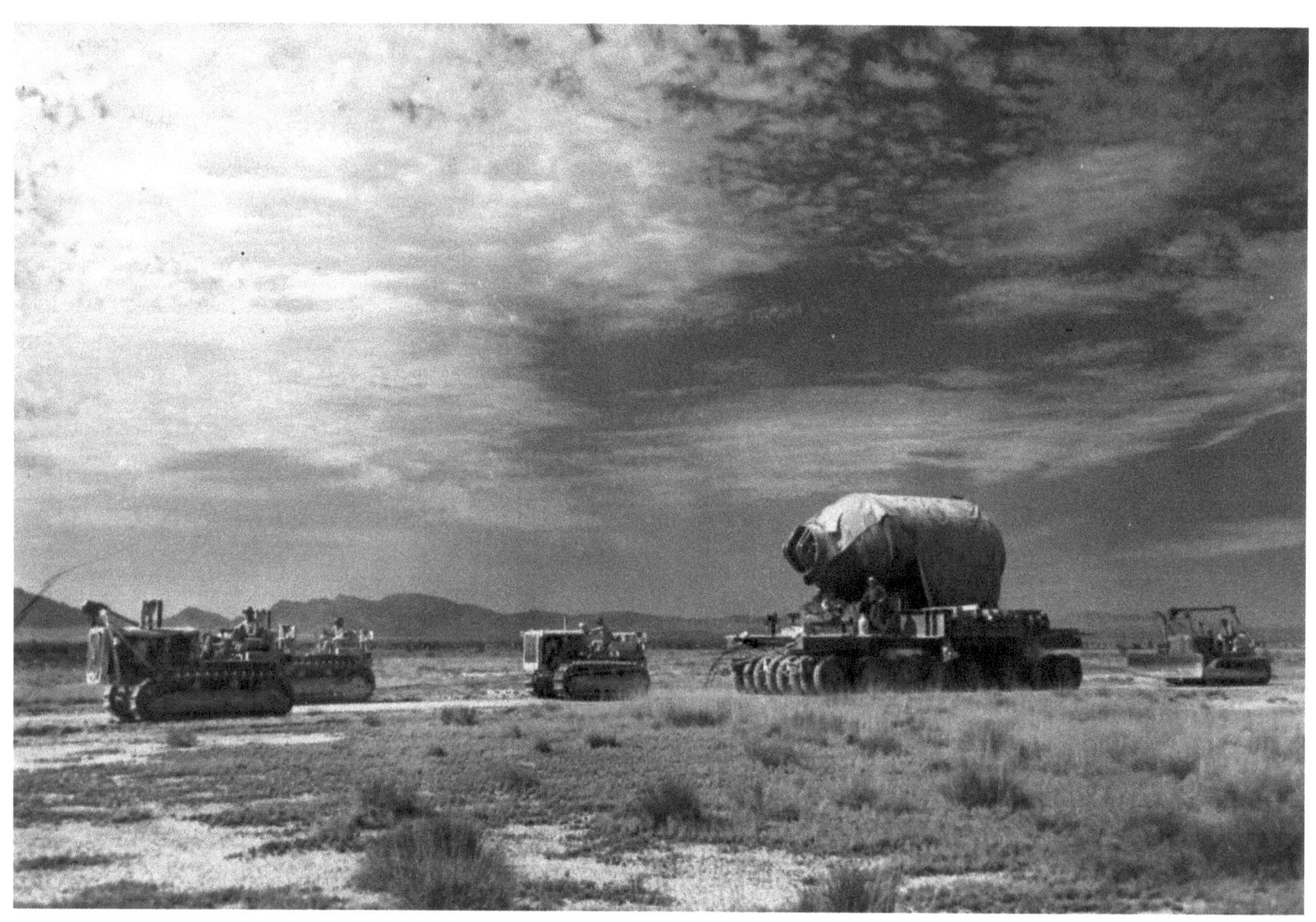

This 214-ton container called "Jumbo" was delivered at a railroad siding and is on a 64-wheeled trailer being towed to the Trinity test site. It was intended to house the bomb in the event the explosion fizzled, so that the highly valuable plutonium, if released, could be recaptured. As the supplies of plutonium increased and calculations showed that chances of success were increasing, it was decided not to use Jumbo.

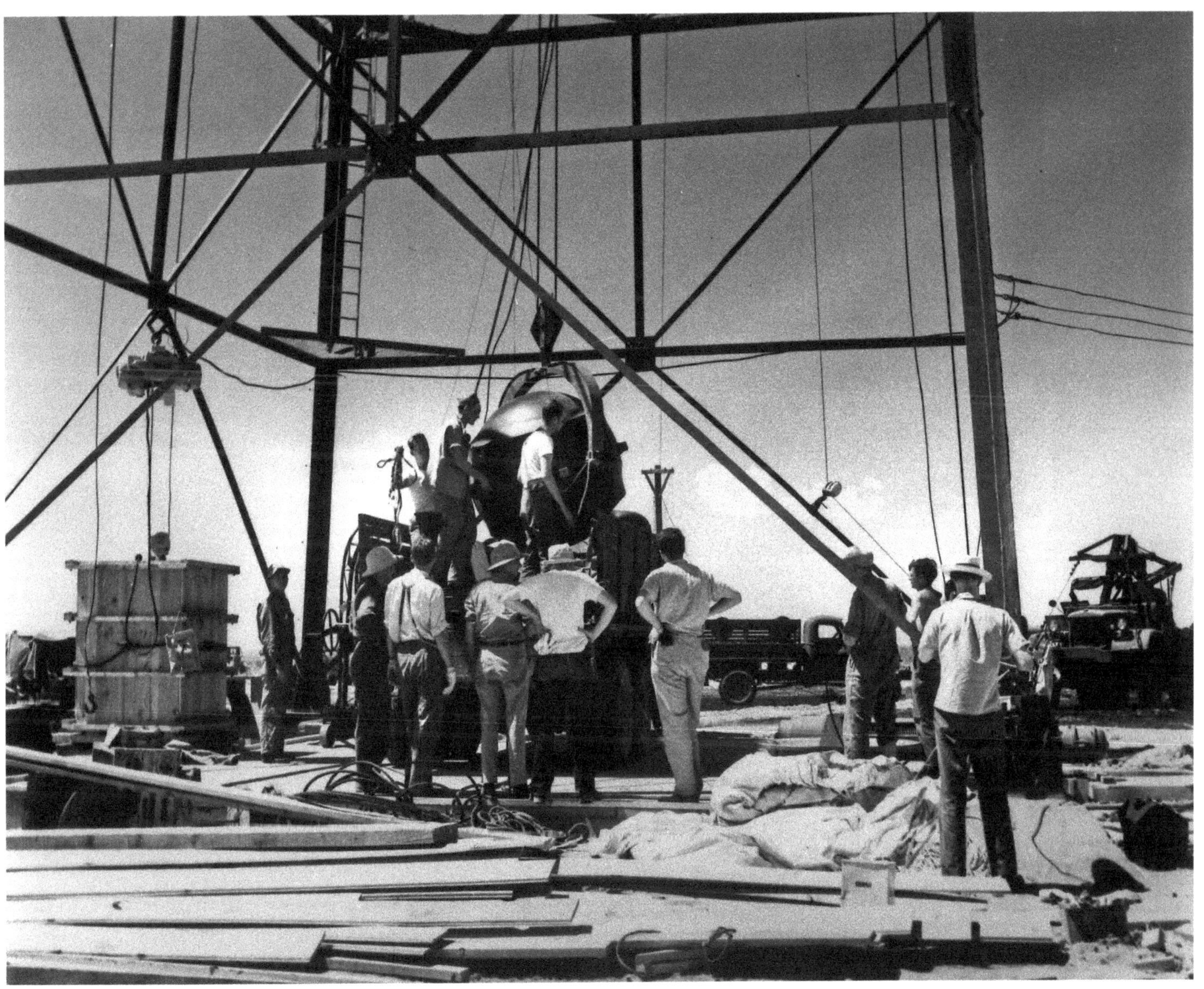

The first test device looked like some weird gadget, the genesis of the name "the Gadget," when final assembly was completed inside the tower shed. In this view, a group of scientists at the base of the Trinity tower at ground zero prepare to hoist the Gadget into position. The explosive component of the device rested inside the sphere, which was to be raised to the top of the tower, wired, and detonated.

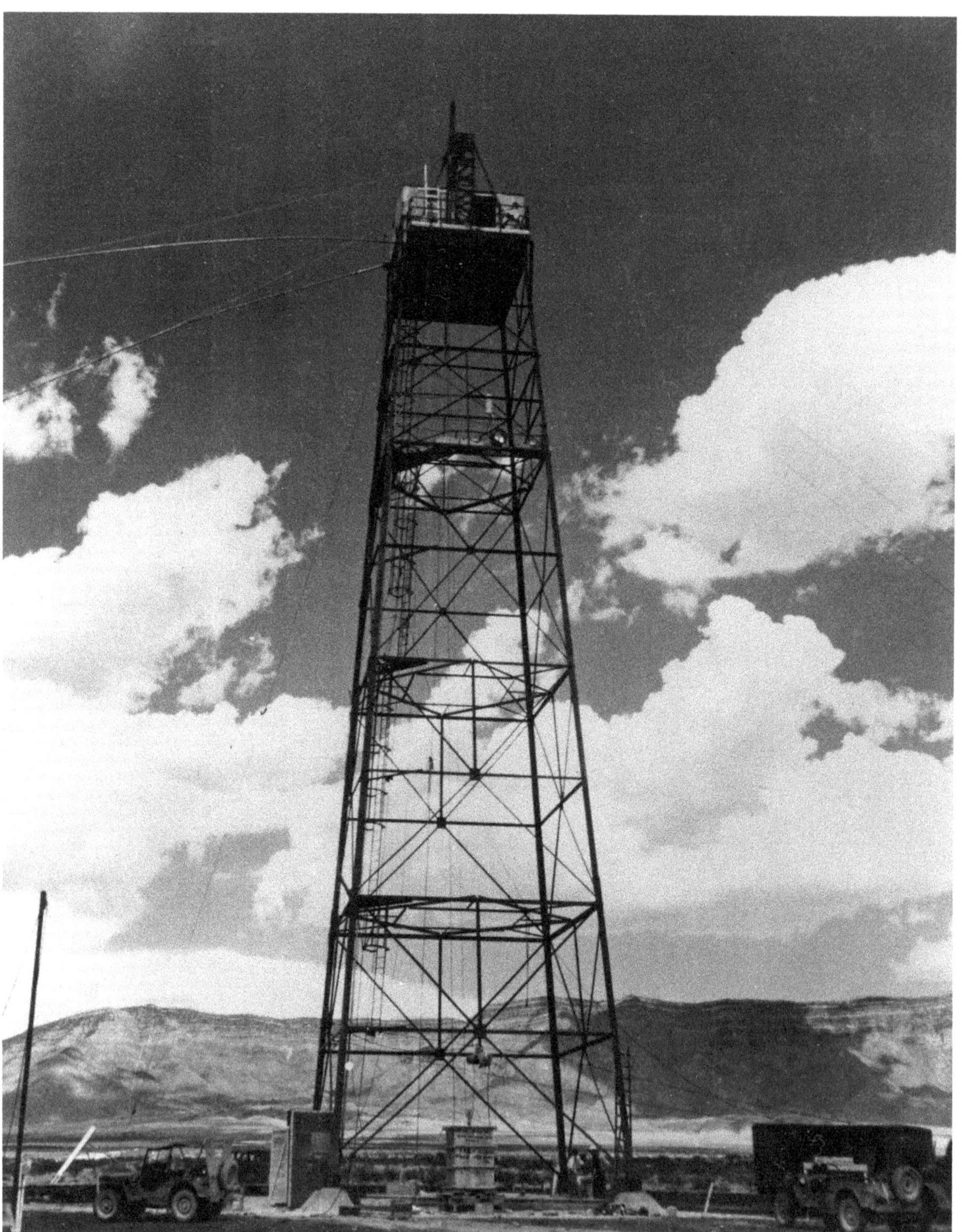

The Gadget sits inside the steel shed at the top of this tower at the Trinity test site, awaiting detonation in July 1945.

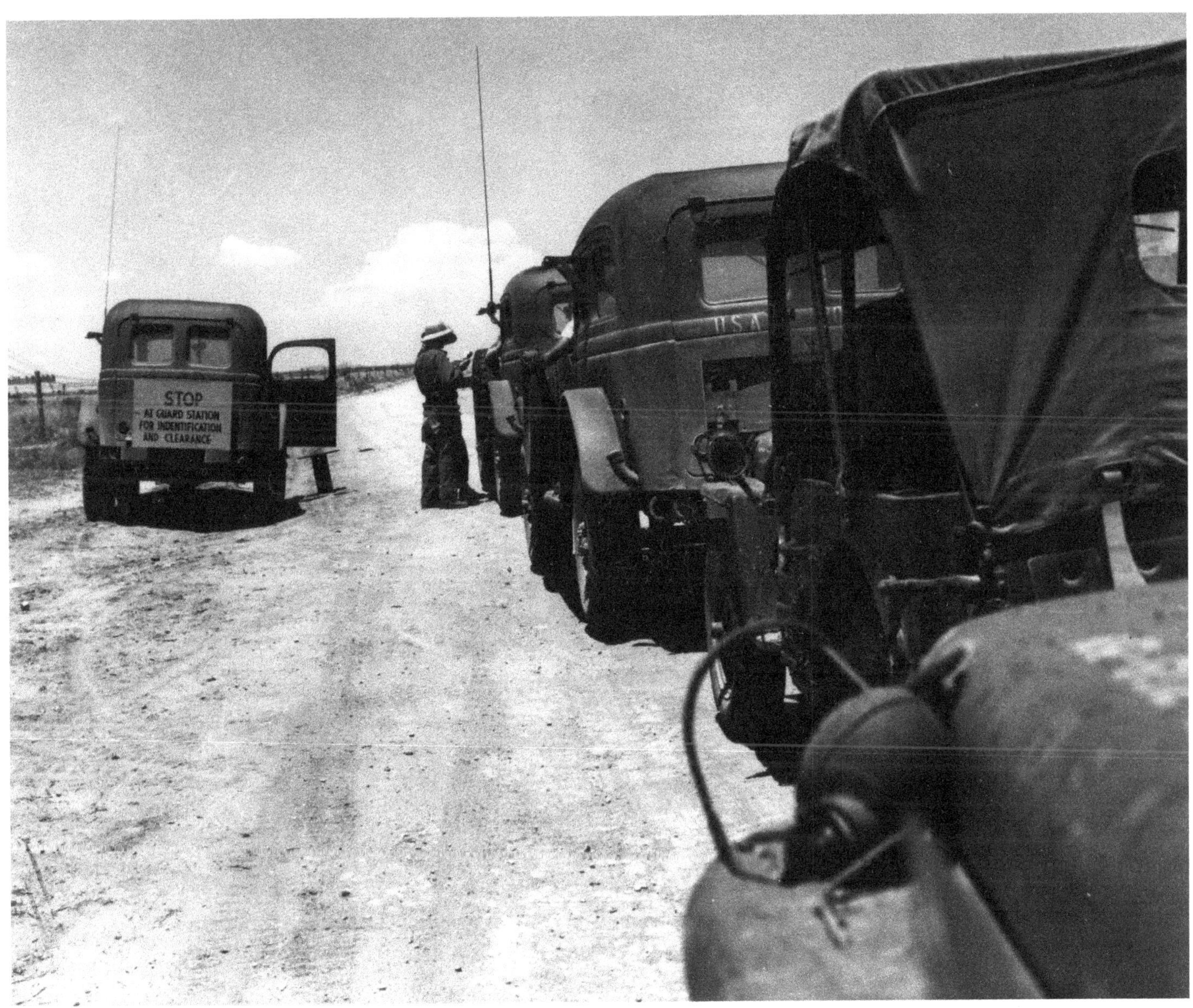

This makeshift security checkpoint in the middle of the desert was set up to inspect all vehicles and personnel prior to entering the Trinity test site each time a test was performed.

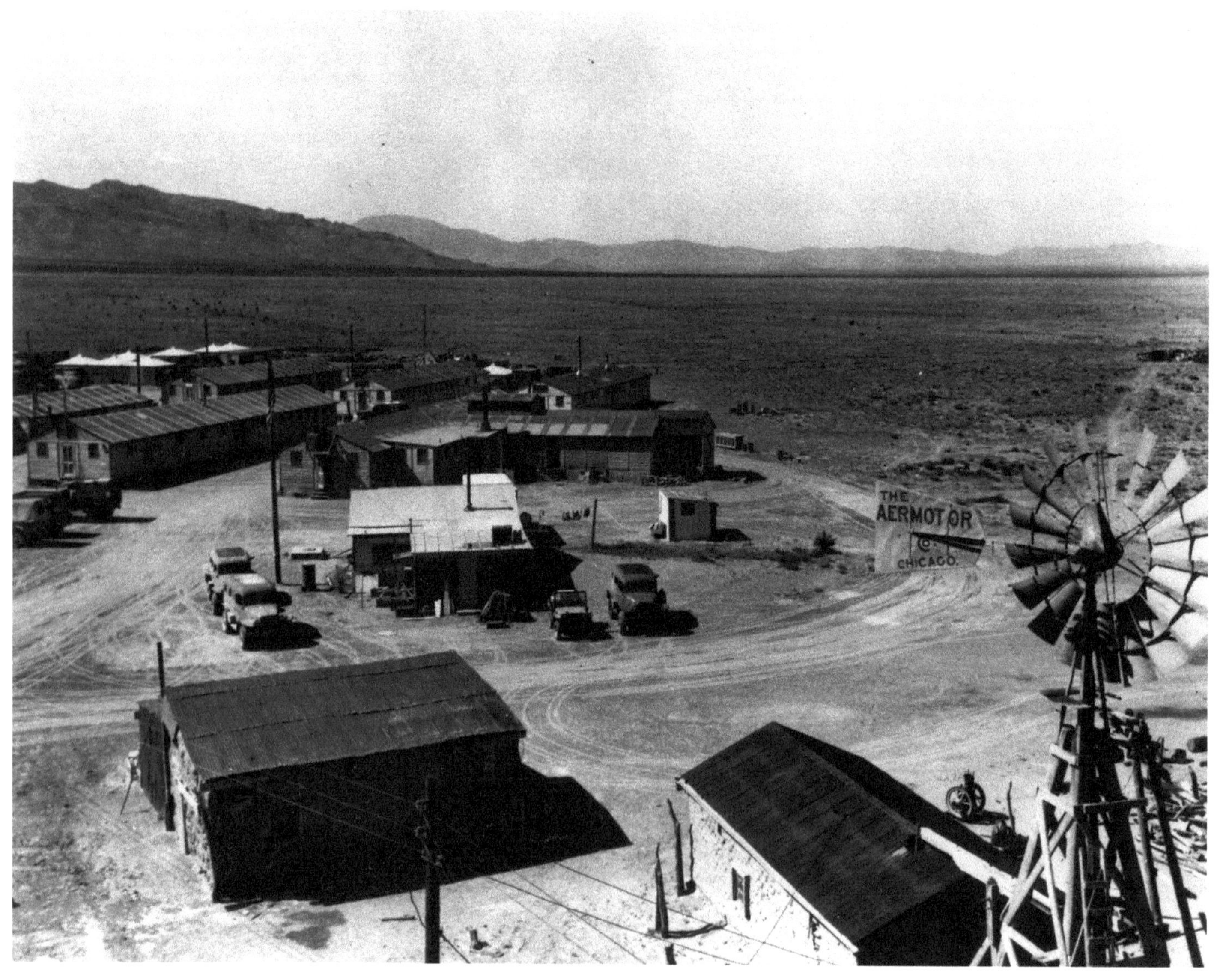

This is the Trinity test site base camp at Alamogordo, New Mexico. The desolate desert expanse had been chosen as the ideal testing area.

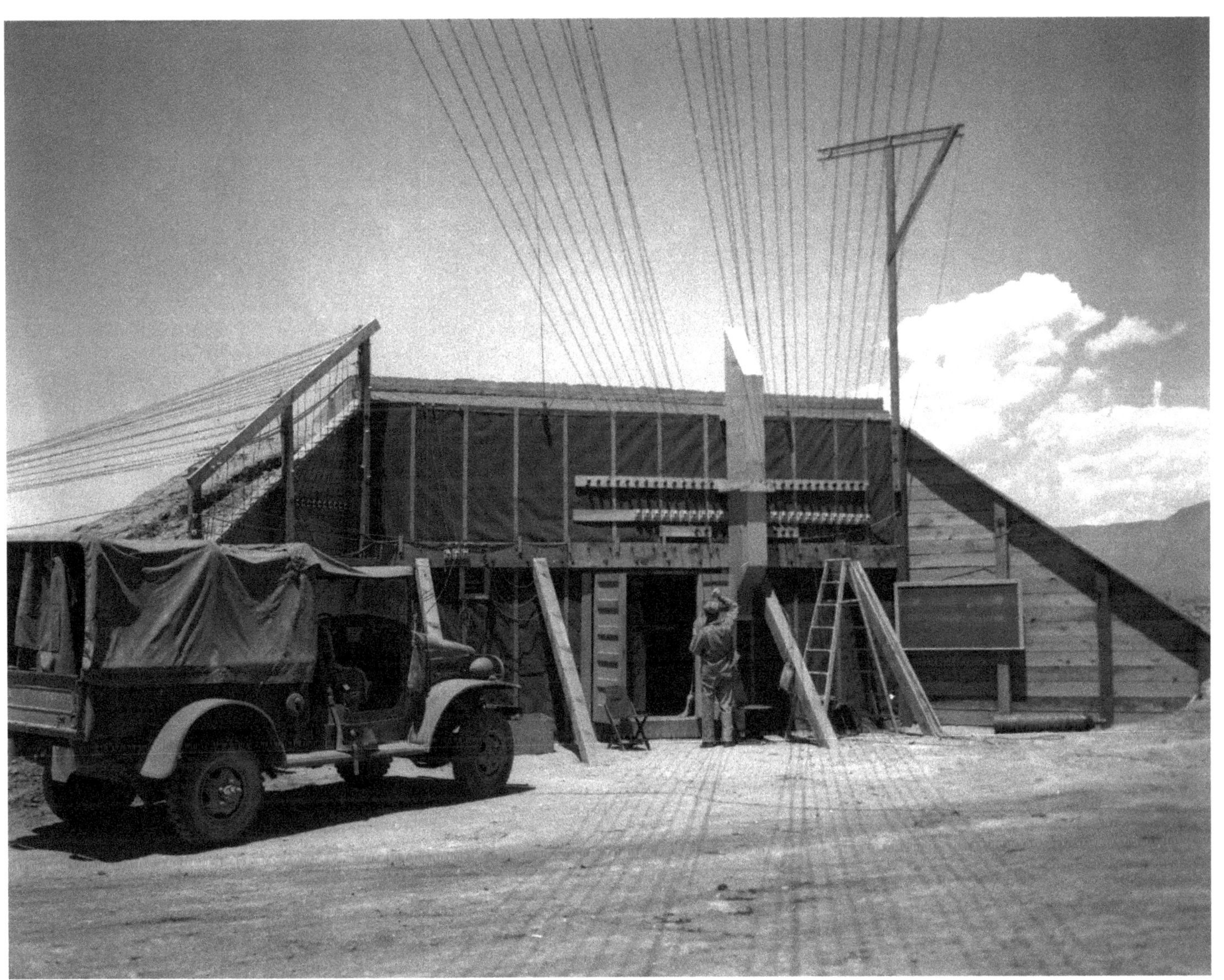

There were three observation bunkers located 10,000 yards (more than 5.5 miles) north, west, and south of ground zero built to determine the symmetry of the blast and to estimate the amount of energy it would release. The one in view here was called the S-10,000 Control Shelter and served as the main control point. Robert Oppenheimer, Kenneth Bainbridge, General Farrell, and others would witness the first Trinity test from inside this bunker.

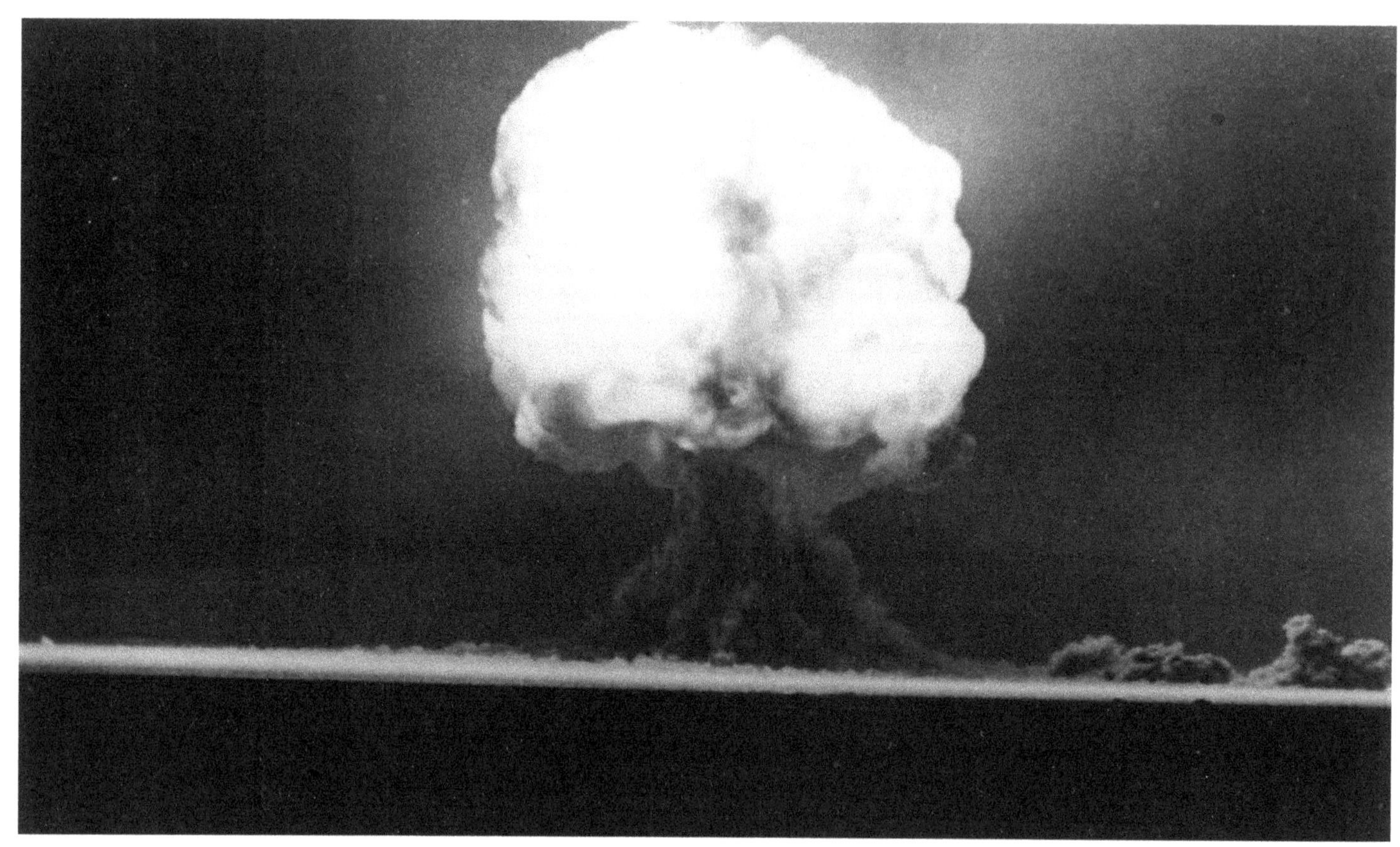

The world's first atomic device was detonated at 05:29:45 on July 16, 1945, confirming that the atomic age, ushered in by the chain reaction at CP-1, was under way. In a quarter of a second an enormous ball of pure energy was unleashed, equivalent to 20,000 tons of TNT. It was felt 100 miles away and the mushroom cloud it created rose to a height of 7.5 miles. John Lugo flying a Navy transport 30 miles away at 10,000 feet said he thought the sun was coming up in the south—the ball of fire was so bright it lit up the cockpit. He radioed Albuquerque, received no explanation, and was told, "Don't fly south." This photo was taken 15 seconds after detonation. The fireball was immense, and the shock wave moving across the desert floor is visible. When asked about what he had created, Dr. Oppenheimer wiped a tear from his eye and quoted a passage from Hinduism's Bhagavad Gita: "I am become death the destroyer of worlds." He then said, "I suppose we all thought that."

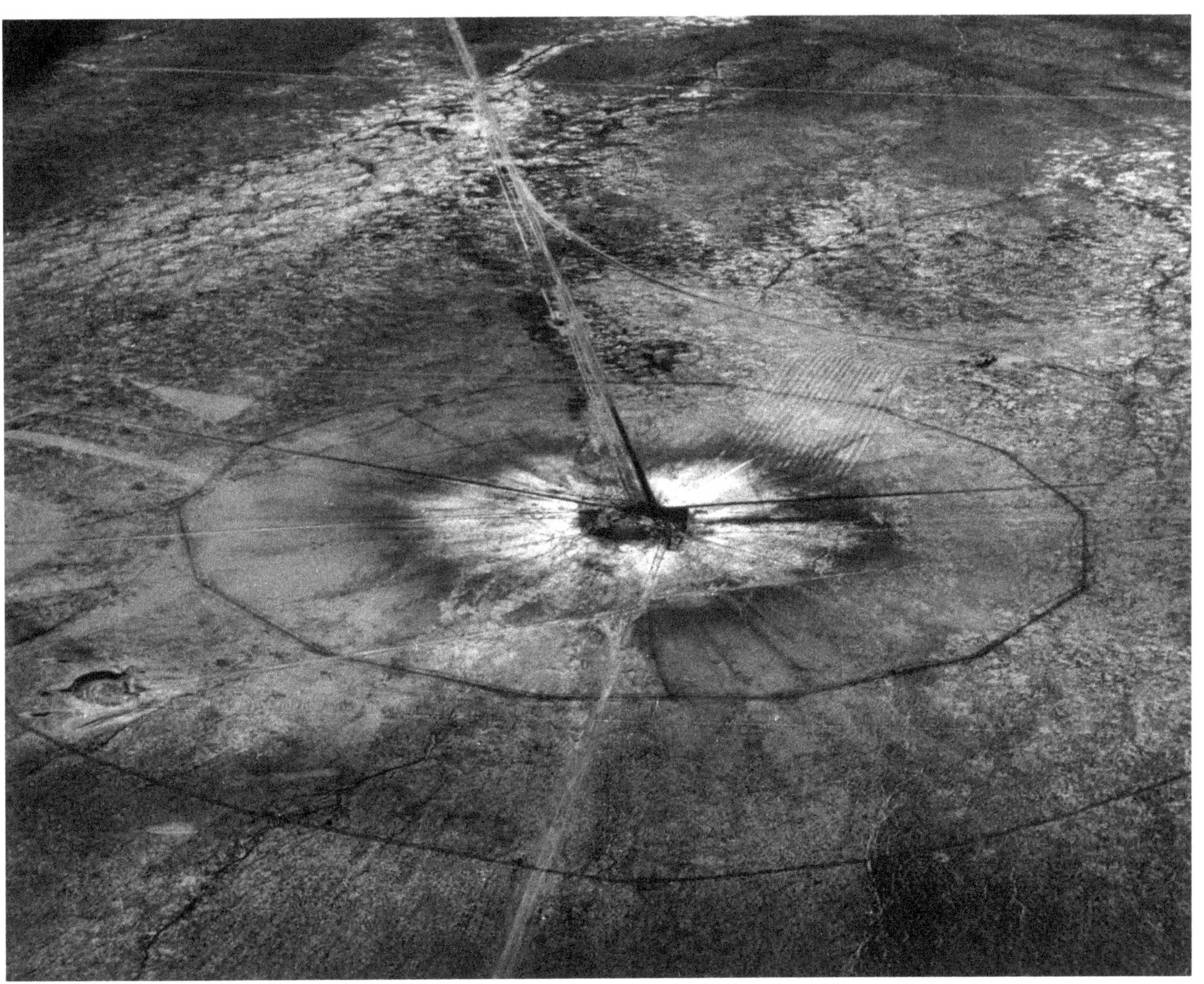

This is ground zero following detonation of the Gadget on top of the tower, leaving a crater of radioactive glass 10 feet deep and 1,100 feet wide. In a bid to keep the bomb a secret, a press release stated, "A remotely located ammunitions magazine containing a considerable amount of high explosives and pyrotechnics exploded, there was no loss of life or limb to anyone." What had actually taken place remained unreported until after the Hiroshima bomb was dropped in August.

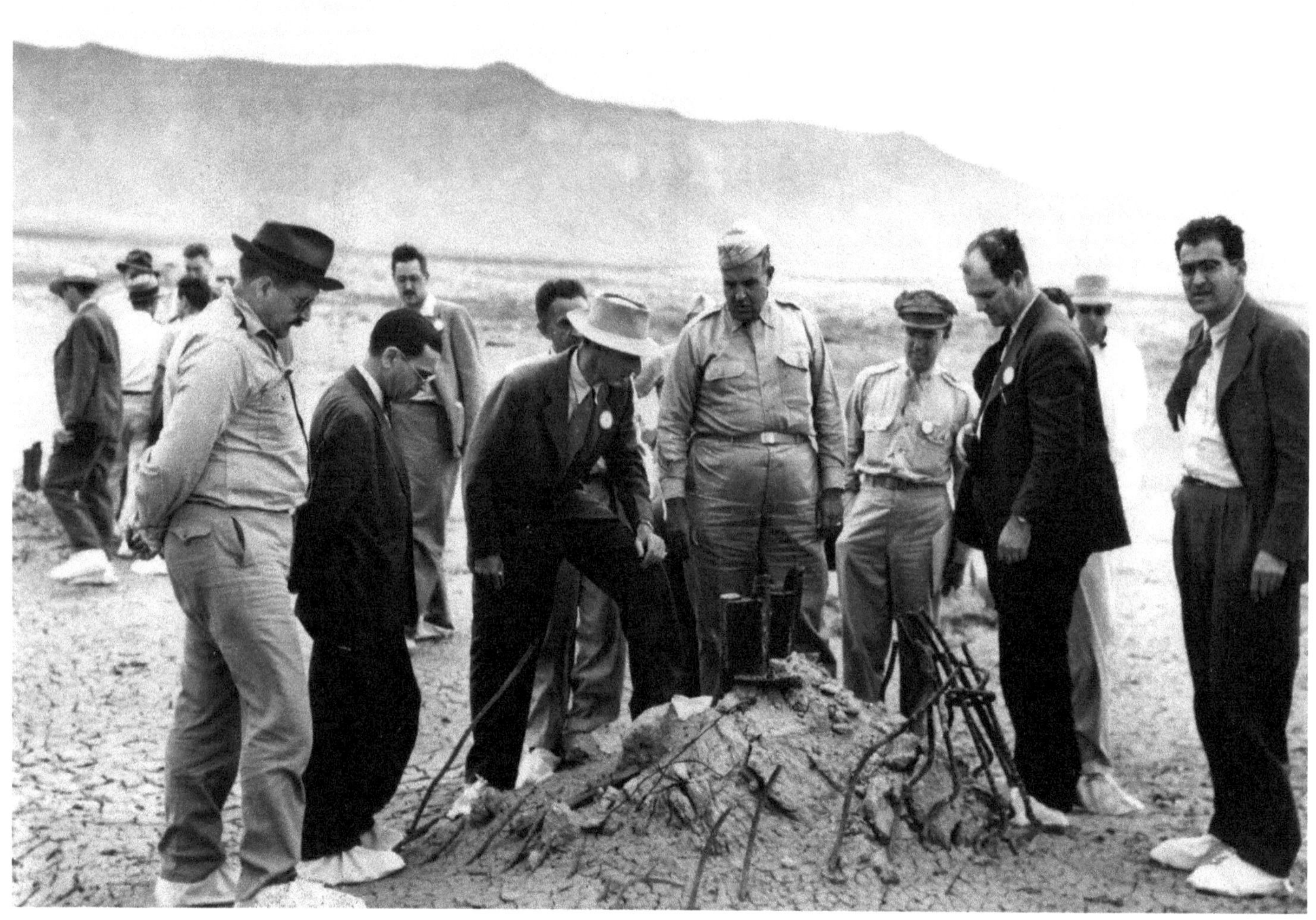

When the Gadget was detonated, the steel tower holding it was instantly vaporized. Weeks after the blast, General Groves (at center), Dr. Oppenheimer (to Groves' right wearing the light-colored hat), and other scientists and military officials examine the only fragment of the tower to weather the detonation. Everyone is wearing protective shoe coverings called booties to keep radioactive contamination off shoes.

The Sadness of Warfare—The Celebration of Peace

A Dichotomy of Evil and Good

When the United States was tragically pulled into World War II with the bombing of Pearl Harbor by the Japanese, all of America rallied around a single goal—to do anything necessary to end the war and bring our soldiers home. The killing of hundreds of thousands of military and civilians around the world drove home the need to bring to bear a threat that could not be ignored. Culmination of the immense effort of the Manhattan Project made that threat a reality—two bombs that would change the course of world history.

On August 6, 1945, at 2:45 A.M., a B-29 bomber piloted by Colonel Paul Tibbets and named after his mother, Enola Gay, rolled down the runway on Tinian Island and headed toward Japan. During the flight, Captain William Parsons completed final assembly in the bomb bay by arming the 9,700-pound uranium bomb "Little Boy." It was released at an altitude of 31,060 feet, fell for 43 seconds, and detonated 1,900 feet above Hiroshima at 08:16:02. Everything within a circle of two miles diameter was instantly vaporized and vanished. Seconds later 90 percent of Hiroshima's buildings were completely destroyed, severely damaged, or on fire.

Shortly after the bombing President Truman announced, "If they do not now accept our terms, they may expect a rain of ruin from the air the like of which has never been seen on this earth." On August 8, 1945, millions of leaflets were dropped over major Japanese cities warning of future atomic bomb attacks if surrender did not come, and warnings were given by Radio Saipan. Surrender did not come.

At 3:47 A.M. on August 9, 1945, Major General Charles W. Sweeney lifted off Tinian in the B-29 later named *Bockscar* with the plutonium bomb "Fat Man" in its belly, and headed for Kokura, Japan. Cloud cover obscured the city, and after three runs and fuel running low owing to a faulty mechanical pump, the crew headed to Nagasaki. It too was clouded in, but at 11:01 bombardier Captain Kermit Beahan saw the target through a break in the clouds and released Fat Man. Forty-seven seconds later at about 1,650 feet, the plutonium device detonated and imploded, creating an immense explosion with a temperature estimated at 7,000 degrees, winds of 625 M.P.H., and a force of 21 kilotons of TNT.

Another bomb was being assembled and three more were to be completed by September, and another three in October. Leslie Groves told General George C. Marshall, Chief of Staff, that the next bomb would be ready after August 17.

The Emperor of Japan, Hirohito, delivered his capitulation announcement to the people of Japan on August 15, stating in a recorded message: "The enemy now possesses a new and terrible weapon with the power to destroy many innocent lives and do incalculable damage. Should we continue to fight, not only would it result in an ultimate collapse and obliteration of the Japanese nation, but also it would lead to the total extinction of human civilization. Such being the case, how are we to save the millions of our subjects, or to atone ourselves before the hallowed spirits of our imperial ancestors? This is the reason why we have ordered the acceptance of the provisions of the Joint Declaration of the Powers." Those words clearly credited the surrender of Japan and the end of the war to the products of the Manhattan Project.

Victory over Japan, V-J Day, was official, yet some Japanese soldiers committed suicide and more than a hundred American as well as many Australian and British prisoners of war were tragically executed by the Imperial Japanese Army, angry at their emperor's surrender.

When newspapers hit the streets in the United States, the entire country erupted in celebration. Especially proud were the thousands of men and women of the Manhattan Project who, each in his own way, had made peace a reality. They understood that their efforts and contribution had brought the war to its final end, and no pride could be stronger or more deserved.

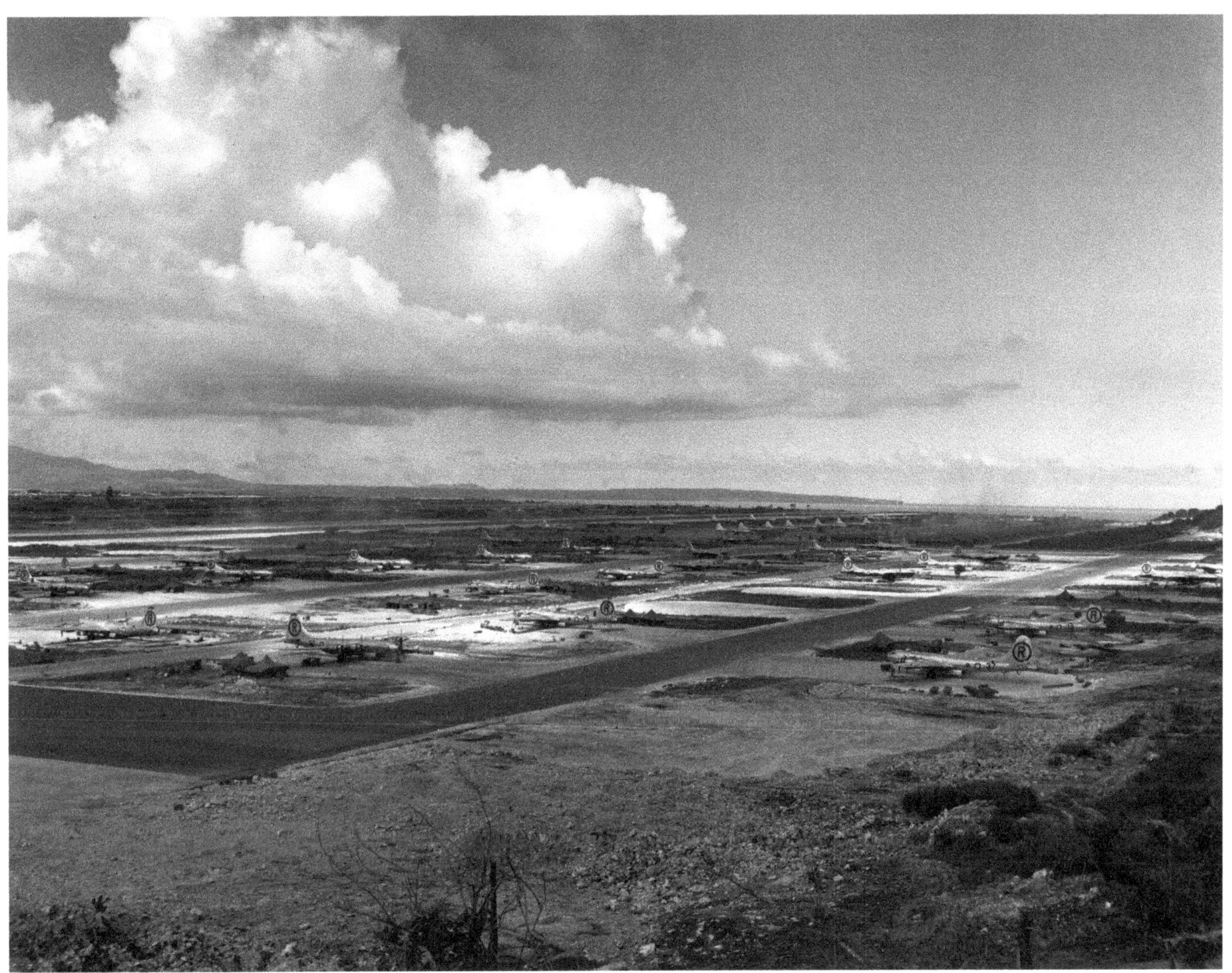

After 13 days of naval bombardment, U.S. Marines assaulted and captured Tinian Island from the Japanese on July 24, 1944. More than 5,000 Japanese were killed and 328 Marines lost their lives. Tinian had three good airfields and eleven miles of taxiways. The unarmed atomic bombs were flown here, where final assembly took place. The trigger assembly was not completed until *Enola Gay* and *Bockscar* reached the correct altitude during the bombing missions.

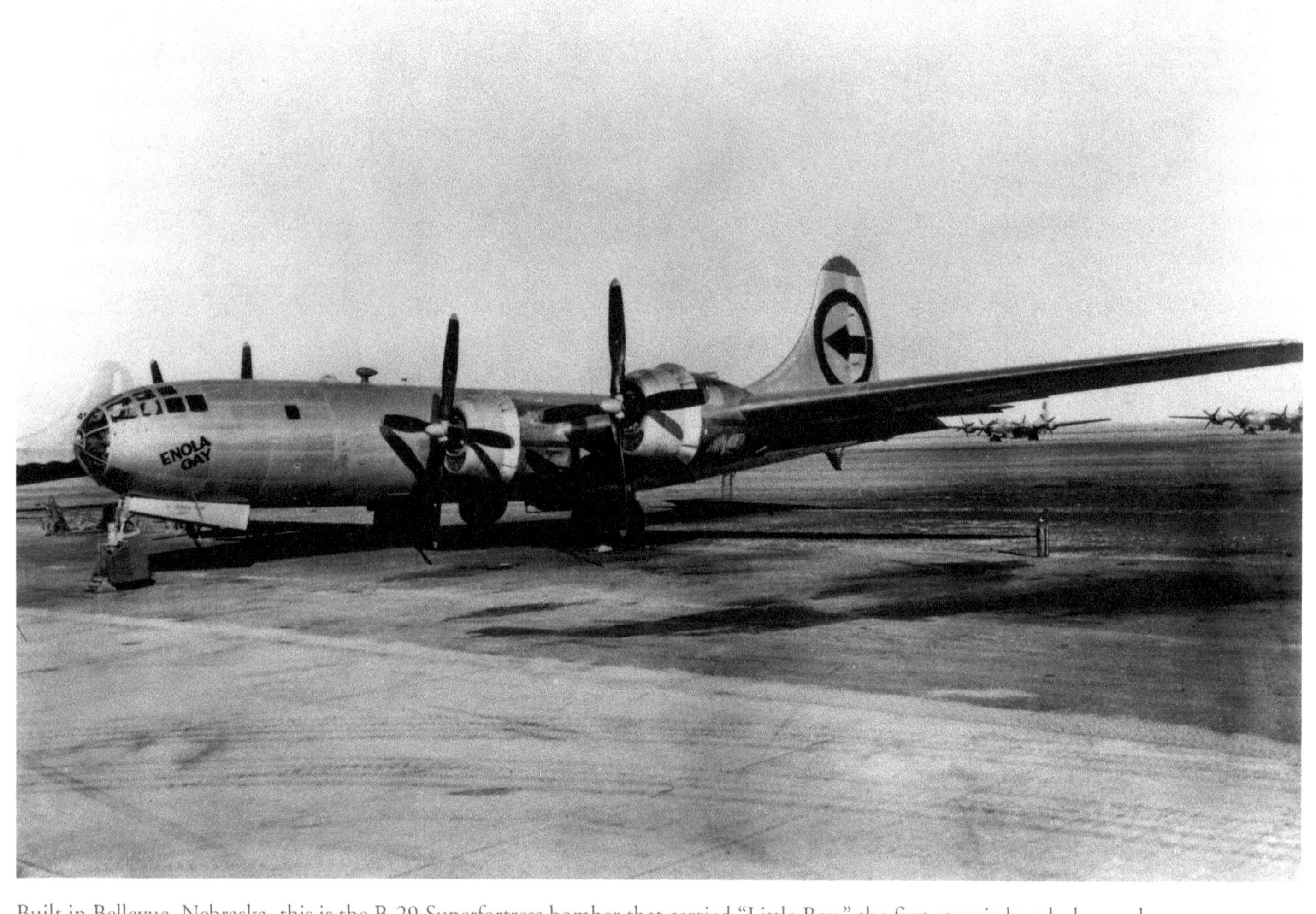

Built in Bellevue, Nebraska, this is the B-29 Superfortress bomber that carried "Little Boy," the first atomic bomb dropped on Japan. Colonel Paul W. Tibbets, Jr., the pilot, named the plane *Enola Gay* after his mother. It was accompanied by two other B-29s, *Necessary Evil,* used as a camera plane to photograph the explosion, and *The Great Artiste,* which was outfitted with instrumentation to measure the blast.

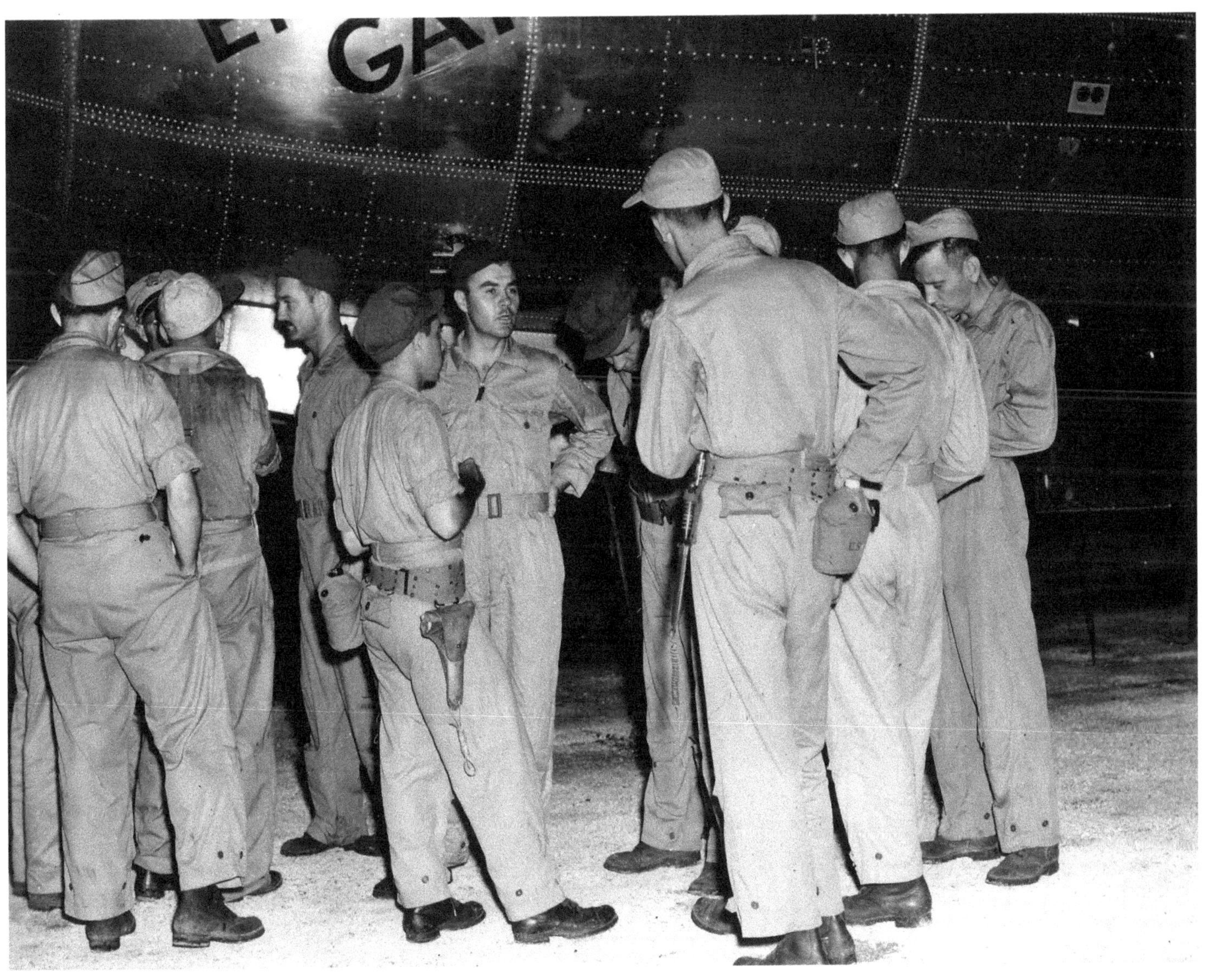

On August 6, 1945, the crew of the *Enola Gay* receives last-minute instructions from Colonel Tibbets just before lifting off Tinian Island in what was perhaps the most top-secret flight ever. The crew did not know what was ahead, not learning the specifics until the plane was in flight. Owing to fear of an accident during take-off, Little Boy was not armed until the aircraft was out over the ocean on its way to Hiroshima.

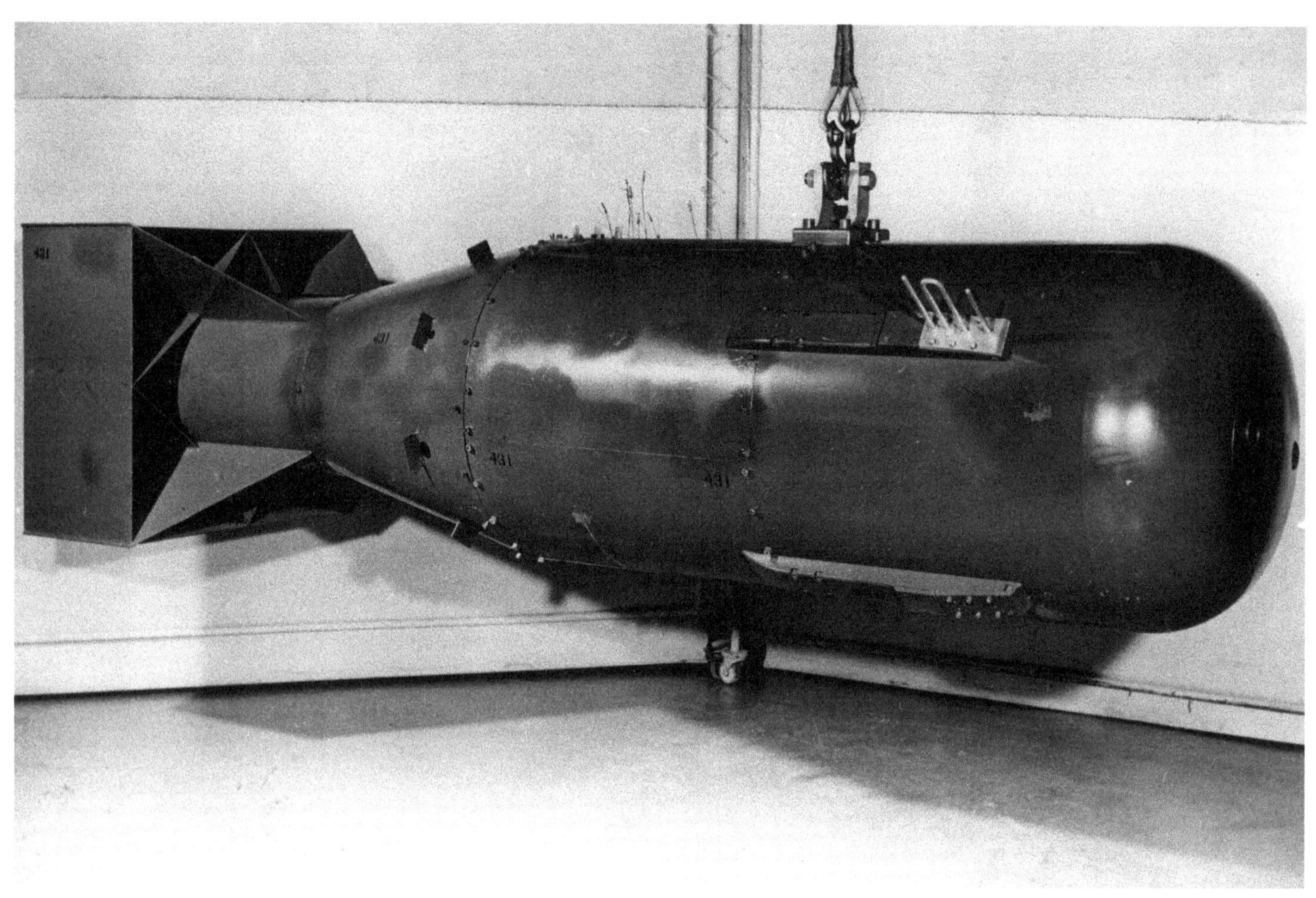

Little Boy was 10 feet long, 28 inches in diameter, and weighed 8,900 pounds. Inside was a gun barrel used to shoot a hollow subcritical mass of uranium some inches in diameter onto a smaller, solid target spike, thus creating a supercritical mass and setting off the nuclear chain reaction. The bomb's explosive force was equivalent to roughly 15,000 tons of TNT.

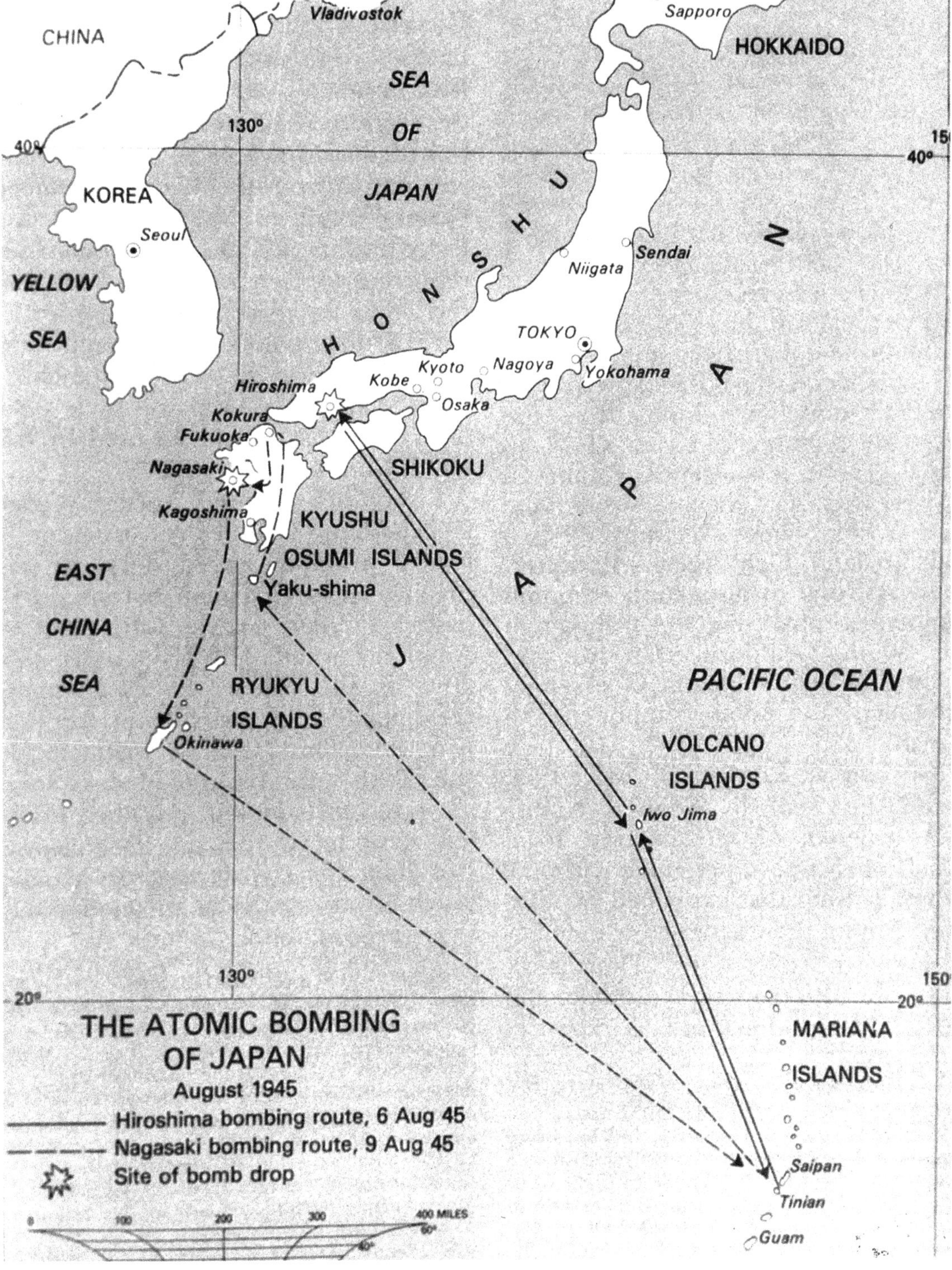

This map shows the flight paths between Tinian Island, from which the planes were deployed, and Hiroshima and Nagasaki, their destinations. The Hiroshima run went as planned. The second bombing run, planned for Kokura, did not. Because the bombing coordinates required a visual sighting and the city was shrouded by clouds, Superfortress no. 77 flew to the alternative city, Nagasaki. It too was clouded in, but at the last minute a break in the clouds permitted identification of the target.

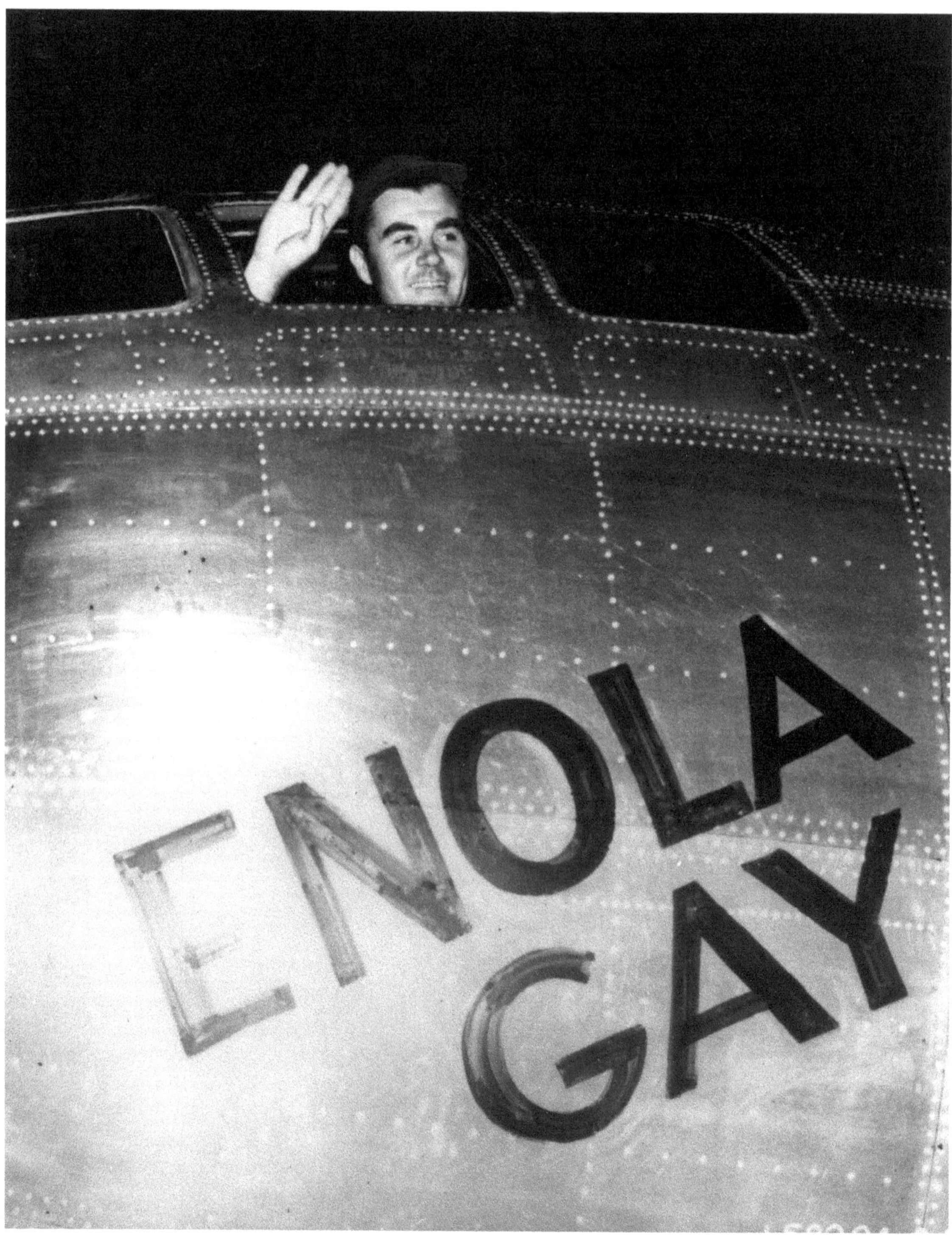

In this famous photograph taken on August 6, Colonel Tibbets gives a final wave prior to taxiing to the runway at Tinian for takeoff. During an interview after the bombing, he said he wasn't sure it had been such a good idea to use his mother's name on a plane with such a sad mission, but he never regretted the mission's objective to save lives and end the war.

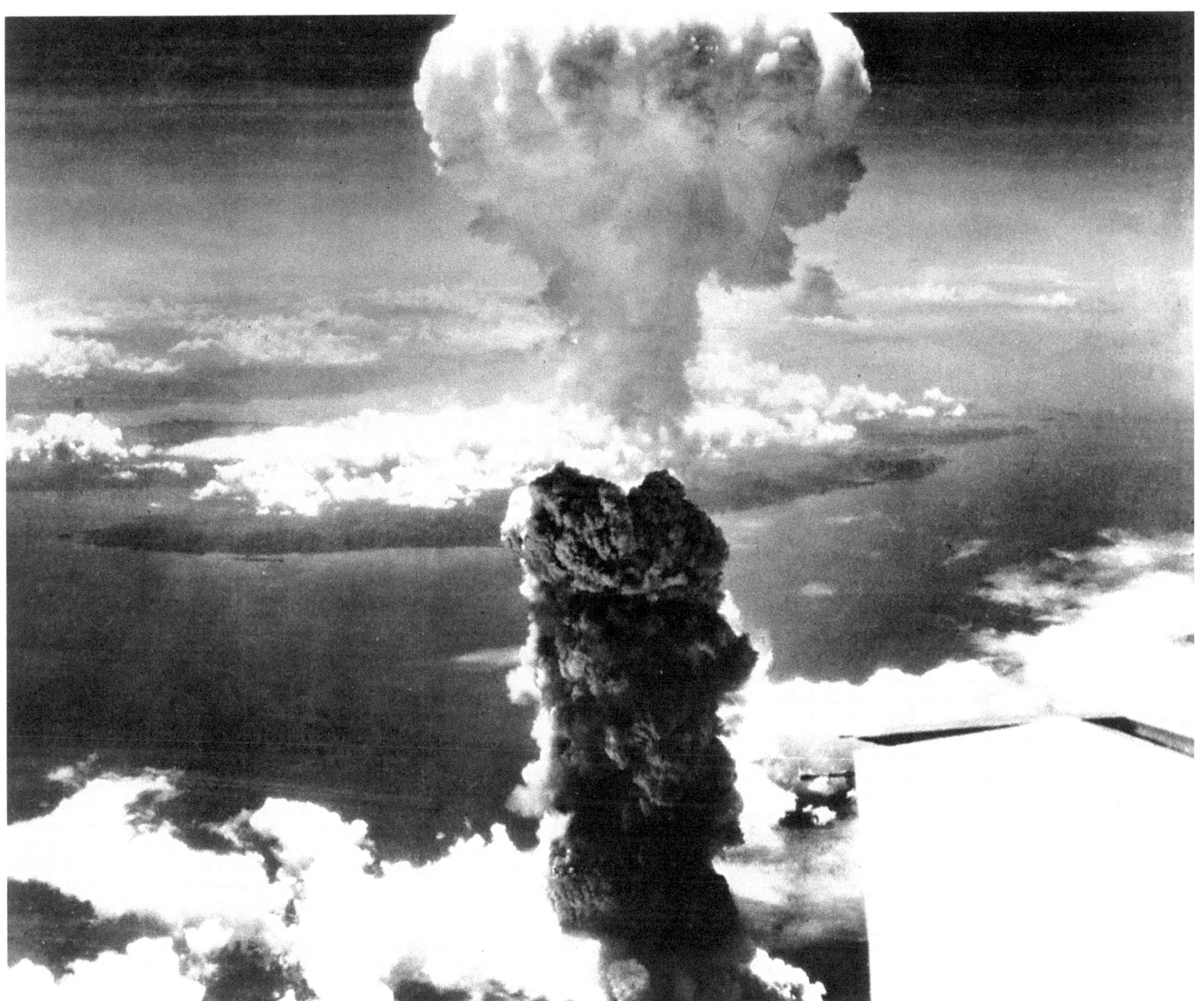

On August 6, 1945, at 8:15 A.M., Little Boy was released at 32,000 feet over Hiroshima and took 57 seconds to fall to 1,900 feet above the city, where it detonated. Everything within a circle about two miles across was completely destroyed, and fires instantly raged across nearly 4.5 square miles. It was estimated that 90 percent of Hiroshima's infrastructure was seriously damaged or completely destroyed. The planes were detected by radar but the Japanese didn't sound an air-raid siren because the number of planes was considered too small to mean much and they didn't want to waste the fuel to intercept them.

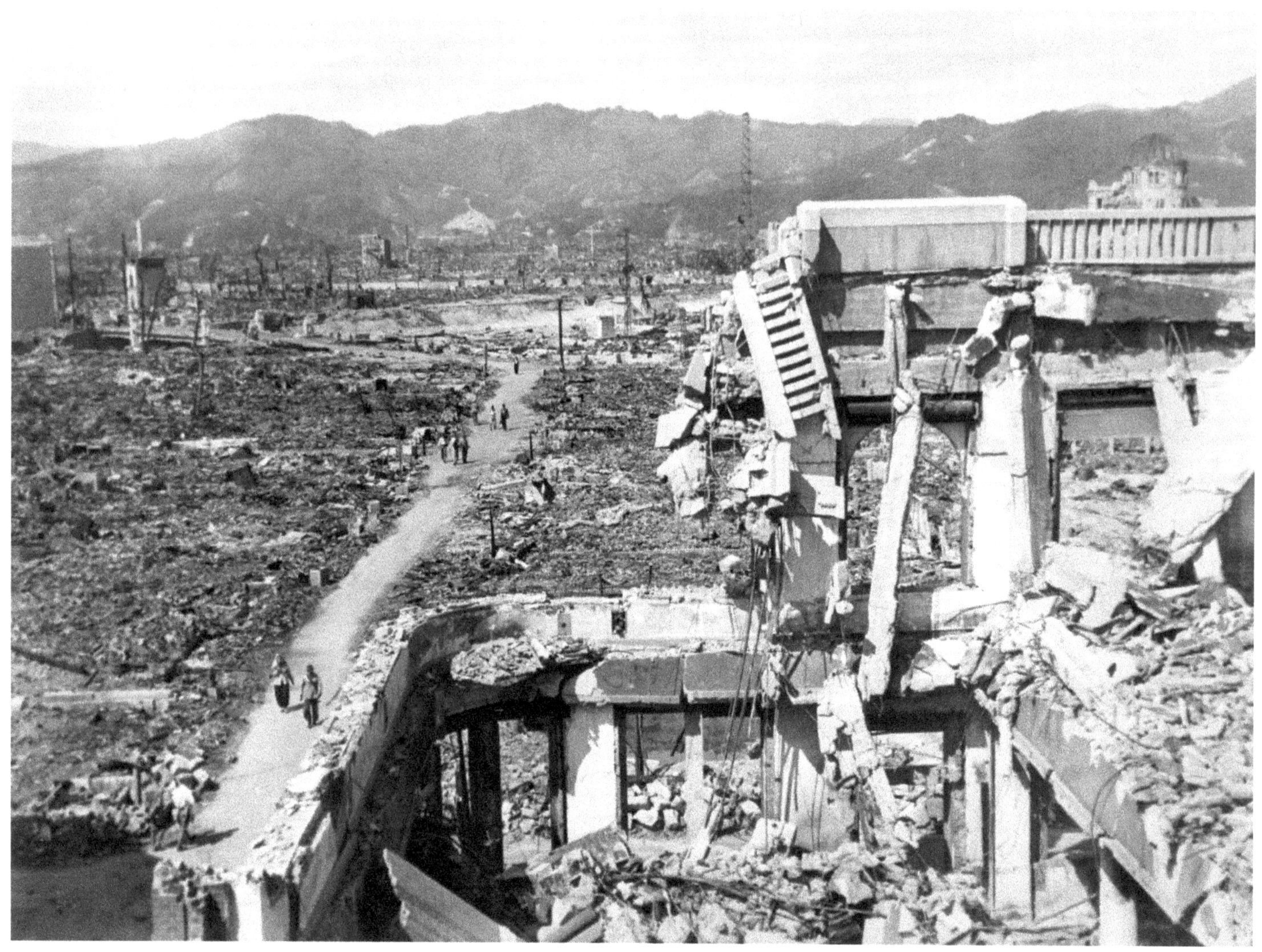

Facing west at approximately 165 yards from ground zero in Hiroshima. This view shows the collapsed portion of the Mitsui Products building facing the hypocenter. The dome of the Industrial Promotion Hall can be seen in the background. Its remains have been preserved and are currently referred to as the Hiroshima A-Bomb Dome.

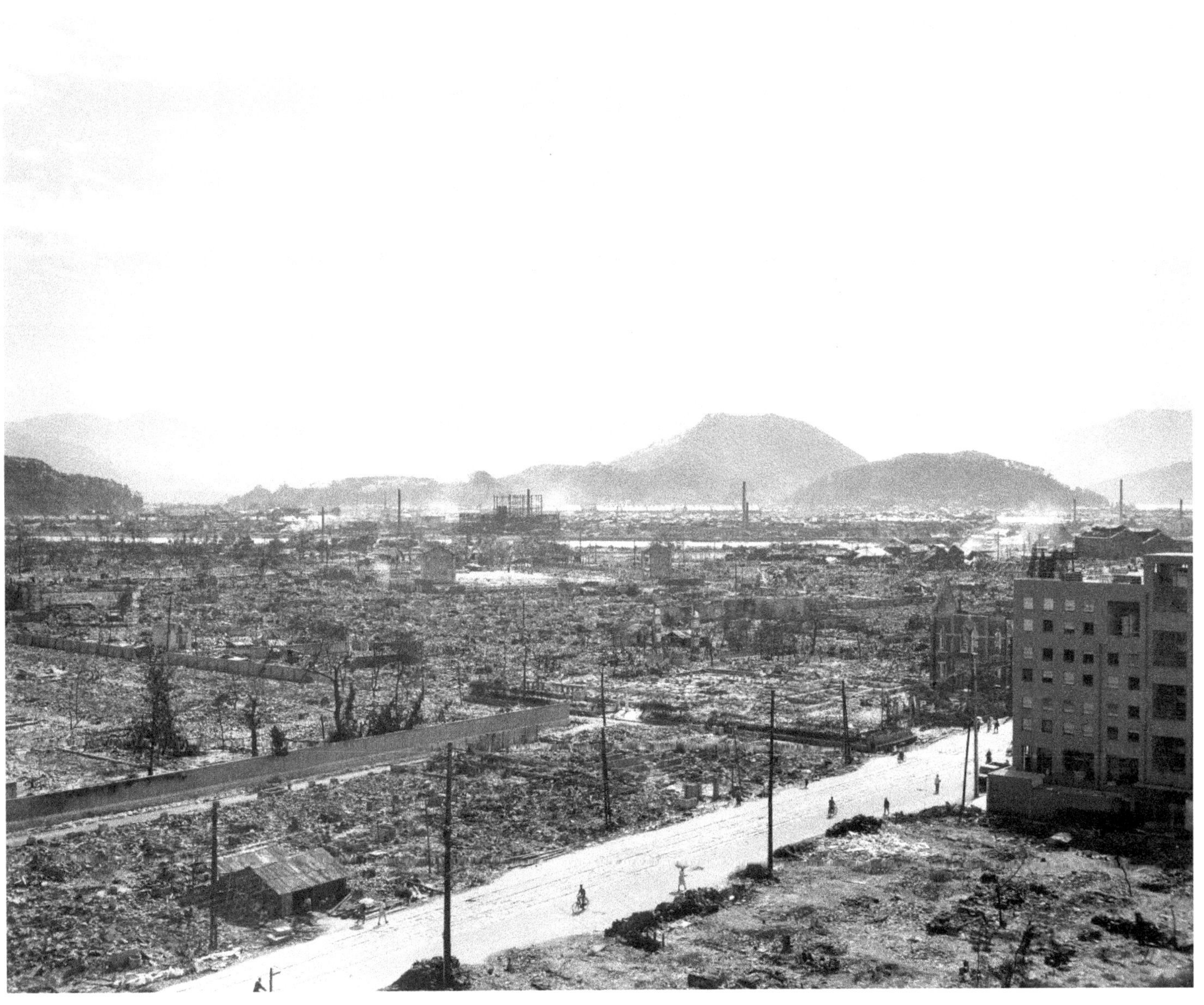

This view faces east from the Red Cross Hospital located approximately 1,650 yards south of ground zero. The masonry wall in the foreground at left was the southeast corner of Hiroshima University.

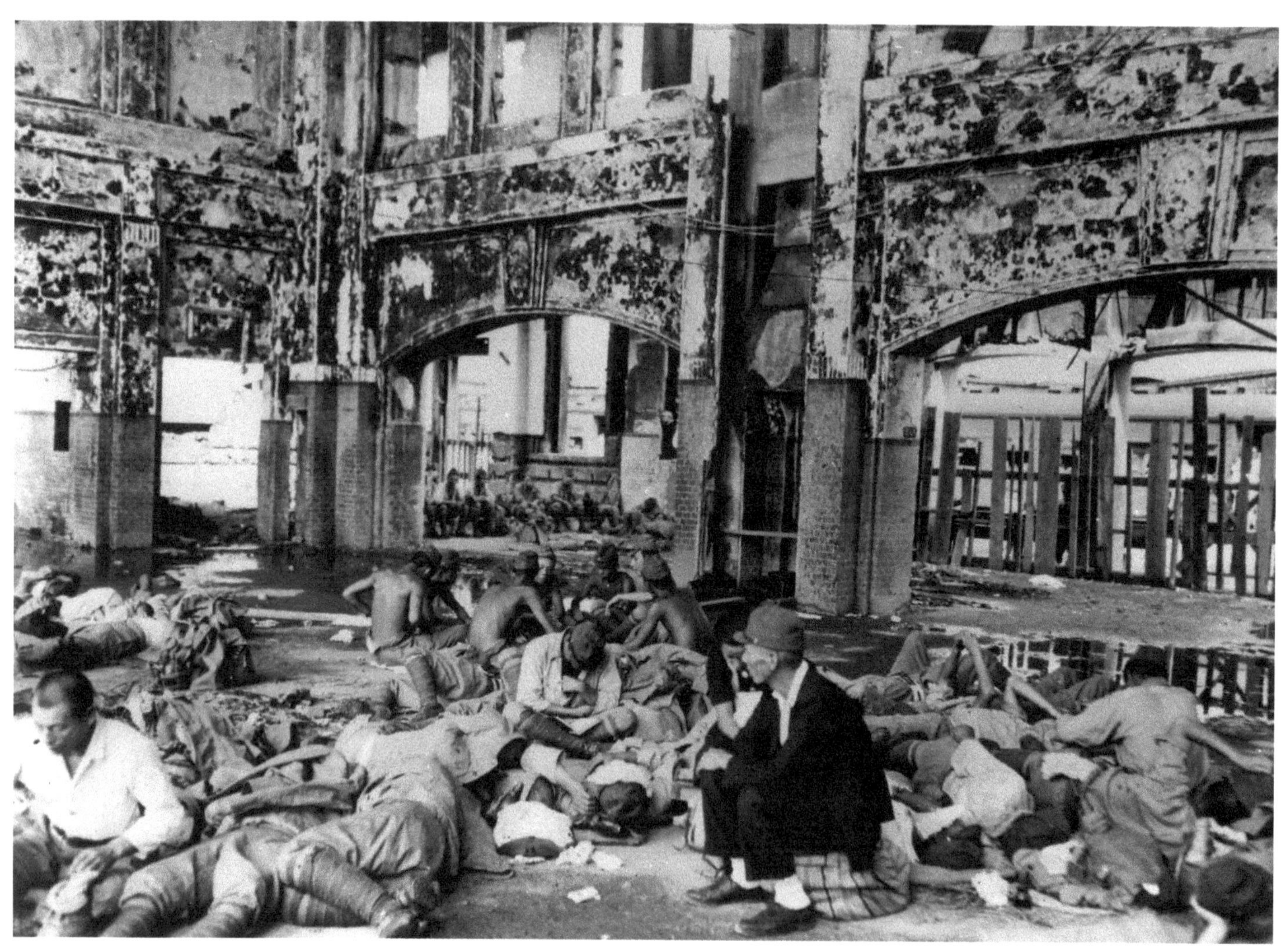

Japanese troops rest in what remains of the bombed-out railway station. Nothing was left on the inside but pitted walls, yet walls meant shelter for many.

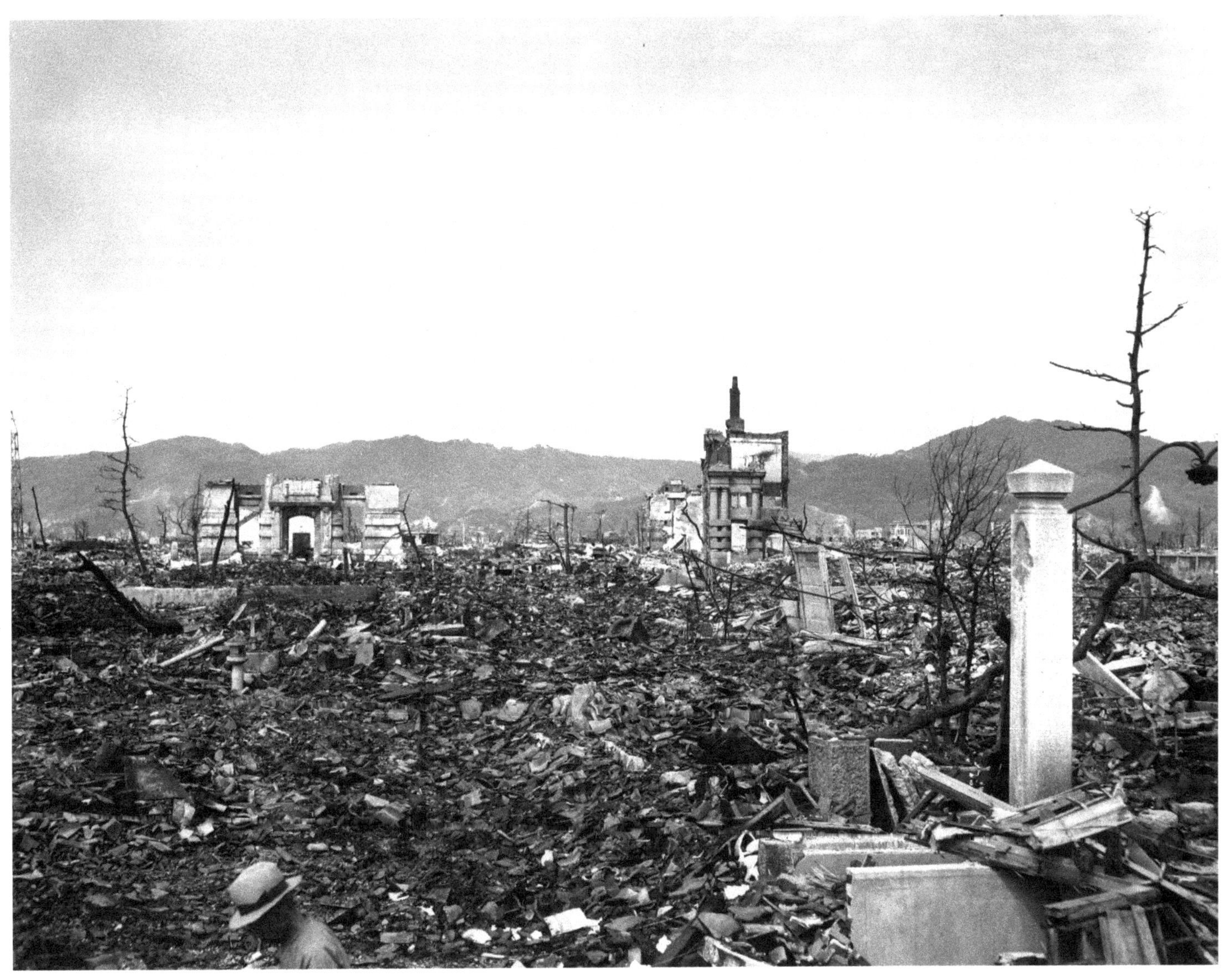

This photo looks west from a point approximately 165 yards south of ground zero. Portions of the walls of two masonry buildings remain standing. These walls ran parallel to the direction of the blast.

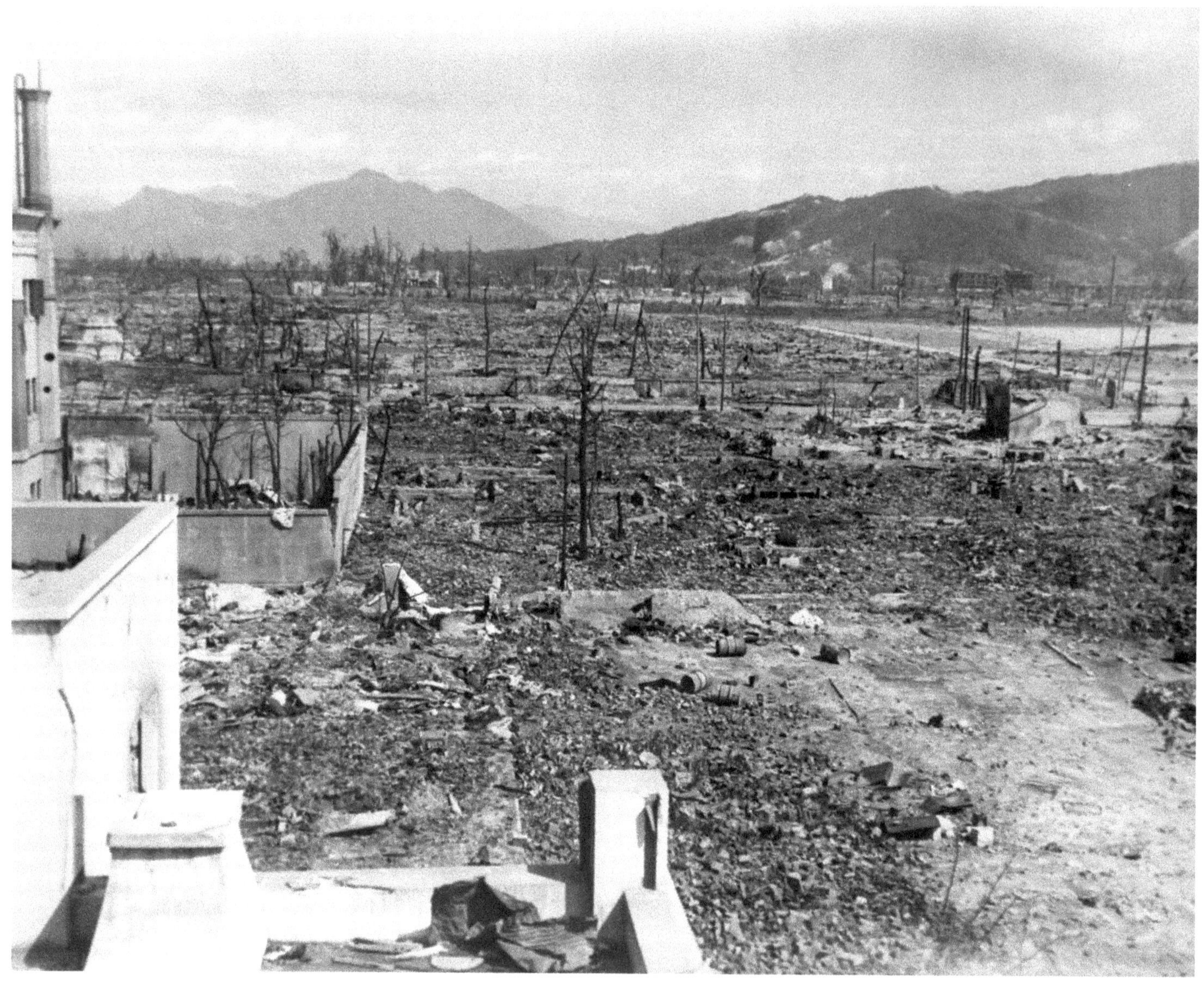

View from the roof of the Mitsui Products building at approximately 165 yards from ground zero. This view shows the military area toward the north. The building at far-left is the Chiyoda Life Insurance Company.

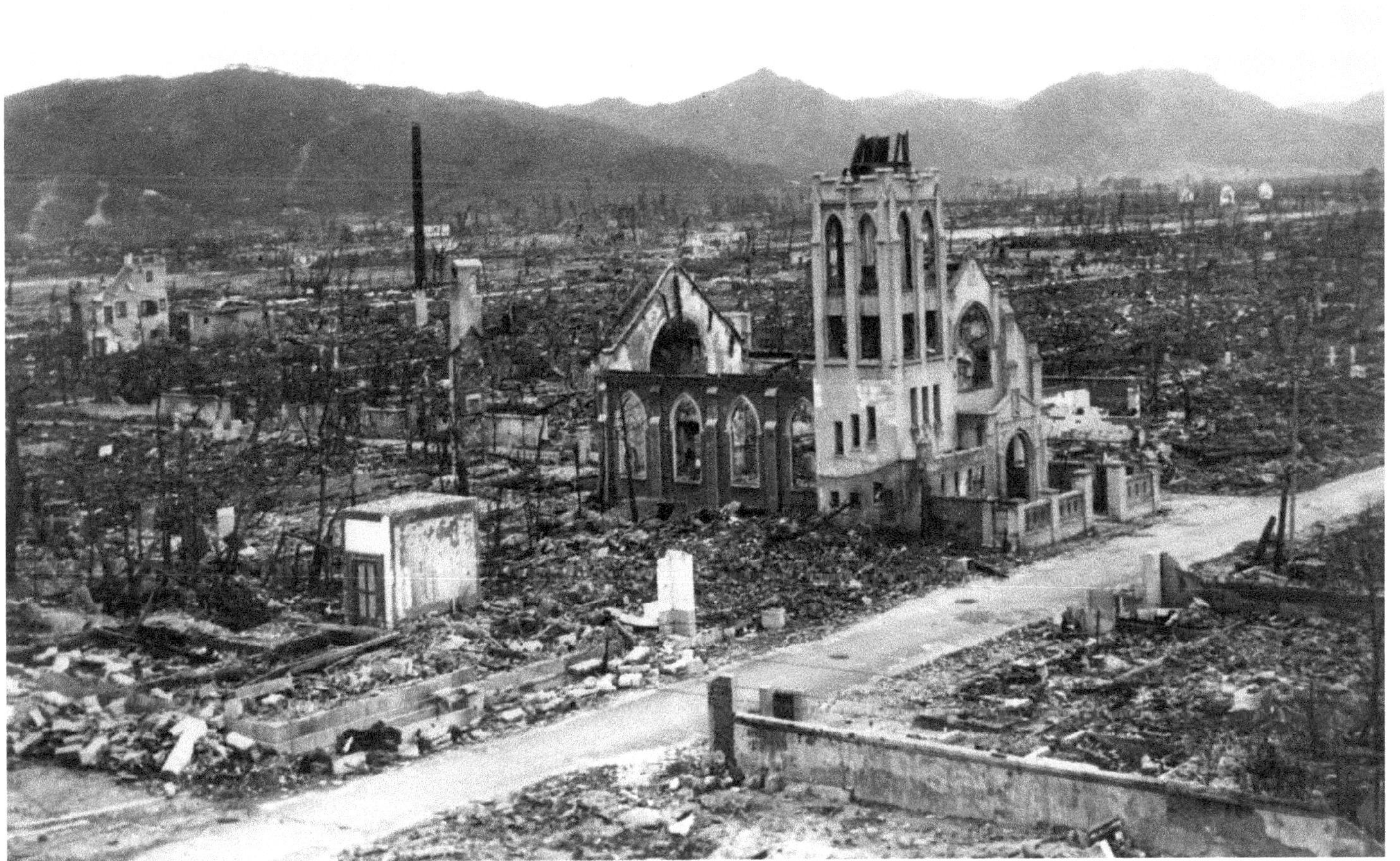

View from the Sumitoma Bank Building approximately 275 yards east of ground zero showing what remained of the Nagarekawa church and the devastation all around. The military area of Hiroshima was located at left in the background.

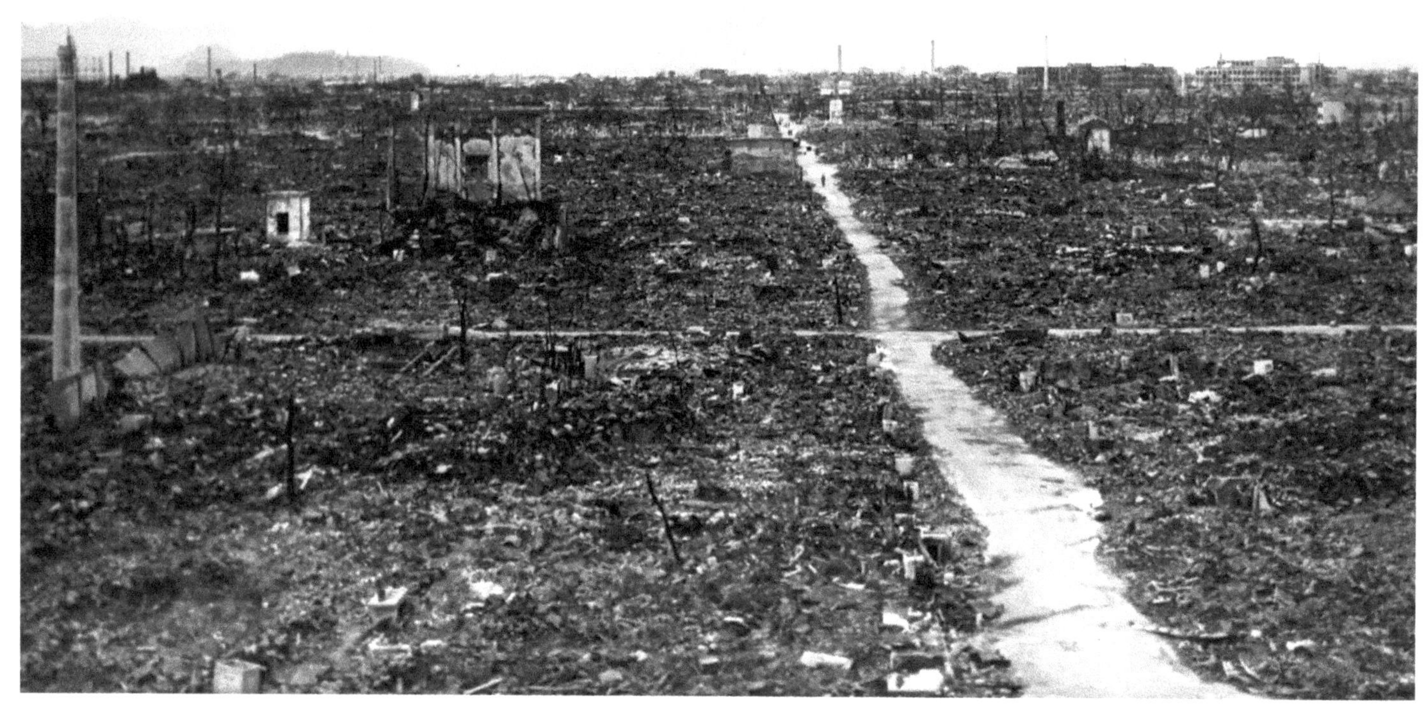

View from the roof of the Sumitoma Bank showing the devastation south of the bank building. Hiroshima University and the Red Cross Hospital are visible at right in the background.

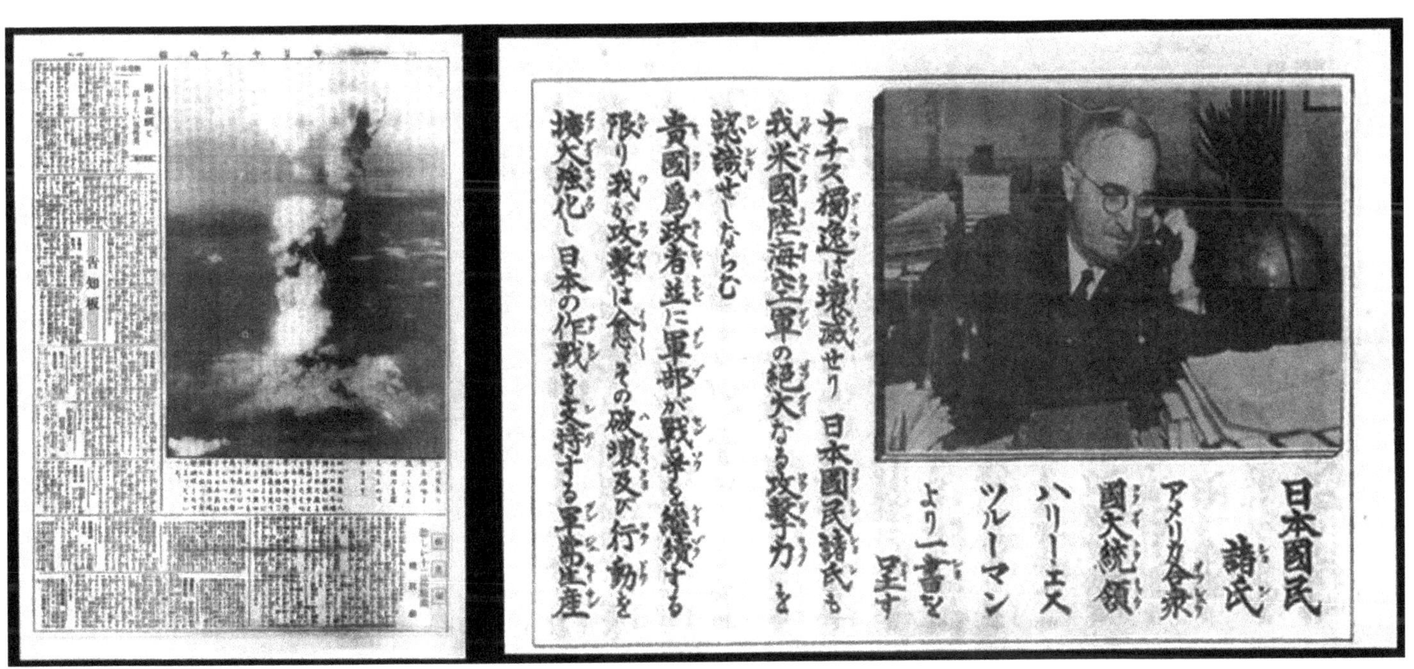

Following the dropping of the first bomb, U.S. bombers released hundreds of thousands of leaflets over major Japanese cities. Several different leaflets were printed. One showed the mushroom cloud and said that more bombs would be dropped unless Japan surrendered immediately; another showed President Truman and also said that immediate surrender was necessary if no more bombs were to be dropped.

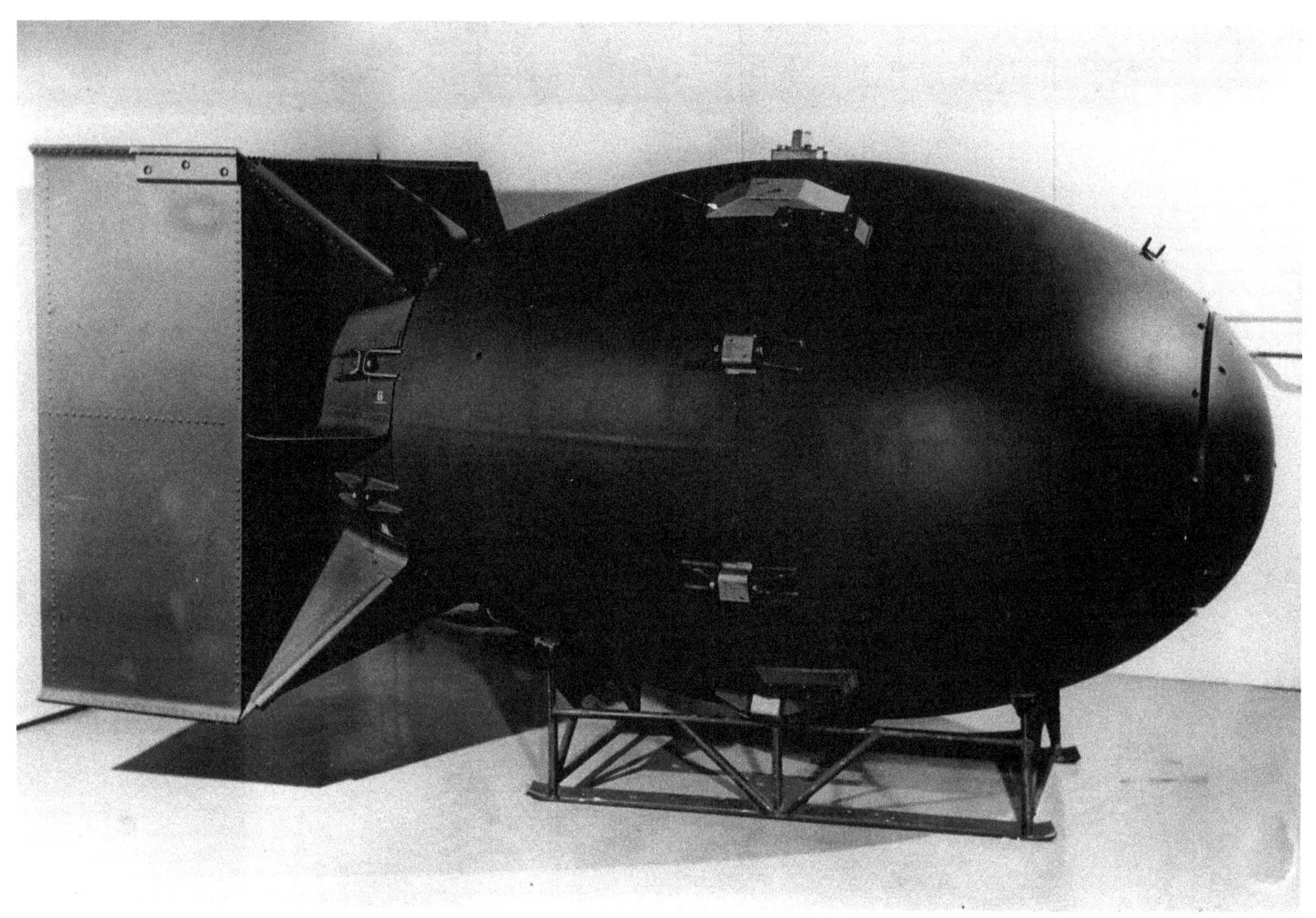

Fat Man, the plutonium implosion bomb being prepared on the heels of Little Boy, was 10 feet 8 inches long, 5 feet in diameter, weighed about 10,200 pounds, and carried an amount of plutonium-239 roughly the size of a softball. It was loaded into B-29 Superfortress no. 77, and the plane headed to the target, Kokura, Japan. Clouds shrouded the city so the mission flew on to Nagasaki. Fat Man was dropped August 9, 1945, at 11:01 A.M.

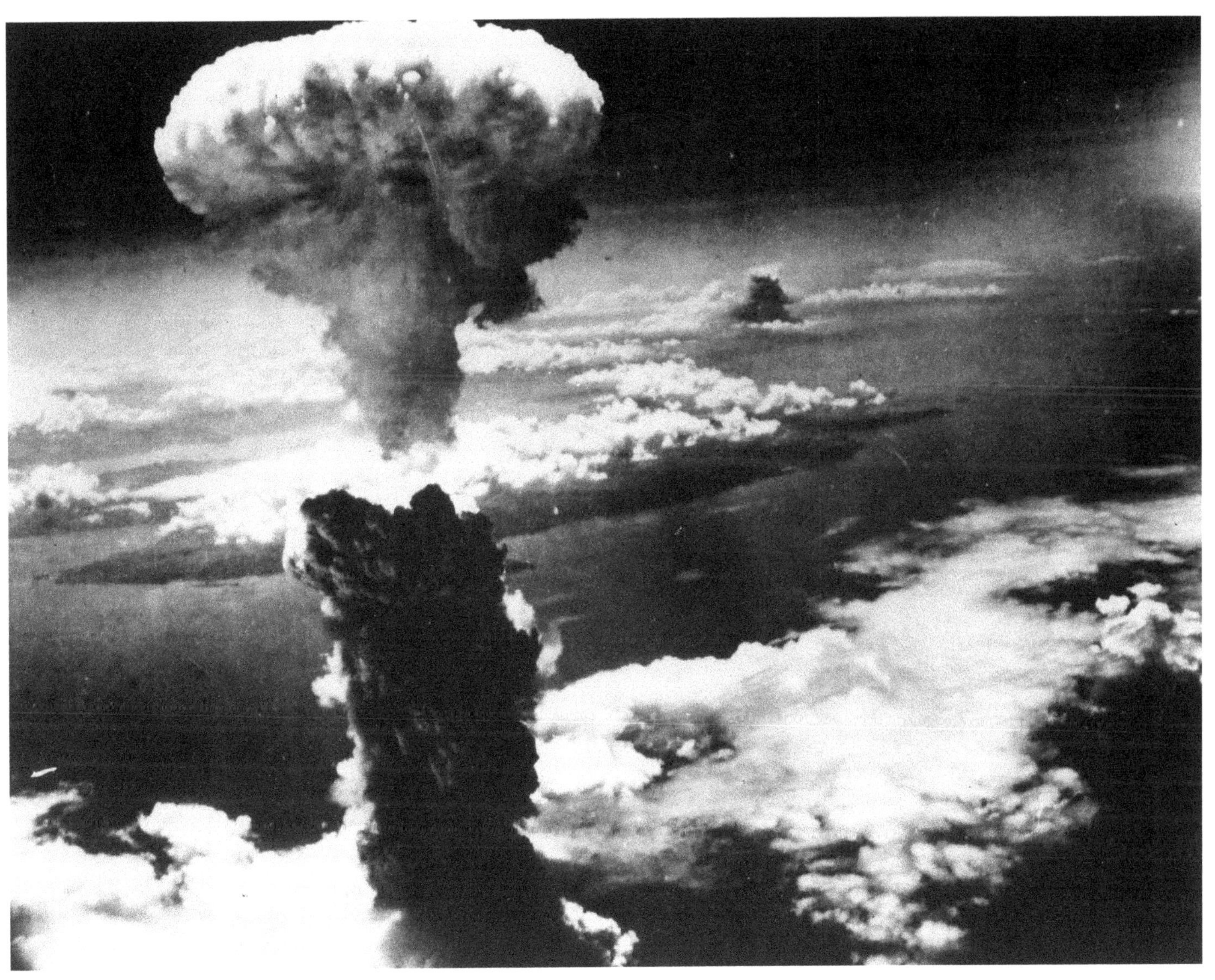

At about 1,650 feet above Nagasaki on August 9, 1945, Fat Man imploded, yielding an explosive force estimated at 21,000 tons of TNT. The explosion produced 7,000-degree temperatures and winds of 625 M.P.H. Buildings were immediately vaporized and a tremendous firestorm ensued. A mushroom cloud rose to an altitude of 11 miles.

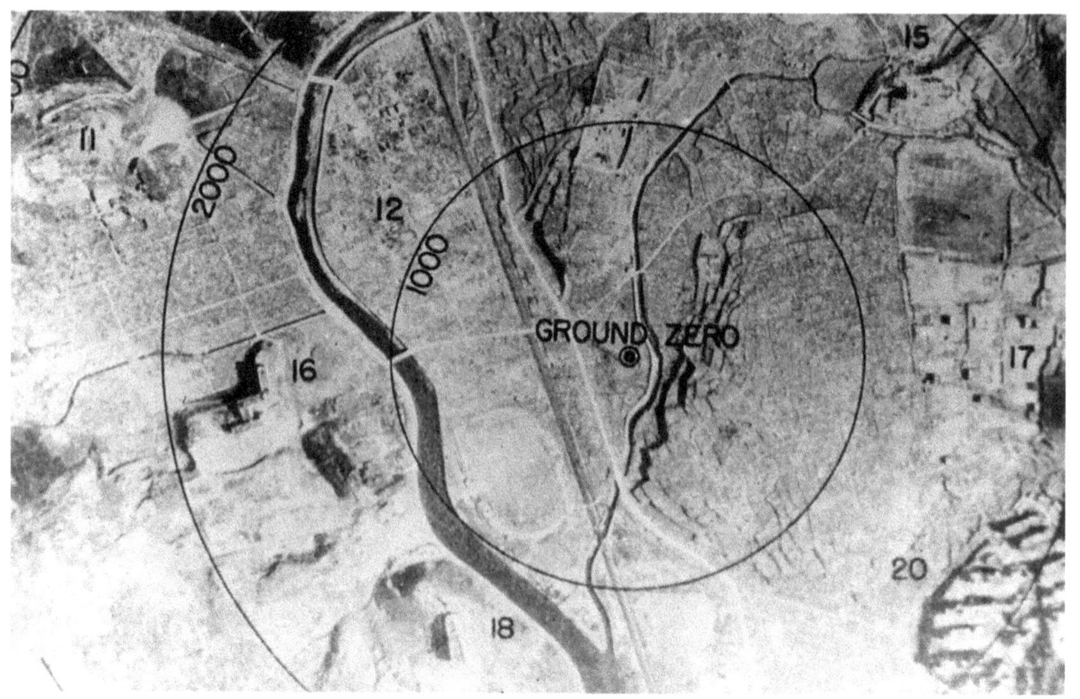

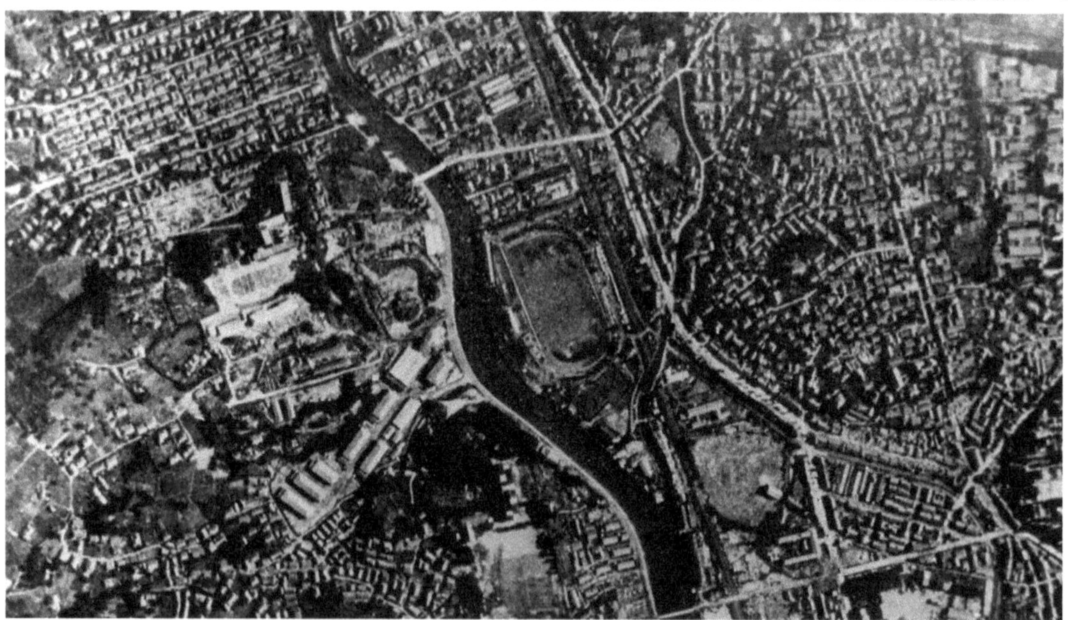

These aerial photos of Nagasaki show ground zero before and after the bomb blast. In the lower photo, buildings of all sizes and clearly outlined business and residential areas can be seen. In the upper photo, all distinguishing features have been obliterated. The blast and the ensuing firestorm turned nearly everything to ash.

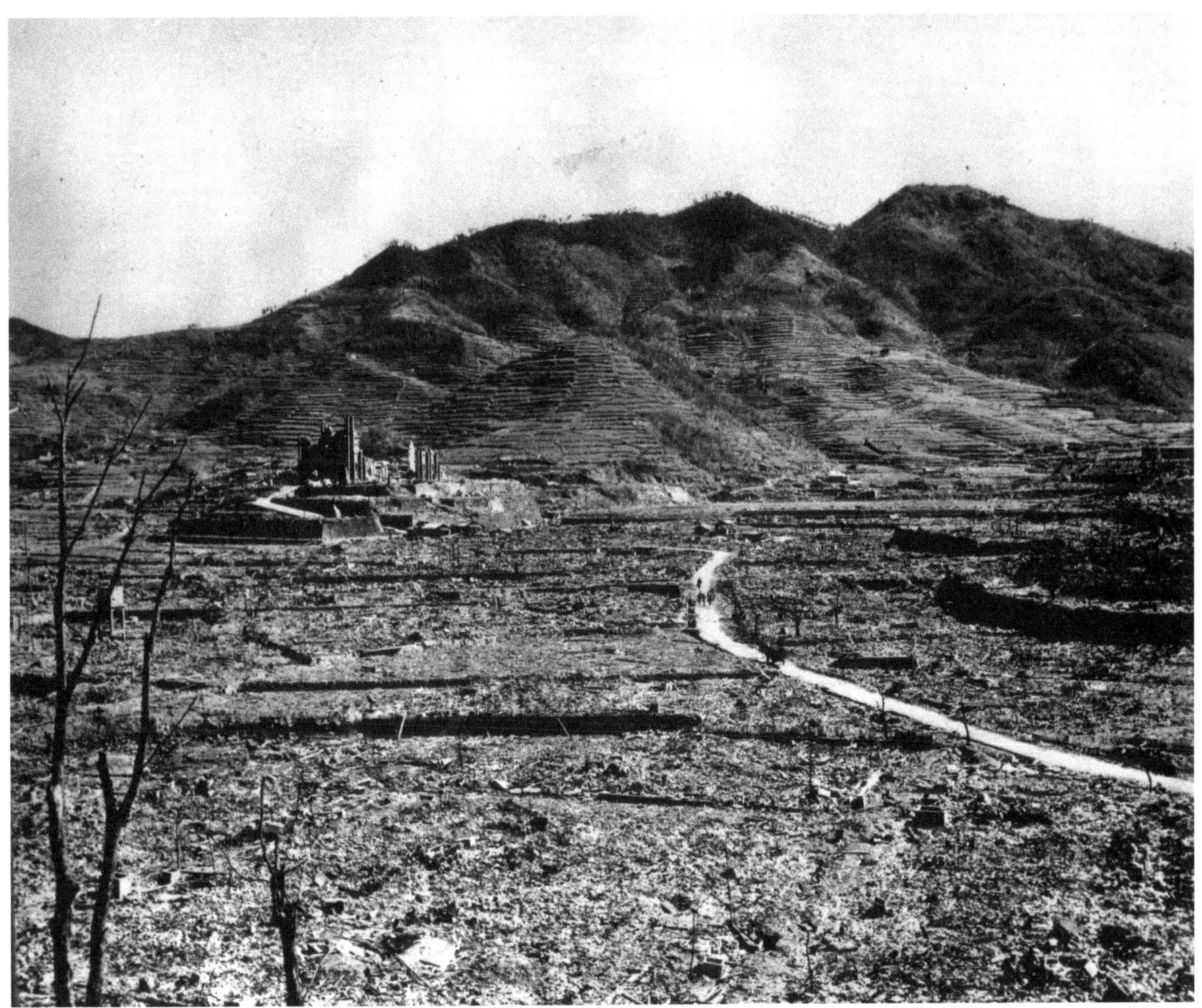

What the immediate blast didn't destroy the firestorm that followed consumed. The fires engulfed a large portion of city structures, many made of wood, and could not be stopped. It simply burned itself out. Very little remained standing.

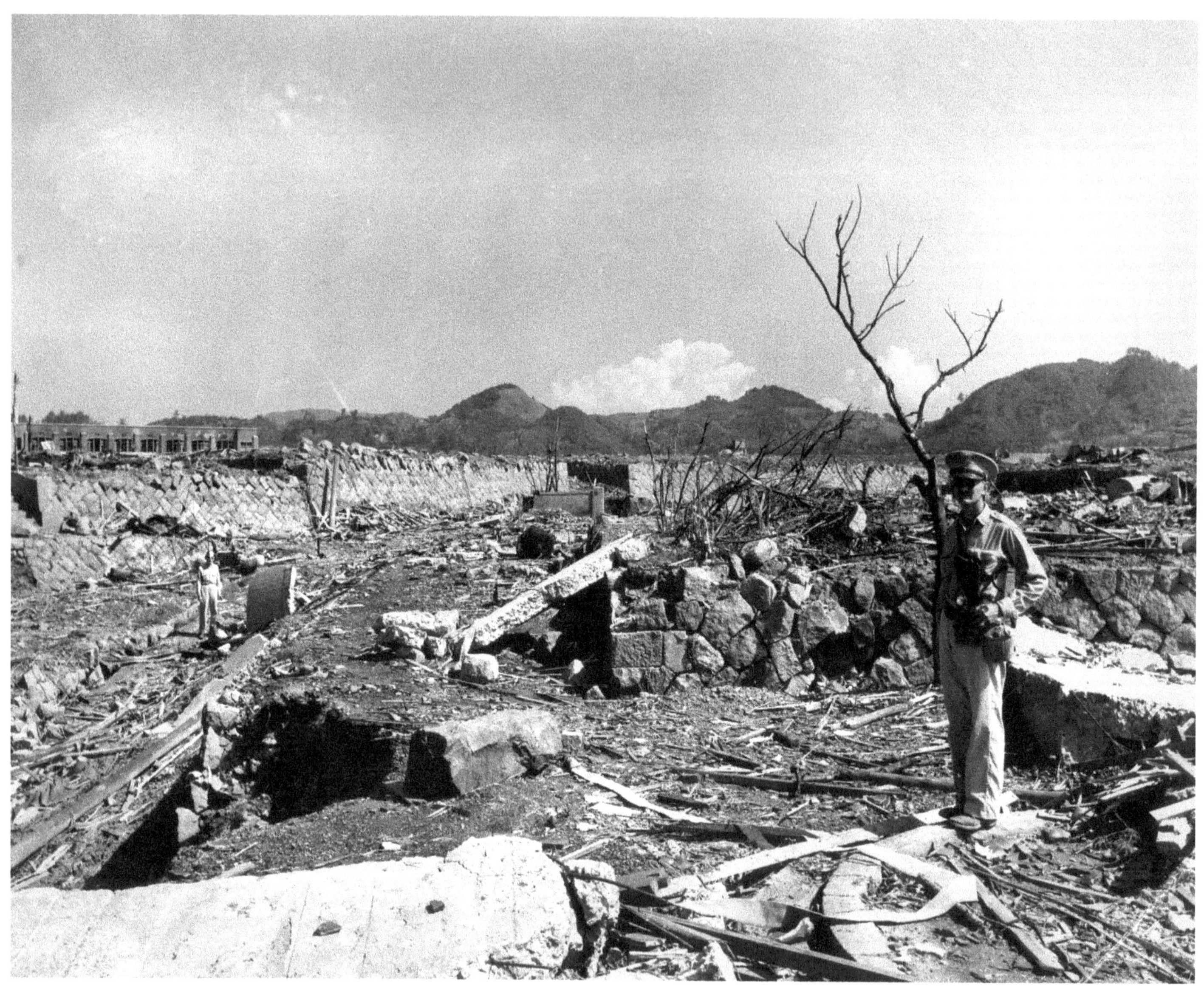

In view here are the remains of a prison located approximately 220 yards north of ground zero in Nagasaki. The wreckage of the concrete and masonry buildings and walls of the prison is complete. U.S. Army soldiers, at left and right, survey the devastation.

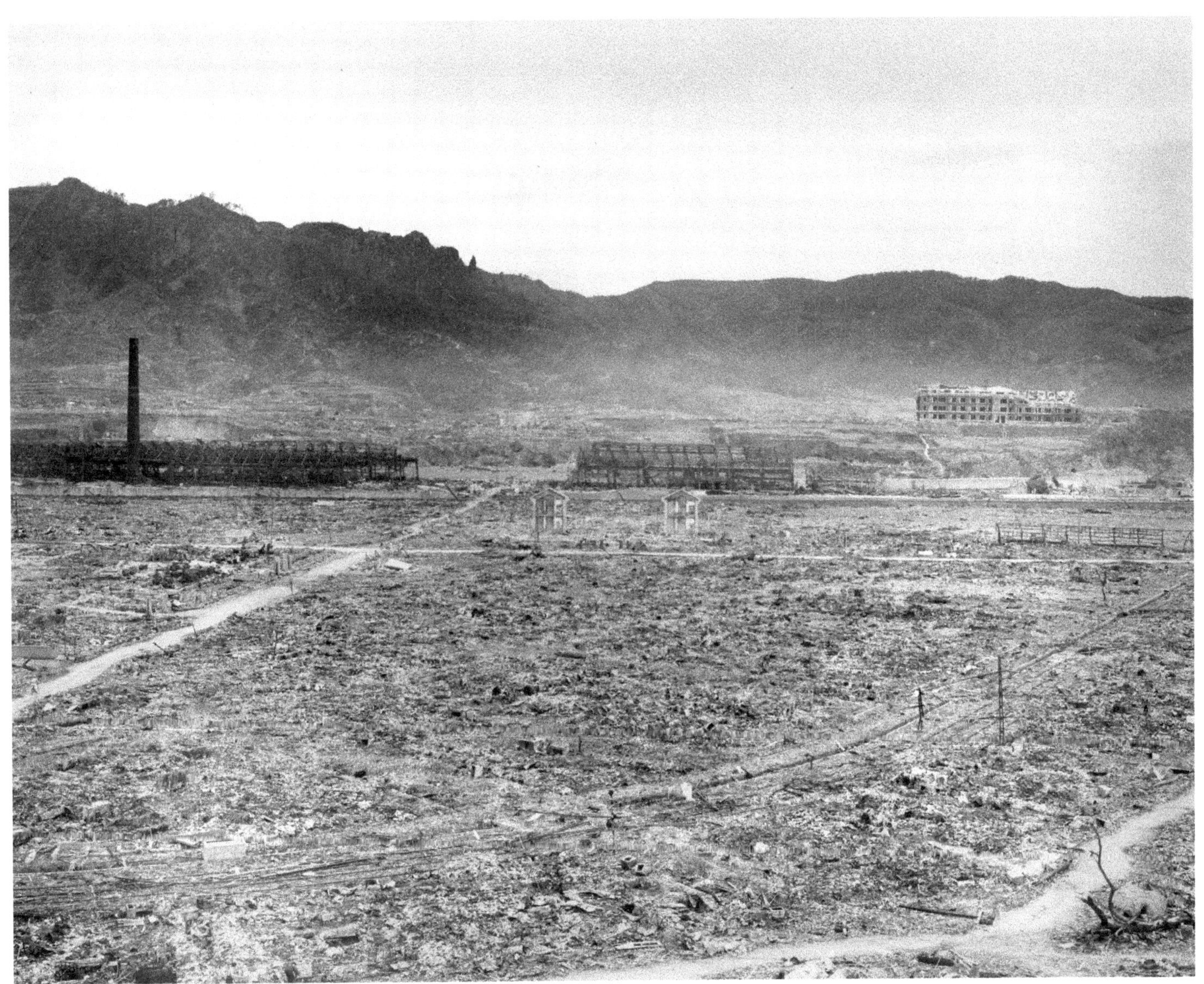

This view shows the nearly complete destruction in the industrialized Urakami Valley of Nagasaki. The Mitsubishi Steel and Arms Works are visible at center. The Chinzei Middle School can be seen in the background at the foot of the hills.

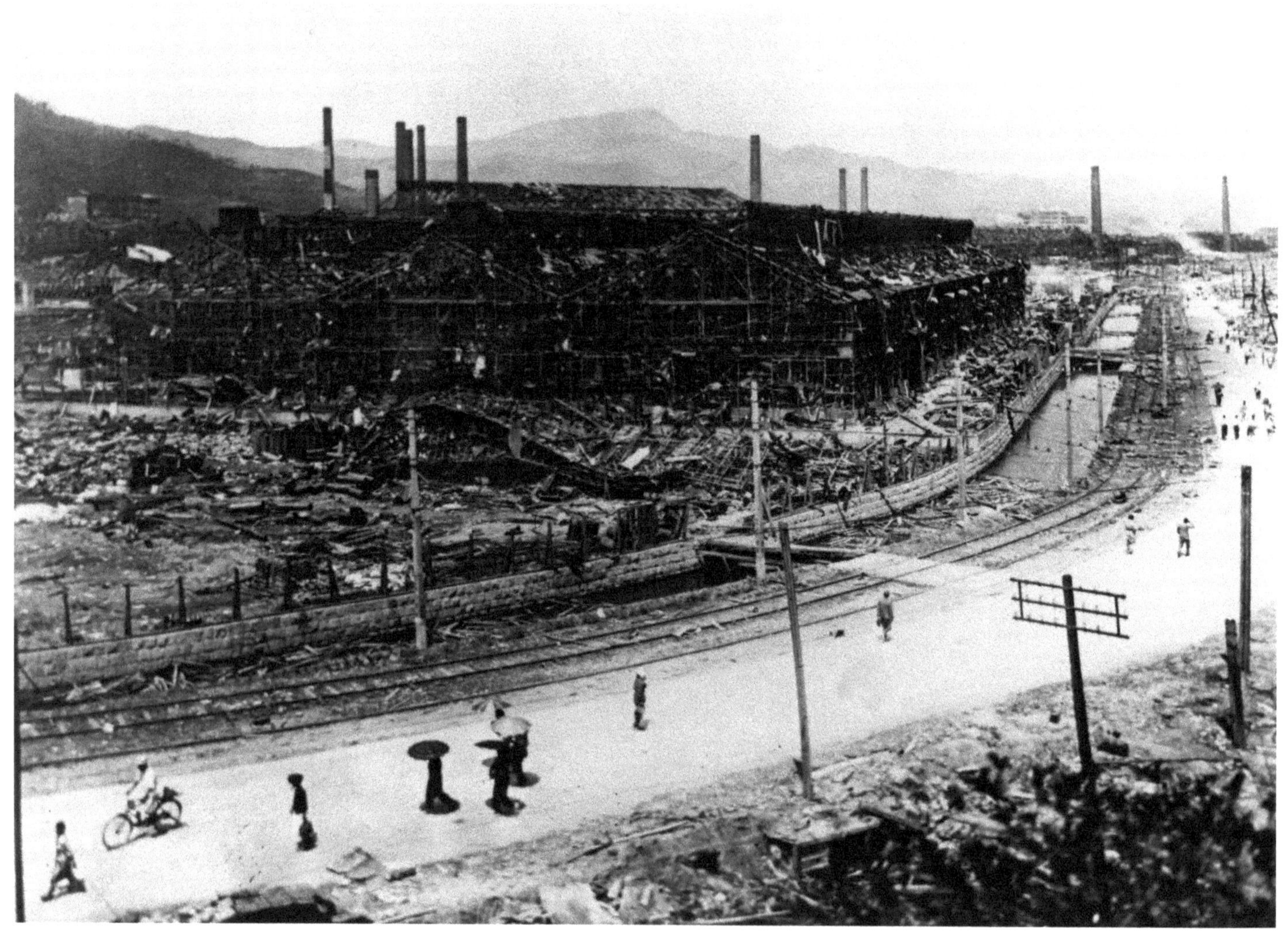

Only the steel superstructure of the Nagasaki shipbuilding factory shown here remains standing. The roadways were cleared of debris, but everywhere else only rubble remained.

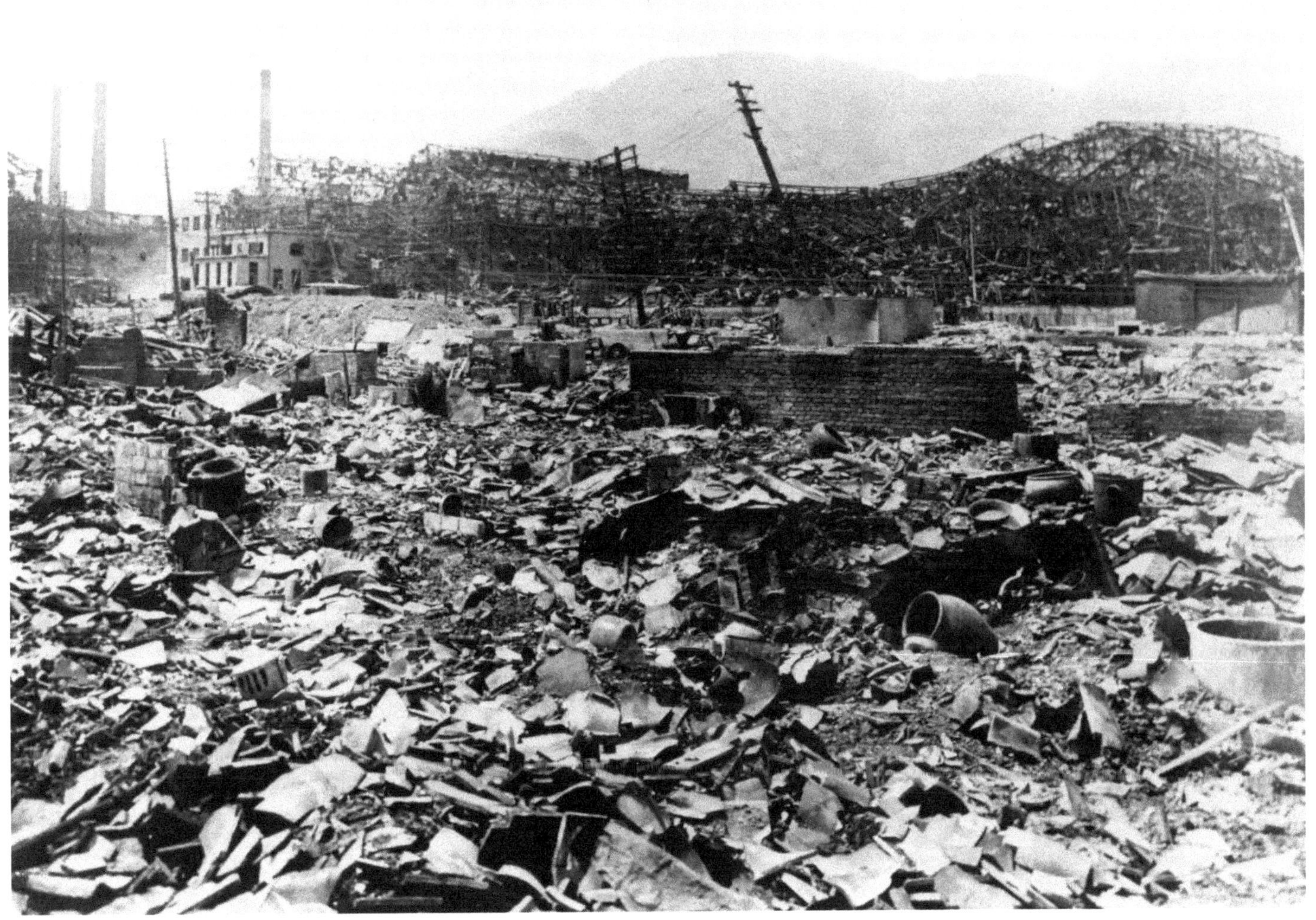

Away from ground zero the only things to survive the blast and firestorm were brick, tile, plaster, concrete, and heavy steel. Wood, fabric, plants, trees, and other organic material were instantly vaporized by the blast or consumed in the fires.

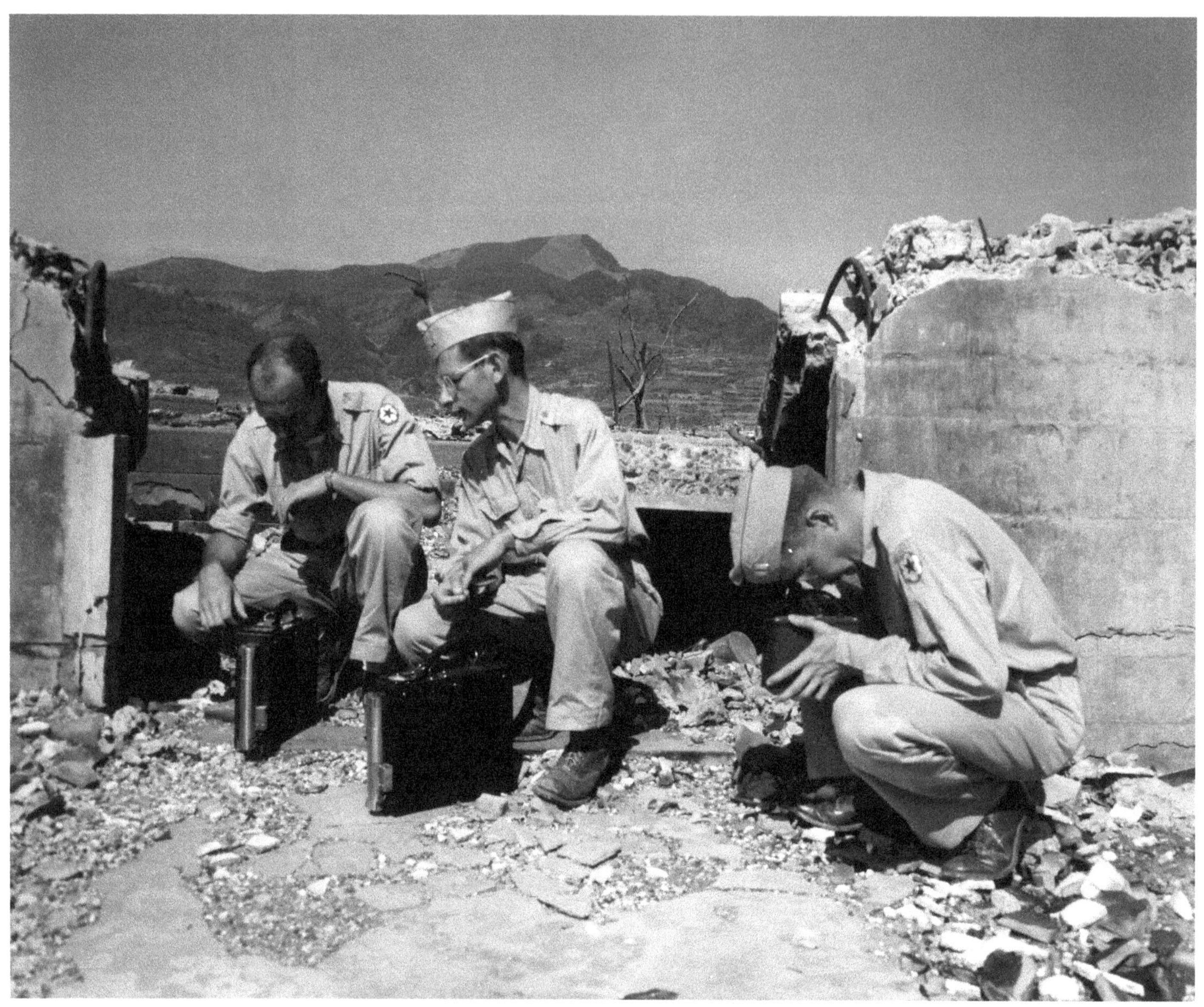

Using Geiger-Muller instruments Captain Henry Barnett and Dr. Robert Serber, both physicists, and Captain Harry Whipple measure the radioactivity of the concrete at what is left of a prison on a hill 75 feet higher than the surrounding area. The prison was a quarter of a mile from ground zero.

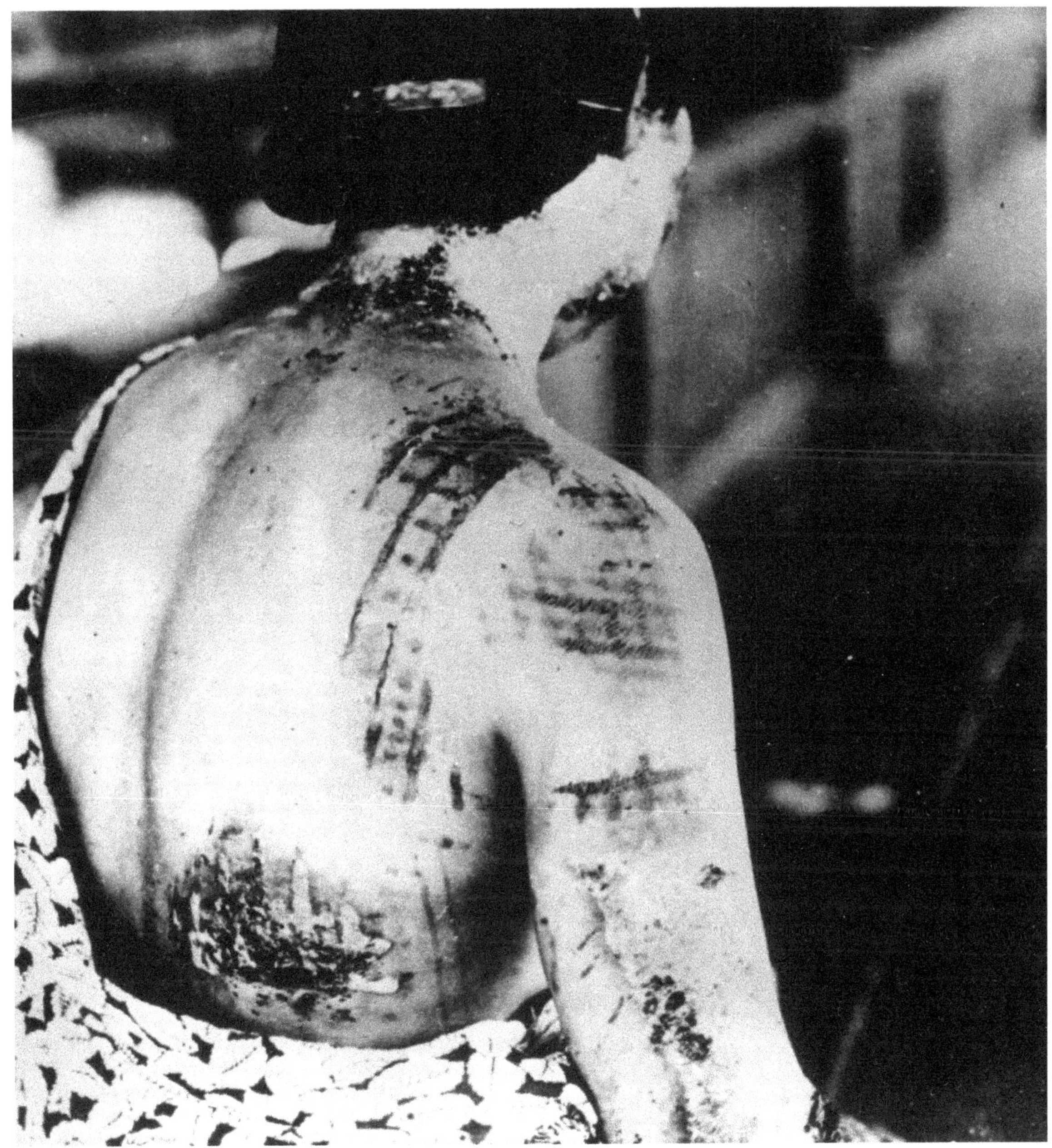

The white and ultraviolet light from the flash of the initial blast burned any dark pattern of clothing into the injured's skin. This woman was wearing a checkered garment when the blast went off. The heat of the blast burned unprotected pavement, brick, and concrete such that anything that shadowed the blast, such as a post, bridge rail, or human being, left behind an unburned imprint of the shadow. These imprints could be seen all over the city, documenting the precise location where people died.

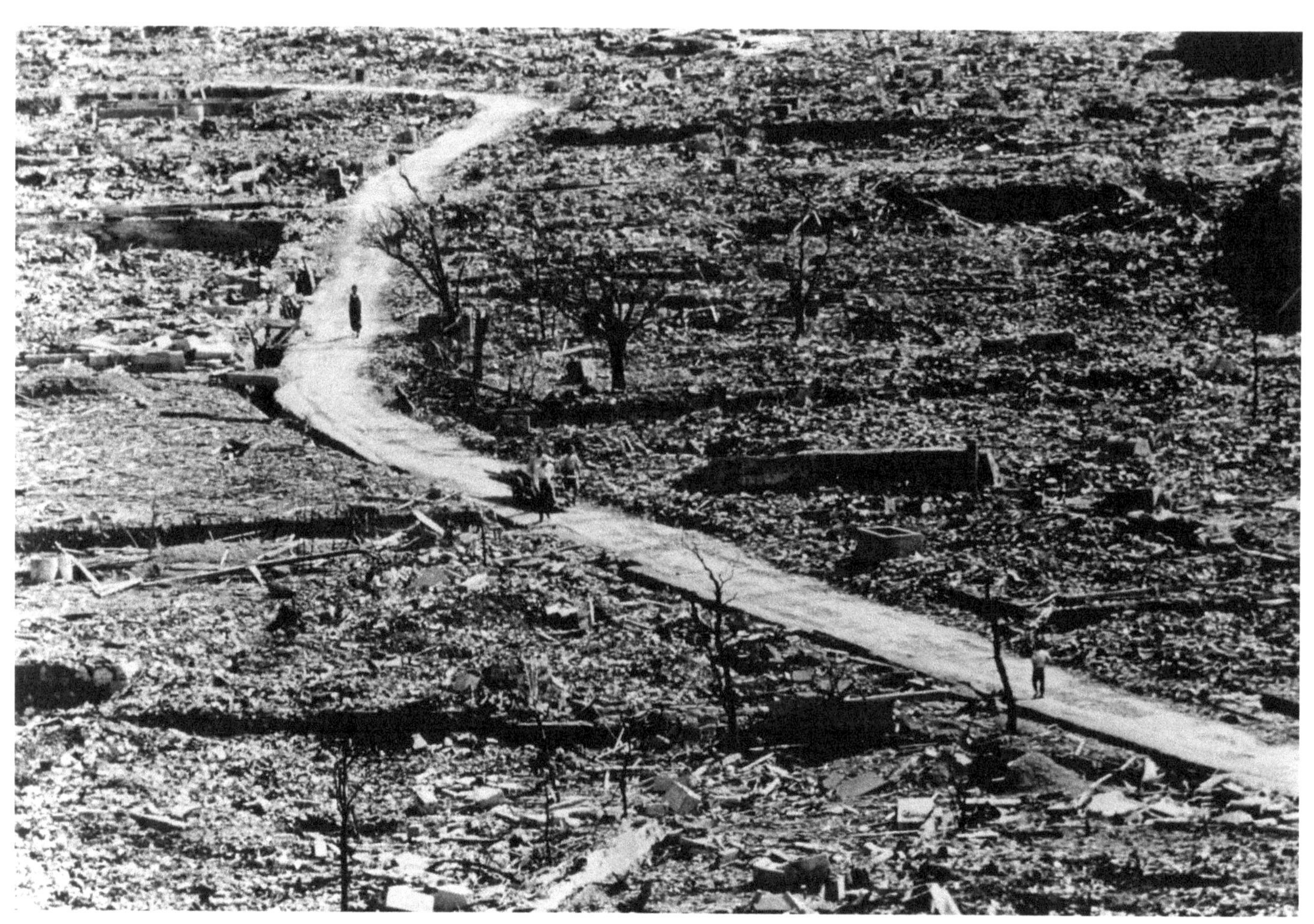

Almost nothing remains of this residential area. The roadway has been cleared and individuals are using an old cart to collect usable building materials. Almost immediately, residents began building small shelters with anything they could find.

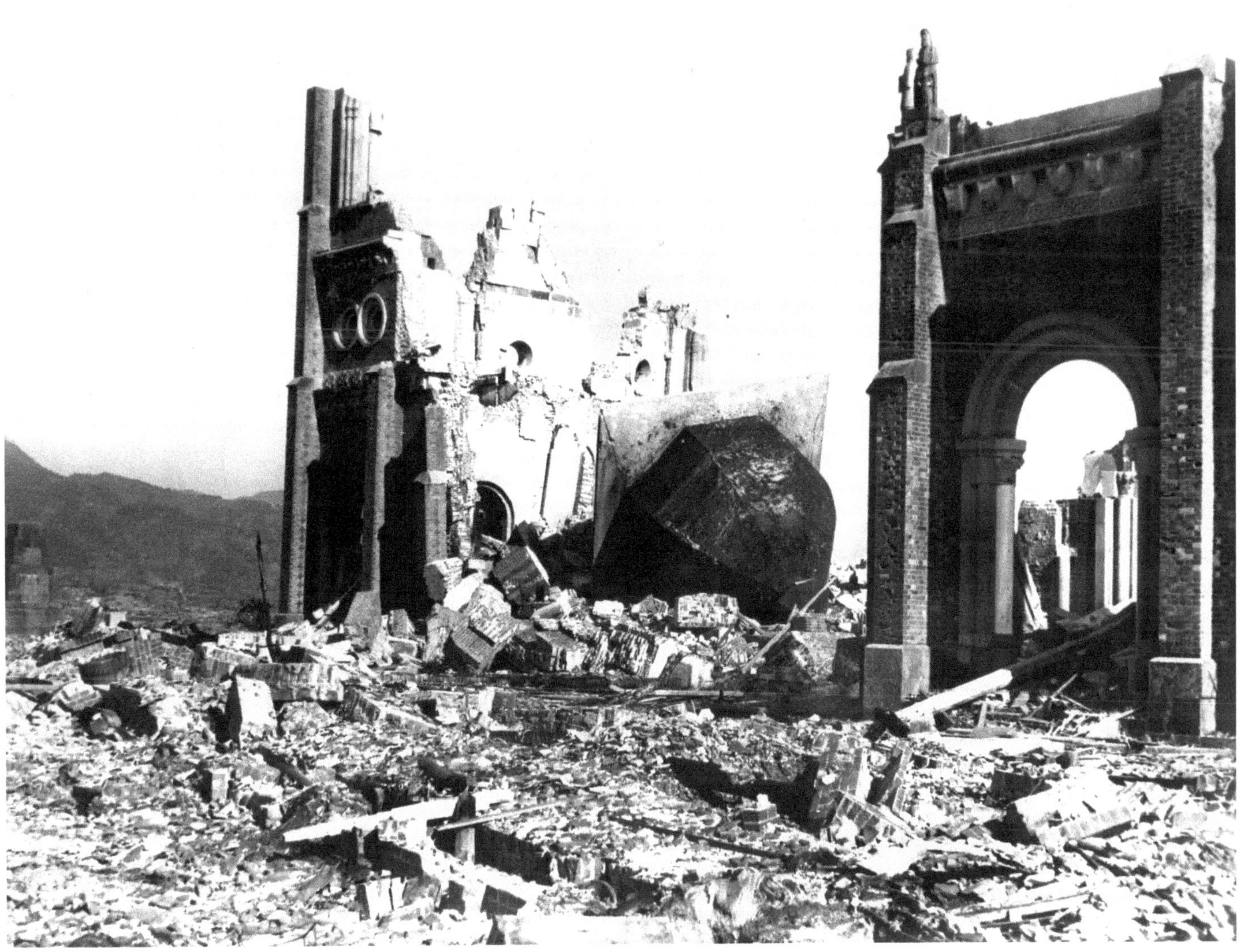

About four-tenths of a mile northeast of ground zero, was this large, brick Catholic church, Urakami Tenshudo. It was totally destroyed, including its two reinforced-concrete domes, one of them visible here toppled over in the rubble. The other dome fell into a nearby creek bed.

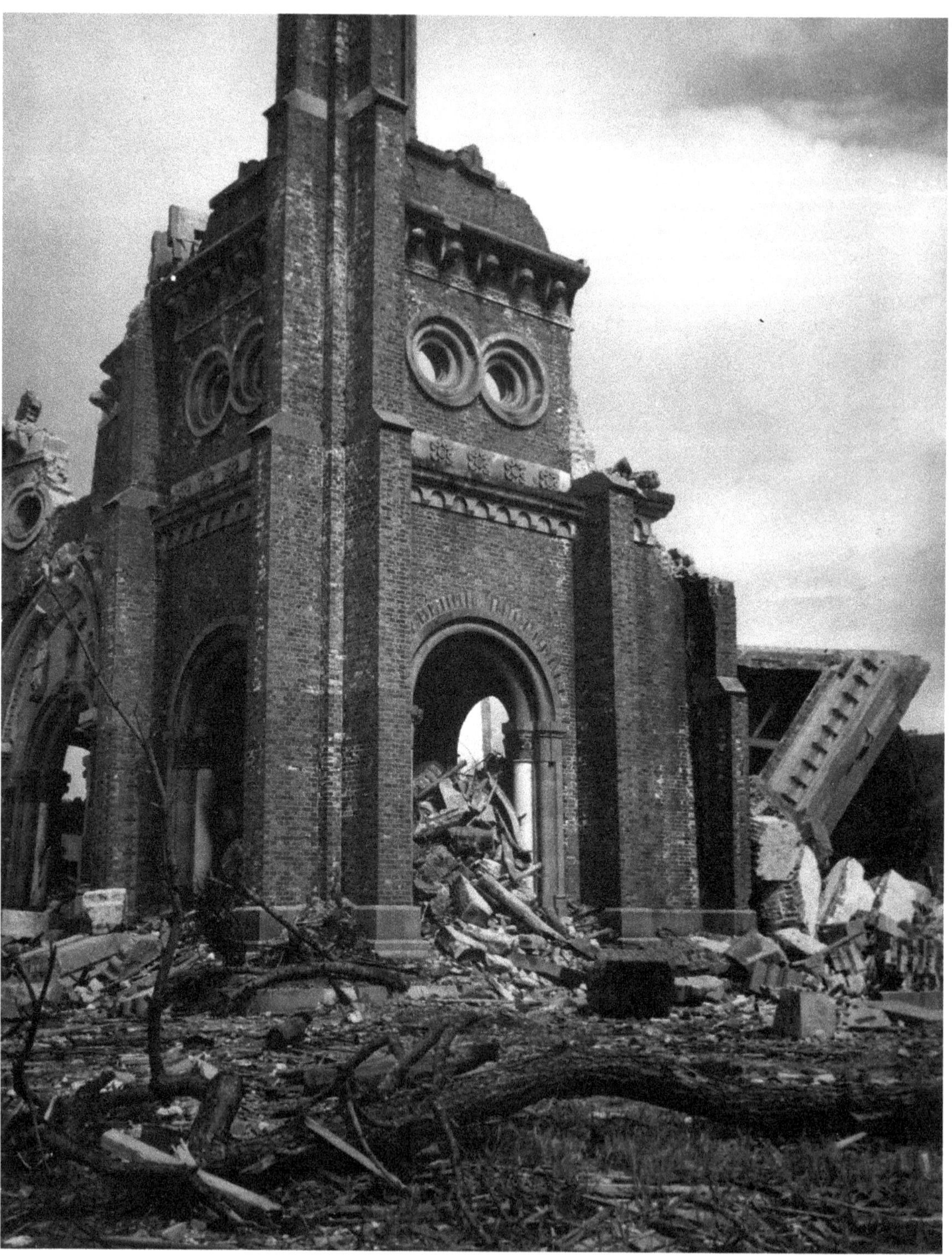

Another view of Urakami Tenshudo, the destroyed Catholic church.

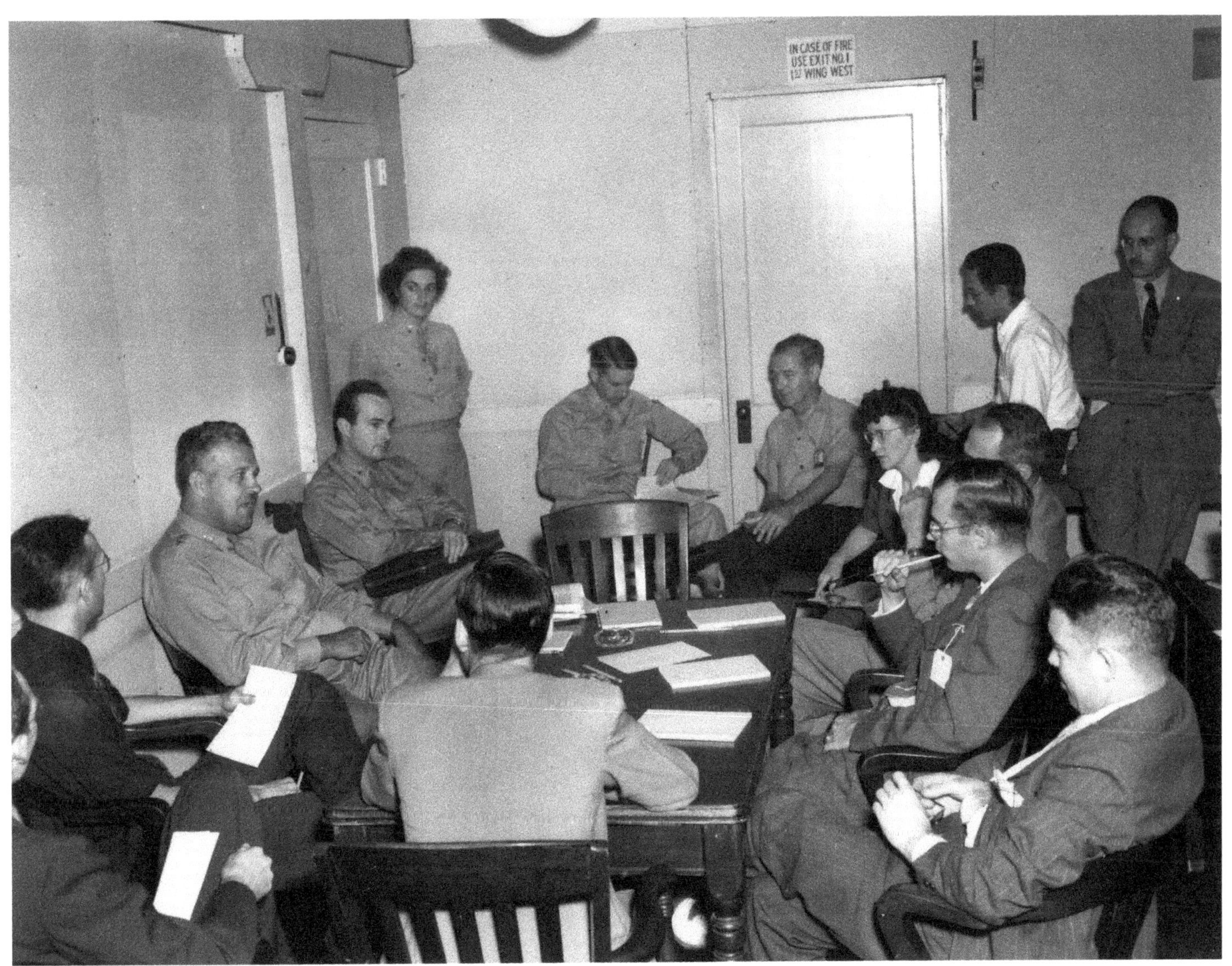

General Leslie Groves holds his first press conference in Oak Ridge following the two bomb drops and war's end, August 30, 1945. Left to right are Horace Wells, Virgil Adams, General Groves, Lieutenant Philip Fell, Colonel Earl Marsden, George Dobbs, Frances Gates, Ed Smith, LaFitte Howard, Loye Miller, and (with back to camera) Willard Yarbrough. In the background are Lieutenant Catherine Filippi, Richard Behman, and Daniel Stern.

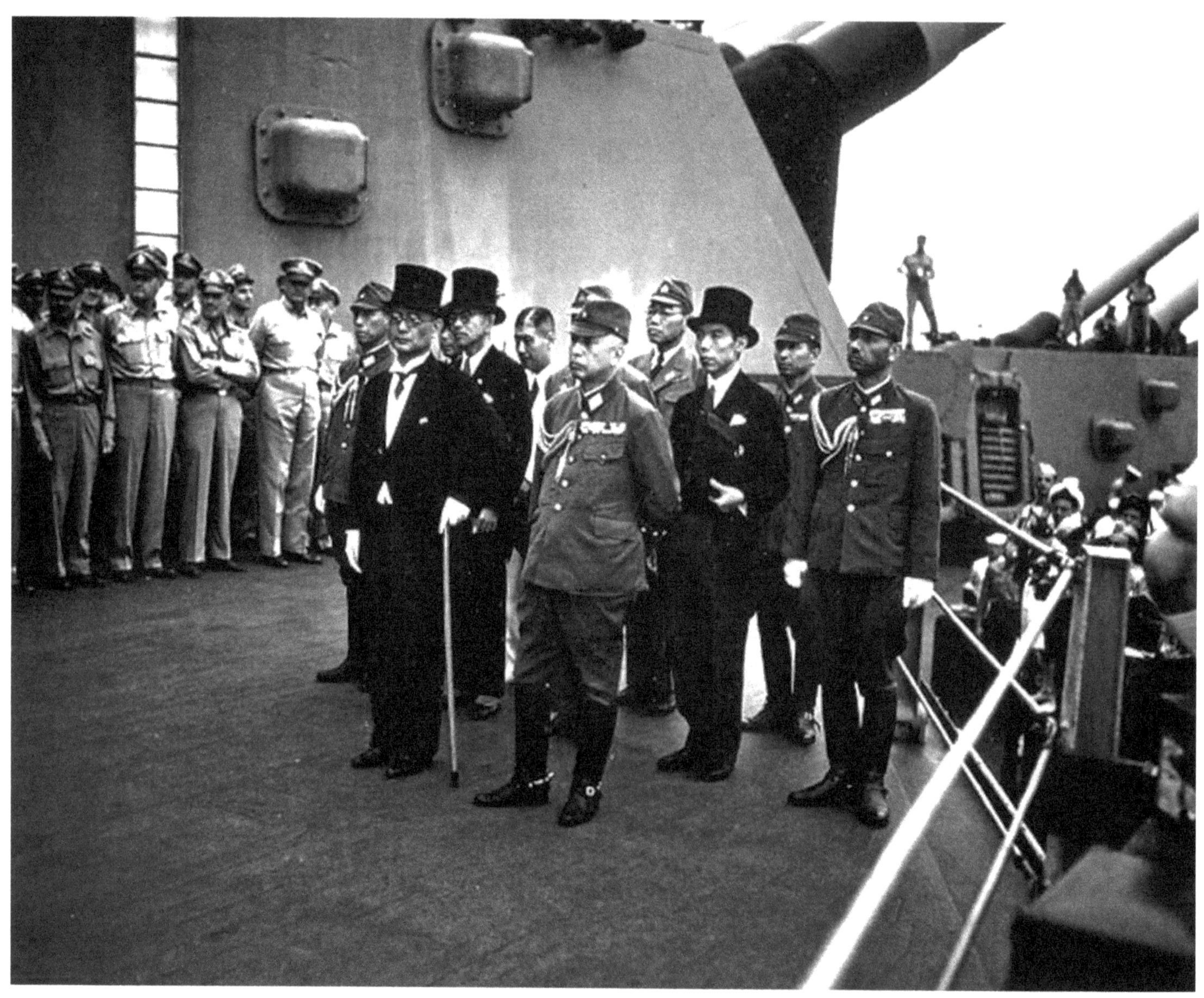

The delegation of Japanese wait to surrender on the deck of the USS *Missouri* anchored in Tokyo Bay on September 2, 1945. In the front are Foreign Minister Mamoru Shigemitsu and General Yoshijiro Umezu. Left to right, front to back rows, are believed to be Major General Yatsuji Nagai, Katsuo Okazaki, Rear Admiral Tadatoshi Tomioka, Toshikazu Kase, Lieutenant General Suichi Miyakazi, Rear Admiral Ichiro Yokoyama, Saburo Ota, Captain Katsuo Shiba, and Colonel Kaziyi Sugita. One can only imagine the disgrace they must have been feeling.

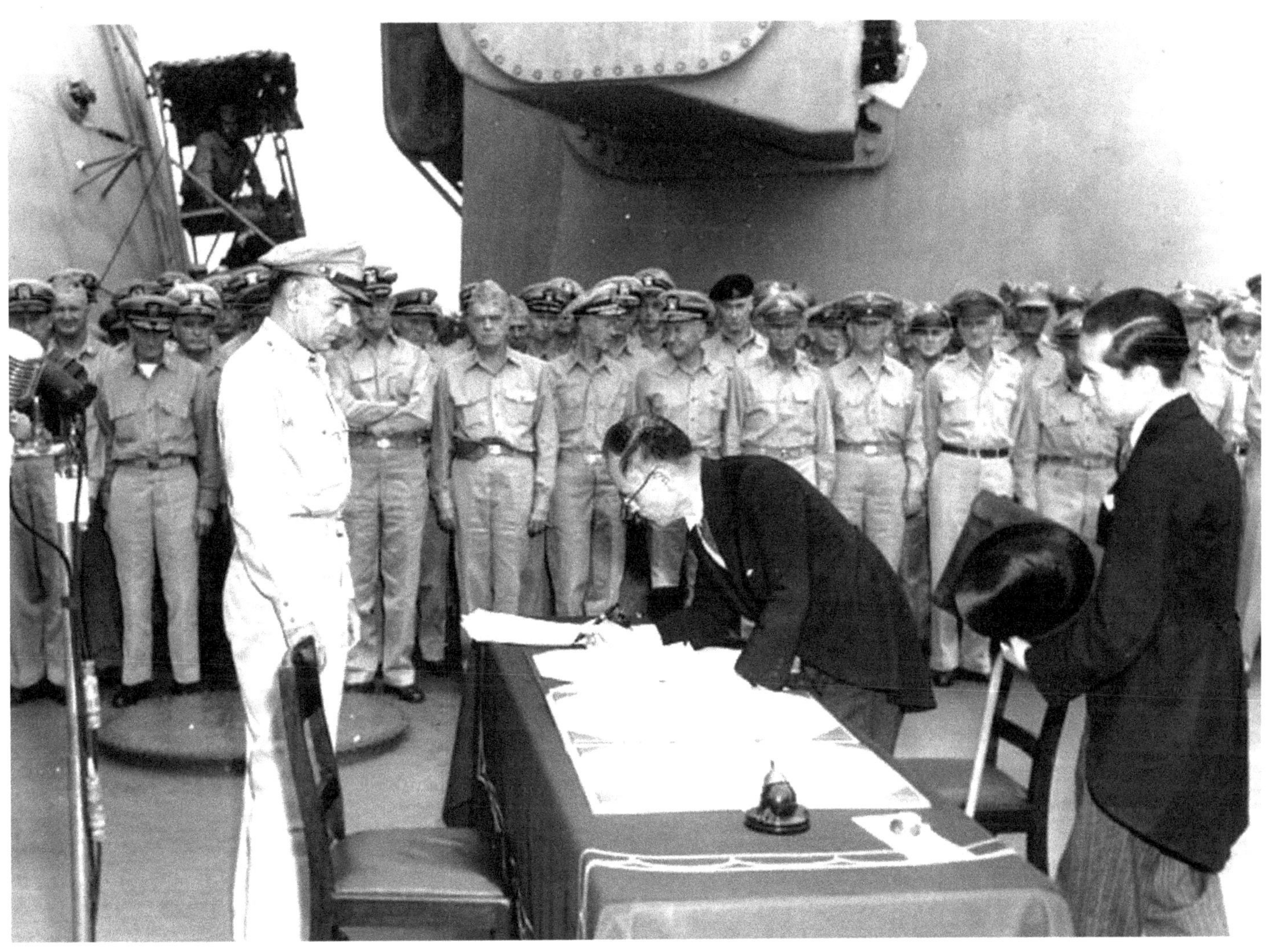

On behalf of the Japanese government, Mamoru Shigemitsu, Japan's foreign minister, signs the Instrument of Surrender at the table set up on the deck of the USS *Missouri.* U.S. Army lieutenant general Richard K. Sutherland stands at attention observing him, and Japan's Foreign Ministry representative Toshikazu Kase holds Mr. Shigemitsu's top hat.

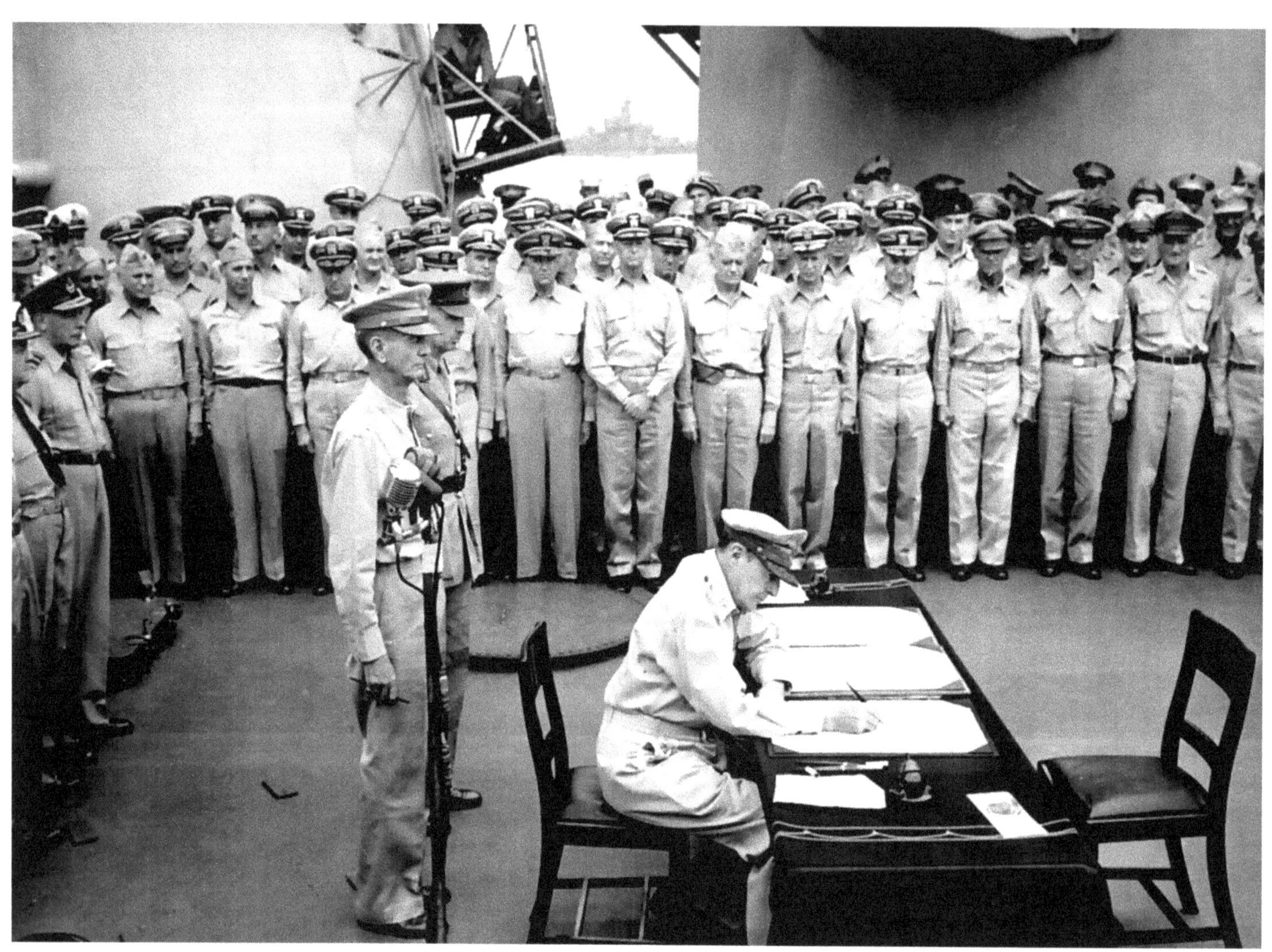

General Douglas MacArthur makes some changes to the Instrument of Surrender and signs the document during the formal surrender ceremony of Japan on September 2, 1945, aboard the USS *Missouri.* Led by U.S. troops, Japan was occupied by Allied Powers for about six years. The Treaty of Peace with Japan was signed by Japan and 49 nations on September 8, 1951, in San Francisco, California, officially ending World War II. Japan was again an independent state, on its way to recovery with the rebuilding assistance of the United States.

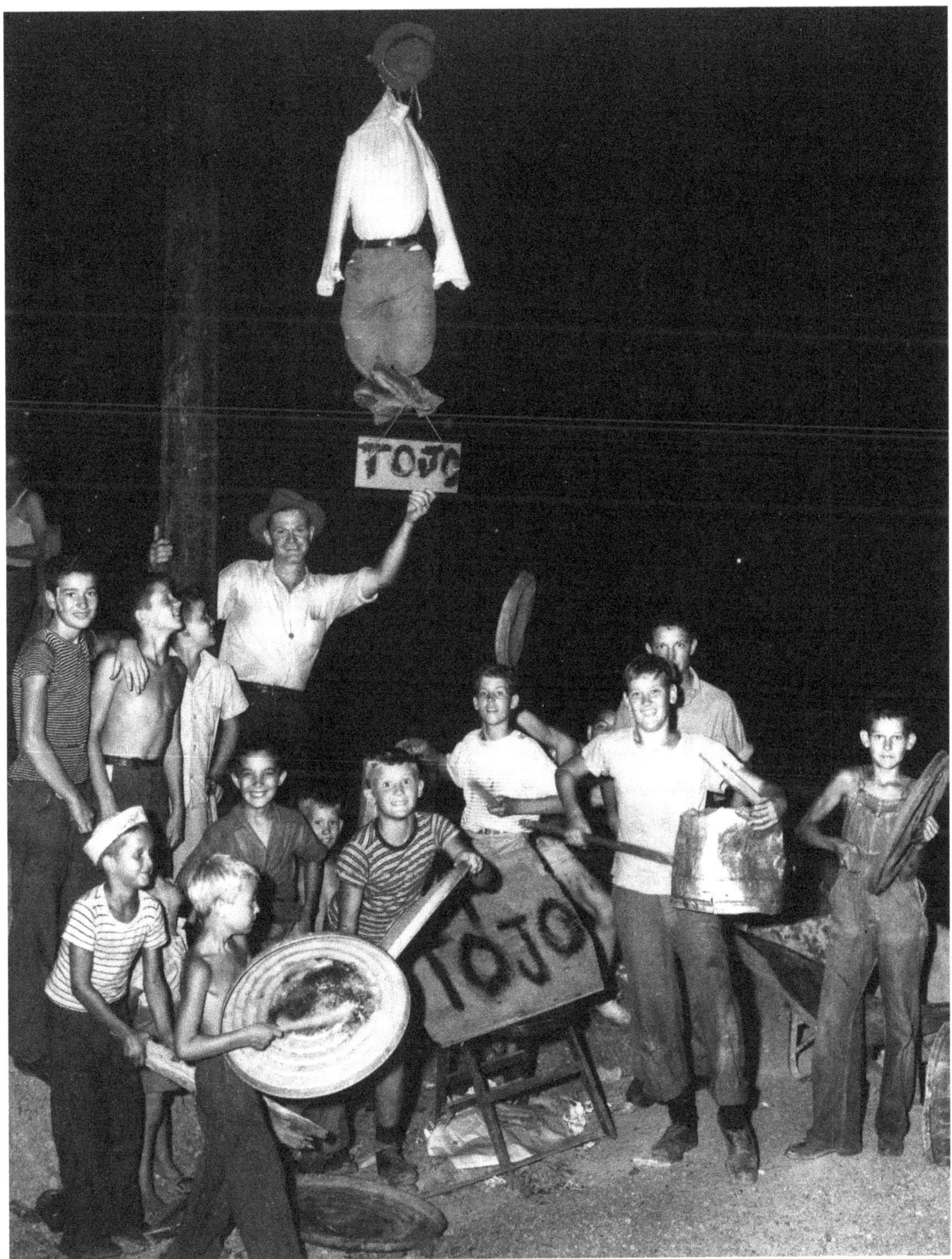

Peace hit the radio stations and papers, and in every part of Oak Ridge parties broke out and people celebrated VJ-Day in different ways. These young people hang Tojo in effigy to signify Japan's defeat.

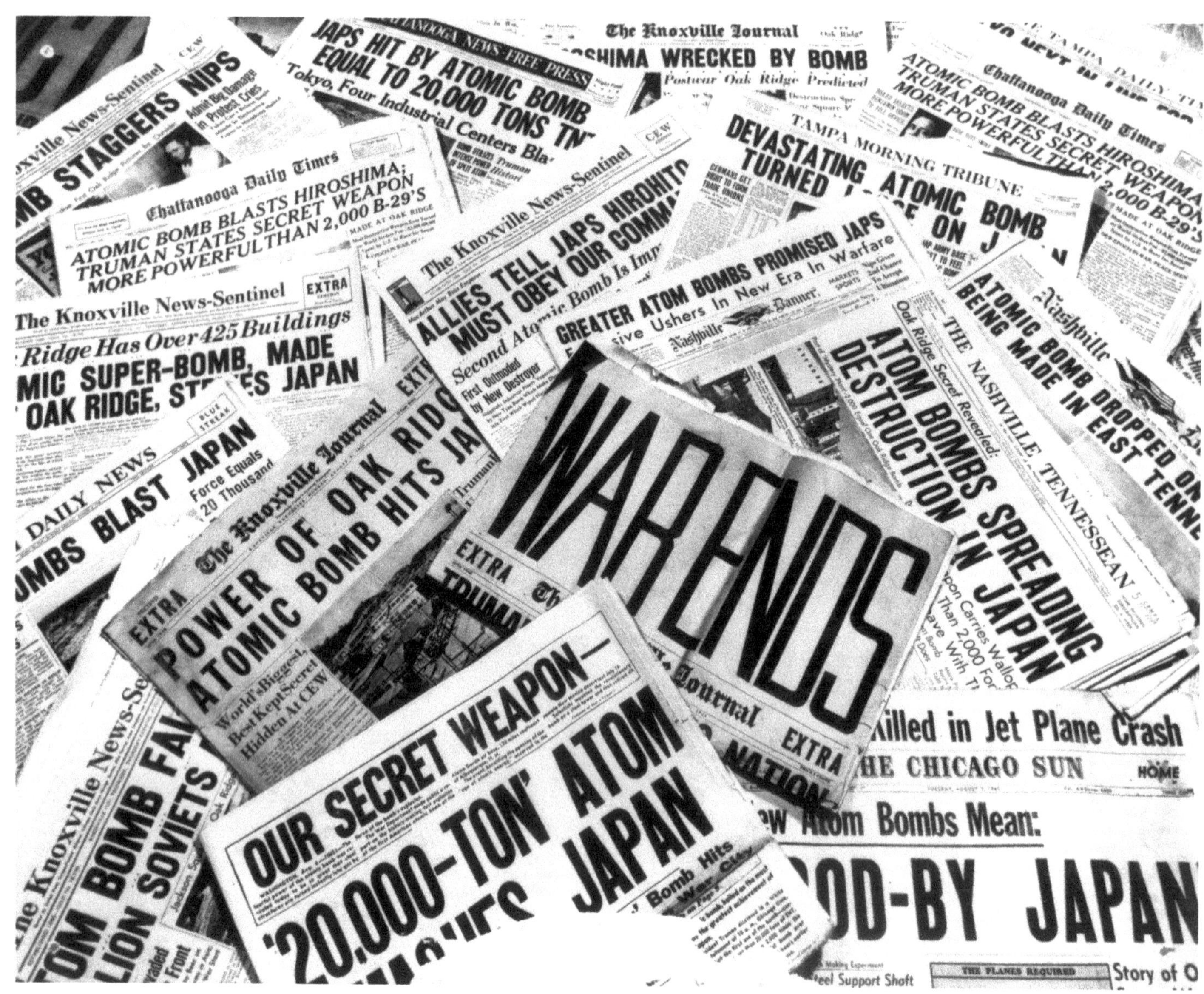

Newspaper headlines around the world announced the end of the war.

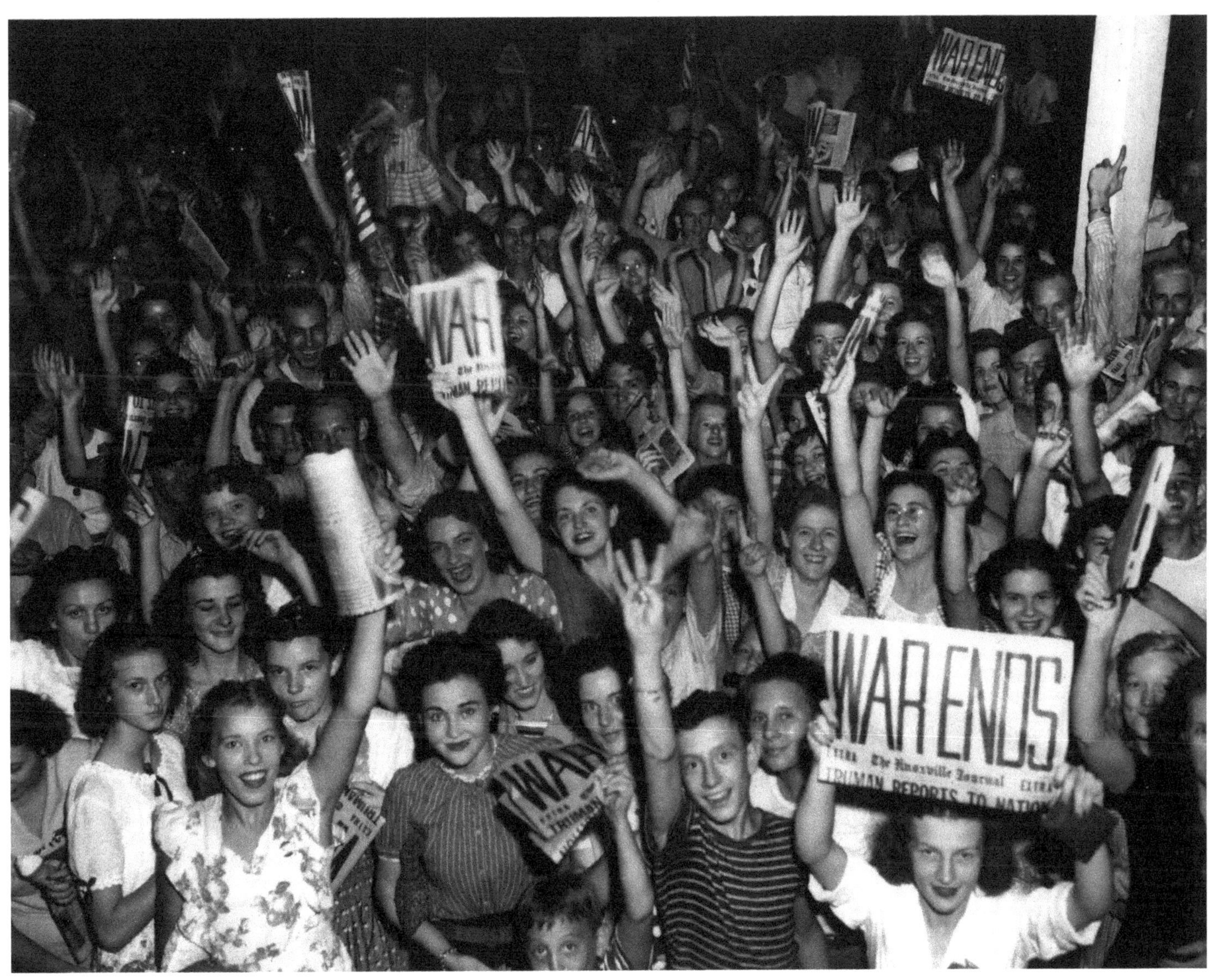

This famous photograph taken in Oak Ridge August 14, 1945, says it all—the war and the killing of our soldiers were over. Newspapers that ordinarily cost a quarter sold for a dollar but all quickly sold out. Everyone wanted one.

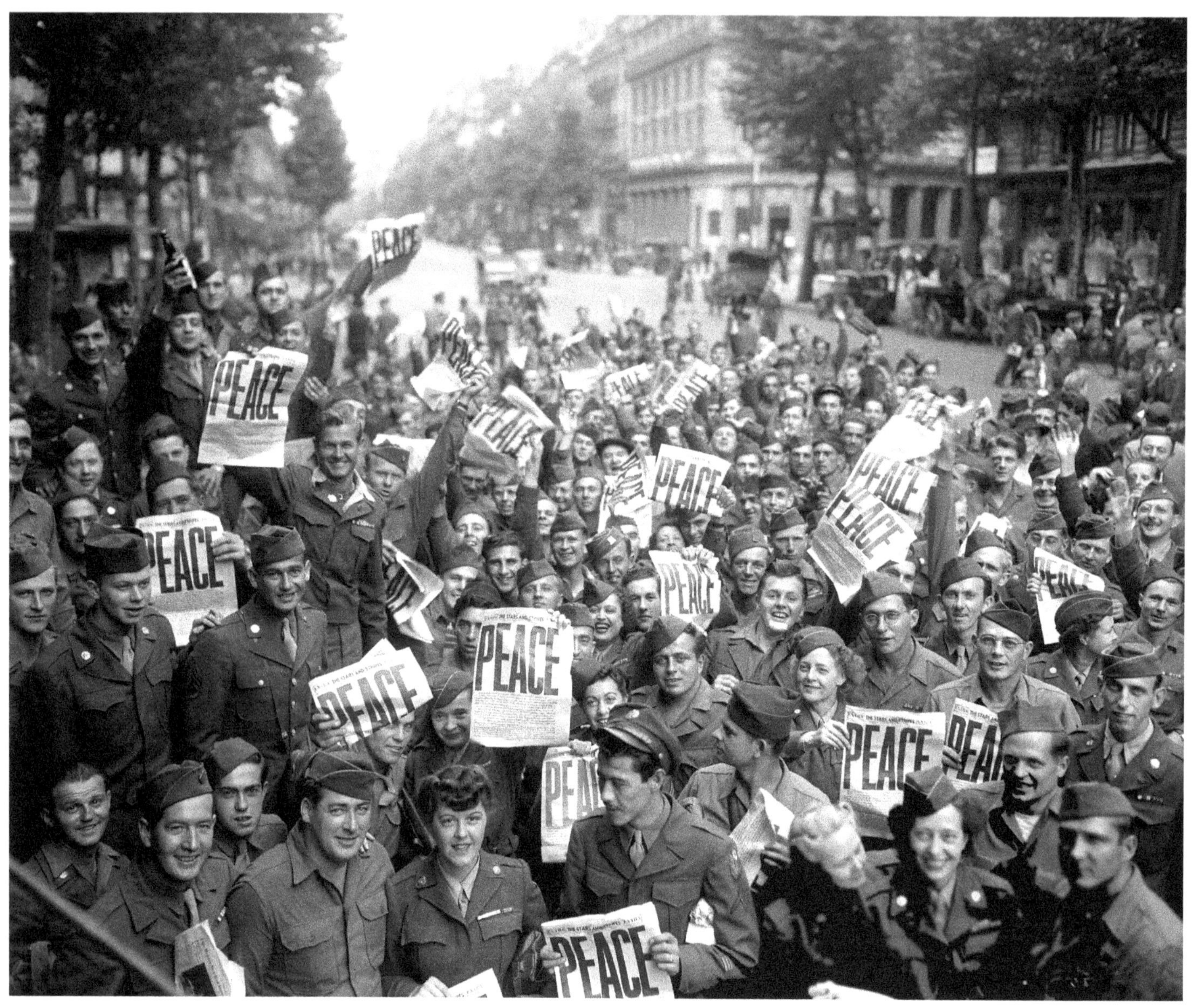

In the streets outside the Red Cross Club in Paris, French and American servicemen and women celebrate "Peace."

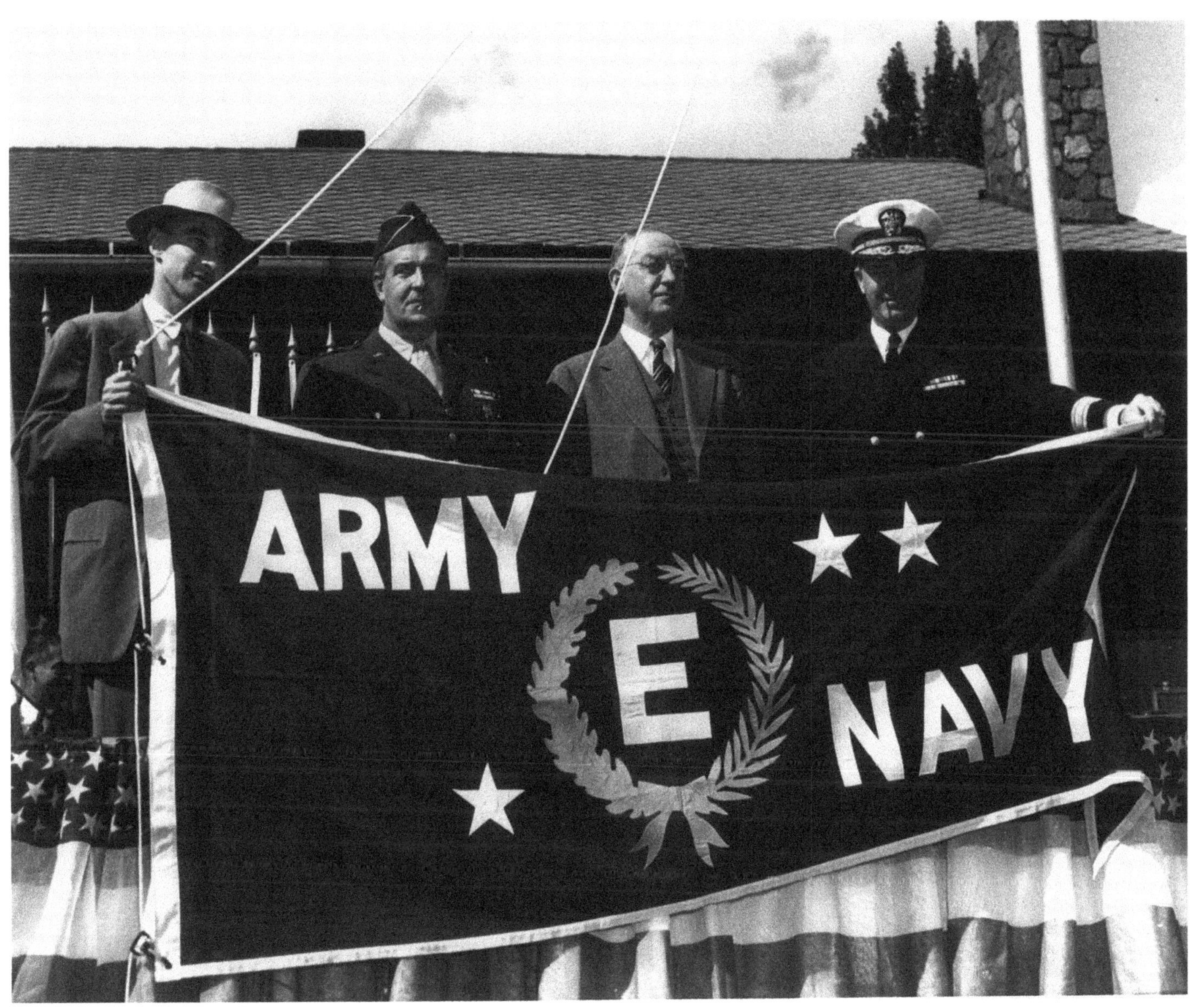

The Los Alamos Laboratory receives the Army-Navy E (for excellence) Award at the end of the war.

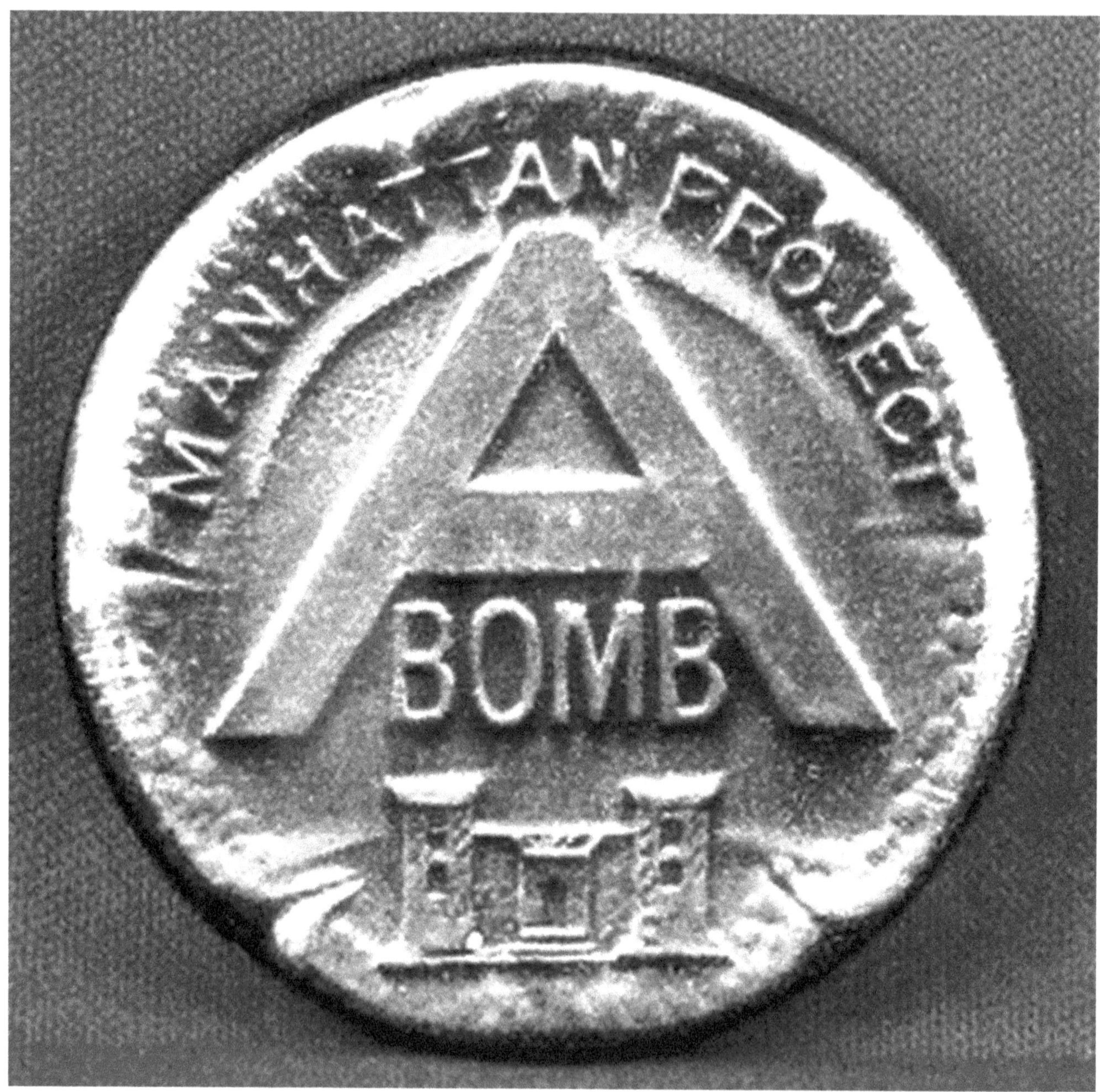

Manhattan Project workers received a small pin called the A-Bomb pin in recognition of their service to the government. The symbol of the Corps of Engineers appeared at the bottom. The pin was bronze or silver depending on the length of time the recipient worked on the project.

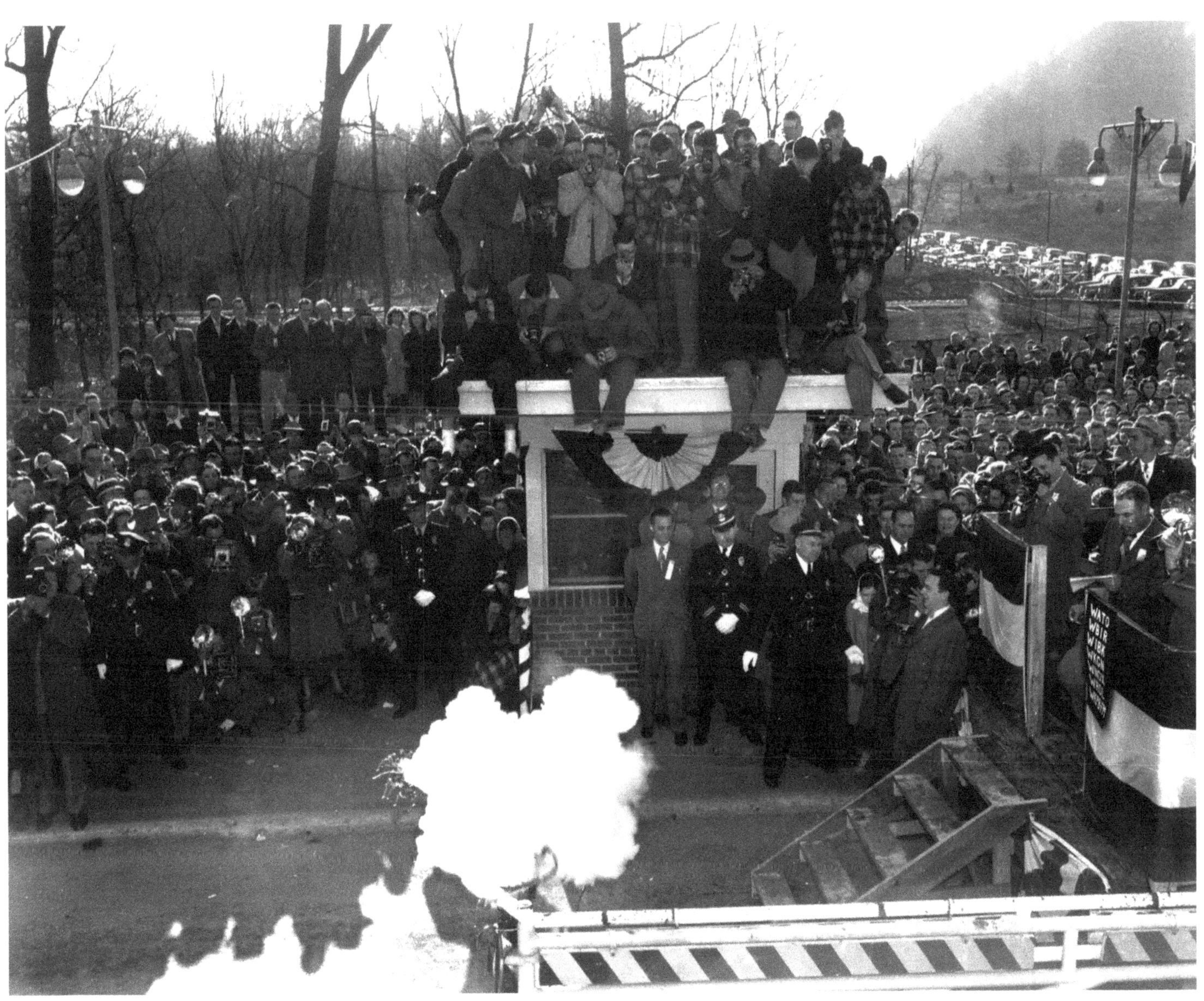

The Secret City of Oak Ridge officially opened its gates on March 19, 1949. The three nuclear facilities remained behind security fences and gates, but the city itself was now open. President Truman sent his vice-president, Alben Barkley, to attend the opening ceremony. This photo was taken at the Elza Gate entrance, with a magnesium flare set off to symbolize the bombs made possible by the secret city.

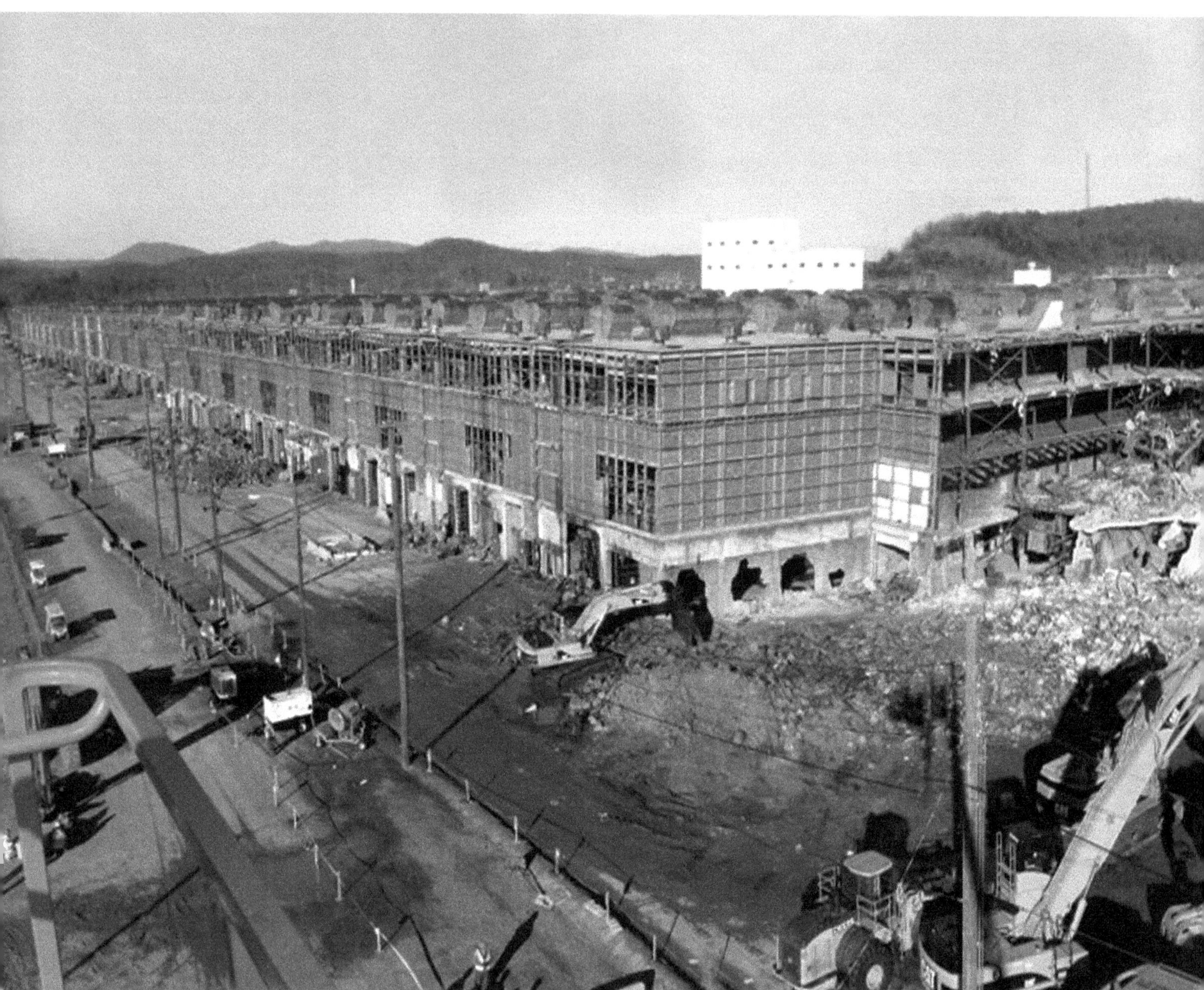

Perhaps the most famous building of the Manhattan Project is the mile-long gaseous diffusion building at the K-25 site in Oak Ridge, Tennessee. History was made in this building, both in its construction and in the incredibly complex science that went on under its roof. It was one of the most secret facilities in the world, yet required thousands of people to build and operate. This photo, taken in December 2008, shows the beginning of its end, and for many symbolizes the true end of the Manhattan Project. For more than half a century, this building represented that incredible project, and though the building will soon be gone, what it represented and what was accomplished inside its walls is a central piece of this nation's history.

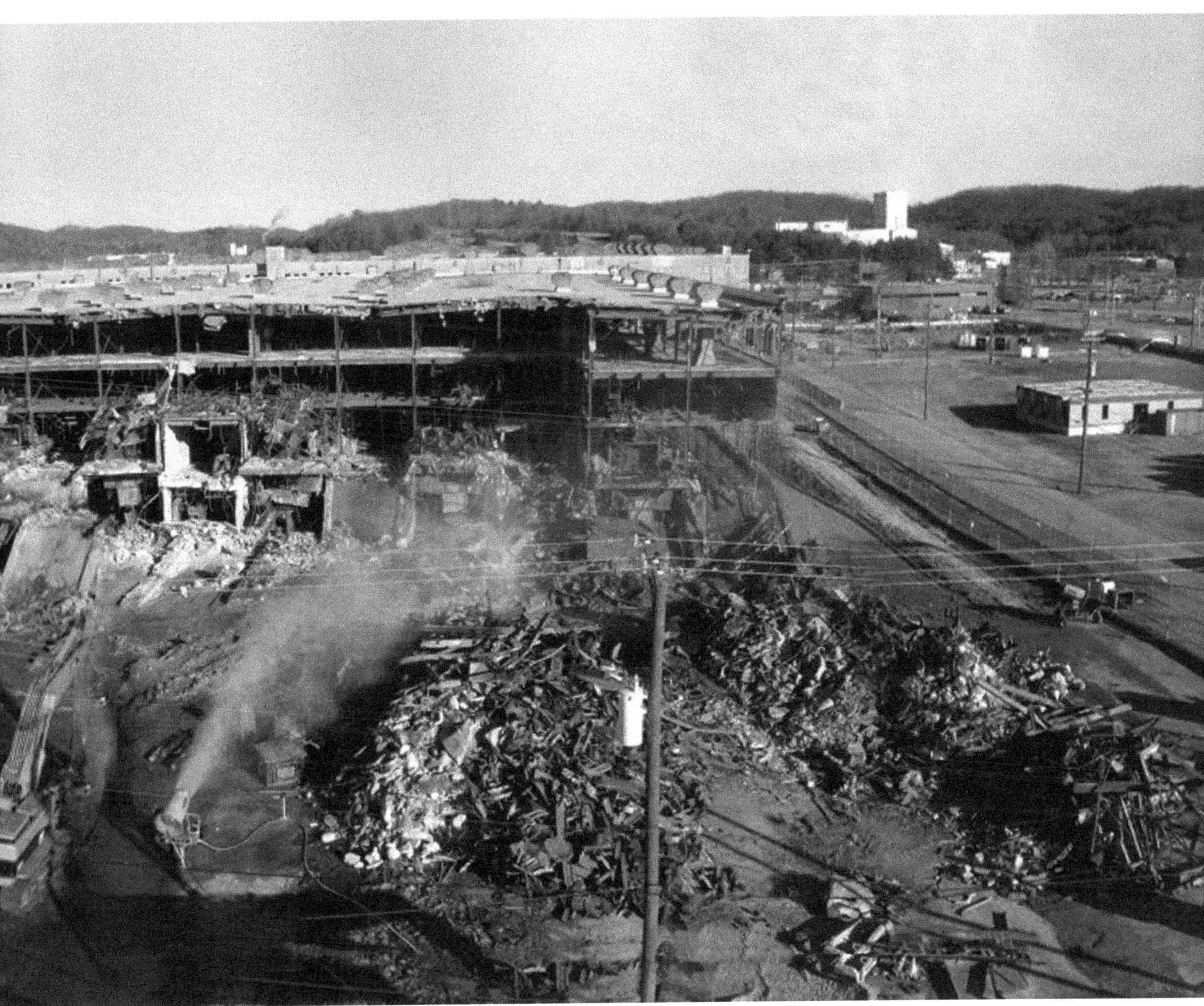

Epilogue

The End of a Project, the Beginning of an Era

The Manhattan Project successfully completed its unique wartime mission and in doing so can be credited with bringing about the end of World War II. Some will argue that the war would have ended without the use of nuclear bombs, which of course is true, but no one knows how long it would have taken or how many more people on both sides would have died. After the war, Japan made the strongest effort of any nation to show the international community that nuclear disarmament was imperative for the world, pushing for complete elimination of nuclear weapons.

The Manhattan Project gave birth not only to the atomic age, but to an era of incredible scientific discovery. It gave this nation the clear realization of the ardent need to lead the world in the pure sciences. The Manhattan Project brought together science, industry, and the military. It demonstrated clearly that the role of science in the security and future of the United States was without equal.

After much debate and disagreement regarding military versus civilian custody of atomic weapons and nuclear research, on August 1, 1946, President Truman signed the Atomic Energy Act calling for the transfer of nuclear authority from the Army to the United States Atomic Energy Commission. With it went all weapons and peacetime nuclear research. The Manhattan Project ended on January 1, 1947, when the AEC took over.

In a very real way the Manhattan Project never truly ended, it was simply given many different names. Looking around this nation today we see that those same Manhattan Project facilities are now world-renowned scientific research laboratories which continue to make breakthrough discoveries. These facilities born of the Manhattan Project did not close their doors, they went on to accomplish countless scientific advances and inventions. And proudly their groundbreaking work continues today in the very same facilities built so quickly in the rush to build an atomic bomb.

The Manhattan Project left behind a considerable legacy of radiological and chemical contamination. Much of it has been successfully cleaned up, and efforts to clean up the remainder continue.

This photographic history of the Manhattan Project closes with a Department of Energy photo taken while the book was being prepared. Being demolished is one of the most important buildings of the project, the mile-long gaseous diffusion building at the K-25 site in Oak Ridge, Tennessee, now called the East Tennessee Technology Park. Perhaps the razing of this structure is an appropriate way to end this story of the Manhattan Project, an effort that can be seen as the most important race in world history, a race won by all those special people some of whom appear in these pages. To each of them goes a deep appreciation and genuine "Thank You."

Notes on the Photographs

These notes, listed by page number, attempt to include all aspects known of the photographs. Each of the photographs is identified by the page number, photograph's title or description, photographer and collection, archive, and call or box number when applicable. Although every attempt was made to collect all data, in some cases complete data may have been unavailable due to the age and condition of some of the photographs and records.

II **Oak Ridge Aerial**
United States Department of Energy, Oak Ridge Office
1225

VI **Elsa Gate Portal**
National Archives

X **Enrico Fermi et Al.**
United States Department of Energy, Washington, D.C.

3. **Albert Einstein and Leo Szilard**
National Archives

4. **Site of First Chain Reaction**
United States Department of Energy, Oak Ridge Office
MED316

5. **World's First Nuclear Reactor**
Argonne National Laboratory

6. **The Blocks of Solid Graphite**
National Archives

7. **Another View of Chicago Pile-1**
National Archives

8. **Lawrence and Fellow Atomic Scientists**
National Archives
MED-240

9. **Julius Robert Oppenheimer**
National Archives

10. **CP-1 Scientists**
United States Department of Energy, Oak Ridge Office
MED 362

11. **Leslie R. Groves**
National Archives
MED 352

12. **Groves at Y-12**
National Archives

13. **Groves and His Secretary, Mrs. J. M. O'Leary**
United States Department of Energy, Oak Ridge Office
2044

14. **Groves, Nichols, and Taylor**
Oak Ridge Public Library

17. **Clinch River Pull-Ferry**
National Archives
MED-229

18. **Oak Ridge Security Gate**
Oak Ridge Public Library
sec0110

19. **Gamble Valley Residential Area**
Oak Ridge Public Library
aer0260

20. **Aerial of Dormitories**
Oak Ridge Public Library
aer0090

21. **Jackson Square**
National Archives

22. **Vacuum Pump at K-25**
National Archives

23. **The K-25 Facility**
National Archives

24. **Workers on Bus**
United States Department of Energy, Washington, D.C.
HD.H.046

25. **K-25 Bus Terminal**
National Archives
MED 202

26. **Aerial of Gaseous Diffusion Building**
Oak Ridge Public Library
aer0430

27. The Y-12 Facility
United States Department of Energy, Oak Ridge Office
PRO3522

28. Construction of Building 9731
United States Department of Energy, Oak Ridge Office
25-2

29. Another View of Y-12
United States Department of Energy, Oak Ridge Office
photo 2013

30. Y-12 Racetrack Under Construction
United States Department of Energy, Washington, D.C.
23-15

31. The Y-12 Alpha Racetrack
United States Department of Energy, Washington, D.C.
HD.4B.004

32. Shift Change at Y-12
National Archives

33. K-25 Welder
United States Department of Energy, Washington, D.C.
OR-Weldwe K-25

34. The X-10 Facility
Oak Ridge Public Library Archives
x100870

35. Uranium Slugs
United States Department of Energy, Oak Ridge Office
7579

36. Plutonium Production at X-10
United States Department of Energy, Oak Ridge Office
7578-2

37. Extracting Radioactive Material
United States Department of Energy, Oak Ridge Office
243897

38. The X-10 Graphite Reactor from Above
United States Department of Energy, Oak Ridge Office
7582

39. Another View of the X-10
United States Department of Energy, Washington, D.C.

40. Reactor Reactions
United States Department of Energy, Oak Ridge Office
243891

41. Connie Bolling and Workers at Y-12
National Archives

42. Security Guard at Y-12
National Archives

43. K-25 Rally
National Archives
PRO 199-9

44. K-25 Dials and Meters
National Archives

45. K-25 Control Area
National Archives

46. K-25 Workmen
National Archives

47. K-25 Machine Shop
National Archives

48. K-25 Wash Station
National Archives

49. The Main Switchboard
Oak Ridge Public Library
srv0220

50. S-50 Construction
United States Department of Energy, Oak Ridge Office
S-50-42

51. Aerial of S-50 and Power Plant
United States Department of Energy, Oak Ridge Office
#3539

52. S-50 Diffusion Columns
Oak Ridge Public Library
s-50-0020

53. Aerial View of K-25 Gaseous Diffusion Building
United States Department of Energy, Oak Ridge Office
59-0435

54. X-10 Waste Storage Tanks
United States Department of Energy, Oak Ridge Office
44-24

55. General Groves Speaking to Workers
National Archives
PRO 976-3

56. Alabama Ordnance Works
National Archives
MED 38-4

57. Los Alamos Security Patrol
United States Department of Energy, Washington, D.C.

58. Los Alamos Highway Construction
United States Department of Energy, Washington, D.C.

59. Los Alamos Scientific Laboratory
United States Department of Energy, Washington, D.C.

60. The Fuller Lodge
United States Department of Energy, Washington, D.C.

61. Site-Y Technical Area-1
United States Department of Energy, Washington, D.C.

62. Los Alamos Parking
National Archives
MED 330

63. WACs at Los Alamos
National Archives
MED 348

64. Radioactive Methods
United States Department of Energy, Oak Ridge Office
91-132

65. Slotin Accident at Los Alamos
United States Department of Energy, Washington, D.C.

66. **Hanford Site Meeting**
United States Department of Energy, Oak Ridge Office
91-211

67. **General Groves at Hanford**
United States Department of Energy, Washington, D.C.

68. **Aerial View of Hanford Hutments**
United States Department of Energy, Washington, D.C.

69. **Hanford Security Check Station**
National Archives
MED 587

70. **Hanford B-Reactor Construction**
Library of Congress
HAER WA-164-3

71. **Hanford 181-8 Pump House Construction**
Library of Congress
HAER WA-164-12

72. **Aerial View of B-Reactor**
Library of Congress
HAER WA-164-1

73. **The Hanford Reactor**
Library of Congress
HAER WA-164-7

74. **Hanford T-41 Tank Farm Construction**
United States Department of Energy, Washington, D.C.

75. **Reservation Barbershop**
United States Department of Energy, Washington, D.C.

76. **The 1701-B Main Gate House**
Library of Congress
HAER WA-164-31

77. **Hanford's 300-Area**
Oak Ridge Public Library
aer 0760

78. **Hanford 221-T and 221-U Construction**
National Archives
MED 386

79. **Hanford Rally**
National Archives
MED 601

80. **Sunday Punch B-25 Presentation**
Department of Energy, Oak Ridge Office
pro303-3

81. **Day's Pay B-17 Presentation**
National Archives
MED 375

82. **War Bonds for Victory**
United States Department of Energy, Washington, D.C.

85. **All the Comforts of Home**
United States Department of Energy, Washington, D.C.

86. **Pasco Liberty Theatre**
United States Department of Energy, Washington, D.C.

87. **Happy Valley Esso Station**
National Archives
MED-230

88. **Army Post Exchange**
United States Department of Energy, Washington, D.C.

89. **Oak Ridge Dentistry Visit**
National Archives

90. **Chapel-on-the-Hill**
National Archives
PRO 889

91. **First Election at Oak Ridge**
Oak Ridge Public Library
el0010

92. **Trailers for Workers**
United States Department of Energy, Washington, D.C.

93. **Y-12 Check Station Queues**
National Archives
PRO 761-7

94. **Christmas 1943**
United States Department of Energy, Washington, D.C.
784-neg (1943)

95. **Santa's Visit to Hanford**
United States Department of Energy, Washington, D.C.
792-neg (1943)

96. **Santa Gift Bag Security Check**
National Archives
191

97. **War Bond Posters**
National Archives
PRO 137-2

98. **Oak Ridge War Bond Rally**
National Archives
Roll 264-28

99. **Oak Ridge High School Cafeteria**
National Archives
PRO-90

100. **Elm Grove Grocery Store**
National Archives
PRO 661-1

101. **Reservation Snack Bar**
National Archives
Roll 226

102. **Oak Ridge Dormitory Linen Room**
National Archives
PRO 414-4

103. **Grove Center Post Office**
National Archives

104. **Oak Ridge Rhythm Engineers**
United States Department of Energy, Washington, D.C.

105. **Meyers Brothers Skating Rink**
United States Department of Energy, Washington, D.C.

106. **Oak Ridge Girl Scouts**
National Archives

107. Grove Center Swimming Pool
National Archives
PRO 928-2

108. Reservation Office Close-up
Oak Ridge Public Library
dl0160

109. City Directory Office
Oak Ridge Public Library
dl0160

110. Middletown Trailer Camp
Oak Ridge Public Library
hsq0460

111. Downed Enemy Plane Cockpit Visit
Oak Ridge Public Library
arm0270

112. The Safety Patrol
National Archives
PRO 32-1

113. Comic Books for Sale
Oak Ridge Public Library
dl0400

114. Mock Plane The Atom
United States Department of Energy, Oak Ridge Office
1122

115. Oak Ridge Swimming Hole
United States Department of Energy, Oak Ridge Office
PR0766

116. Reservation Bookmobile
Oak Ridge Public Library
srv0230

117. Coal Delivery by the Bucket
Oak Ridge Public Library
bus0320

118. Refuse Truck
United States Department of Energy, Oak Ridge Office
Pro884-4

119. Oak Ridge Outhouses
United States Department of Energy, Oak Ridge Office
X10-14

120. Surgery in Progress
Oak Ridge Public Library
med0030

121. Shots in the Arm
Oak Ridge Public Library
med0130

122. Dominoes Game
Oak Ridge Public Library
dl0260

123. Radio Station Dancing
Oak Ridge Public Library
bus0240

124. Victory Garden
Oak Ridge Public Library
dl0270

125. Poultry Production
Oak Ridge Public Library
bus0340

126. The Central Cafeteria
Oak Ridge Public Library
dl0310

127. Cafeteria for Blacks
Oak Ridge Public Library
bus0280

128. Reservation Billboard
United States Department of Energy, Oak Ridge Office
228-15

129. Reservation Billboard no. 2
United States Department of Energy, Oak Ridge Office
197-2

130. Charitable Cigarette Donations
Oak Ridge Public Library
bus0370

131. Combat Veteran Morale Boost
Oak Ridge Public Library
arm0130

132. Barracks Play Rehearsal
Oak Ridge Public Library
arm0140

133. Piano Entertainment at Gamble Valley
Oak Ridge Public Library
arm0250

134. Alonzo and Guards at Blair Security Gate
Oak Ridge Public Library
sec0120

135. Row of Hutments
Oak Ridge Public Library
hsg0670

136. Reservation Strip Mall
Oak Ridge Public Library
bus0360

137. Hutment Interior
Oak Ridge Public Library
hsq0540

138. Outside Hanford Auditorium
United States Department of Energy, Washington, D.C.

139. Hanford Lunchtime Cafeteria
National Archives
MED 376

140. Jukebox at the Army Post Exchange
National Archives

143. Aerial of Los Alamos Hill Road
United States Department of Energy, Washington, D.C.

144. Lehr with Gadget Component
National Archives
MED

145. Plymouth Plutonium
National Archives
MED 317

146. Jumbo's Journey
United States Department of Energy, Washington, D.C. LA

147. The Gadget at Trinity Tower
National Archives
MED 318

148. The Gadget Awaiting Detonation
National Archives
MED 316

149. Trinity Checkpoint
National Archives
MED 373

150. Trinity Base Camp at Alamogordo
National Archives
MED 325

151. S-10,000 Control Shelter
United States Department of Energy, Washington, D.C.

152. Detonation of First Atomic Bomb
National Archives
MED 334

153. Trinity Ground Zero Following Detonation
National Archives
MED 339

154. Results of the Blast
National Archives
MED 314

157. Tinian Island Airfield
National Archives
MED 359

158. The Enola Gay
National Archives
MED 357

159. Colonel Tibbets and Crew of Enola Gay
National Archives

160. Little Boy
National Archives

161. Map of the Bombing Missions
United States Department of Energy, Washington, D.C.

162. Colonel Tibbets Before Takeoff
National Archives

163. Bombing of Hiroshima
U.S. Army Photo
personal collection of George Kerr

164. Ruins of Hiroshima
U.S. Army Photo
personal collection of George Kerr

165. Ruins of Hiroshima no. 2
U.S. Army Photo
personal collection of George Kerr

166. Bombed Railway Station
National Archives

167. Ruins of Hiroshima no. 3
U.S. Army Photo
personal collection of George Kerr

168. Ruins of Hiroshima no. 4
U.S. Army Photo
personal collection of George Kerr

169. Ruins of Hiroshima no. 5
U.S. Army Photo
personal collection of George Kerr

170. Ruins of Hiroshima no. 6
U.S. Army Photo
personal collection of George Kerr

171. Leaflet Warnings
United States Department of Energy, Oak Ridge Office

172. Fat Man
National Archives

173. Bombing of Nagasaki
National Archives
AEC-72-9692

174. Nagasaki Before and After
National Archives

175. Ruins of Nagasaki
National Archives

176. Ruins of Nagasaki no. 2
U.S. Army Photo
personal collection of George Kerr

177. Ruins of Nagasaki no. 3
U.S. Army Photo
personal collection of George Kerr

178. Ruins of Nagasaki no. 4
National Archives
AEC-52-4447

179. Ruins of Nagasaki no. 5
National Archives
AEC-52-4420

180. Nagasaki Radioactivity Measurements
National Archives

181. Injured Woman
National Archives

182. Ruins of Nagasaki no. 6
National Archives

183. Ruins of Nagasaki no. 7
U.S. Army Photo
personal collection of George Kerr

184. Ruins of Nagasaki no. 8
National Archives

185. Groves Press Conference
National Archives

186. Japanese Delegation Aboard USS Missouri
U.S. Army Photo
National Archives

187. Japanese Signing Surrender Papers
U.S. Army Photo
National Archives

188. Douglas MacArthur Presiding at Surrender
U.S. Army Photo
National Archives

189. Tojo Hanged in Effigy
National Archives
PRO 946-12

190. War's End Newspapers
United States Department of Energy, Oak Ridge Office
85-423

191. Oak Ridge Victory Celebration
National Archives
PRO 946-26

192. Victory Celebration in France
National Archives

193. Army-Navy E Excellence Award
United States Department of Energy, Washington, D.C.

194. The A-Bomb Pin
United States Department of Energy, Oak Ridge Office

195. Secret City Opened to the Public
United States Department of Energy, Oak Ridge Office

196. Razing the Gaseous Diffusion Building
Department of Energy
Oak Ridge Office

HISTORIC PHOTOS OF THE MANHATTAN PROJECT

The atomic age began at 5:30 A.M. on July 16, 1945, with the explosion of "the Gadget" at Trinity near Alamogordo, New Mexico. Prelude to the bombing of Hiroshima and Nagasaki, which forced the capitulation of Japan and ended World War II, the Trinity test was the culmination of herculean efforts by scientists, civilians, and the military of the United States to tap the potential of the atom for a wartime emergency. If Nazi Germany could engineer the bomb first, an Allied victory against Hitler was all but lost.

Historic Photos of the Manhattan Project is a look back at the epic struggle to build the world's first atomic bomb. Nearly 200 images in vivid black-and-white reveal the project as it unfolded, from its secretive origins at Oak Ridge, Hanford, and Los Alamos, to the day Americans celebrated triumph over the Axis powers with victory over Japan. A pinnacle moment in the history of the United States, the Manhattan Project's application of Einstein's famous equation $E = MC^2$ shows, perhaps better than any other single endeavor, what can be achieved by human ingenuity when the citizens of a great nation are united in freedom against a fearsome and despotic foe.

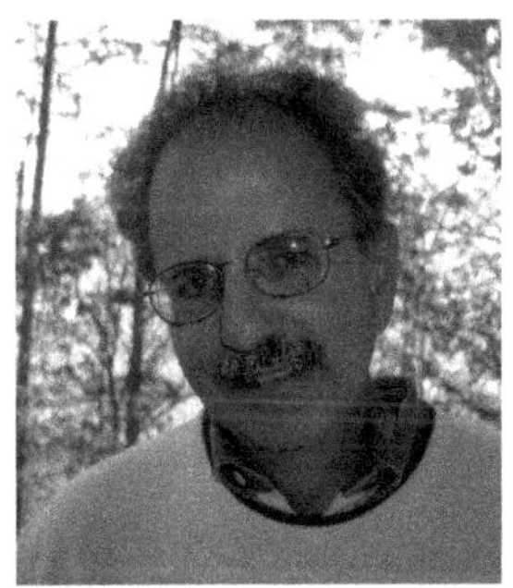

Timothy Joseph is a former high school teacher, college professor, and corporate manager and consultant. He holds a Ph.D. in biology, was a senior scientist and project manager for the U.S. Department of Energy for 24 years in Chicago, Illinois, and Oak Ridge, Tennessee, and is involved in the government assessment of radiation doses to past workers, many from the Manhattan Project. Tim is a freelance technical writer, consultant, and novelist with four published books. He gives creative writing talks to young people to instill interest in and awareness of the personal rewards of writing and reading. Tim lives in Knoxville with his wife, Marsha.

WWW.TURNERPUBLISHING.COM